The Bible as Political Artifact

The Bible as Political Artifact

Artifact

On the Feminist Study of the Hebrew Bible

Susanne Scholz

Fortress Press
Minneapolis

THE BIBLE AS POLITICAL ARTIFACT

On the Feminist Study of the Hebrew Bible

Cover image: Thinkstock: 611784572/Jumpeestudio/Abstract colorful geometric and modern overlapping triangles on white

Cover design: Alisha Lofgren

Print ISBN: 978-1-5064-2047-9

eBook ISBN: 978-1-5064-2048-6

The paper used in this publication meets the minimum requirements of American National Standard for Information Sciences — Permanence of Paper for Printed Library Materials, ANSI Z329.48-1984.

Manufactured in the U.S.A.

Dedicated to my treasured feminist professors of my student years at the University of Mainz, Germany, and Union Theological Seminary in the City of New York, nurturing my commitment to reading the Bible in one hand and the newspaper in the other:

Phyllis Trible

Luise Schottroff

Dorothee Sölle

Beverly W. Harrison

Contents

Acknowledgments

First and foremost, thanks are due to several publishers for granting permission to republish the following essays in this book:

1. "Redesigning the Biblical Studies Curriculum: Toward a 'Radical-Democratic' Teaching Model." In *Transforming Graduate Biblical Education: Ethos and Discipline*, edited by Elisabeth Schüssler Fiorenza and Kent Richards, 269–91. Atlanta: SBL Press, 2010. Reprinted by permission.

2. "Occupy Academic Bible Teaching: The Architecture of Educational Power and the Biblical Studies Curriculum." In *Teaching the Bible in the Liberal Arts Classroom*, edited by Jane S. Webster and Glenn S. Holland, 28–43. Sheffield: Sheffield Academic Press, 2012. Reprinted by permission.

3. "Standing at the Crossroads with Räisänen's *Programme*: Toward a Future of Biblical Studies in Post-Biblical Societies." In *Moving Beyond New Testament Theology? Essays in Conversation with Heikki Räisänen*, edited by Todd Penner and Caroline Vander Stichele, 161–78. Publications of the Finnish Exegetical Society 88. Helsinki: Finnish Exegetical Society; Göttingen: Vandenhoeck & Ruprecht, 2005. © 2005 Finnish Exegetical Society. Reprinted by permission.

4. "Tandoori Reindeer or the Limitations of Historical Criticism." In *Her Master's Tools? Feminist Challenges to Historical-Critical Interpretations*, edited by Todd Penner and Caroline Vander Stichele, 46–69. Global Perspectives on Biblical Scholarship Series. Atlanta: Society of Biblical Literature, 2005. Reprinted by permission.

5. "Back Then It Was Legal: The Epistemological Imbalance in Readings of Biblical and Ancient Near Eastern Rape Legislation." *The Bible and Critical Theory* 1, no. 4 (December 2005): 36.1–36.22. ©2005 Monash Press. Used with permission.

6. *"Lederhosen* Hermeneutics: Toward a Feminist Sociology of White Male German Old Testament Studies." In *Crossing Textual Boundaries: A Festschrift in Honor of Professor for Archie Chi Chung Lee for His Sixtieth Birthday*, edited by Lung Kwong Lo, Nancy N. H. Tan, and Ying Zhang, 334–53. Hong Kong: Divinity School of Chung Chi College, 2010. Reprinted by permission from Divinity School of Chung Chi College in Hong Kong.

7. "The Forbidden Fruit for the New Eve: The Christian Right's Adaptation to the (Post)modern World." In *Interreligious Hermeneutics in Pluralistic Europe: Between Texts and People*, edited by David Cheetham, Ulrich Winkler, Oddbjørn Leirvik, and Judith Gruber, 289–315. Current of Encounter 40. Amsterdam: Rodopi, 2011. Reprinted by permission from Koninklijke Brill NV.

8. "Discovering a Largely Unknown Past for a Vibrant Present: Feminist Hebrew Bible Studies in North America." In *Feminist Interpretation of the Hebrew Bible in Retrospect: Social Locations*, edited by Susanne Scholz, 2:118–47. Sheffield: Sheffield Phoenix Press, 2014. ©2014 Sheffield Phoenix Press. Used with permission.

9. "Was It Really Rape in Genesis 34? Biblical Scholarship as a Reflection of Cultural Assumptions." In *Escaping Eden: New Feminist Perspectives on the Bible*, edited by Harold Washington, Susan L. Graham, and Pam Thimmes, 182–98. New York: New York University Press, 1998. Reprinted by permission.

10. "'Belonging to All Humanity": The Dinah Story (Genesis 34) in the Film *La Genèse* (1999) by Cheick Oumar Sissoko." Translated by the author from the original German titled: "'Belonging to All Humanity:' Die Dina Episode (Gen. 34) und ihre Aktualisierung im Film 'Die Erben von Kain und Abel' (*La Genèse*, F/Mali 1999) von Cheick Oumar Sissoko." In *Religion und Gewalt im Bibelfilm*, edited by Reinhold Zwick, 55–75. Köthen: Schüren Verlag, 2013. Reprinted by permission.

Second, I would like to express my scholarly gratitude to my employing institution, Perkins School of Theology at Southern Methodist University (SMU), for the financial support that enabled me to present one of my previously unpublished conference papers at the annual meeting of the Society of Biblical Literature in November 2014. This modified and expanded paper appears here with the title "Biblical Studies Is Feminist Biblical Studies, and Vice Versa: About the Conceptualization of Feminist Biblical Studies as the Core of Biblical Studies."

I thank the SMU University Research Council (URC) for a travel grant that allowed me to attend the meeting of the European Society for Translation Studies (EST) at the Johannes Gutenberg University of Mainz, Germany, in August 2013. The revised and expanded essay, titled "Barbaric Bibles: The Scandal of Inclusive Translations," is based on the paper I presented during the meeting.

I am grateful to two colleagues, Davina C. Lopez, professor of religious studies, and Doug McMahon, director and chaplain of the Center for Spiritual Life, for inviting me to give a talk sponsored as the Burchenal Lecture for the Center for Spiritual Life at Eckerd College in Petersburg, Florida, in September 2015. The occasion gave me the opportunity to develop my thoughts for the essay titled "How to Read Biblical Rape Texts with Contemporary Title IX Debates in Mind."

Last but not least, I thank my colleague Deborah Rooke, associate lecturer in Old Testament hermeneutics, Regent's Park College at the University of Oxford, who organized a scholarly conference in July 2011. The conference was titled "What Do You Think You Are? Gender and the Transmission of Identity in the Hebrew Bible, Dead Sea Scrolls, and Related Literature." Colleagues from a wide spectrum of ancient text studies gathered in Lecture Room 1 of the Oriental Institute on Pusey Lane in Oxford for four days. We listened to each other's papers, sat in the pub around the corner to debate postpaper ideas, and experienced the Oxford summer heat, which means air conditioning was entirely unnecessary. One of the essays included in this book goes back to this conference, and it is now titled, "Tell Me How You Read This Story and I Will Tell You Who You Are: Post-postmodernity, Radicant Exegesis, and a Feminist Sociology of Biblical Hermeneutics."

Susanne Scholz
Dallas, Texas
March 2017

Abbreviations

BibInt   *Biblical Interpretation*

BJS   Brown Judaic Studies

BWANT   Beiträge zur Wissenschaft vom Alten und Neuen Testament

BZAW   Beihefte zur Zeitschrift für die alttestamentliche Wissenschaft

CBQ   *Catholic Biblical Quarterly*

CC   Continental Commentaries

EUZ   Exegese in unserer Zeit

FCB   Feminist Companions to the Bible

FOTL   Forms of Old Testament Literature

GCT   Gender, Culture, Theory

IBC   Interpretation: A Bible Commentary for Teaching and Preaching

IDB   *The Interpreter's Dictionary of the Bible*. Edited by George A. Buttrick. 4 vols. New York: Abingdon, 1962

JAAR   *Journal of the American Academy of Religion*

JAOS   *Journal of the American Oriental Society*

JBL   *Journal of Biblical Literature*

JEA   *Journal of Egyptian Archaeology*

JFSR   *Journal of Feminist Studies in Religion*

JSOT   *Journal for the Study of the Old Testament*

JSOTSup   Journal for the Study of the Old Testament Supplement Series

JTSA   *Journal of Theology for Southern Africa*

NIB	*The New Interpreter's Bible.* Edited by Leander E. Keck. 12 vols. Nashville: Abingdon, 1994–2004
NICOT	New International Commentary on the Old Testament
OTL	Old Testament Library
RB	*Revue biblique*
RelEd	*Religious Education*
SJOT	*Scandinavian Journal of the Old Testament*
StBibLit	Studies in Biblical Literature (Lang)
TThRel	*Teaching Theology and Religion*
UF	*Ugarit-Forschungen*
VT	*Vetus Testamentum*
WBC	World Biblical Commentary
ZAW	*Zeitschrift für die alttestamentliche Wissenschaft*

Introduction: Feminist Readings of the Bible as a Political Artifact

This book is the result of two decades of teaching, researching, and writing in the field of Hebrew Bible studies, always with feminist concerns in mind. It is profoundly indebted to the insistence of my many teachers of Protestant theological, religious, and biblical studies that biblical meanings are never objective, universal, and value neutral, but always embedded and accountable to the contexts from which they emerge. For me, so far, the most important context has always been related to issues of feminism, gender, and sexuality in their various intersectional manifestations. This is my scholarly bias, my hermeneutical interest, and my theo-ethical commitment as a diasporic German, "naturalized" US-American, post-Holocaust, and feminist biblical exegete who approaches the Hebrew Bible, also known as the Old Testament, the First Testament, or simply the Bible, as a political artifact. In all of my work, I have always wanted to know the manifold routes taken by biblical interpreters to make this ancient and highly prominent text meaningful. In this way, I have learned firsthand that the Bible has contributed heavily to the past and present quest for knowledge, understanding, and living in the world, not only in religiously oriented but also in secular settings.

Thus biblical literature offers much to those who make an effort to study it and its readers throughout history. When we do, we come to recognize existing connections, long forgotten and assumed concepts, as well as new possibilities about all kinds of things we take for granted. The Bible read as a political artifact always indicates why things are ordered the way they are or, alternatively, how they could be reordered so that justice, peace, and the integrity of creation would prevail, as the World Council of Churches articulated it so powerfully in the last two decades of the twentieth century.[1]

Yet most people, even and perhaps especially some Bible scholars, do not read the Bible as a political artifact. Usually they insist on reading it as the literal word of God, favoring a privatized, personalized, and sentimentalized hermeneutics that looks for spiritual refreshment divorced from the troubles of the world. Especially when they are Bible scholars, they will favor a historical-antiquarian approach, what Elisabeth Schüssler Fiorenza designates as the "scientific positivist paradigm."[2] This approach is fixated on the quest for historical origins, authorial intention, and how life was in ancient Israel. This modern epistemological drive permeates the field of biblical studies because it successfully released biblical scholarship from ecclesial supervision and theological dogmatism in the nineteenth century. Although in certain settings the historical-antiquarian approach is still effective, especially when the Bible is upheld as doctrinal authority in Christian fundamentalist and religiously conservative communities, the hegemony of this approach has been seriously challenged since the waning decades of the twentieth century. Cultural critics of the Bible have been on the forefront of this challenge, and this book owes a debt of gratitude to them. In fact, this book aims to endorse and, if this is not too immodest, further the agenda of cultural criticism in biblical research from a feminist hermeneutical stance.

This volume contains ten previously published essays and four essays that had been the basis of unpublished conference papers. The idea to collect various published and unpublished essays and put them into one volume goes back to a fateful meeting with a young and enthusiastic colleague who wanted to chat with me over coffee at the regional meeting of the Southwest Commission in Religious Studies (SWCRS) in Irving, Texas, in March 2015. To make a long story short, after the coffee meeting I had the idea to put a proposal together for a book that would contain several of my published essays, scattered around in anthologies, and unpublished works that I did not yet have

---

1. For details on these theological principles, see, e.g., D. Preman Niles, "Justice, Peace, and the Integrity of Creation," *WCC ecumenical dictionary*, November 2003, http://www.wcc-coe.org/wcc/who/dictionary-article11.html. See also his monograph *Between the Flood and the Rainbow: Interpreting the Conciliar Process of Mutual Commitment (Covenant) to Justice, Peace and the Integrity of Creation* (Geneva: WCC, 1992).
2. Elisabeth Schüssler Fiorenza, *Rhetoric and Ethic: The Politics of Biblical Studies* (Minneapolis: Fortress Press, 1999), 41.

the time to expand into full-blown essays. The goal of the book would be to provide a twenty-year selective but significant survey of my exegetical, hermeneutical, and methodological contributions to the field of biblical studies thus far.

That Fortress Press saw merit in such a volume fills me with scholarly gratitude. The work of the biblical researcher and scholar is an introverted endeavor, and one never knows if the hours spent in library stacks and in front of the computer screen will amount to anything. During all of those years, I have been lucky to test out my ideas with students in the classroom, in office-hour conversations, and during conferences, as well as with colleagues over lunch or coffee (although I prefer a first-flush Darjeeling or Phoenix Oolong tea anytime). The reworking of the published essays into the required Word-document format was relatively easy. The rethinking and rewriting of the four conference papers created more work, but was also gratifying because the time for excuses was over and I had to expand these papers into publishable compositions. Although I tinkered with a few jots and tittles, the substance of all essays remains the same.

It is a marvel to me that I am still in agreement with my earlier thinking about the politics of biblical studies and the reading of the Bible. I have reread every sentence and every footnote, and it is humbling and a great relief that this is so, as the possibility for disagreeing with one's previous positions always exists. And so I continue to agree with my work, whether it was articulated twenty years ago in "Was It Really Rape in Genesis 34? Biblical Scholarship as a Reflection of Cultural Assumptions," or whether it is an exploration of the reasons for the vicious responses to the first inclusive German Bible translation in "Barbaric Bibles: The Scandal of Inclusive Translations," going back to a conference paper presented in 2013. The essay titled "Biblical Studies Is Feminist Biblical Studies, and Vice Versa: About the Conceptualization of Feminist Biblical Studies as the Core of Biblical Studies" was delivered at the 2014 annual meeting of the Society of Biblical Literature (SBL) when the adverb *still* began sneaking up in feminist research. Is feminist biblical scholarship "still" needed? Are feminist studies outdated or do they need to be revised?

My scholarly assessment on the matter is clear. In light of the relentless permeation of androcentric structures of domination in their various manifestations, feminist analysis is far from being finished. It is "still" pushed to the margins like an edge plant, such as sweet alyssum or barrenwort, beautifying the field on the edges but never placed at the center. The challenge is to make feminist research central without creating another form of domination. Obviously, after only a few decades of feminist scholarship, human societies are only at the beginning of taking seriously feminist challenges to androcentric and, yes, patriarchal infrastructures that have created such havoc on planet earth for several millennia. The essays of this book aim to contribute to understanding the serious and pervasive nature of this relentless structural problem. Thus, whether the essays deal with rape, the architecture of the biblical studies curriculum, or feminist biblical readings in the era of the Title IX debates, all fourteen essays represent my conviction that feminist biblical studies are needed more rather than less.

Importantly, the order of the fourteen essays is not arranged chronologically but in three main parts, to indicate the movement of my work in three related but nevertheless separate fields of inquiry. The first part includes three essays that investigate the pedagogical politics of (feminist) biblical studies in institutions of higher education and society. The second part contains five essays that explore the politics of exegetical methods. The third part includes six essays about the politics of hermeneutical and cultural alternatives in the feminist interpretation of the Hebrew Bible; it is perhaps the broadest in scope and approach, as it also contains three of the four unpublished conference papers that I expanded specifically for the inclusion in this book. Together, the fourteen essays investigate from a critical feminist stance how biblical texts, themes, and issues are constructed in the sociopolitical, cultural, and religious settings in which they have been read, with the goal of deconstructing and illuminating past and present epistemologies, sociologies, and hermeneutics of biblical interpretation in the world. As such, the Hebrew Bible emerges as an artifact of considerable political implications and ramifications in society, whether it is construed as Western, Christian, African, barbaric, or as being part of past and present rape cultures.

Finally, the question emerges what I mean by "artifact" and why I consider the Bible a "political" artifact. For such definitional considerations, I always like to check a dictionary and in the case of the English language, the *Oxford English Dictionary* (OED). It explains that, etymologically, the word *artifact* (US spelling) is loaned from the classical Latin noun *arte*, which is the ablative of *ars* in the sense of art, and *factum*, which is the neuter past participle of *facere* (to make). Accordingly, the explanations emphasize the human-made qualities of an artifact. For instance, the first explanation states: "An object made or modified by human workmanship, as opposed to one formed by natural processes." An artifact can also refer to an archaeologically "excavated object that shows characteristic signs of human workmanship or use." Or in yet another main sense, an artifact is "a non-material human construct," such as mathematics understood as a "mental artifact." The first mention of the phrase "political artifact" comes from no other than the US-American Protestant theologian Richard Niebuhr, who in 1949 relied on the expression in an essay titled "The Illusion of World Government," published in the journal *Foreign Affairs*.[3] Interestingly, Niebuhr uses the phrase "political artifact" in the negative when he asserts: "The police power of a government cannot be a purely political artifact. It is an arm of the community's body. If the body is in pieces, the arm cannot integrate it."[4] He classifies police power as a political artifact that is only effective when the people accept it as its governing and controlling authority and are loyal to it. Niebuhr proposes an important meaning for a political artifact; it is human-made, but it also receives its significance from people. Without their loyalty to a political artifact, the "thing" is powerless, ineffective, and useless. Something else has to happen for a political artifact to be of consequence, worth, and substance. In Niebuhr's view, what is needed are "organic forces of cohesion in the world community,"[5] and so political artifacts fulfill their functions and purposes only when communities are cohesively integrated into the world.

One of the most comprehensive discussions on the notion of political artifacts comes from Langdon Winner in his essay "Do Artifacts Have Politics?"[6] Winner explains that artifacts embody social relations and thus distribute and enhance power, authority, and privilege "of some over others."[7] To Winner, artifacts are tools that are not neutral, apolitical entities. Rather, they "build order in our world,"[8] "structure decision," and "establish a framework for public order that will endure over many generations."[9] In this sense, then, artifacts "correlate with particular kinds of political relationships," and so they are "inherently political."[10] To Winner, artifacts are linked to "specific ways of

---

3. Reinhold Niebuhr, "The Illusion of World Government," *Foreign Affairs* 27 (1949): 379–88.
4. Ibid., 384.
5. Ibid., 385. The *Oxford English Dictionary* also lists references to "cultural," "sacred," "magical," and "psychic" artifacts, but here I am only interested in developing the meaning of "political artifacts."
6. Langdon Winner, "Do Artifacts Have Politics?," *Daedalus* 109, no. 1 (Winter 1980): 121–36.
7. Ibid., 125.
8. Ibid., 127.
9. Ibid., 128.

organizing power and authority,"[11] which raises the important question: "Does this state of affairs derive from an unavoidable social response to intractable properties in the things themselves, or is it instead a pattern imposed independently by a governing body, ruling class, or some other social or cultural institution to further its own purposes?"[12]

In my view, it is important to relate Winner's question to the study of the Bible. In fact, every essay included in this book considers it, asking whether the Bible itself, in its "essence," contributes to the misogyny, androcentrism, sexism, patriarchy, or heteronormativity in their various intersectional manifestations, or whether religious bodies, individual believers, scholars, exegetes, and "ordinary readers" do not construct the various genderized structures of domination with the Bible. Since I assert the latter, this book classifies the Bible as a political artifact, a human-made construct, that has been intimately immersed in, related to, and shaped by those societies in which biblical texts have been read, painted, filmed, talked about, shared, or even rejected. Its frameworks have been used to shape the social, economic, political, and religious order in the world, ensuring that the Bible has endured over many generations.

It needs to be emphasized that the attribution of interpretative agency and perhaps even primacy to biblical readers does not imply that biblical texts are innocent or free of ideological signification. Feminist exegetes have shown convincingly and abundantly the androcentric nature of biblical literature. Yet, in my view, in our post-postmodern era feminist analyses need to focus on the readers as the creators of (biblical) meanings, because only this approach promises to move our cultural-political and religious-theological moment beyond fundamentalist literalism and the modern obsession with originalism. Such a move enables feminist interpreters to hold readers accountable, pointing to their complicity and co-optation into the order of things. By investigating, uncovering, and deconstructing examples of the disorder of things, the various essays of this volume explain how to contribute to alternative views and to a future of more just relations when the topic relates to gender, misogyny, heteronormativity, and sexism in their intersectional manifestations. This is a tall order for one book. Indeed, it has cost me twenty years of thinking and working on the

---

10. Ibid., 123.
11. Ibid., 131.
12. Ibid.

selected texts, topics, and issues to demonstrate in a highly selective fashion what is at stake in the field of biblical studies and in biblical interpretations when we read the Bible with a focus on readers as agents and creators of biblical meanings.

The essays also indicate that the discussion, analysis, and evaluation of biblical meanings wherever they occur require a painstaking consideration of the meaning-making standards with which to read and study the Bible. This is a complicated matter that cannot be solved with arguments about the intentional or original meanings of the Bible or with references to the text itself. When readers are recognized, acknowledged, and taken seriously as the meaning-producing agents, it becomes clear that the meaning-making standards of reading and studying a text like the Bible come from somewhere. Meanings do not exist just by themselves in a vacuum. Readers, grounded in their social locations, create them even when they believe that this is not so. Since the discussion goes far beyond the limits of this introduction, suffice it to mention that meaning-making standards are closely linked to readerly convictions about ethics, values, and politics. Readers have to become aware of their ethical assumptions and belief systems. Do they read with the oppressed, marginalized, and disempowered groups and individuals in support of their efforts to live their lives in economically, socially, culturally, and politically just ways? Or do they hinder such efforts and endorse the status quo? And how do past and present biblical meanings advance or prevent readers from recognizing their complicity with or resistance to the status quo? Answering these and related questions takes a long time, and so it is an involved process to determine the meaning-making standards. In short, when readers acknowledge that they are the agents and endorsers of this or that biblical meaning, they also have to accept responsibility for their interpretations. Several essays included in this book offer more detailed discussions and analyses of what is involved in this process. The task, however, is not another totalizing move, as some critics observe in a "gotcha" kind of mode. It is an old problem already mentioned in Plato's great dialogue *Theaetetus*, written in approximately 360 BCE.

One thing is certain. There are no quick and easy answers to any of these exegetical, hermeneutical, and epistemological issues. It takes time, patience, and energy to develop alternative ways of seeing the world, which depends on the critical analysis of what is. In my view, the world would be less out of sync, less violent, and less unjust if more people were interested in critically interrogating their positions about gender, misogyny, androcentrism, and heteronormativity in their various intersectional manifestations. Many people do not even realize that the Hebrew Bible has anything to do with these issues, and has shaped our world to the extent it has. It is my hope that the following fourteen essays shed some light on some of these dynamics and perhaps surprise one or the other reader about the possibilities that the academic feminist study of the Bible has to offer us even today.

PART I

The Pedagogical Politics in Academia and Society

1

Redesigning the Biblical Studies Curriculum: Toward a "Radical-Democratic" Teaching Model

The academic field of biblical studies faces serious challenges during the early years of the twenty-first century. It must compete with flashy, noisy, and attention-seeking modes of engaging the world; and that is just the beginning. A visit to any technology store presents a variety of computers, printers, televisions, iPods, cell phones, and cameras of any size and price that is simply overwhelming to the senses. But an equally challenging fact is that very few people have ever heard of the existence of biblical studies and many are quite comfortable defending literal biblical meaning,[1] as if scholars had not long disproved, dismantled, or deconstructed it. For instance, the tensions

---

1. For an example of the popular insistence on the Bible's literalist meaning, see www.gafcon.org, the website of an Anglican group that has formed within the Anglican Church in opposition to LGBT people's ordination in Episcopal churches in the United States and Canada. In a statement at the end of a meeting in Jerusalem in June 2008, the group asserts: "The Bible is to be translated, read, preached, taught and obeyed in its plain and canonical sense, respectful of the church's historic and consensual reading"; see the statement here: "GAFCON: Final Statement," GAFCON website, June 28, 2008, http://tinyurl.com/l43oetx. For reports in the press, see, e.g., Robert Pigott, "Rival Meeting Deepens Anglican Rift," *BBC*, June 22, 2008, http://tinyurl.com/lu7fadv; Laurie Goodstein, "Rival Conferences for Anglican Church," *New York Times*, June 20, 2008, http://tinyurl.com/n2jd5ej.

within the Anglican Communion over the ordination of LGBTQ people in US-American and Canadian congregations have again proved the ongoing popularity of literalist biblicism despite abundant research on the topic in biblical studies.[2]

Yet the challenges come not only from the outside but also from within the field; one in particular pertains to the curricular design of teaching biblical studies. Current curricula illustrate that the field has remained aloof from a world, not only distracted by the newest technological gadgets and often intellectually caught in literalist biblicism, but also endangered by nuclear destruction, environmental pollution, military devastation, poverty, hunger, illness, disease, and economic, racial, ethnic, and gender violence. There is a curricular apathy toward these challenges that does not foster pedagogical innovation, intellectual curiosity, and sociopolitical, religious, and cultural change. In contrast, Elisabeth Schüssler Fiorenza calls for "a radical democratic emancipatory form" of teaching biblical studies today.[3]

This essay asserts that the curricular structure of biblical studies, as taught at *all* levels of academic learning, is firmly stuck in a nineteenth-century Christian-Protestant vision as initially articulated by Friedrich Schleiermacher. Because of its orientation toward past accomplishments, biblical curricular design at all levels has adapted little to continual sociocultural and epistemological-political developments. Recently, Schüssler Fiorenza suggested that "some creative thinking and educational transformation [has been] happening at the Masters of Divinity and College levels" but that no such pedagogical creativity seems to occur at the doctoral level.[4] Schüssler Fiorenza's assessment about undergraduate and master's level teaching is perhaps too optimistic. At these levels, too, the curriculum remains largely frozen in the "philological-historical or exegetical-doctrinal disciplinary paradigm"[5] developed during the nineteenth century as part of the "new

---

2. See, e.g., John Boswell, *Christianity, Social Tolerance and Homosexuality: Gay People in Western Europe from the Beginning of the Christian Era to the Fourteenth Century* (Chicago: University of Chicago Press, 1980); Bernadette Brooten, *Love between Women: Early Christian Responses to Female Homoeroticism* (Chicago: University of Chicago Press, 1998); Robert E. Goss and Mona West, eds., *Take Back the Word: A Queer Reading of the Bible* (Cleveland: Pilgrim, 2000); Deryn Guest, ed., *The Queer Bible Commentary* (London: SCM, 2006); Theodore W. Jennings Jr., *Jacob's Wound: Homoerotic Narrative in the Literature of Ancient Israel* (London: Continuum, 2005); Dale B. Martin, *Sex and the Single Savior: Gender and Sexuality in Biblical Interpretation* (Louisville: Westminster John Knox, 2006); Ken Stone, ed., *Queer Commentary and the Hebrew Bible* (Cleveland: Pilgrim, 2001).

3. Elisabeth Schüssler Fiorenza, "Rethinking the Educational Practices of Biblical Doctoral Studies," *TThRel* 6 (2003): 69, 72–73. See also the revised version of her essay in Schüssler Fiorenza, *The Power of the Word: Scripture and the Rhetoric of Empire* (Minneapolis: Fortress Press, 2007), 239–66.

4. Schüssler Fiorenza, "Rethinking the Educational Practices," 68. See also Schüssler Fiorenza, *Power of the Word*, 241, 261.

model for the production of knowledge and higher education . . . of German scientific research."[6]

The reticence toward curricular change in biblical studies does not surprise when one recognizes the interrelationship of graduate and undergraduate teaching and learning, the hiring practices in the field, and the credentialing requirements of aspiring Bible professors. All of these areas are connected, and so curricular changes need to be made at all teaching levels. For instance, if curricular changes were to be made only at the doctoral level, it would take decades to implement them in the undergraduate and master's-level curriculum. Until then, newly minted PhD scholars applying to teaching positions would be ill-prepared for the expected teaching assignments and most likely not be offered positions, perhaps drop out in frustration, or enter only graduate programs that promised adequate training for future job openings. Even if young professors, trained at innovative graduate programs, landed positions at master's-level and undergraduate institutions, rank issues would make it difficult for them to create lasting curricular modifications. If, on the other hand, curricular changes were made only at the undergraduate level, these changes would probably be regarded as less legitimate and scholarly than if they came from graduate institutions, due to existing hierarchies between graduate and undergraduate institutions. The implementation of curricular change is difficult because issues of authority, power, and hierarchies burden the process. Only when the scholarly conversation on curricular design reaches the entire field will creative thinking and educational transformation become sustainable, desirable, and executable at all levels.

Based on this insight, the following analysis takes a closer look at the undergraduate curriculum in biblical studies to suggest that improved interaction among graduate, master's-level, and undergraduate curricular needs, expectations, and opportunities would benefit all of them if they want to successfully confront the curricular challenge. The article looks at three different areas of undergraduate teaching to illustrate the close connections to the graduate curricular design in biblical studies. The article begins by describing the nineteenth-century curricular model of theological studies as developed by Schleiermacher. It then examines two teaching instruments to demonstrate the ongoing popularity of this curriculum both in undergraduate and graduate education. Among the teaching instruments are course

---

5. Schüssler Fiorenza, "Rethinking the Educational Practices," 68.
6. Ibid., 70.

descriptions at several US-American undergraduate institutions and undergraduate Bible textbooks of major textbook publishers. The article then discusses ideas about an alternative curriculum based on a "radical-democratic" model of biblical studies education[7] that develops in students intellectual-religious maturity, historical-cultural understanding, and literary-ethical engagement of the world. The briefly outlined alternative implies modified curricular goals, strategies, and techniques for both graduate and undergraduate teaching. Overall, then, the article argues for a comprehensive curricular redesign at all levels of graduate, master's-level, and undergraduate teaching of biblical studies.

Friedrich Schleiermacher's Curricular Vision of Biblical Studies

Rarely did a curriculum reform enjoy as much success as the one envisioned by Friedrich Schleiermacher in his *Brief Outline on the Study of Theology*, published in 1811.[8] The vision that theological education should cover the trilogy of historical, theological-philosophical, and practical investigation still shapes many biblical studies programs. The genius of this curriculum, persuading generations of theology professors, was its distinction between the quest for knowledge of God and the academic task of theological education, namely, the training of future clergy. To Schleiermacher, theological education should be conceptualized as a purely academic pursuit. Its foundational method is historical criticism.[9] Schleiermacher believed that theology had to be founded on this method since otherwise it would not be part of the scientific enterprise as defined, promoted, and established by the universities of his time.

This conviction also applied to biblical studies since Schleiermacher considered historical criticism as the key to scientific-modern knowledge. Academic Bible study was considered historical work because only "the historically situated scientific method"[10] creates the kind of

---

7. For an elaboration on these and other pedagogical models, see ibid., 69. See also her other publications that include further explanations on the models: Schüssler Fiorenza, *But She Said: The Practices of Feminist Biblical Interpretation* (Boston: Beacon, 1992); Schüssler Fiorenza, *Wisdom Ways: Introducing Feminist Biblical Interpretation* (Maryknoll, NY: Orbis, 2001).

8. Friedrich Schleiermacher, *Brief Outline on the Study of Theology*, trans. of the 1811 and 1830 eds., with essays and notes, by Terrence N. Tice (Lewiston, NY: Mellen, 1990); Friedrich Schleiermacher, *Kurze Darstellung des Theologischen Studiums zum Behuf einleitender Vorlesungen: Kritische Ausgabe herausgegeben von Heinrich Scholz* (Darmstadt: Wissenschaftliche Buchgesellschaft, 1993).

9. Robert W. Ferris, "The Role of Theology in Theological Education," in *With an Eye on the Future: Development and Mission in the Twenty-First Century; Essays in Honor of Ted W. Ward*, ed. D. H. Elmer and L. McKinney (Monrovia: MARC, 1996), 101–11.

knowledge that furthers the understanding of the church. Historical investigation is essential to Schleiermacher's curricular vision because "historical criticism is the all-pervasive and indispensable organ for the work of historical theology, as it is for the entire field of historical studies."[11] Only when the Christian religion is related to past developments, Schleiermacher maintained, would scholars be able to address the church's future. He explained: "The present simply cannot be regarded as the kernel of the future that is to correspond more nearly to the full conception of the Church, or to any other notion, unless one recognizes how it has developed out of the past."[12] Or put more succinctly: "The present, however, can only be understood as a result of the past."[13]

Schleiermacher was primarily interested in Christianity and the New Testament. To him, the New Testament is the "first" discipline of "historical theology" because "[knowledge of primitive Christianity] rests entirely upon the correct understanding of these writings."[14] It was difficult for him to integrate the Hebrew Bible into this Christian framework, an anti-Jewish bias characteristic of much of Christian thought that also affected his curricular vision. He addressed the New Testament more frequently than the Hebrew Bible because, in his view, the Old Testament had little to contribute to Christian doctrine. He wrote: "That the Jewish codex does not contain any normative statements of faith regarding distinctively Christian doctrines will doubtless be recognized almost universally."[15] Nevertheless, he still believed that the Old Testament should receive the same exegetical treatment as the New Testament. In one brief sentence he affirmed that the Old Testament should also be examined with historical methods, stating: "The same applies to the ordering of the books of the Old Testament in our Bible."[16]

Not only did he define biblical studies as a historical discipline, but he also structured the exegetical process. He directed scholars to begin with the biblical text, to create an exegetical apparatus based on philological standards, and to work with the original languages—all of which

---

10. Ibid.
11. Schleiermacher, *Brief Outline*, §102 (p. 57); Schleiermacher, *Kurze Darstellung*, 43.
12. Schleiermacher, *Brief Outline*, §26 (p. 16); Schleiermacher, *Kurze Darstellung*, 11.
13. Schleiermacher, *Brief Outline*, §82 (p. 47); Schleiermacher, *Kurze Darstellung*, 35.
14. Schleiermacher, *Brief Outline*, §88 (p. 50); Schleiermacher, *Kurze Darstellung*, 38.
15. Schleiermacher, *Brief Outline*, §115 (p. 63); Schleiermacher, *Kurze Darstellung*, 47. Yet he also wanted to continue early church practice that united "the Old Testament with the New Testament to one whole book."
16. Ibid.

was not yet regularly done at the time. Schleiermacher dismissed commentary literature as academically inadequate when it "lack[s] philological spirit and art," "remain[s] within the bounds of general edification," and "only produce[s] confusion by its pseudo-religious tendency."[17] His unwavering commitment to developing an academically rigorous and methodologically sound biblical studies curriculum, grounded in historical analysis, has shaped the teaching of the Bible at universities, divinity schools, seminaries, and colleges worldwide ever since.[18]

It should also be mentioned that this curricular vision encountered repeated attempts of scholarly critique. In 1899, W. R. Harper questioned some of Schleiermacher's assumptions, followed by critique from William Adams Brown and Mark A. May in 1934, H. Richard Niebuhr in 1956, and Edward Farley in 1983.[19] In 1992 and 1993, David H. Kelsey noted that the curriculum at theological schools is a cause for the "fragmentation of theological education."[20] Kelsey reminds his readers that the division into biblical, historical, systematic-theological, and practical fields emerged in the late eighteenth-century pietist and the nineteenth-century "Berlin" model. He also notes that this model has become so pervasive that it shapes the theological curriculum of theological schools almost everywhere.

Most importantly, Kelsey worries that due to its modern scientific assumptions Schleiermacher's curricular vision rejects the original task of educating clergy, which he defines as the preparation of future clergy toward a better understanding of God. The existing curriculum alienates students from their professional tasks because it introduces them to the latest scholarly discourse and lacks a systemic focus on spiritual-theological issues. Accordingly, the agenda of academic disciplines in (Protestant) theology is "more deeply shaped by interests currently central to the relevant guild"[21] than most mission statements of seminaries would indicate. As a consequence, curricular tensions

17. Schleiermacher, *Brief Outline*, §148 (p. 77); Schleiermacher, *Kurze Darstellung*, 58.
18. Shanta Premawardhana, "Preparing Religious Leaders for Our Time," *TThRel* 9 (2006): 71.
19. Edward Farley, *Theologia: The Fragmentation and Unity of Theological Education* (Philadelphia: Fortress Press, 1983); Richard H. Niebuhr, Daniel Day Williams, and James M. Gustafson, *The Purpose of the Church and Its Ministry: Reflections on the Aims of Theological Education* (New York: Harper & Brothers, 1956); William Adams Brown et al., *The Education of American Ministers*, 4 vols. (New York: Institute of Social and Religious Research, 1934); William Rainey Harper, "Shall the Theological Curriculum Be Modified and How?," *American Journal of Theology* 3 (1899): 45–66.
20. David H. Kelsey, *To Understand God Truly: What's Theological about a Theological School* (Louisville: Westminster John Knox, 1992), 232–34; Kelsey, *Between Athens and Berlin: The Theological Education Debate* (Grand Rapids: Eerdmans, 1993).
21. Kelsey, *To Understand God Truly*, 234.

characterize theological education that is torn between research interests on the one hand and professional training on the other. Kelsey explains:

> Disciplines tend to develop an agenda of their own as sets of practices with interests rooted in the social location of those practices (e.g. universities). They tend, in short, to take on a life of their own, having the power to order and govern the courses comprising a course of study. In this context, commitment to specialization and its central disciplines may lead to a commitment to preserving one's own area . . . thereby preserving the particular fragmentation. . . . For that reason, in the present state of inquiry in theological schooling it may be difficult for theological schools to embrace the disciplines without threat to the theological integrity of their theological task.[22]

To Kelsey, the theological curriculum threatens the integrity of theological education because it invites disciplinary fragmentation. Some educators, such as Pheme Perkins, want to ease this tension by combining historical criticism with a theological vision.[23] This is a compromise, an "add-on" approach with its own set of problems, but it is part of a "tradition" that searches for alternatives to the Schleiermacher curriculum.

Another such voice comes from Catholic educator Lawrence E. Boadt in a discussion on the purpose of biblical studies at Catholic universities and seminaries. Boadt, too, hopes for a biblical studies curriculum that moves beyond the narrow confines of historical criticism. He suggests including what he calls a "post-critical interpretation" that values the "existence and active role [of the Bible] in the believing community from which it arose and for and to which it speaks."[24] Boadt distinguishes between a strict academic and a faith-oriented study of the Bible when he writes: "University scholarship may limit its task to the examination of how this relationship works itself out in the actual composition of the biblical text and its history of interpretation, but seminary biblical studies must also communicate to its students how to translate this into the lives of a believing community."[25] This proposal is theologically conservative—after all, Boadt favors a religious

---

22. Ibid.
23. Pheme Perkins, "Revisioning the Teaching of Scripture," *Current Issues in Catholic Higher Education* 7 (1987): 29–32.
24. Lawrence E. Boadt, "Biblical Studies in University and Seminary Theology," in *Theological Education in the Catholic Tradition: Contemporary Challenges*, ed. Patrick W. Carey and Earl C. Muller (New York: Crossroad, 1997), 262.
25. Ibid., 263.

and liturgical approach to the Bible. Still, it is important to recognize that Boadt's assessment questions the universal validity of Schleiermacher's model. Like other theological educators, Boadt envisions a curriculum that goes beyond the historical paradigm. Yet he and the other critics have not been able to advance a comprehensive reform of the dominant curriculum in biblical studies.

The curricular situation is different for undergraduate (and graduate) institutions that adhere to Christian-fundamentalist, evangelical-conservative positions. They promote a biblical studies curriculum divorced from the theo-pedagogical and academic-scientific developments that characterize Schleiermacher's vision. Embracing the Bible as the literal or "infallible Word of God,"[26] doctrinal positions shape the biblical curriculum of many Christian fundamentalist and evangelical-conservative schools of higher education. An example is Grace College in Winona Lake, Indiana, "an evangelical Christian community of higher education which applies biblical studies values in strengthening character, sharpening competence, and preparing for service."[27] Its "covenant of faith" states:

> We believe in THE HOLY SCRIPTURES: accepting fully the writings of the Old and New Testaments as the very Word of God, verbally inspired in all parts and therefore wholly without error as originally given of God, altogether sufficient in themselves as our only infallible rule of faith and practice (Matt 5:18; John 10:35, 16:13, 17:17; 2 Tim 3:16; 2 Pet 1:21).[28]

When the Bible is publicly proclaimed as the inerrant word of God in the context of higher education, it is studied abundantly, but the Schleiermacher curriculum is discarded because such schools assert the separation of faith and academic theological work. Theologically conservative schools want to claim academic rigor in their undergraduate biblical studies curriculum, but more often than not their faith convictions get in the way.[29] By contrast, academically "mainstream" seminaries and colleges stand in the tradition of Schleiermacher's curricular vision that shapes their Bible courses today. They exemplify the close connections between undergraduate

---

26. See, e.g., the website of Trinity Christian College, a four-year liberal arts college southwest of Chicago: http://tinyurl.com/lqyoqtw.
27. See "Mission and Values," Grace College and Seminary, http://tinyurl.com/k9lqmbz.
28. See "The Covenant of Faith," Grace College and Seminary, http://tinyurl.com/mtyaonz.
29. A list of colleges with a similar outlook can be found at the "National Christian College Athletic Association," www.thenccaa.org.

and graduate biblical studies, yet provide little room for curricular innovation and educational transformation.

The Hebrew Bible at US-American Liberal Arts Colleges

Many course descriptions at several liberal arts colleges in the United States give evidence of a biblical studies curriculum that advances the "philological-historical or exegetical-doctrinal disciplinary para-digm"[30] and emphasizes content description and historical-literal pre-sentation of biblical literature. The following discussion illustrates the prevalence of this paradigm as it appears in the online course descrip-tions of several undergraduate academic catalogs.[31] The selected col-leges share several traits but also exhibit some differences. All of them are located in the United States; they are four-year, private, liberal arts colleges, and all of them have name recognition. A few are denomi-nationally (Christian) affiliated, several are women's colleges, and one is a historically black college. They are the College of the Holy Cross, Kalamazoo College, Wellesley College, Pomona College, Barnard Col-lege, Agnes Scott College, and Morehouse College. This is a relatively small number of institutions, but cursory study of the curriculum at other schools indicates the overall validity of the following observa-tions. For the sake of disciplinary coherence the focus is on the Hebrew Bible.

It is important to remember that, before going further, the obser-vations made in this essay do not claim universality. They describe curricular tendencies and trends, and they *suggest* the validity of the charge that the dominant approach in undergraduate classrooms emphasizes content description and historical-literal presentation of biblical literature. Since a comprehensive study of the undergrad-uate biblical studies curriculum does not currently exist and because it is always difficult to undertake such a review due to the shifting dynamics in any teaching environment, this article invites readers to add their professional experiences of undergraduate teaching in biblical studies when they consider the validity of the following observations.

---

30. Schüssler Fiorenza, "Rethinking Educational Practices," 68.
31. The discussion was also enhanced by personal correspondence with several professors who teach at the selected colleges.

A relatively consistent pattern emerges from the various Hebrew Bible course descriptions. Historical analysis shapes the pedagogical agenda, although other methodological and hermeneutical developments are sometimes included. For instance, the Department of Religious Studies at the College of the Holy Cross in Worcester, Massachusetts, a Catholic liberal arts college, offers a "bread and butter course"[32] on the Hebrew Bible titled "Religious Studies 126—Introduction to the Old Testament." The course places the Bible in "the social and cultural worlds that produced the texts, examines the biblical texts themselves, and investigates the assumptions and methods employed by pre-modern, modern (post-Enlightenment), and postmodern interpreters of the Bible."[33] Another course listed in Holy Cross's catalog is "Women and/in the Bible," which analyzes "the function of patriarchy in the biblical texts, in the ancient world that produced the texts, and in the interpretations of the Scriptures throughout history."[34] According to Alice Laffey, professor of Old Testament at Holy Cross, the specifics of the course have changed since it was first offered in the early 1980s. Yet other markers have remained the same. The description still refers to the "Bible" because originally the course covered both the Old and New Testaments.

Other courses not listed in the online catalog but taught in recent years include "Old Testament and Contemporary Prophets" as well as seminars and tutorials on prophetic literature, the Psalms, and Hebrew language. Since, according to Laffey, Holy Cross students do not usually register for advanced courses in Old Testament, the department does not often offer them. She explains that "most of [our undergraduate] students . . . are not interested in an advanced course in Old Testament."[35] In contrast, the departmental online catalog lists five intermediate and advanced New Testament courses in addition to a New Testament introduction course, although none of the courses promote a Roman Catholic or other denominational faith perspective.[36] In general, then, this curriculum stands in the Schleiermacher tradition, favoring historical analysis and emphasizing the New Testament.

---

32. I acknowledge gratefully Dr. Alice Laffey, who took the time to correspond with me about the department's curriculum and who used this phrase in an email message on June 28, 2008.
33. See the Old Testament course description at the website of College of the Holy Cross, http://tinyurl.com/n75p3dj.
34. Ibid.
35. In an email message to me on June 28, 2008.
36. Dr. Laffey made this point in an email message on June 28, 2008.

Similar tendencies appear at Kalamazoo College in Kalamazoo, Michigan, originally founded as a Baptist college in 1833. The online catalog lists an introduction course to the Old Testament, which is described as the "study of ancient Israel's sacred literature in its historical and religious development."[37] Again, historical analysis shapes the outlook, although the lack of details leaves room for developing the course in various directions. In 2008, the catalog also listed another course, titled "Studies in Old Testament," which consisted of a "detailed examination of some aspects of the Old Testament, for example the Wisdom literature: Job, Proverbs, Ecclesiastes, etc, and their relationship to the wisdom heritage of the ancient Near East and to the sacred traditions of Israel." According to the available information at Kalamazoo College, students encounter the academic study of the Hebrew Bible primarily as a historical project.

Likewise, the curriculum of Wellesley College in Wellesley, Massachusetts, limits Hebrew Bible courses as a historical project, although literary approaches appear in several course descriptions. For instance, the course titled "REL 104 Study of the Hebrew Bible/Old Testament" promises the "critical introduction to the Hebrew Bible/Old Testament, studying its role in the history and culture of ancient Israel and its relationship to ancient Near Eastern cultures." Yet it also includes a story of "the fundamental techniques of literary, historical, and source criticism in modern scholarship, with emphasis on the Bible's literary structure and compositional evolution."[38] Another course, "REL 243 Women in the Biblical World," locates biblical studies in the historical paradigm. The blurb specifies the content: "The roles and images of women in the Bible, and in early Jewish and Christian literature, examined in the context of the ancient societies in which these documents emerged. Special attention to the relationship among archaeological, legal, and literary sources in reconstruction to status of women in these societies."[39]

Other Bible courses follow this pattern, such as a seminar titled "The Sacrifice of the Beloved Child in the Bible and Its Interpretation," which examines both the historical and cultural significance of Genesis 22, or the topical course "Jerusalem: The Holy City,"[40] which also

---

37. See the website of Kalamazoo College, www.kzoo.edu/programs/?id=28&type=2 (accessed on August 17, 2010). The Wayback Machine provides access to archived webpages at http://archive.org/web/web.php.
38. See www.wellesley.edu/Religion/courseofferings/courseofferings.html (accessed on August 17, 2010).
39. See www.wellesley.edu/Religion/professors/Geller/geller.html (accessed on August 17, 2010).

includes cross-religious references to Judaism, Christianity, and Islam. The course catalog in biblical studies for 2007–2008 lists three Old Testament and five New Testament courses. The trend is clear: undergraduate Hebrew Bible courses focus on historical methodology and so reinforce the paradigm that emerged in the nineteenth century. Sometimes courses also include approaches such as literary criticism and, especially at the introductory level, they emphasize content description.

Yet several undergraduate religion departments stretch their biblical studies curriculum in more innovative hermeneutical directions. Among them is the department of religious studies at Pomona College in Claremont, California. Its academic catalog includes courses that explore biblical literature with decidedly cultural and postmodern methodologies. For instance, a course titled "The Biblical Heritage" acknowledges the Bible as "important for the formation and ongoing structure of U.S. American culture" and promises to "explore the [biblical] texts through careful reading and critical analysis, using a variety of interpretive strategies, including historical, literary, and ideological critical analyses."[41] Other courses give a nod to the historical context of the Bible, such as the course "Life: Love and Suffering in Biblical Wisdom and the Modern World" or a course, firmly grounded in historical methodology, titled "New Testament and Christian Origins." Yet courses on film ("Celluloid Bible: Hollywood, the Bible, and Ideology") and queer theory ("Queer Theory and the Bible") examine the Bible's intersection with culture. In these courses, cultural-theoretical concerns prevail, as the following course description exemplifies:

> 184. Queer Theory and the Bible. This course will look at how the Bible can be read productively through queer theory. We will examine biblical passages that are central to prohibitions on homosexuality, and the larger discourses of heteronormativity (constructed around gender, sexuality, class, national identity, state formations, kinship, children etc.) in which homophobic readings of the Bible emerge. We will also look at the ways in which these discourses and the identities they shore up can be "queered," as well as at biblical that can be read as queer friendly. This process of queering will allow and require us to approach the biblical text in new ways.

40. See www.wellesley.edu/Religion/courseofferings/coureofferings.html (accessed on August 17, 2010).
41. For all courses mentioned here, visit www.pomona.edu/academics/departments/religious-studies/courses/all-courses.aspx (accessed on August 17, 2010).

Not even referencing the historical paradigm, this course focuses on queer theory as a lens for examining biblical texts and the history of interpretation. It is grounded in cutting-edge biblical scholarship that engages biblical literature as a hermeneutically relevant resource for contemporary readers in today's world.

Similar curricular innovation is part of the religious studies department of Barnard College in New York City. Next to traditional courses, such as "Rel 3501 Hebrew Bible: Introduction to the Literature of Ancient Israel against the Background of the Ancient Near East," other courses advance newer hermeneutical developments. An example is the following course:

4730 Exodus & Politics: Religious Narrative as a Source of Revolution: Examination of the study of the Israelite exodus from Egypt, as it has influenced modern forms of political and social revolution, w/ emphasis on political philosopher Michael Walzer. Examination of the variety of context this story has been used in: construction of early American identity, African-American religious experience, Latin American liberation theology, Palestinian nationalism, and religious feminism.[42]

The course investigates the book of Exodus through its history of interpretation and relates the academic study of the Bible to society, politics, culture, and religion. Perhaps these are the kind of courses Schüssler Fiorenza had in mind when she thought of creativity and innovation at the undergraduate level. Yet they appear to be rare in a biblical studies curriculum that accentuates historical methodology.

Sometimes the undergraduate curriculum also perpetuates another dynamic that has haunted Christian theology for millennia. Although the data are limited here, it may serve as a cautionary note on the inherent difficulties of teaching the Bible to broad audiences, as in the case at the undergraduate level. The problem is that sometimes the undergraduate curriculum contains a total of one Hebrew Bible course. As a result, in-depth courses are rare, and generic courses emerge. Such a situation seems to have evolved at the religious studies department at Agnes Scott College in Decatur, Georgia, which lists only a single Hebrew Bible course, titled "100 Hebrew Bible." The blurb states: "Religious history and society of the people of ancient Israel as contained in their sacred Scriptures with a link to contemporary Jewish practice and interpretation."[43] Grounded in historical analysis,

42. See www.barnard.edu/catalog.pdf (accessed on August 17, 2010).
43. Agnes Scott's academic catalog of 2007–2009 lists only one Hebrew Bible course, but other courses

the course covers two broad areas, Israelite history and contemporary Judaism, and so the course connects the study of the Hebrew Bible with Judaism. But locating the Hebrew Bible as part of Judaism only is problematic because it marginalizes the Old Testament as an integral part of the Christian canon. It assumes that the Old Testament is secondary to Christian theology. The second-century Christian theologian Marcion is among the most renowned proponents of this anti-Jewish attitude toward the Old Testament, a position that the early church rejected.[44]

The Agnes Scott catalog lists an introductory course on the New Testament that aggravates the problem. In parallel design to the Hebrew Bible course, the New Testament blurb promises to examine the New Testament literature "with links to contemporary Christian practice and interpretation."[45] The course reinforces the notion that the Hebrew Bible belongs only to Judaism and Christian practices and the New Testament is more important to Christians than the Hebrew Bible. It would be advantageous theologically and pedagogically to include Jewish and Christian practices and interpretations in a single Hebrew Bible course to avoid misunderstandings about the Hebrew Bible's significance to Christianity.

Similarly, Kenyon College in Gambier, Ohio, mentions in its online course catalog only one Hebrew Bible course, titled "RLST 310 Hebrew Scriptures/Old Testament." The description states:

> This course will serve as an introduction to the Hebrew Scriptures (Old Testament), as they reflect the myths, history, and institutions of ancient Israel. Topics to be explored will include biblical narrative and poetry, law codes, prayers and ritual, the prophetic critique of religion and society, and wisdom literature. Students will be given an opportunity to read a selection of short fiction and poetry that have been inspired by biblical literature.[46]

include the study of Judaism and Christianity. Among them are New Testament; Jesus in History and Culture; Introduction to Christianity; Judaism, Christianity, and Islam; Sacred Texts and World's Religions; Jewish Faith and Practice; Roman Catholic Faith and Practice; Protestant Faith and Practice; Gender in U.S. Religion; Feminist and Womanist Ethics and Spirituality. See www.agnesscott.edu/academics/catalog (accessed on August 17, 2010).

44. See, e.g., Padraic O'Hare, *The Enduring Covenant: The Education of Christians and the End of Antisemitism* (Valley Forge, PA: Trinity Press International, 1997); Craig A. Evans and Donald A. Hagner, eds., *Anti-Semitism and Early Christianity: Issues of Polemic and Faith* (Minneapolis: Fortress Press, 1993); Charlotte Klein, *Anti-Judaism in Christian Theology*, trans. Edward Quinn (Philadelphia: Fortress Press, 1978).

45. The complete course blurb states: "101 Literature of the New Testament and its origins and development in the early Jesus movement and early Christianity, with links to contemporary Christian practice and interpretation."

46. See www.kenyon.edu/x11447.xml (accessed on August 17, 2010). Two additional courses in biblical studies appear in the online catalog; one introduces the New Testament ("RLST 225 New Tes-

This course places the study of the Hebrew Bible firmly within the historical paradigm, although it also promises to trace the Hebrew Bible in literature. The historical outlook evades the curricular problem of the Agnes Scott curriculum, but it too does not move beyond the nineteenth-century model.

Other colleges pursue yet a different route by developing a comprehensive "mini-seminary" curriculum. This is the case at the Department of Philosophy and Religion at Morehouse College in Atlanta, Georgia, where an Old Testament introduction course is followed by the New Testament equivalent and several specialized Bible courses, such as "235 The Eighth Century Prophets" and "230 Understanding the Bible," followed by courses on church history, systematic theology, and psychology of religion.[47]

In short, then, these undergraduate departments conceptualize Hebrew Bible courses primarily as history courses that illuminate ancient Near Eastern and Israelite history. Sometimes they also include literary approaches, and only a few courses investigate the Hebrew Bible with contemporary hermeneutics and methodologies. Overall, then, the undergraduate curriculum remains closely tied to the Protestant vision of Schleiermacher, which conceptualizes biblical studies as a historical enterprise.

Admittedly, only a few examples substantiate the points made above, but another indicator supports the accuracy of the observations. This one comes from undergraduate textbooks that illustrate that the undergraduate curriculum mimics the graduate curriculum of Schleiermacher's vision. The books are published in edition after edition because there are many Bible courses that require them. Accordingly, they preserve a curriculum that fosters historical-literalist description of biblical texts. The next section examines popular textbooks in Hebrew Bible to demonstrate the prevalence of this curricular pattern.

---

tament") and another investigates the phenomenon of prophecy in biblical and contemporary literatures and sociopolitical movements ("RLST 382 Prophecy").

47. The course blurb explains: "210 Introduction to the Old Testament: Survey of the literature of the Old Testament, bringing to bear upon it the fruits of modern historical and archaeological research." See Morehouse College, Department of Philosophy and Religion, http://tinyurl.com/n75p3dj.

Undergraduate Textbooks on the Hebrew Bible

Anyone who teaches at the undergraduate level receives textbooks that arrive in the office mailbox without request. Publishers send them because they know that professors are continually looking for new books to be used in future semesters. Many of these books outline the biblical story line in accessible prose aided by graphs, photos, and art pictures. As a whole, the books simplify complex historical, linguistic, and scholarly discussions, and they summarize seemingly straightforward Israelite history, events, and characters. Usually, they omit details on postmodern hermeneutical advances or the difficulties of historical reconstruction. Discussion on multiple meanings, newer exegetical methods, and the significance of social location are largely absent, as is information on the use of the Bible in contemporary US-American society such as the Ten Commandments or the creationist controversy. Content overviews, historical dates, and abbreviated historical analyses predominate.

A good example is Stephen L. Harris's *Understanding the Bible*, a book that describes the Christian canon in 533 pages.[48] The book follows the canonical order of the Bible and surveys biblical content and historiographical discussions. Devoting a single page to "the Bible read from different social perspectives,"[49] Harris mentions hermeneutical issues. He acknowledges that "in recent years, scholars have become increasingly aware that the meaning of any book—including the Bible—is to a large extent dependent on the reader's individual experience and viewpoint."[50]

Harris's statement is not entirely accurate since debates on social location are not often defined by "individual" experiences or viewpoints but are instead a matter of collective historical, cultural, and political developments in society, politics, economics, and religion. Furthermore, the ensuing short description on African American, Native American, and feminist hermeneutics is too brief to give readers a sense of the research as it has developed since the 1970s. For instance, Harris states that "as feminist critics have pointed out, women of all nationalities may read the Bible from a perspective different from that of most men."[51] This short comment shortchanges feminist

---

48. Stephen L. Harris, *Understanding the Bible*, 7th ed. (Boston: McGraw Hill, 2006).
49. Ibid., 33.
50. Ibid.
51. Ibid.

accomplishments and makes feminist goals seem naive. Feminist interpretations are not grounded in essentializing notions that emphasize
differences between women and men, but they investigate the relationship between the Bible and androcentrism and in its intersectional
manifestations.[52]

A specific reference to Pauline gender politics does not remedy Harris's cryptic discussion of feminist biblical scholarship. In a literalist
statement on Pauline and post-Pauline passages, Harris writes:

> Paul's flat refusal to permit a woman to teach in his churches (1 Cor
> 14:34–35) or the Pastor's insistence that the first woman must be blamed
> for humanity's downward spiral into sin and death (1 Tim 2:13–14) may
> spark feelings of incredulity or resentment unknown to the men listening
> to the same passage. But, as feminist scholars have also observed, the
> same apostle who allegedly forbade women to address the congregation
> also recognized the role of women prophets (1 Cor 11:5) and women as
> church officeholders, as well as "fellow workers" in the Christian fold
> (Rom 16:1–5). At his most insightful, Paul endorses a vision of radical
> equality—legal, ethnic, social, and sexual. . . . (Gal 3:28).[53]

In this brief statement on women's places in early Christian movements, Harris refers to popular New Testament passages as if this short
description summarized the complex results of feminist research. Content description of selected verses becomes a substitute for a thorough
representation of the pertinent scholarly positions. This nod at contemporary hermeneutical accomplishments confirms the overall
impression that Harris promotes a curriculum mostly based on the
historical-literalist paradigm. Many similar textbooks also engage the
literalist-descriptive strategy evident in Harris's book, advancing the
Schleiermacher paradigm.[54]

---

52. For information on these developments in Hebrew Bible Studies, see Susanne Scholz, *Introducing
the Women's Hebrew Bible* (London: T&T Clark, 2007), esp. 100–121.
53. Harris, *Understanding the Bible*, 33.
54. Barry L. Bandstra, *Reading the Old Testament: An Introduction to the Hebrew Bible* (Belmont, CA:
Wadsworth/Thomson Learning, 2004); Bernhard W. Anderson, with Steven Bishop and Judith H.
Newman, *Understanding the Old Testament*, 5th ed. (Upper Saddle River, NJ: Prentice Hall, 2007);
Corrine L. Carvalho, *Encountering Ancient Voices: A Guide to Reading the Old Testament* (Winona, MN:
Saint Mary's Press, 2006); Christian E. Hauer and William A. Young, *Introduction to the Bible* (Upper
Saddle River, NJ: Prentice Hall, 2005); Adam L. Porter, *Introducing the Bible: An Active Learning
Approach* (Upper Saddle River, NJ: Prentice Hall, 2005); John J. Collins, *Introduction to the Hebrew
Bible* (Minneapolis: Augsburg Fortress Press, 2004); Stephen Harris and Robert Platzner, *The Old
Testament: An Introduction to the Hebrew Bible* (New York: McGraw-Hill, 2002); Henry Jackson Flan-
ders, Robert W. Crapps, and David A. Smith, *People of the Covenant: An Introduction to the Hebrew Bible*
(New York: Oxford University Press, 1996); Frank S. Frick, *A Journey through the Hebrew Scriptures*
(Fort Worth: Harcourt Brace College Publishers, 1995).

Another textbook that is solidly grounded in historical analysis tries to accomplish more. Written by J. Bradley Chance and Milton P. Horne,[55] *Rereading the Bible: An Introduction to the Biblical Story*, is not limited to canonical content description interspersed with historical research because, as the authors state, "it is virtually impossible to survey the sixty-six books of the Bible in a typically fifteen-week semester" and "inevitably, professors must be selective."[56] Thus Chance and Horne make "no pretense to cover everything."[57] They organize the materials according to the scholarly conviction that "the Bible came to be as a result of interpretive readings of earlier texts and traditions."[58] The pedagogical goal is that students learn "how the Bible came to be."[59] Thus Chance and Horne start with the latest "rereading" contained in the Hebrew Bible canon, the postexilic books of Ezra and Nehemiah. This hermeneutical decision puts the postexilic books into a prominent and unusual position. In contrast to other textbooks, Ezra and Nehemiah appear in the initial chapters of the book. In addition, postexilic Jewish topics organize the entire presentation of the Hebrew Bible, among them "the Temple, the Torah, and an ideology of self-exclusion endorsed by many Jewish people of this era."[60]

Yet even this innovative approach is limited to traditional conventions of the biblical studies curriculum. Emphasizing historical origins and authorial meaning, it excludes the rich postcanonical history of interpretation. It also does not include discussions on the rhetorical functions of biblical texts in the past and present context, or an examination of the ideological meanings in variously located sociopolitical and religious discourse. Although the book tries to break with a linear description of biblical content mixed with historical-critical information, it too does not go beyond the nineteenth-century paradigm. Chance and Horne aim for a "radical-democratic" curricular model, but ultimately they do not succeed because they limit themselves to historical methodology and content description.

These and other books, then, demonstrate the pervasiveness of the traditional nineteenth-century curriculum. Similar to Hebrew Bible courses, they emphasize historical-literalist analysis. Kelsey observes

55. J. Bradley Chance and Milton P. Horne, *Rereading the Bible: An Introduction to the Biblical Story* (Upper Saddle River, NJ: Prentice Hall, 2000).
56. Ibid., xviii.
57. Ibid., xviii.
58. Ibid., xix.
59. Ibid., xx.
60. Ibid.

that theological teaching, research, and writing reinforce each other. They are discipline-preserving activities that make change difficult to attain, whether on the undergraduate or graduate level.

A "Radical-Democratic" Model for Teaching Biblical Studies

Elisabeth Schüssler Fiorenza contends that research and teaching of biblical studies need to "articulate a radical democratic religious imaginary that sustains wo/men, in transnational struggles against the injustice and devastations of global empire and for the survival and well-being of all."[61] This rhetorical-emancipatory model is based on "an ethical-political turn"[62] that "investigates and reconstructs the discursive arguments of a text, its socioreligious location, and its diverse interpretations in order to underscore the text's possible oppressive as well as liberative/performative actions, values, and possibilities in ever-changing historical-cultural situations."[63] This is the abstract agenda of a radical-democratic curriculum in biblical studies. It teaches how to understand a text's discursive arguments, examines the various socioreligious and political contexts within which these arguments are made and read, and recognizes the oppressive and liberative textual histories and potentials within multiple reading contexts.

Schüssler Fiorenza's proposal is clear. A biblical studies curriculum cannot be limited to content description and historical-literal presentation. Schleiermacher's vision, modified or not, is insufficient in an era in which human and ecological needs are perhaps greater than ever. Is it then preferable and more effective to nurture students' faith, as evangelical departments of theology and religion tend to do? Schleiermacher rejected vehemently this option during a time in which historiography counted as superior intellectual work. Yet his priority does not match contemporary needs, which are increasingly characterized by "multicultural versus fundamentalism" sensibilities.[64] Our times are different from the nineteenth-century European enthusiasm for historically defined truth, valid anywhere and for anyone.

---

61. Elisabeth Schüssler Fiorenza, *The Power of the Word: Scripture and the Rhetoric of Empire* (Minneapolis: Fortress Press, 2007), 27.
62. Ibid., 253.
63. Ibid., 253–54.
64. See, e.g., the informative discussion on this dynamic by Jeffrey W. Robbins, "Terror and the Postmodern Condition: Toward a Radical Political Theology," in *Religion and Violence in a Secular World: Toward a New Political Theology*, ed. Clayton Crocket (Charlottesville: University of Virginia Press, 2006), 187–205.

Taking these ideas into account, I developed an anthology titled *Biblical Studies Alternatively*, which contains scholarly resources for teaching Bible courses grounded in the radical-democratic teaching model.[65] More specifically, the materials help in correlating the study of the Bible to gender, race/ethnicity, and class. They are a resource for interpreting biblical literature as a site of theo-ethical and sociopolitical struggle in the past and the present, "as a site of struggle over authority, values, and meaning" with "public character and political responsibility."[66] Some articles in the volume do not reject the historical-literalist model. Yet all of them provide perspectives and resources to enhance a radical-democratic approach. The anthology promotes multiplicity of meanings, reader centeredness, and sociopolitical explorations in biblical literature and interpretation.

Suffice it to say that the book aims to bring biblical literature "back" into the intellectual debates on today's social, political, cultural, and religious issues, and to release the Bible from its academically isolated, undervalued, and privatized space.[67] As one of my students said: "In this Bible course we have talked about everything: money, sexuality, race, religion, politics—is this still a course on the Bible?" I told the student that, yes, this is a course on the Bible, and I also asked them why they would not expect to learn about all of these issues in a biblical studies course. What followed was a good discussion on the inclination of many Western readers to historicize, sentimentalize, and privatize the Bible and its academic study.

An example shall demonstrate how the resources in *Biblical Studies Alternatively* foster a radical-democratic approach that develops in students' intellectual-religious maturity, historical-cultural understanding, and literary-ethical engagement. The book includes several articles that investigate the issues of class in relation to particular biblical texts. Debates on classism are not a popular topic in US-American society, and undergraduate students whom I taught during the past ten years are rarely asked to think critically about poverty and wealth. These mostly white undergraduate students typically take for granted that they belong to the numinous "middle class," and they tend to be firm believers in the ideology of the "American Dream." It takes several handouts and meetings to explore why most US-Americans

---

65. Susanne Scholz, ed., *Biblical Studies Alternatively: An Introductory Reader* (Upper Saddle River, NJ: Prentice Hall, 2003).
66. Schüssler Fiorenza, *Power of the Word*, 254.
67. For an analysis of this problem, see Hector Avalos, *The End of Biblical Studies* (Amherst, NY: Prometheus, 2007).

believe that they belong to the middle class, whether they are poor or independently wealthy or receive a paycheck each month. Students also learn that contemporary US-American society allows for less class mobility than contemporary European societies.

The work benefits from data on the overwhelming number of poor people in today's world, which challenges students to think about their ethical responsibilities toward economic inequality.[68] Students are usually appalled about the level of inequality in the United States, but they find it difficult to let go of politically conservative ideas about social welfare, charity, and the acquisition of wealth. They believe in the merits of a capitalist economy: "If you work hard, you will make it." They also often reject expanding foreign aid to poor nations because, in their opinion, too much money already flows into impoverished countries. Additional handouts quickly dispel these notions.[69]

Once the contemporary context is at least sufficiently scanned, the work continues with biblical texts and interpretations on wealth, poverty, and economic justice. For instance, we read Jon L. Berquist's "Dangerous Waters of Justice and Righteousness: Amos 5:18–27." This essay examines the famous prophetic passage in Amos that Christians and Jews like to mention in debates on socioeconomic injustice.[70] Berquist presents three interpretive traditions that focus particularly on verse 24. In the early twentieth century, interpreters emphasize the aspect of punishment in the prophetic announcement. The Revised Standard Versions (RSV) illustrates this viewpoint in its use of the noun "judgement" for the people's failings, condemning them to punishment. Amos is seen as a prophet of doom whose prophecy gives the people one last opportunity for change.

Later in the twentieth century, another interpretive tradition becomes prevalent that highlights the poem's positive ethical dimensions. It rejects the idea that God performs punitive justice, and instead stresses that people have to commit themselves to the doing of justice. Ethics solves the problem of religious ritual. Thus, for instance, Martin

---

68. Jeffrey Selingo and Jeffrey Brainard, "The Rich-Poor Gap Widens for Colleges and Students," *Chronicle of Higher Education*, April 7, 2006, A1, A13; Jo Blanden, Paul Gregg, and Stephen Machin, "Intergenerational Mobility in Europe and North America: A Report Supported by the Sutton Trust," *Centre for Economic Performance*, April 2005, http://tinyurl.com/k2xtdcj; Bob Herbert, "The Mobility Myth," *New York Times* (6 June 2005): 19; see also websites such as www.undp.org/poverty; www.globalissues.org/TradeRelated/Poverty.asp?p=1; and www.policyalmanac.org/social_welfare/poverty.shtml.
69. See, e.g., "Relief Agency Criticizes Rich Lands," *New York Times*, December 6, 2004, A12.
70. Jon L. Berquist, "Dangerous Waters of Justice and Righteousness," in Scholz, *Biblical Studies Alternatively*, 327–41.

Luther King Jr. quotes verse 24 to instill hope for social change. This reading is optimistic about people's ability to function as agents for social justice. It assumes that we can change society for the better if we believe that working toward social change is doing God's work. In contrast to the earlier interpretive tradition, then, the prophet is not seen as a bringer of doom. The second tradition affirms the human ability to create justice on earth and views humans as the potential doers of God's will.

Berquist describes yet another interpretive tradition that stresses the significance of "the waters" in verse 24. Here the poem does not address a problem with ritual or worship practice, a position that sometimes has led to anti-Jewish views in Christian commentaries. Rather, the poem wrestles with the problem of unequal distribution of wealth and power. It offers a unique solution by calling for the total destruction of society because anything less would compromise divine justice and righteousness. Without such comprehensive and all-destructive change, the inconsistency between religious practice and societal justice would result in blasphemy.

This third interpretation requires an in-depth look at the terminology, especially the meaning of "the waters" in verse 24. Berquist explains that "the waters" should not be imagined as soothing and refreshing liquids, but instead as having dangerous and all-destructive qualities. They are forceful like Noah's flood that destroyed everything in its way. "The waters" contain the raw force of a tsunami that wipes out everything and everybody in its path. They are harbingers for divine justice and righteousness, eliminating unjust social conditions and ushering in a new beginning. The poem suggests that justice and righteousness, to be worthy of divine affiliation, arrive only after the annihilation of known society.

According to this interpretive tradition, then, God is seen as destroying all people to restore justice and righteousness in society. Like religious fundamentalists of any persuasion, Amos emerges as a prophet who calls for complete, uncompromised, and total change. Neither divine purging nor human intervention suffice to implement the divine order or to eradicate socioeconomic injustice, but rather the implementation of the divine order. It requires "the destruction of known society with the fulfillment of divine intention."[71] At best, then, the poem is "extremely countercultural."

71. Ibid., 340.

Students in my classes find the third interpretative tradition that characterizes Amos as a religious fundamentalist completely unacceptable. They associate fundamentalism with people flying planes into buildings, and they favor socioeconomic moderation and compromise. They do not support a position that solves the problem of poverty by calling for the total destruction of unjust society. It is difficult for them to view social injustice as such a grave problem to merit such extreme action. When students learn that other biblical passages, such as the book of Proverbs, address issues of wealth and poverty, yet are differently interpreted than the Amos poem, students are usually astonished at the plurality of biblical and interpretive viewpoints. They also begin to grasp the complexities of reading the Hebrew Bible with socioeconomic issues in mind. Exam after exam shows their growing intellectual-religious maturity, historical-cultural understanding, and literary-ethical engagement. It is a rewarding process, and, if space allowed it, additional examples could illustrate that this approach creates important pedagogical and intellectual learning in the undergraduate teaching of biblical studies.

In short, a radical-democratic approach—according to this specific example—examines the structures of globalized inequalities and injustices in the social, political, economic, and religious realms of human societies and relates them to the reading of biblical texts such as Amos 5:24. Understood as "a site of struggle over authority, values, and meaning,"[72] this kind of a biblical studies curriculum defines the academic study of the Bible as helping students understand the contributions of biblical interpretations to past and present political, societal, and economic Bible readings. It educates students toward an active participation in society and religion, freeing "them from all forms of kyriarchal inequality and oppression."[73]

In Conclusion

This essay has described the biblical studies curriculum as articulated by nineteenth-century theologian Friedrich Schleiermacher. It has investigated the ongoing contemporary dominance of this curriculum and illustrated the benefits of an alternative approach that envisions the teaching of biblical studies according to the radical democratic model as defined by Elisabeth Schüssler Fiorenza. This model is not

---

72. Schüssler Fiorenza, *Power of the Word*, 254.
73. Ibid.

often practiced in biblical studies, and the essay has shown that many undergraduate Bible courses and textbooks mimic a graduate curriculum committed to Schleiermacher's influential design of biblical studies as a historical-literalist enterprise.

This, then, is the pedagogical challenge for the field of biblical studies: to move from curricular apathy to a radical-democratic practice that educates students toward an understanding of the complexities and challenges in our world and toward an increase of "knowledge, values and skills that will prepare them for active and effective participation in society."[74] It is not an easy task for various reasons, not the least of which is the fact that the nineteenth-century model of theological education is well and alive.[75] Furthermore, many contemporary Western people are "allergic" to Christian fundamentalism and prefer to eliminate *all* religious study from higher education. In turn, Christian fundamentalists try to combat the secular disregard for religion. They fear a critical examination of the Bible because, in their view, it leads to religion's demise in the first place. For sure, the Christian Right in the United States works hard to reclaim the Bible—alas, in a religiously and sociopolitically conservative fashion. The result is a tug-of-war in which neither side wants to use rational arguments, and so the pedagogical aim of a radical-democratic curriculum runs into resistance from many sides.

Still, it is time to develop a biblical studies curriculum on all levels of higher education that teaches biblical studies as an academic field of inquiry, needed for a comprehensive understanding of culture, politics, and religion. Can the biblical studies curriculum be reshaped to account for the social, political, religious, and intellectual struggles in our world today? It is good to remember that Schleiermacher did not get discouraged when he saw little of the theological education he had in mind. Of course, in 1811, he was in a powerful academic position—really at the heart of the academic enterprise in Berlin, and able to implement changes as he saw fit. Many of us are not located at places of academic power, and nowadays it often seems as if changes arrived there last anyway. But a move toward the radical-democratic teaching model is possible wherever we teach, and a sustained conversation on the biblical studies curriculum at all levels ensures that we develop

74. Carol M. Barker, "Liberal Arts Education for a Global Society," Carnegie Corporation of New York, 2000, http://tinyurl.com/n49bq8e.
75. Another difficulty relates to the changing socioeconomic dynamics in US-American universities as institutions of higher learning; see Marc Bousquet, *How the University Works: Higher Education and the Low-Wage Nation* (New York: New York University Press, 2008).

a viable future for the field. This is, perhaps, more urgent now than in the nineteenth century because, as William M. Plater states, "the entire system of American postsecondary education is undergoing a profound transformation."[76] The next chapter elaborates on these university-wide developments with a focus on the external political and economic forces that inhibit the curricular redesign in biblical studies today.

---

76. William M. Plater, "The Twenty-First-Century Professoriate: We Need a New Vision if We Want to Create a Positive Future for the Faculty," *American Association of University Professors* (July-August 2008); available at http://www.redorbit.com/news/education/1533208/the_twentyfirst-century_professoriate/.

2

Occupy Academic Bible Teaching: The Architecture of Educational Power and the Biblical Studies Curriculum

If the Occupy movement[1] included a critical analysis of the structures in which the academic teaching of the Bible takes place today, it would find that the power dynamics shaping the academic curriculum of the Bible in North American and European colleges and universities is extremely slanted, so much so that a comprehensive transformation of the biblical studies curriculum may even be futile. Internal and external forces have contributed to this curricular situation. In the previous essay of this book,[2] I examined some of the *inner-disciplinary* dynamics in need of change for an alternative curriculum to emerge. I made the claim there that the teaching of biblical studies in liberal arts settings faces similar curricular challenges to graduate school settings because "the curricular structure of biblical studies, as taught at all levels of academic learning, is firmly stuck in a

---

1. For a brief description of the Occupy movement, see *Wikipedia*, s.v. "Occupy Movement," updated May 9, 2017, http://tinyurl.com/mw7378g.
2. Susanne Scholz, "Redesigning the Biblical Studies Curriculum: Toward a 'Radical Democratic' Teaching Model," in *Transforming Biblical Studies Education: Ethos and Discipline*, ed. Elisabeth Schüssler Fiorenza and Kent Harold Richards (Atlanta: SBL Press, 2010), 269–92.

nineteenth-century Christian-Protestant vision, as initially articulated by Friedrich Schleiermacher."[3] I substantiated this claim by highlighting three areas in the curricular design of biblical studies courses: I showed that the nineteenth-century curricular model still controls the basic assumptions of many undergraduate and graduate curricula; I examined teaching instruments, such as introductory books, to illustrate the ongoing popularity of teaching the Bible within the Schleiermacher model; and I outlined an alternative curricular vision for the teaching of biblical studies.

By examining the inner-disciplinary dynamics of the biblical studies curriculum, I maintained that a curricular transformation seemed not only necessary but also possible and even mandatory if we want biblical studies courses to meet the expectations of a liberal arts education, sometimes defined as "provid[ing] students with knowledge, values and skills that will prepare them for active and effective participation in society."[4] I suggested that a transformed biblical studies curriculum ought to be based on a "radical-democratic" educational vision developing in students "intellectual-religious maturity," "historical-cultural understanding," and "literary-ethical engagement" with the world. A few examples illustrated this vision, which champions a comprehensive redesign of the undergraduate and graduate curriculum, and fosters, develops, and encourages in students a thorough understanding of culture, politics, and religion. In a sense, then, the analysis of the inner-disciplinary status quo argues for a social-justice-oriented vision of the biblical studies curriculum.[5]

Although no extensive curricular debate currently takes place in the field, my proposal does not stand alone. Some renowned Bible scholars envision curricular redesigns. For instance, R. S. Sugirtharajah explains:

> Those who teach biblical studies need to come up with fresh plans to increase students' knowledge of the Bible, but the success of these renewed plans to deepen biblical literacy depends largely on how biblical courses prepare students for responsible citizenship in an increasingly globalized world as well as in Western countries whose populations now have their roots in an array of cultures and histories.[6]

3. Ibid., 270.
4. Carol M. Barker, "Liberal Arts Education for a Global Society," Carnegie Corporation of New York, 2000, http://tinyurl.com/n49bq8e.
5. I have been committed to this curricular vision and published accordingly; see, e.g., Susanne Scholz, ed., *Biblical Studies Alternatively: An Introductory Reader* (Upper Saddle River, NJ: Prentice Hall, 2003).

In the forefront of Sugirtharajah's vision for the biblical studies curriculum stands the development of "responsible citizenship" in a "globalized world." In other words, he wants biblical studies courses to contribute constructively and critically to democratic society. Other scholars report of already transformed curricula. Archie Lee describes a curriculum for "multiscriptural contexts." More specifically, the graduate program of the Department of Cultural and Religious Studies at the Chinese University of Hong Kong promotes a "cross-textual hermeneutic" that acknowledges the existence of Asian sacred texts and takes seriously students and their cultural contexts.[7] Prominent scholars urge moving the biblical studies curriculum from a historically defined curriculum toward a design that advances interdisciplinary, cross-cultural, and cross-textual hermeneutical explorations.[8] In accordance with these scholarly observations, the previous essay in this book maintains that "a move toward the radical democratic teaching model is possible whenever we teach, and a sustained conversation on the biblical studies curriculum at all levels ensures that we develop a viable future for the field."[9] It is an optimistic assessment for transforming the Bible curriculum. It is one of a few inner-disciplinary efforts to systematically redesign the academic teaching of biblical studies.

Yet the previous essay also hints at the fact that the relative lack of developing alternative curricula is not only related to a general lack of interest in the field. Powerful external forces impede such attempts, having put considerable pressures on many institutions of higher education during the past few decades. As William M. Plater, an English professor and former executive vice chancellor and dean of the faculties at Indiana University, explains, faculty members have increasingly become arbitrary to the curricular design because many of them only hold contingent appointments and perform disaggregated work. They lack job security and comprehensive institutional integration that earlier generations of the professoriate took for granted. Plater observes:

> Most American colleges and universities can no longer sustain an academic workforce based on an ideal of the "complete scholar" engaged

6. R. S. Sugirtharajah, "The End of Biblical Studies?," in *Toward a New Heaven and a New Earth: Essays in Honor of Elisabeth Schüssler Fiorenza*, ed. Fernando F. Segovia (Maryknoll, NY: Orbis, 2003), 136.
7. Archie C. C. Lee, "Cross-Textual Biblical Studies in Multiscriptural Contexts," in Schüssler Fiorenza and Richards, *Transforming Biblical Education*, 44.
8. See also, e.g., Elisabeth Schüssler Fiorenza, *Democratizing Biblical Studies: Toward an Emancipatory Educational Space* (Louisville: Westminster John Knox, 2009).
9. Scholz, "Redesigning the Curriculum," 292.

in coherent, integrated, and self-directed work across the full range of teaching, research, service, and governance. The predictable career path leading from graduate student to tenured full professor is no longer the norm.[10]

Plater's dire observation is part of a growing body of literature arguing that professors have increasingly joined America's low-wage workers. English professor John Champagne finds that this situation "proletarianizes the professoriate, subjecting it to increasing surveillance and regulating in greater detail how its work time is spent."[11] In addition, accreditation agencies evaluate the health and viability of academic programs, departments, and, in fact, the teaching and research agendas of entire universities and colleges based on "models of corporate business management."[12] The future of higher education looks grim indeed.[13] The call by biblical scholar Abraham Smith that we "use our analytical skills—as public intellectuals—to help to expose the full panoply of power arrangements in biblical discourse, whether our attention is devoted to texts, interpreters, or the larger productive processes that seek to control thought, desire, and behavior,"[14] demands to be heeded.

My previous essay, recognizing these developments, suggests that Bible scholars need to look beyond the inner-disciplinary debates when we think about the viability of transforming the biblical studies curriculum. The current essay thus turns to the external forces that limit curricular transformation. The pervasive architecture of educational power, having come to shape institutions of higher education, prevents the creative, innovative, and comprehensive redesign of the biblical studies curriculum at the undergraduate and graduate levels. In my view, these "geometries of power"[15] do not give reason for much

10. William M. Plater, "The Twenty-First-Century Professoriate: We Need a New Vision if We Want to Create a Positive Future for the Faculty," *Academe Online* (July-August 2008): www.aaup.org/AAUP/pubres/academe/2008/JA/Feat/plat.htm (accessed on July 2, 2012; use the Wayback Machine to access the original webpages at http://web.archive.org/).
11. John Champagne, "Teaching in the Corporate University: Assessment as a Labor Issue," *AAUP Journal of Academic Freedom* 2 (2011): 4, www.academicfreedomjournal.org/VolumeTwo/Champagne.pdf (accessed on July 2, 2012).
12. John W. Powell, "Outcomes Assessment: Conceptual and Other Problems," *AAUP Journal of Academic Freedom* 2 (2011): 9, www.academicfreedomjournal.org/Previous/VolumeTwo/Powell.pdf (accessed on July 2, 2012).
13. See, e.g., Marc Bousquet, *How the University Works: Higher Education and the Low-Wage Nation* (New York: New York University Press, 2008).
14. Abraham Smith, "Taking Spaces Seriously: The Politics of Space and the Future of Western Biblical Studies," in Schüssler Fiorenza and Richards, *Transforming Biblical Education*, 68.
15. A. E. Mazawi and R. G. Sultana, "Editorial Introduction," in *Education and the Arab "World": Political Projects, Struggles, and Geometries of Power*, ed. André E. Mazawi and Ronald G. Sultana, World Year-

optimism. They do not solely apply to biblical studies but also to religious studies, to the humanities, and in fact, to institutions of higher education. My concerns, however, remains focused on biblical studies. I examine in three steps how primarily three components form a pervasive architecture of educational power that discourages curricular transformation in the field. First, I highlight the neoliberal agenda prevalent in society during the early decades of the twenty-first century and correlate this agenda to the status of the biblical studies curriculum. Second, I turn to the notion of the university as a corporation and its effects on the biblical studies curriculum. Third, I elaborate on the pressures of degree marketability and what its absence means for the biblical studies curriculum. In short, the following discussion sheds light on *external* political and economic forces that inhibit the transformation of the academic curriculum in biblical studies today.

One final thought in this introduction: Since the Occupy movement has called for opposition to the political and economic forces of Wall Street that also threaten institutions of higher education,[16] biblical scholars ought to be ready to ask why relatively little curricular change has been realized despite the hermeneutical and methodological innovations in the field since the 1970s. Is it not the case that powerful external forces have sidelined those academic disciplines that do not directly advance neoliberal and money-driven goals, and thus curricular practices in biblical studies—and in the humanities in general—attempt to preserve at least the status quo? At worst, are these external forces not steadily nibbling away at any curricular ambition to offer a thriving humanities curriculum, including biblical studies, and to develop in students "critical thinking, dialogue, and those values that engage matters of social responsibility and civic engagement?"[17] The following analysis aims to contribute to a discussion about the institutional conditions in which we teach, and to encourage bold proposals toward a transformed biblical studies curriculum at the undergraduate and graduate levels.

---

book of Education 2010 (New York: Routledge, 2009), 12. See also, e.g., Debbie Epstein et al., eds., *Geographies of Knowledge, Geometries of Power: Framing the Future of Higher Education*, World Yearbook of Education 2008 (New York: Routledge, 2007). See also Smith, "Taking Space Seriously," 64.

16. See, e.g., Henry A. Giroux, "Why Faculty Should Join Occupy Movement Protestors on College Campuses," *Truthout*, December 19, 2011, www.truth-out.org/why-faculty-should-join-occupy-movement-protestors-college-campuses/1324328832 (accessed on July 2, 2012).

17. Giroux, "Why Faculty Should Join."

Neoliberalism, Historical Criticism, and
the Biblical Studies Curriculum

When biblical studies were established as an academic discipline in Western counties during the early to mid-nineteenth century, the socioeconomic and political conditions of contemporary capitalist societies were also in the making.[18] European societies had moved into the industrial age under newly emerging economic and political conditions. The renowned 1904 study by the sociologist Max Weber entitled *The Protestant Ethic and the Spirit of Capitalism* describes the "elective affinities" between the Calvinist work ethic and the capitalist system.[19] Weber observed that Protestant theologies endow moral and spiritual significance to hard work and economic success. In fact, they provide religious justification for an economic system that requires the suppression of immediate gratification and stresses potential economic gains in the future.

The evolving historical method in biblical scholarship does not challenge this ethos. On the contrary, it supports it. The focus on the past, presumably divorced form issues prevalent at the time of those reconstructing biblical history, teaches every reader to disregard contemporary concerns because they are classified as unscientific and thus irrelevant for understanding the Bible. In other words, historical criticism divorces biblical texts from the social locations of readers and establishes biblical meanings in the distant past. Interestingly, historical criticism was initially contested by the theologically and methodologically conservative generation of Bible scholars in nineteenth-century Europe, as the career of Ernst Hengstenberg illustrates. Hengstenberg was a professor in Berlin from 1826 until 1869, and during these decades he prevented the appointment of any historical critic to the theological faculty. Only his retirement changed this situation, and predictably the next group of scholars advanced the new method with full force. They also convinced colleagues in other fields that biblical studies fit into the scientific framework of the modern university,[20] and they established biblical studies as a legitimate academic discipline. Michael C. Legaspi describes the institutionalization of biblical

---

18. Sugirtharajah, "End of Biblical Studies," 135.
19. Max Weber, *The Protestant Ethic and the Spirit of Capitalism*, trans. Talcott Parsons (Mineola, NY: Dover, 2003).
20. For an analysis of the early stages of this development in the eighteenth century, see Michael C. Legaspi, *The Death of Scripture and the Rise of Biblical Studies* (Oxford: Oxford University Press, 2010).

scholarship in the eighteenth century and early nineteenth century, affirming that "the discipline is best understood as a cultural-political project shaped by the realities of the university."[21]

Today, the social, political, economic, cultural, and educational status quo is in great upheaval again, and what was taken for granted forty years ago is now in flux. Intellectuals talk about "the end" of everything: history, journalism, newspapers, the nation-state, America, Europe, and even biblical studies.[22] Since 2008, most everybody in the Western world realizes that capitalist economies are in crisis mode, and some even speak of the end of capitalism, the economic system that in 1989 moved globally into the neoliberal mode, a development that began in the West in the 1970s.[23] Neoliberalism is defined as "a market-driven approach to economic and social policy based on neoclassical theories of economics that stresses the efficiency of private enterprise, liberalized trade and relatively open markets, and therefore seeks to maximize the role of the private sector in determining the political and economic priorities of the state."[24] A fundamental principle of neoliberalism concerns the privatization of public functions in society because of the conviction that private companies "produce a more efficient government and improve the economic health of the nation."[25] Privatization, deregulation, and "financialization"[26] are key processes that have increasingly come to dominate Western societies.

Neoliberal interests endorse investments in business, engineering, and science departments while the humanities receive neoliberal glances of suspicion. This is a time of retrenchment in which curricular

---

21. Ibid., 7.
22. Hector Avalos, *The End of Biblical Studies* (Amherst, NY: Prometheus, 2007). See also Francis Fukuyama, *The End of History and the Last Man* (New York: Free Press, 1992); Jean-Marie Guéhenno, *The End of the Nation-State* (Minneapolis: University of Minnesota Press, 1995); Naomi Wolf, *The End of America: Letter of Warning to a Young Patriot* (White River Junction, VT: Chelsea Green, 2007); Marie Bénilde, "The End of Newspapers?," *New York Times*, March 16, 2010, http://tinyurl.com/jwz5qyq; David Marquand, *The End of the West: The Once and Future Europe* (Princeton: Princeton University Press, 2011).
23. See, e.g., Joel Kovel, *The Enemy of Nature: The End of Capitalism or the End of the World?* (New York: Zed Books, 2002); Anthony Faiola, "The End of American Capitalism?," *Washington Post*, October 10, 2008, http://tinyurl.com/kr4mxe8; Eugene McCarraher, "The End of Capitalism and the Wellspring of Radical Hope," *The Nation*, June 27, 2011, http://tinyurl.com/mpjhaq8.
24. *Wikipedia*, s.v. "Neoliberalism," en.wikipedia.org/wiki/Neoliberalism (accessed on July 2, 2012).
25. Ibid.
26. For a definition of "financialization," see *Wikipedia*, s.v. "Financialization" (accessed on July 2, 2012), en.wikipedia.org/wiki/Financialization: "an economic system or process that attempts to reduce all value that is exchanged (whether tangible, intangible, future or present promises, etc.) either into a financial instrument or a derivative of a financial instrument. The original intent of financialization is to be able to reduce any work-product or service to an exchangeable financial instrument, like currency, and thus make it easier for people to trade these financial instruments."

innovation in the humanities or biblical studies is marginalized, especially since neither area of learning holds much gain to neoliberal interests. Hence, academic disciplines in the humanities, including biblical studies, seek to preserve the status quo; they are in survival mode. Money is tight, sociocultural and political support often minimal, and intellectual space for curricular exploration rare. Neoliberal authorities demand justifications of the curricular status quo, and if they are not forthcoming, degrees, departments, and even entire schools disappear.[27] When scarce job opportunities are added on top of these conditions, curricular transformation is seldom a goal.

In European countries, too, changes in the educational infrastructure are underway due to neoliberal advances. European universities developed "solely as national institutions, in an era when economies were national," but nowadays "the economic fulcrum is increasingly moving to a supernational level."[28] This is important because some scholars posit that the economic and political pressures placed on institutions of higher education reflect "the changing nature of the relationship between capitalism and modernity."[29] The societal developments in Europe affect departments of theology and religion in which biblical studies are housed. The departments operate in secularized societies that recognize religious traditions merely as historical relics. I am stating the following based on anecdotal evidence only, but it seems to me that theological departments at European universities exist on the margins, holding on to past accomplishment, status, and method.[30]

The situation is worse in developing nations, in which institutions of higher education are often in crisis mode. They face "increasing demand, a lack of basic physical resources such as classrooms, a small number of skilled and committed academic and administrative staff and the absence of academic resources such as journals and basic scientific equipment."[31] Educational imperialism and a growing dependence

27. Champagne, "Teaching in the Corporate University," 7–8. See also, e.g., Richard Lake, "Proposal Would Eliminate Nevada State College, Other Schools," *Las Vegas Review-Journal*, March 10, 2011, http://tinyurl.com/kll9e37; Laurel Rosenthal, "Some California University Degrees Disappear amid Budget Cuts," *Sacramento Bee*, July 9, 2011, http://tinyurl.com/la57mak.
28. Roger Dale, "Repairing the Deficits of Modernity: The Emergency of Parallel Discourses in Higher Education in Europe," in Epstein et al., *Geographies of Knowledge*, 15.
29. Ibid., 16.
30. See, e.g., Erhard Gerstenberger, "Liberation Hermeneutics in Old Europe, Especially Germany," in *The Bible and the Hermeneutics of Liberation*, ed. Alejandro F. Botta an Pablo Andiñach (Atlanta, GA: SBL Press, 2009), 61–84.
31. Rajani Naidoo, "Higher Education: A Powerhouse for Development?," in Epstein et al., *Geographies of Knowledge*, 252.

on neoliberal benefactors aggravate a situation that also applies to Christian educational institutions. Financial support comes often from organizations subscribing to neoliberal ideologies and located in developed countries, especially the United States.[32] Firoze Manji and Carol O'Coill elaborate on the effects of the neoliberal austerity measures that the International Monetary Fund (IMF) implemented in Africa during the 1980s: "The outcome of these deliberations [by the IMF and African governments] was the 'good governance' agenda of the 1990s and the decision to co-opt NGOs and other civil society organizations to a repackaged programme of welfare provision, a social initiative that could be more accurately described as a programme of social control."[33]

Since then, international and some local NGOs, including churches, have been involved in charitable development, and many of them have been co-opted by neoliberal interests. As a result, social institutions in health, education, and social welfare suffer under the externally imposed constraints in most African countries. More specifically related to the academic teaching of the Bible, this situation has fostered theological conservatism and adherence to the literal-historicist hermeneutical paradigm with little concern for curricular innovation in biblical studies. However, it has to be stressed that progressive Christian organizations, churches, and select biblical studies scholars have organized to oppose these neocolonial forces; they also attempt to develop alternative and indigenized readings of the Bible.[34]

It should therefore not surprise us that some politically progressive economists state that neoliberals have created "a big structural crisis" in capitalist Western societies. To them, this crisis is grounded in a "civilizational crisis."[35] For instance, the members of the International

---

32. For an analysis see, e.g., Kingsley Banya, "Globalization, Social Justice, and Education in Africa: Neoliberalism, Knowledge Capitalism in Sub-Saharan Africa," in *Globalization, Education, and Social Justice*, ed. Joseph I. Zajda, Series Globalization, Comparative Education and Policy Research 10 (New York: Springer, 2010), 15–31. For a general discussion beyond the educational realm see James Ferguson, *Global Shadows: Africa in the Neoliberal World Order* (Durham, NC: Duke University Press, 2006).

33. Firoze Manji and Carl O'Coill, "The Missionary Position: NGOs and the Development of Africa," *International Affairs* 78, no. 3 (2002): 578.

34. See, e.g., James Howard Smith and Rosalind I. J. Hackett, *Displacing the State: Religion and Conflict in Neoliberal Africa* (Notre Dame: University of Notre Dame Press, 2011); World Council of Churches, "African Women's Statement on Poverty, Wealth and Ecology" (November 5–6, 2007, Dar Es Salaam, Tanzania), http://tinyurl.com/mv6hdas); World Alliance of Reformed Churches, "Neoliberalism Contradicts Christian Faith, Argentine Forum Says," May 2003, www.warc.ch/pc/confess/00.html (accessed on July 2, 2012). See also Gerald O. West and Musa W. Dube, eds., *The Bible in Africa: Transactions, Trajectories and Trends* (Leiden: Brill, 2000).

35. Wim Dierckxsens et al., eds., *XXI Century: Crisis of Civilization; The End of History or the Birth of a*

Observatory of the Crisis—a group located at the Departmento Ecuménico de Investigaciones (DEI) in San José in Costa Rica and closely affiliated with the liberationist theological movements in Latin and Central America—have looked at the financial crash of 2008 in conjunction with the ecological crisis, the increasing diminishment of natural resources, and the ongoing food and water crisis. They predict that the capitalist system is nearing its collapse. They see an urgent need for an alternative economic system based on values that "reaffirm the lives of the majorities"[36] and built on "the desire of the majority of the world population to live at peace with liberty, justice, mutual respect and integral democracy."[37]

The question is how the Bible curriculum has contributed to these dire developments. It would also be interesting to explore how a biblical studies curriculum would look if it sought to focus on economic injustice as part of an alternative economic vision that is not based on greed and the exploitation of the 99 percent. To be sure, teaching students how to do a word study on "money in the Bible" would not satisfy the learning goals of such a newly transformed curriculum. Dramatic and radical curricular changes are necessary, but it seems unlikely that universities and colleges, driven and shaped by neoliberal political and economic forces, would support faculty teaching in opposition to neoliberal forces prevalent today. And although academic freedom continues to be officially affirmed,[38] self-censorship among the faculty and intricate hiring processes ensures widespread silence on issues overtly critical of the political and economic status quo. Hence, like many other academics, scholars of the Bible often practice a preferential option for the curricular status quo in liberal arts colleges and elsewhere.

The University as a Corporation and Its Effects on the Humanities

One of the first articles that classified universities as corporations appeared in 1931. The author, M. M. Chambers, delivered a generally positive assessment of US-American universities as corporations

New Society? (San José, Costa Rica: DEI, 2010), www.observatoriodelacrisis.org/what-encourages-us/?lang=en.

36. Dierckxsens, *XXI Century*, 110.
37. Ibid., 111.
38. For a critical perspective on this statement, see, e.g., John M. Elmore, "Institutionalized Attacks on Academic Freedom: The Impact of Mandates by State Departments of Education and National Accreditation Agencies on Academic Freedom," *AAUP Journal of Academic Freedom* (2011): www.academicfreedomjournal.org/VolumeOne/Elmore/pdf (accessed on July 2, 2012).

because this status made universities no longer "merely a creature of the legislature."[39] Chambers outlined how various state universities moved from legislative control to "the status of a constitutional corporation,"[40] a welcome advancement because it enabled schools to grow and flourish undeterred from legislative interference.

This assessment has changed because perhaps the perception of the nature and function of corporations has dramatically changed. Nowadays, the word *corporation* has significant negative connotations. For instance, David C. Korten describes the global spread of corporate power as "enriching the few at the expense of the many, replacing democracy with rule by corporations and financial elites, destroying the real wealth of the planet and society to make money for the already wealthy, and eroding the relationships of trust and caring that are the essential foundation of a civilized society."[41] Or as a review in *Publishers Weekly* states: Corporations are "a malignant cancer exercising a market tyranny that is gradually destroying lives, democratic institutions, and the ecosystem for the benefit of greedy companies and investors."[42] These and other studies have contributed to an understanding of corporations as antidemocratic, profit-driven, unethical, and hierarchical entities that aim for the concentration of economic and political power.[43] When institutions of higher education turn to corporate principles, even though they are mostly nonprofit organizations, some scholars express concern. They challenge the idea that universities or colleges should operate like corporations and be guided by profit-driven and efficient management principles. They argue that universities and colleges do not deliver measurable products but enable the cumbersome and long-winded processes of learning, teaching, and doing research.

Yet the scholarly criticism is not loud and influential enough. Increasingly, educational institutions rely on corporate management principles. Is there a professor left who has not heard the ubiquitous call for learning outcomes? Some critics thus classify institutions of

39. M. M. Chambers, "The University as a Corporation," *Journal of Higher Education* 2, no. 1 (January 1931): 24.
40. Ibid.
41. David C. Korten, *When Corporations Rule the World*, 2nd ed. (West Hartford, CT: Kumarian, 2001), 5.
42. See the quote on the back cover of Korten's book, *When Corporations Rule the World*.
43. See also, e.g., Russell Mokhiber and Robert Weissman, *On the Rampage: Corporate Power and the Destruction of Democracy* (Monroe, ME: Common Courage, 2005); Susanne Soederberg, *Corporate Power and Ownership in Contemporary Capitalism: The Politics of Resistance and Domination* (New York: Routledge, 2010); Luis Suzrez-Villa, *Globalization and Technocapitalism: The Political Economy of Corporate Power and Technological Domination* (Burlington, VT: Ashgate, 2011). See also the work of the International Forum on Globalization, available at ifg.org.

higher education as "ruined institutions." Bill Readings is one of them, stating "that the market structure of the posthistorical University makes the figure of the student as a consumer more and more a reality, and that the disciplinary structure is cracking under the pressure of market imperatives."[44] Readings also observes that "the professoriate is being proletarianized as a body and that the number of short-term or part-time contracts at major institutions increases" while the production of knowledge becomes "equally uncertain."[45] In his view, the legitimizing struggles within the humanities as well as the disputes over methods and theories within individual disciplines indicate the "contemporary shifts in the University's function as an institution . . . [which] is now up for grabs."[46] Readings's dire observation is alarming: "It is no longer clear what the place of the University is within society nor what the exact nature of that society is, and the changing institutional form of the University is something that intellectuals cannot afford to ignore."[47]

Things have certainly heated up since Readings. Nowadays, even mainstream newspapers and magazines publish analyses and commentaries on these issues. As Jane Kenway and Johannah Fahey note, contemporary universities are most "interested in scientific and technological knowledge that can be applied and commercialized"[48] as institutions aim for international recognition and fame. Articles with titles like "The End of Tenure"[49] and "The Crisis in Higher Education"[50] try to inform the general public that untenured and time-limited positions constitute the majority of academic appointments while tenured and tenure-track professors represent "no more than 35% of the American faculty."[51] William Deresiewicz summarizes the reason for these developments in one word: efficiency. He comments: "Contingent academic labor, as non-tenure-track faculty, part-time and full-time, are formally known, is cheaper to hire and easier to fire. . . . Good, secure, well-paid positions—tenured appointments in the academy, union jobs

44. Bill Readings, *The University in Ruins* (Cambridge, MA: Harvard University Press, 1996), 177.
45. Ibid., 1.
46. Ibid., 2.
47. Ibid.
48. Jane Kenway and Johannah Fahey, "Policy Incitements to Mobility," in Epstein et al., *Geographies of Knowledge*, 171.
49. Christopher Shea, "The End of Tenure?," *New York Times*, September 3, 2010, http://tinyurl.com/lwb6l8s.
50. William Deresiewicz, "Faulty Towers: The Crisis in Higher Education," *The Nation*, May 4, 2011, http://tinyurl.com/lf9j6st.
51. Ibid.

on the factory floor—are being replaced by temporary, low-wage employment."[52] He elaborates:

> What we have in academia . . . is a microcosm of the American economy as a whole: a self-enriching aristocracy, a swelling and increasingly immiserated proletariat, and a shrinking middle-class. The same devil's bargain stabilizes the system: the middle, or at least the upper middle, the tenured professoriate, is allowed to retain its prerogatives—its comfortable compensation packages, its workplace autonomy and its job security—in return for acquiescing to the exploitation of the bottom by the top, and indirectly, the betrayal of the entire enterprise.[53]

In an academic environment in which the "middle class," that is, tenured and tenure-track faculty, is squeezed, curricular innovation and change are not a priority.

Institutional disparities are further aggravated when the discrepancies between public and private institutions are taken into account. State schools enroll three-quarters of America's college students, and yet their budgets are constantly attacked and reduced. Simultaneously, political and parental pressures push students into vocational programs, further sidelining the liberal arts curriculum in favor of so-called practical job skills. Attitudes about college education advance utilitarian principles because it has become too expensive to acquire an undergraduate education that does not translate into immediate employment skills after graduation.[54] As a result, the humanities, as well as the social and some natural sciences (e.g., anthropology, physics) experience draconian faculty reduction, and entire departments are closed when they do not advance instant educational payoff.[55] In short, money is at the center of the educational enterprise, which C. John Sommerville bemoans when he writes:

---

52. Ibid.
53. Ibid.
54. See also Patricia Cohen, "In Tough Times, the Humanities Must Justify Their Worth," *New York Times*, February 25, 2009, C1.
55. See, e.g., Reeve Hamilton, "Budget Woes, Calls for Efficiency Imperil Physics," *Texas Tribune*, September 16, 2011, http://tinyurl.com/lyf4lq7; Kayla Johnson and Gianna Cruet, "Cost of Cutting: Philosophy Tied to Campus," *The Nevada Sagebrush*, April 25, 2011, nevadasagebrush.com/blog/2011/04/25/cost-of-cutting-philosophy-tied-to-campus (accessed on July 2, 2012); Lisa W. Foderaro, "Budget-Cutting College Bid Some Languages Adieu," *New York Times*, December 5, 2010, MBI; Scott Jaschik, "Turning Off the Lights," *Inside Higher Ed*, March 4, 2010, www.insidehighered.com/new/2010/03/04/clark (accessed on July 2, 2012); Stanley Fish, "The Crisis of the Humanities Officially Arrives," *Opinionator* (blog), *New York Times*, October 11, 2010, http://tinyurl.com/n29j4mg; "Reading Confirms Physics Closure," *BBC*, November 21, 2006, http://tinyurl.com/mvtgqmd.

The secular research university has gotten caught up in the values of a secularized economy . . . now money has become the measure of them all. Students all too often want the majors that promise the highest starting salaries. Faculty are eager to leave one college if they hear of a "better" job elsewhere. Administrators make their decisions with an eye to the financial advantage or security of their institutions. Taxpayers want the cheapest faculty available. Parents want the cheapest education on offer—unless they think a higher investment will guarantee an even higher return—and then too often wring their hands when they found out their children have chosen "impractical" majors.

The corporate model is essentially the view that a university has a product. The product is a degree, or more properly, the "human capital" holding that degree. . . . Its corporate character draws our attention to the one pseudo-value of money.[56]

The architects of corporate universities and colleges define education as a skill set that adapts students to the mainstream of the global economy. In this educational model, "impractical" majors have no future; hence the declining prestige of a humanities education. This scenario also applies to the workers at degree-granting institutions, as English professor Marc Bousquet observes succinctly: "Campus administrators have steadily diverged from the ideals of faculty governance, collegiality, and professorial self-determination. Instead they have embraced the values and practices of corporate management."[57] In the same vein, education scholar Terri Kim states: "Universities are now managed as if they are corporations, competing in a global knowledge economy, in which hierarchies of power and wealth are generated by transactions in a new mode of knowledge production."[58] In this corporate environment curricular transformation of biblical studies courses seems like a quaint idea in which the study of religion and the Bible has little employment purpose for degree-seeking students.

In a nutshell, then, and to state the obvious, these developments have not benefited the academic study of the Bible. There are very few teaching positions, whether part or full time, tenure-track or tenured. The pressure to conform to curricular expectations is intense. An overloaded teaching and service schedule produces workdays filled with little time left for curricular explorations. Scholars choose narrow,

---

56. C. John Sommerville, *Religious Ideas for Secular Universities* (Grand Rapids: Eerdmans, 2009), 27–28.
57. Bousqet, *How the University Works*, 1. For an argument that universities cannot be labeled as corporations, see Lars Engwall, "The University: A Multinational Corporation?" (London: Portland Press, 2008), http://tinyurl.com/kufw8k2.
58. Terri Kim, "Transnational Academic Mobility in a Global Knowledge Economy," in Epstein et al., *Geographies of Knowledge*, 326.

safe, and conventional research topics in the hope of eventually being offered one of the few coveted tenure-track positions. Furthermore, teaching positions in biblical studies and other disciplines in theological and religious studies are often limited to religiously affiliated institutions that are theologically, hermeneutically, and ideologically conservative. Finally, salaries start low and remain relatively low, and few students major in biblical studies. Certainly, these conditions apply not only to the biblical studies field but also to the humanities in general. As Champagne puts it bluntly, it is a situation in which "the corporate university has colonized the humanities."[59] Under such circumstances, the transformation of the biblical studies curriculum remains elusive.

On the Marketability of Biblical Studies Courses

Then there is the issue of marketability of the academic study of the Bible. In secular-defined departments of religious studies a heavy emphasis on the Bible is too specialized, appears to lack comparative perspective, and seems to endorse a religious-cultural heritage linked to Western imperialism. In short, it seems biased, value-driven, and normative. The field is virtually unknown outside of theological and religious studies departments and not a safe bet for a postgraduation job. Biblical scholar Jacques Berlinerblau describes the situation in the following way:

> Consider that "biblical studies" as a college major is not exactly a booming industry. In secular universities, a department devoted solely to biblical studies is virtually unheard of. When an undergraduate takes a class in Scripture, it will most probably be a survey course.... Consider that many secular universities don't even have a full-time position in biblical studies. Biblical scholarship is underwritten by theological seminaries—be they independent or affixed to universities.[60]

Berlinerblau's observations depict a profound institutional reality. Can and should the field be changed under such circumstances? Who would be in favor, and why? Whose hermeneutic would be required, and whose would be silenced? And most importantly, how does the academic location of biblical studies limit curricular transformation?

Yet, perhaps surprisingly, the biblical curriculum is precarious also

---

59. Champagne, "Teaching in the Corporate University," 5.
60. Jacques Berlinerblau, "What's Wrong with the Society of Biblical Literature?," *Chronicle of Higher Education*, November 10, 2006, B13–B15.

at mainline Christian theological schools despite the general acknowledgment, often repeated in a somber tone, that the academic study of the Bible is essential for future clergy and religious leaders. The situation may be different for Jewish seminaries, but the mainline Christian seminary curriculum does not include many innovative courses in biblical studies, and if it does, these courses do not usually constitute the core curriculum. Instead historical criticism rules and the curriculum covers the basics: introductory courses to the Old and New Testaments and courses on the Prophets, the wisdom books, the Gospels, Jesus, and Paul. In contrast, courses on feminist/womanist, postcolonial, and newer hermeneutical and methodological topics are rarely among the electives.

In short, biblical studies courses are not usually a market priority at liberal arts colleges, and perhaps they should not be. Whenever universities or colleges expand into "new markets," they develop degrees in "new industries with new needs for expertise." Such degrees are then found "in industries like cybersecurity, health informatics and project management, matching programs with . . . industries and labor needs."[61] The point is that the quest for marketable degrees does not include Bible courses, and hence the curricular status quo does not attract many learners beyond a perhaps required introductory course.

Corporate Interests, Institutional Power Dynamics, and Occupying Academic Bible Teaching: Concluding Observations

When Friedrich Schleiermacher outlined the theological curriculum in 1811, he was at the pinnacle of academic power at the University of Berlin in Germany. European nations were formed into their current shapes and the industrialized-capitalist era began. Much was in flux and Schleiermacher became the visionary and builder of "the quintessential German university,"[62] the Humboldt Universität, influencing the curricular infrastructure of universities worldwide for almost two centuries. As a theologian, Schleiermacher succeeded "over the course of the nineteenth century . . . in assimilating theology to the realities of the modern state in order to ensure the continued survival of their discipline."[63] He had the institutional and political power to envision,

---

61. Tamar Lewin, "Joining Trend: College Grows beyond Name," *New York Times*, December 28, 2011, A1, A12.
62. Legaspi, *Death of Scripture*, 29.
63. Ibid.

build, and implement a curriculum that fit the political and economic interests of his era. Today, these interests have changed considerably and significantly sidelined the humanities in general and biblical studies in particular.

In fact, institutions of higher education are undergoing such profound institutional changes that all academic disciplines, faculty, students, and the very vision about the purpose of a college degree have become uncertain.[64] Do scholars, theologians, and professors of religious studies and the humanities engage in substantive and pragmatic debate that articulate the purpose of the academic study of the Bible and of other research areas not conforming to neoliberal market trends? In this regard, the provocative position of biblical scholar Hector Avalos on the end of biblical studies is not even broad enough. Avalos blames biblical scholars for the field's predicament but fails to address the corporate interests and institutional power dynamics that shape so considerably all educational settings.[65]

Another anthology, titled *Academic Repression: Reflections from the Academic-Industrial Complex*, addresses these larger societal-educational dynamics.[66] The various authors illuminate the conditions within the neoliberal economic and corporate infrastructures of higher education, making connections to a wide range of sociopolitical, economic, and cultural developments. Although none of them addresses the state of religious, theological, or biblical studies, the editors assert unambiguously that "higher education [is] a place of hierarchical domination, bureaucratic control, hostility to radical research and teaching, and anathema to free thinking."[67] They recognize that universities and colleges depend on corporate interests and seek conformity to and compliance with the corporate status quo. The volume thus documents the silencing effects of the corporate educational infrastructure on faculty, students, and even administrators.

---

64. See, e.g., the various online lists of wealthy entrepreneurs who did not complete their college education but were nevertheless successful: Lauren Drell, "We Don't Need No Education: Meet the Millionaire Dropouts," February 9, 2011, http://www.huffingtonpost.com/2011/02/09/we-dont-need-no-education-millionaire-dropouts_n_916319.html (accessed June 21, 2017); Tina Barseghian, "How Valuable Is a College Degree?," *Mindshift* (blog), *KQED News*, May 27, 2011, http://tinyurl.com/n4twd2o.

65. Hector Avalos, *The End of Biblical Studies* (Amherst, NY: Prometheus, 2007). For another critique of the field as inherently religious and neglectful of secular approaches to the Bible, see, e.g., Jacques Berlinerblau, "'Poor Bird, Not Knowing Which Way to Fly': Biblical Scholarship's Marginality, Secular Humanism, and the Laudable Occident," *Biblical Interpretation* 10, no. 3 (2002): 267–304.

66. Anthony J. Nocella II, Steven Best, and Peter McLaren, eds., *Academic Repression: Reflections from the Academic-Industrial Complex* (Baltimore: AK Press, 2010).

67. Ibid., 13.

Certainly, the decline of academic freedom is not a problem created by corporate-driven college campuses alone. Limitations to academic freedom have prevailed in religiously affiliated institutions of higher education for a long time, although they have usually operated undercover. Berlinerblau refers to this problem when he exclaims:

> As for academic freedom, something needs to be done—urgently. The obvious move is to call for a "blue-ribbon panel" of SBL members to investigate disputes regarding alleged infringements of scholarly freedom. Then again, how would any given seminary feel about having its internal affairs judged by scholars who themselves are members of seminaries affiliated with rival denominations? . . . Here I have no answer. I only know that the problem exists, and the SBL is the only entity that can even begin to address it.[68]

Berlinerblau, a pragmatic thinker, makes important suggestions to resolve limitations to academic freedom in the scholarly study of the Bible, certainly not prevalent only in seminar settings. For instance, he advises that we collect data on Bible scholars and that the Society of Biblical Literature (SBL) as the premier academic society of biblical studies in North America commit to gathering it. The data would provide insight into the institutional conditions of teaching the Bible as an academic discipline and provide a better understanding of why there is such a reticence to curricular transformation. Berlinerblau offers a whole array of questions about the field's teaching and research contexts:

> What percentage of members practice in theological institutions? What percentage work in a university not affiliated with any denomination? Of the latter, how many did their graduate work in seminaries? What is the denominational breakdown of the society? Is the persistent rumor that the SBL is dominated—if not overrun—by conservative Christians true? Does this explain the oft-heard accusation that the society takes an overly reverent, uncritical attitude toward the Bible and religion in general? And does this explain why the society has done so little to explore Scripture's aforementioned comeback in American politics?[69]

It would be interesting to have answers to these questions because they would certainly help in getting a clear picture about the innerdisciplinary power dynamics that define the field today. However, the

---

68. Berlinerblau, "What's Wrong with the Society of Biblical Literature?," B13.
69. Ibid.

questions are also limiting because they do not deal with the external forces. As I discussed above, these forces are remarkably widespread, pervasive, and influential in today's academic world. The neoliberal economic system, the increasing move toward fashioning universities and colleges like corporations, and the lack of marketability do not encourage systemic curricular changes in the field. Most of us teach in money-driven educational contexts in which biblical studies lack the economic cachet of powerful markets, individual attempts notwithstanding.

Again, this situation is not limited to biblical studies but affects many disciplines in the arts and sciences. The curricular state in biblical studies thus reflects the conditions of higher education in a world in which money, greed, and speedy results rule.[70] It is high time then to occupy not only academic Bible teaching but also institutions of higher education as a whole. But then there is society as a whole. What ought the future of the Bible and biblical studies to look like in Western societies, beyond Christian fundamentalist revival efforts? The next chapter illuminates the possibilities by looking closely at the work of a prominent Bible scholar, Heikki Räisänen, who helps us envision alternative strategies that need to be pursued if biblical scholars want to remain part of the intellectual, cultural, and political debates taking place in postbiblical societies.

---

70. Wade Rowland, *Greed, Inc.: Why Corporations Rule Our World and How We Let It Happen* (Toronto: Thomas Allen, 2005).

3

Standing at the Crossroads with Räisänen's Program: Toward a Future of Biblical Studies in Postbiblical Societies

Obviously, we are on our way into a culturally (even if not statistically) post-Christian period.

—Heikki Räisänen[1]

The Status of the Bible and Biblical Studies in Postbiblical Societies

We live in a postbiblical world—a world that increasingly sentimentalizes the Bible, ignores it, and cares little for the sacred text of the Christian and Jewish religions. By "we" I mean those of us who live in North America or Western Europe and who belong to the culturally and politically dominant group of white, middle-class, and fairly educated people. We live in societies that are largely secularized, perhaps even "antireligiously" oriented, increasingly digitalized, and economically organized by a capitalist system that eradicates equal and just

---

1. Heikki Räisänen, *Beyond New Testament Theology: A Story and a Programme*, 2nd ed. (London: SCM, 2000), 157.

distribution of wealth nationally and internationally. In our world, the Bible plays, at best, a privatized, individualized, and societally marginalized role. To be sure, especially in the United States of America, Christian fundamentalist and evangelical groups of ethnically and racially diverse communities organize politically to foster change, which includes their efforts to reinstate the political centrality of the Bible. The placement of a stone monument of the Ten Commandments in the Alabama state courthouse or the insistence on the validity of creationism as a subject to be taught in general educational curricula are prominent examples of the Christian fundamentalist involvement in the secularizing trends of Western societies.[2] Mostly, however, such attempts meet with an indifferent majority that favors the Western scientific worldview over biblical primacy.

As a consequence of the Bible's diminishing public presence in Western societies, familiarity with biblical literature is dramatically lower among people younger than forty-five years of age than among those older than that. The so-called Generation X (those born after 1960) and Generation Y (those born after 1984) know little of the Bible and take little interest in it, unless they are committed members of Christian or Jewish organizations. This fact raises important questions: If younger generations in postbiblical societies by and large do not read the Bible, what is the future of this sacred text in the West? Will it simply turn into a relic of the past? And what does this trend indicate for the academic field of biblical research?

Biblical scholarship—until the 1980s a largely Western endeavor—is still unconcerned about these generational developments in our societies. For many biblical scholars, the fact that we are living in a postbiblical world is a nonissue; it does not affect their daily work as exegetes. Accordingly, many, if not most, publications continue to operate within a nineteenth-century mind-set that regards the church as a powerful opponent of the historical and literary study of the Bible, even though so-called mainstream religion has little cultural, political, and religious authority left. Furthermore, laypeople remain mostly ignorant of the issues discussed in the field of biblical studies, and even scholars who advocate for independence from religious institutions seldom reflect on the limited relevance of their work for larger society.

Perhaps oblivious to changed circumstances or unable to relate to

---

2. See, e.g., Jeffrey Gettleman, "Judge Suspended for Defying Court on Ten Commandments," *New York Times*, August 23, 2003, A7; and Francis X. Clines, "Ohio Board Hears Debate on an Alternative to Darwinism," *New York Times*, March 12, 2002, A16.

postbiblical discourse in Western societies, many exegetes thus do what they know best: they apply historical and literary methods to biblical texts, as if nothing else is needed in our time. Accordingly, many Bible scholars hardly notice that they talk only with, and among, each other. They seem undisturbed that their work rarely, if ever, has an impact on cultural, religious, or political discourse. In fact, many of them would not even agree that the Bible and biblical studies face a severe crisis. Yet the lack of institutional investment in biblical research, the small and decreasing number of academic positions, and the lack of interest in biblical research by scholars outside the field are reasons enough to worry. Is there still a future for the Bible and biblical studies in postbiblical societies beyond Christian fundamentalist revival efforts?

Looking Back: Räisänen's Program
in *Beyond New Testament Theology*

The work of Heikki Räisänen represents a remarkable exception to the indifference among researchers regarding the marginal role of the Bible and biblical studies in secular-dominated Western societies. Räisänen's frankness and sincerity about the diminishing role of the Bible in the secularized West is unusual. Not many exegetes of his generation, stature, or geographical location admit to the problems the field confronts at the dawn of the twenty-first century CE. For instance, he warns biblical scholars that they "will soon find themselves at a crossroads. Will they remain guardians of cherished confessional traditions, anxious to provide modern man with whatever normative guidance they still manage to squeeze out of the sacred texts? Or will they follow those pioneering theologians and others congenial to them on their novel paths, fearlessly reflecting on the biblical material from a truly ecumenical, global point of view?"[3] Räisänen suggests that "the central task of theology in the present situation is to ascertain just what beliefs or concepts inherited from the tradition are still viable, and to determine in what ways they should be reconstructed so that they will continue to serve human intellectual and religious needs."[4] He therefore recommends taking seriously contemporary questions about the "effect" of the Bible on culture, politics, and religion—areas of investigation traditionally ignored by biblical scholarship.[5] He wants

3. Räisänen, *Beyond New Testament Theology*, 209.
4. Ibid., 205.

biblical research to "confront the Bible with present-day questions,"[6] and therefore suggests moving the current mode of scholarly inquiry from an exclusively, text-oriented task to one that examines biblical literature, history, and traditions in relation to the global contexts of our world.

While Räisänen pushes for a kind of "opening up" of biblical studies, he also insists that a responsible scholarly reading must understand biblical literature in its original context. Accordingly, an exegete has to perform two tasks: to explain what texts meant when they were written and to discuss what they mean to readers today. This "two-level strategy" is not a novel idea. Krister Stendahl, another renowned Scandinavian scholar, developed this distinction more than forty years ago.[7] For Räisänen, the second step is crucial to ensure a vibrant future for the field since "present-day concerns ... keep alive the interest of most readers in the subject in the first place."[8]

Räisänen's effort to contemporize biblical literature is connected to his conviction that biblical studies should promote a global and ecumenical perspective. New Testament research has to seek its "horizon" beyond ecclesiastical settings and address "humanity as a whole."[9] Räisänen approvingly mentions those exegetes who refused to conform to the limitations of an ecclesial agenda, beginning with William Wrede, a hero in Räisänen's story of New Testament historiographers. Räisänen also favorably mentions contemporary scholars such as Gerd Petzke, a German scholar who likes to orient "post-Christian exegesis" to the concerns of society rather than of "the church."[10] Räisänen, agreeing with this position, illustrates elsewhere that biblical literature, examined as part of historical, cultural, and religious histories and traditions, "contribute[s] to the encounter of faiths and worldviews."[11] To demonstrate what such scholarship might look like, Räisänen describes, for instance, Marcion's position on the biblical canon or

5. Heikki Räisänen, "The 'Effective History' of the Bible: A Challenge To Biblical Scholarship?," in Challenges to Biblical Interpretation: Collected Essays 1991-2000, Biblical Interpretation Series 59 (Leiden: Brill, 2001), 280. For a recent publication that addresses questions about the "effect" of biblical texts, see J. Cheryl Exum and Stephen D. Moore, eds., Biblical Studies/Cultural Studies: The Third Sheffield Colloquium, JSOTSup 266; GCT 7 (Sheffield: Sheffield Academic, 1998).
6. Räisänen, Beyond New Testament Theology, 158.
7. Krister Stendahl, "Biblical Theology, Contemporary," IDB 1:418–32.
8. Räisänen, Beyond New Testament Theology, 204.
9. Ibid., 96. Beyond New Testament Theology, however, describes the work of Western scholarship that often emerged within an ecclesiastical context.
10. Ibid., 154.
11. Räisänen, Marcion, Muhammad and the Mahatma: Exegetical Perspectives on the Encounter of Cultures and Faiths (London: SCM, 1997), ix.

the portrayal of Jesus in the Qur'an, both important appropriations of the Bible inside and outside the Christian tradition.

However, not all Bible scholars agree with Räisänen's global vision for biblical scholarship. Old Testament scholar, James Barr, believes that Räisänen's work carries out "important research in other fields."[12] This comment testifies to the resistance of exegetes to expanding the field's traditional parameters. For Barr, the Bible's ecumenical and global history of interpretation goes beyond the task of biblical studies. For biblical researchers like Barr, Räisänen's approach is no longer considered to be part of biblical studies. Yet for others, Räisänen's proposal hardly represents a dramatic departure from long-established boundaries. He is not an innovator but a traditionalist who stresses the importance of historical methodology. His proposal allows for a contemporizing approach only because of the perceived need to revitalize biblical studies in a "post-Christian world." Accordingly, Räisänen holds dear the central tenets of the discipline, not intending to challenge them.

The conservative character of Räisänen's position is instantly apparent in *Beyond New Testament Theology*. When I read this book for the first time, I felt thrown back to my years as a student of Protestant theology in Germany. Even then, during the 1980s, German theology professors candidly and repeatedly expressed their conviction that any biblical scholarship worthy of its name emerged from German theology departments alone. Räisänen, a Finnish scholar, seems to share this conviction. He takes for granted the superiority of much of German New Testament studies, and includes only selected researchers from other countries.[13] His survey is thus rather limited, and even if it were not, why would Räisänen not explain how German scholarship came to play such a crucial role in New Testament research? Yet unfortunately Räisänen's descriptions do not analyze the cultural, political, economic, and religious dynamics that have led to the domination of German biblical studies in his exegetical framework.

The conservative character of *Beyond New Testament Theology* is readily apparent in other omissions too. Räisänen refers to only one female

---

12. James Barr, *The Concept of Biblical Theology: An Old Testament Perspective* (Minneapolis: Fortress Press, 1999), 530 (emphasis added).

13. Examples of non-German scholars whom Räisänen discusses are Alan Richardson (Räisänen, *Beyond New Testament Theology*, 65–66), the "three Nordic contributions" of Harold Riesenfeld, Aimo T. Nikolainen, and René Kiefer (ibid., 68–73), James D. G. Dunn (ibid., 98–101), and Luke Timothy Johnson and Christopher Rowland (ibid., 107–9).

scholar, Elisabeth Schüssler Fiorenza, whose work he discusses in one paragraph. Here it is:

> In a somewhat similar vein, Elisabeth Schüssler Fiorenza, objecting to alleged "value-free objectivism" . . . , argues for "a paradigm shift in the ethos and rhetorical practices of biblical scholarship." Biblical studies ought to accept public-political responsibility . . . to develop into "a critical reflection on rhetorical practice encoded in the literatures of the biblical world and their social or ecclesial functions today." In preparing the first edition of this book I thought that Schüssler Fiorenza's programme did not abandon the distinction between two stages of work, or at least that between two different foci. Subsequently she has severely criticised what she deems positivistic and scientistic antiquarianism. I do not think that she is quite fair to the scholarship that she is castigating. But, independently of that, historical study of the Bible is not bound to be insensitive to the issues raised by her—even if it remains historical. Biblical study is to continue its "descriptive analytic work, utilising all the critical methods available for illuminating our understanding of ancient texts and their historical location." But this study should also include "a hermeneutic-evaluative" practice exploring "the power/knowledge relations inscribed in contemporary biblical discourses and in biblical texts themselves." A scholarly community thus engaged in public discourse could be "a significant participant in the global discourse seeking justice and well-being for all."[14]

Räisänen's paragraph, astounding for its omissions, illustrates the limitations of a traditional androcentric perspective. He dedicates not a single word to Schüssler Fiorenza's pioneering feminist work in New Testament research. Moreover, Räisänen does not refer to any other nontraditional perspectives.[15] Neither the first edition of 1990 nor the revised and expanded second edition of 2000 mention postcolonial, African American, or so-called Third World scholarship, as if such work had not made significant contributions to New Testament studies during the last years.[16] Does Räisänen think that his male-dominated, Western European genealogy of biblical studies is more comprehensive

---

14. Ibid., 106. He mentions the German feminist New Testament scholar Luise Schottroff only in two footnotes; see ibid., 263n25 and 269n27.
15. He mentions briefly "feminist, ideological and post-colonial criticisms," only to characterize these approaches as a "continuation (in a new framework) of the content criticism that was practiced by liberal scholars a century ago"; see ibid., 169.
16. See, e.g., the following sample studies that appeared between the first and second editions of Räisänen's *Beyond New Testament Theology*: Carol A. Newsom and Sharon H. Ringe, eds., *Women's Bible Commentary with Apocrypha* (Louisville: Westminster John Knox, 1992); Fernando F. Segovia and Mary Ann Tolbert, eds., *Social Reading from This Place*, vol. 1, *Location and Biblical Interpretation in the United States* (Minneapolis: Fortress Press, 1995); Rasiah S. Sugirtharaja, ed., *Voices from the*

than one that would acknowledge the multifaceted contributions of feminist and postcolonial research? This viewpoint is as hard to believe as it is difficult to sustain.

Sadly, Räisänen, limited by traditional perspectives, values German male scholarship above all else. Unaware of this bias, Räisänen is quite unapologetic for his historical-critical stance, as he acknowledges elsewhere: "Am I being too apologetic? Well, of course I too am 'speaking from a place,' from a social location. . . . I owe it all to the clear-headed Scandinavian tradition which appreciates Religionswissenschaft, and emphasizes keeping historical and theological interpretations apart."[17] Others equally recognize his defensive stance. Schüssler Fiorenza, for instance, writes: "His misreading of my work becomes understandable when one recognises the apologetic character of Räisänen's discourse, that seeks to defend the centrality of historical-criticism in biblical studies and attributes central status to it."[18] As a result, Räisänen's program is a statement more about the past of New Testament theology than its future. What we really need, however, are alternatives that relate the Bible and biblical studies to the political, cultural, and religious discourses of our time and beyond.

Looking Around for Alternatives: Reading the Bible in a Postbiblical World

The fundamental problem with Räisänen's agenda is that it assumes a Bible-centered intellectual discourse even though such discourse is losing its relevance in postbiblical societies of the West. It is perhaps difficult for many women and men of Räisänen's generation to renounce the notion of the Bible's centrality since in their perception religious institutions remain powerful. But for many younger people of the West, who are not religiously committed, these institutions appear on the sidelines of society, counting little in politics, economics, or societal life. In their experience, these institutions serve highly privatized needs, are apparently removed from the power struggles in the world, and are quite ineffective in shaping political or societal life. Younger

---

Margin: Interpreting the Bible in the Third World (Maryknoll, NY: Orbis, 1991); Cain Felder, ed., *Stony the Road We Trod: African American Biblical Interpretation* (Minneapolis: Fortress Press, 1991).

17. Heikki Räisänen, "Biblical Critics in the Global Village," in *Challenges to Biblical Interpretations: Collected Essays 1991–2000*, Biblical Series 59 (Leiden: Brill, 2001), 300.

18. Elisabeth Schüssler Fiorenza, "Defending the Center, Trivializing the Margins," in *Reading the Bible in the Global Village: Helsinki*, ed. Heikki Räisänen et al. (Atlanta: Society of Biblical Literature, 2000), 33.

people, unfamiliar with the field of biblical studies, may well wonder why Räisänen emphasizes the need for a historical analysis of the New Testament at all. They do not understand his argument because they do not share his belief in the significance of the Bible.

This problem is indeed acute. Many people raised in postbiblical societies are not familiar enough with traditional religious organizations to comprehend what is at stake. They find other issues more urgent than debates about historical versus theological readings of the Bible and ask instead: Why read the Bible in the first place? This question does not occur to Räisänen since he assumes the Bible's superior status. To him, one would want to read biblical texts—always. However, since people of postbiblical societies do not share this position, scholars have to make a case for the Bible's continued relevance in Western postbiblical societies if they do not want their work to disappear into oblivion. So what shall they do?

The following three sections describe strategies that, in my view, need to be pursued if biblical studies is to remain relevant amid the rise of intellectual, cultural, and political discourses of postbiblical societies. The future of the field depends on alternative proposals that take seriously the concerns, debates, and challenges presented by Western postbiblical societies. Indeed, some of the work is already underway, often on the margins of the field, since much of it has not yet made it into the mainstream of biblical scholarship, as hiring announcements, course descriptions, and publications indicate.

Strategy One: Assuming Postmodernity

Contemporary biblical scholarship experiences a lack of credibility because it has insisted for so long on the singularity of biblical meaning, whether such meaning is historical, literary, or religious. Yet the claim of a singular meaning is no longer tenable in postbiblical societies. Not only is the idea of a single, universally true, and objectively valid meaning contested by the polyphony of modern biblical interpretations themselves,[19] but also in postbiblical societies life itself challenges this notion. Ruled by diversity and seemingly endless possibilities, secular societies provide multiple meanings to daily events every day. Particularly the Internet confronts people with the vast array of

---

19. See, e.g., my work on the history of interpreting Genesis 34 in nineteenth-century Germany and the contemporary international scene that demonstrates the multivalence of modem interpretations even when singularity of meaning is assumed: Susanne Scholz, *Rape Plots: A Feminist-Cultural Study of Genesis 34*, StBibLit 13 (New York: Lang, 2000), esp. 45–63, 91–127.

possible meanings on any given aspect of societal, economic, political, cultural, or religious life. People always know they have alternatives: whether their interest is in a piece of soap, the news, or an election campaign. We encounter and embody the postmodern insight of inter- pretative polyphony even while some people—such as Christian funda- mentalists—deny it.

In contrast to Räisänen's proposal, an alternative approach must therefore assume the multivalence of the exegetical enterprise. It has to address the fact that meanings of biblical texts, whether defined his- torically or otherwise, emerge from a variety of choices and convic- tions initiated by the reading process. At the dawn of the twenty-first century, I edited and compiled a volume titled *Biblical Studies Alter- natively*,[20] which presents an alternative by introducing readers to a diverse range of biblical texts and interpretations. The collection illus- trates that biblical meanings emerge through the lenses of different interpreters, and it shows that every text has multiple meanings, shaped by the historical-cultural contexts and perspectives of the read- ers. Even a historical exegesis is only one of many possible meanings, as interpreters always make choices. If we do not share the assumptions, we will develop alternative readings. An objective, universally valid, and value-neutral meaning of the Bible is thus impossible, despite the persistence of that claim. Philosophers speak of the "linguistic turn," which recognizes truth as a social construct. Meaning is no longer regarded as an objective reality, independent from interpreters. Rather, meaning "arises from the subjective, or ideological juxtaposing of text with text on behalf of specific readers in specific historical/ material situations."[21]

The notion of the plurality of meanings is not entirely new to biblical studies.[22] Important publications elaborate on this idea even though resistance to this postmodern insight is strong. New Testament exegete A. K. M. Adam, for instance, states that "scholars who practice postmodern biblical interpretation do not always have ready access to the most prominent venues for promulgating biblical interpretations"

---

20. Susanne Scholz, ed., *Biblical Studies Alternatively: An Introductory Reader* (Upper Saddle River, NJ: Prentice Hall, 2003).
21. George Aichele and Gary Phillips, "Introduction: Exegesis, Eisegesis, Intergesis," *Semeia* 69/70 (1995): 15.
22. See, e.g,, these important publications: The Bible and Culture Collective, *The Postmodern Bible* (New Haven: Yale University Press, 1995); A. K. M. Adam, *What Is Postmodern Biblical Criticism?* (Min- neapolis: Fortress Press, 1995); Adam, ed., *Postmodern Interpretations of the Bible: A Reader* (St. Louis: Chalice, 2001); David Jobling, Tina Pippin, and Ronald Schleifer, eds., *The Postmodern Bible Reader* (Malden, MA: Blackwell 2001).

and "the politics of interpretative association make those venues uncomfortable places even when they open themselves to postmodern interpreters."[23] Traditional scholars reject "antifoundational, antitotalizing, and demystifying"[24] discourse as "anything goes," as shallow, or as unscientific. Their confidence in an unshakeable truth, attained by scientific methodology as developed since the philosopher, René Descartes, articulated his famous *cogito, ergo sum*, does not allow for a multivalent understanding of truth. Traditional biblical scholarship has been based on this modem conviction, and thus created "meta-narratives" about biblical history in the process. Consequently, many exegetes do not want to let go of the singularity of meaning in their work.

Yet biblical research informed by postmodern discourse exposes traditional Bible readings as "false consciousness."[25] It recognizes "that reading and interpretation is always interested, never disinterested; always significantly subjective, never completely objective; always committed and therefore always political, never uncommitted and apolitical; always historically-bound, never ahistorical. The modernist dream of disinterested, objective, distanced, abstract truth is fading rapidly."[26] Postmodern readers consider the Bible as a "polysemous" book, and they reject the possibility of extracting an objective and single truth from it. Biblical texts, understood accordingly, contain many interpretative possibilities, some realized and others still to come. Readers do not simply describe the content of a text or reconstruct its historical meaning. They cannot claim to define the Bible conclusively, but they have to recognize that every interpretative attempt is situated, located, and particular. Different readers create different meanings, and therefore readers have become more important in biblical studies than Räisänen's descriptions acknowledge.

Yet some biblical scholars, focusing on readers and their interpretative interests, recognize the centrality of past and present readers in the meaning-making process. These scholars analyze the social, political, or religious views promoted in biblical interpretations, and they examine how readings relate to the societal status quo.[27] My *Biblical*

23. Adam, *Postmodern Interpretations*, viii.
24. Adam, *What Is Postmodern Biblical Criticism?*, 5.
25. Bible and Culture Collective, *Postmodern Bible*, 11.
26. Robert M. Fowler, "Postmodern Biblical Criticism," *Forum* 5 (1989): 3–30 (here 22).
27. See, e.g., Knut Holter, *Yahweh in Africa: Essays on Africa and the Old Testament*, Bible and Theology in Africa (New York: Lang, 2000); Rasiah S. Sugirtharajah, *The Bible and the Third World: Precolonial, Colonial and Postcolonial Encounters* (Cambridge: Cambridge University Press, 2001); and Vincent L.

Studies Alternatively similarly contributes to the increasing recognition in biblical scholarship that meanings depend on interpreters. The volume encourages students to appreciate the fact that different readers assign to the Bible vastly different and often contradictory meanings. Students learn to view the study of the Bible as an opportunity to look at biblical meanings as reflections of political, cultural, and religious theories and practices. Biblical research, understood in this way, connects to the past and present, and perhaps, most importantly, it invites students to consider society's involvement in the process of interpretation. In short, such an approach to biblical literature is based on the conviction that postmodern assumptions are critical for reading the Bible in today's postbiblical world.

Strategy Two: Working Thematically

A thematic approach characterizes the second strategy that promises to keep biblical research connected to intellectual, cultural, and political discourses in postbiblical societies. Räisänen points in this direction when he criticizes the verse-oriented approach of the field. He states: "Detailed exegesis of each biblical verse . . . is not of much interest to society. . . . The present flood of commentaries is only comprehensive in a church context, as a survival from the good old days when exegesis could still be seen as normative. . . . One might venture to say that there is in fact far too much exposition of the Bible in present-day scholarship."[28] Not only do text-oriented studies presuppose solid knowledge of the Bible, but they also assume an audience that awaits miniscule expositions of individual verses and vocabulary. Yet even today's clergy do not share these assumptions anymore, as Räisänen himself asserts: "Half a century ago the classical reader, for whom commentaries were written, was the minister engaged in a scholarly preparation of his sermon. However, this situation no longer exists; times have changed even in the church."[29] Räisänen thus suggests examining the Bible with contemporary questions in mind, and so to move scholarly work from a textual to a thematic—he calls it "theological"—orientation. He senses that thematically focused studies connect biblical texts more readily to people living in postbiblical societies than text-focused ones.

Wimbush, ed., *African Americans and the Bible: Sacred Texts and Social Textures* (New York: Continuum, 2000).
28. Räisänen, *Beyond New Testament Theology*, 157.
29. Ibid., 269n21.

This redirection of the exegetical task is also beneficial for another reason. It encourages the application of social categories, such as gender, race, ethnicity, and class, to the study of the Bible, and links the reading of biblical literature to contemporary society, politics, and religion. During the past few decades, an increasing number of exegetes have related the Bible to social, political, and religious discourses and life. Prominent examples have emerged from feminist, womanist, African (American), and postcolonial researchers (among others)—none of whom, however, appear in Räisänen's *Beyond New Testament Theology*.

Although thematic approaches make the Bible accessible to laypeople and have the potential to relate to social, political, and religious issues, they are not yet common in introductory courses for several reasons. The book market is still dominated by introductory materials often exclusively focused on historical and text-oriented questions. Teachers often rely on a traditional Bible curriculum because they are trained this way or because they want their students to know the text and its history first. The traditional approach is also quite effective in countering Christian fundamentalist beliefs, especially prevalent in the United States. But perhaps most importantly, thematic introductory textbooks are hard to find. I myself noticed the dire need for a thematically organized volume when I began teaching the obligatory Bible introduction course. For that reason, I developed *Biblical Studies Alternatively*, organizing it according to the categories of gender, race, ethnicity, and class. During the past few decades, American scholars in particular began studying these and related categories under the influence of the political and social movements of the 1960s. In due course, interpreters of biblical literature have also applied these categories to their work, and by now there is a bounty of scholarship available on these issues. *Biblical Studies Alternatively* collects such work in this format for the first time, introducing students to a potpourri of biblical texts, characters, and issues.

A thematic introduction to the Bible has pedagogical merits. In *Biblical Studies Alternatively*, the categories of gender, race, ethnicity, and class enable students to speak from the contexts of their lives—the "known"—and to expand their knowledge of the "unknown," namely, how these categories shape biblical literature and its interpretation both in the past and the present. Students are encouraged, for instance, to wonder why they take androcentric interpretations for granted, but not feminist ones. They also learn to appreciate how practices of slavery or discrimination against women were justified with the use of the Bible. Students become curious about a particular culture and society after reading biblical interpretations, for instance, from Asia. A thematic organization thus encourages the development of a critical stance toward one's views on the Bible and one's experiences in the world. In a time when many people in the West know little about the sacred texts of Judaism and Christianity, a thematic approach helps to increase curiosity about the unfamiliar world of biblical text and interpretation.

The thematic approach to the study of biblical literature has another advantage: it holds considerable potential for conversations with disciplines traditionally disconnected from biblical studies. The field of biblical research has enjoyed a long tradition of interdisciplinary exchange with linguistics, archaeology, and history, but this exchange has often been one-sided. A thematic redirection of exegetical work, as indicated by Räisänen, aims to establish conversations with such disciplines as political science, sociology, and African American and women's/gender studies programs. A thematic focus encourages biblical researchers to relate their work to politics, culture, economics, and religion. In postbiblical societies of the West, a thematic approach communicates the fruits of biblical studies to an audience that does not expect much from the Bible. It makes biblical literature accessible beyond the narrow confines of a shrinking Bible-committed audience.

Strategy Three: Taking Sides

Another important strategy for connecting biblical studies with intellectual discourses in postbiblical societies relates to the notion of ethical accountability. Scholarly work has to clarify the ethical standards with which texts, histories of interpretation, and scholarly discourse are to be examined. When biblical research considers the ethical import of biblical texts and their histories, it encourages readers in postbiblical societies to reflect on the Bible's ongoing value. It teaches postbiblical readers that they cannot simply deduce ethics or morals from the Bible. They have to identify their presuppositions and positions and explain why they read a text this and not another way. They learn to appreciate the multivalency of biblical meanings and to disclose intellectual, political, and/or religious commitments leading to this or that interpretation. Ethical accountability becomes part of the work, as it discloses interpretative interests and assumptions, clarifying social, political, and religious goals as part of the meaning-making process.

In this respect, Schüssler Fiorenza has offered an important theoretical contribution to the discussion on ethics in biblical studies. She contends that an ethically focused approach is necessary because it overcomes "the assumed dichotomy between engaged scholarship (such as feminist, postcolonial, African American, queer, and other subdisciplines) and scientific (malestream) interpretation."[30] An emphasis on the ethical dimensions of biblical scholarship not only affects the ethics of textual readings but it also addresses the "ethics of interpretive practices," the "ethics of scholarship," and the "ethics of scientific valuation and judgment."[31] Schüssler Fiorenza thus considers ethical investigations as central to biblical studies even though mainstream scholarship has barely begun to take notice of it.

Other Bible exegetes also discuss the significance of ethics in biblical studies. For instance, New Testament scholar Daniel Patte offers a more limited proposal about the position of ethics in biblical studies. Patte encourages careful investigation of the ethical implications that interpretations have for "others."[32] In his view, such work includes both the study of individual texts and the history of interpretation, constituting what Patte calls "an androcritical multidimensional exegetical practice."[33] Patte articulates his views in deliberate recognition of his social location as a "male European-American critical exegete" who affirms the necessity to dialogue with people from "other" locations and the need to investigate "our interpretations and how they affect others."[34] According to Patte's proposal, the focus on ethics has an almost redemptive quality that bears the possibility of eliminating oppressive theories and practices once justified by the Bible.

Overall, then, the move toward ethical responsibility in biblical studies is important precisely because it facilitates an appreciation of biblical literature as a medium that educates, strengthens, and exposes the intellectual, political, and religious commitments of people engaged in the reading of the Bible. It becomes clear that the point of biblical interpretation is not to learn "moral lessons" from the Bible, but to

30. Elisabeth Schüssler Fiorenza, *Rhetoric and Ethic: The Politics of Biblical Studies* (Minneapolis: Fortress Press, 1999), 195.
31. Ibid., 196.
32. Daniel Patte, *Ethics of Biblical Interpretation: A Reevaluation* (Louisville: Westminster John Knox, 1995), 12.
33. Ibid., 11.
34. Ibid., 12.

reflect actively on the ethics of particular texts in correlation with the histories of interpretation and developments in the world. In this sense, then, the reading of biblical literature helps people comprehend the ethical dimensions of the Bible within its manifold social-cultural and religious-political reading contexts. It assists them in evaluating the ethical implications of the Bible in the world.

Let me briefly illustrate this process once again with the essays collected in *Biblical Studies Alternatively*, in which several interpreters invite students to reflect on the rhetoric of socioeconomic class, specifically on the subject of "economic justice as a biblical concern."[35] For instance, Jan Botha's discussion of Romans 13, a text that has often been read as a command to obey the political status quo, delineates how social location shapes meaning.[36] Botha shows how South African blacks challenge the traditional (state-obedient) understanding of Romans 13 because of their lived experiences. Their ethical perspectives diverge because of their social location, and hence their readings are vastly different from those of the people in power. By contrast, Luise Schottroff, arguing from a historical perspective, examines the parable of the workers in the vineyard (Matt 20:1–16) as a text that the earliest audience heard as an ethical mandate for radical equality among all human beings.[37] Both of these interpreters connect the Bible with a specific situation in the world—the South African apartheid system on the one hand and the capitalist economy on the other hand, and so both of them advance a particular ethical concern in their interpretations.

Moreover, Botha's and Schottroff's interpretations help students to reflect on their own perspectives. Since the discourse on class represents a neglected area in postbiblical societies dominated by capitalist economies, the various biblical texts and interpretations challenge hegemonic views on the economic order in the West. The discourse on class, as articulated in biblical readings, prepares readers to reflect on the economic status quo and to develop alternative visions. The deliberate focus on the ethics of biblical texts and their interpretations is,

---

35. Scholz, *Biblical Studies Alternatively*, 327–84.
36. Jan Botha, "Creation of New Meaning: Rhetorical Situations and the Reception of Romans 13:1-7," *JTSA* 79 (1992): 24–37 (repr. in Scholz, *Biblical Studies Alternatively*, 368–84).
37. Luise Schottroff, "Human Solidarity and the Goodness of God: The Parable of the Workers in the Vineyard," in *God of the Lowly: Socio-historical Interpretations of the Bible*, ed. Willy Schottroff and Wolfgang Stegemann (Maryknoll, NY: Orbis, 1984), 29–47 (repr. in Scholz, *Biblical Studies Alternatively*, 351–67).

then, another strategy to keep the field in conversation with contemporary postbiblical societies.

Looking Ahead: Toward a Future of Biblical Studies in the Secular West

Despite its limitations, Heikki Räisänen's contribution to the academic study of the Bible in postbiblical societies is appreciated because it supports a critical engagement of biblical texts with contemporary issues. Eventually, however, Räisänen's contribution needs to be left behind at the crossroads when we look ahead and consider strategies for creating a future for the Bible and biblical studies in the secular West. Räisänen's position is steeped in a worldview that postbiblical people recognize as a relic from the past. His interest in the historical task of biblical studies is understandable and in certain circumstances still useful. But overall Räisänen's position does not capture the postbiblical imagination. Although he recognizes the need for "contemporizing interpretations," Räisänen limits his study of the Bible to historical investigations. To his credit, Räisänen recognizes the difficulties of his position when he observes: "Obviously, we are on our way into a culturally (even if not statistically) post-Christian period."[38] He knows that a case needs to be made for reading the Bible, but his solution stems from a time when the Bible played a much larger role than it does in the West today, and as a result his agenda evades the problem.

Alternative strategies are therefore needed, and I offer three of them, encouraging exegetes to assume postmodern principles, working thematically, and embracing ethical accountability. It is certainly open for debate whether these strategies will give the Bible and the field of biblical studies a future beyond the efforts of Christian fundamentalists who often dominate public discussions in postbiblical societies. Much will depend on the practice of the next generation of exegetes. Indeed, Schüssler Fiorenza warns of scientific objectivist frameworks and the "kyriocentric rhetoric" that continue to prevail within the guild of biblical scholarship. They might prevent the necessary transformation toward "an emancipatory allegorical paradigm of interpretation" for the wider public.[39] Will the younger generation merely accept the exegetical doctrines of the past and continue along the established path? Or will organizations for the academic study of

---

38. Räisänen, *Beyond New Testament Theology*, 157.
39. Schüssler Fiorenza, *Rhetoric and Ethic*, 44–55.

the Bible actively support alternative approaches and provide the necessary space and time during conferences and in publications for these pursuits? Hopeful signs exist on the margins of the established field, but even here scholars who are engaged in such work do so with insufficient resources; they also do not always get support and collegial recognition.

Much more will likely be required to shake up a field that seems to be either content with or unwilling to face the realities of postbiblical societies. If fifty million US-Americans are indeed "cultural creatives" who reject traditional forms of religiosity, as sociologist Paul Ray and psychologist Sherry Ruth Anderson suggest,[40] professional interpreters of the Bible need to determine if they have something to say to these people. The three strategies outlined in this essay may serve as a start, but even more adventurous approaches will have to emerge. Perhaps exoteric methodologies need to be enhanced by esoteric approaches and, in so doing, reach people who search for religiosity and spirituality not only beyond the New Testament of the Bible but also beyond organized (and Western) religion as a whole.[41] The future of biblical studies depends on creative visions that emerge at the crossroads. Where will we go with the Bible in our hands?

The following chapter provides a preliminary response to this question as it has presented itself at the end of this discussion of Räisänen's work and what it teaches biblical exegetes today. As historical criticism, though initially subversive, has turned to supporting the political, cultural, and religious status quo, Western societies have become increasingly intercultural, interreligious, and diasporic. East meets West and North encounters South, polycultural sensibilities have become visible, and syncretism is not a "bad" word anymore. The next chapter explores the hermeneutical and methodological possibilities for biblical exegesis in this kind of context and specifically discusses the value of exoteric and esoteric approaches to the contemporary reading of the Bible in Western societies.

---

40. Paul H. Ray and Sherry Ruth Anderson, *The Cultural Creatives: How 50 Million People Are Changing the World* (New York: Three Rivers, 2001).
41. See further my development of this emphasis in Susanne Scholz, "'Tandoori Reindeer' and the Limitations of Historical Criticism," in *Her Master's Tools? Feminist and Postcolonial Engagements of Historical-Critical Discourse*, ed. Caroline Vander Stichele and Todd Penner, Global Perspectives on Biblical Scholarship 9 (Atlanta: Society of Biblical Literature, 2005), 47–69.

PART II

The Politics of Method

4

"Tandoori Reindeer" Exegesis: On the Limitations of Historical Criticism and Two Alternatives

Powerful political, social, economic, and spiritual-religious developments have been underway since the end of the so-called Second World
War in 1945.[1] Anticolonial movements in the Third World emerged
and succeeded in removing colonial rule. Moreover, the Western social
movements of the 1960s and 1970s led to major changes in social and
cultural dynamics. At the same time the human population exploded
to more than six billion. Nuclear and biological-chemical weapons are
threatening to destroy our planet several times over. Corporate capitalism has grown exponentially. Wars, famine, and political unrest
have created hundreds of thousands of refugees and immigration
movements worldwide. Western societies rely on information technology more than ever, while the gap between rich and poor is widen-
ing everywhere,[2] and worldwide 800 million people live in hunger and

---

1. The term "Second World War" is often criticized for its Eurocentric perspective. See, e.g., Enrique
Dussel, "The Sociohistorical Meaning of Liberation Theology: Reflections about Its Origin and
World Context," in *Religions/Globalizations: Theories and Cases*, ed. Dwight N. Hopkins, Lois A.
Lorentzen, Eduardo Mendieta, and David Batstone (Durham, NC: Duke University Press, 2001),
33–45.

starvation. At the same time, institutionalized religious traditions, especially the established Christian churches, have seen their power and influence decline in the West. Many Westerners of mainstream Christian, Jewish, and secular backgrounds are looking elsewhere to satisfy their spiritual needs. Consequently, in many Western countries Christian fundamentalism and the New Age movement have risen to become remarkable religious forces in recent decades. Religious fundamentalism is also on the rise worldwide. These and other developments have far-reaching consequences for humanity and nature on planet earth.

Yet the field of biblical studies seems strangely disconnected from these changes in our world, hardly taking notice of them. In fact, biblical research, at least Western biblical scholarship, is a field that has remained mostly unchanged during the past fifty years, and little change is likely to take place in biblical studies in the near future. Despite the crises in the world, both in wealthy countries located mostly in the Northern Hemisphere and in impoverished countries located mostly in the Southern Hemisphere, established scholars of the Bible are not even expected to relate to social, political, economic, and religious developments in our societies. Thus, courses on biblical literature are usually taught as if not much has changed since they were first designed. How is such detachment possible? I suggest that the dominant methodology in biblical studies—historical criticism—is one of the reasons for this lack of involvement in contemporary affairs. Historical criticism allows interpreters to position biblical literature in a distant past, far removed from today's politics, economics, and religion. Although the exclusion of contemporary questions is not an essential requirement in historical criticism, especially not as understood in the field of history during the last two decades,[3] biblical scholars often continue using historical criticism in a way that keeps the Bible separate from the intellectual-epistemological insights and developments in the world.

2. For more information, see, e.g., Mitchel A. Seligson and John T. Passé-Smith, eds., *Development and Underdevelopment: The Political Economy of Global Inequality*, 5th ed. (Boulder, CO: Lynne Rienner Publishers, 2014). Also see "An Economy for the 1%: How Privilege and Power in the Economy Drive Extreme Inequality and How This Can Be Stopped," 210 Oxfam Briefing Paper (January 18, 2016); available at www.oxfam.org (accessed June 9, 2017).

3. See, e.g., Mary Fulbrook, *Historical Theory* (London: Routledge, 2002); Georg G. Iggers, *Historiography in the Twentieth Century: From Scientific Objectivity to the Postmodern Challenge* (Hanover, NH: University Press of New England, 1997); and Bruce Mazlish and Ralph Buultjens, *Conceptualizing Global History* (Boulder: Westview, 1993). For further references, see footnote 15 below.

From Subversion to the Status Quo

Not all historical critics have used the method in this way; indeed, some, among them feminist interpreters, have examined the Bible's historical context with contemporary questions in mind. For instance, Monika Fander, a feminist critic in New Testament studies, insists on the value of historical criticism for a feminist reading of biblical literature. She explains: "It is not the methods of historical criticism as such that are unsuitable for feminist historical research. The tensions between the historical-critical method and feminist historical study are hermeneutical in character. . . . Every scholar addresses a text in terms of a particular pre-understanding that is marked, consciously or unconsciously, by the cultural context and questions of the researcher's own time."[4] Similarly, the pioneer of feminist New Testament analysis, Elisabeth Schüssler Fiorenza, sees historical analysis as connected to the hermeneutical interests of the exegete when she states:

> A critical feminist analysis takes the texts about wo/men out of their contextual frameworks and reassembles them like mosaic stones in a feminist pattern or design that does not recuperate but counteracts the marginalizing or oppressive tendencies of the kyriocentric text. To that end, one has to elaborate models of historical and socio-cultural reconstruction that can subvert the biblical text's kyriocentric dynamics and place the struggles of those whom it marginalizes and silences into the center of the historical narrative. . . . This calls for an increase in historical imagination.[5]

This viewpoint is still not the norm, however, and so younger scholars often accept traditional methodology uncritically. The pressure to promote and protect the dominance of historical criticism is strong even today[6] because, for the most part, Western biblical scholars do not see the need to engage systematically theological, political, and international issues of our day. This detachment often serves conservative

---

4. Monika Fander, "Historical-Critical Methods," in *Searching the Scriptures*, vol. 1, *A Feminist Introduction*, ed. Elisabeth Schüssler Fiorenza (New York: Crossroad, 1993), 221.

5. Elisabeth Schüssler Fiorenza, *Wisdom Ways: Introducing Feminist Biblical Interpretation* (Maryknoll, NY: Orbis, 2001), 146, 148.

6. For a description of the increasing prominence of historical criticism in the West, see John W. Rogerson, *Old Testament Criticism in the Nineteenth Century: England and Germany* (Philadelphia: Fortress Press, 1985); and Hans-Joachim Kraus, *Geschichte der Historisch-kritischen Erforschung des Alten Testaments von der Reformation bis zur Gegenwart*, 3rd ed. (Neukirchen-Vluyn: Neukirchener Verlag, 1982).

theological and cultural-religious purposes, and so, unsurprisingly, the field of biblical studies is largely dominated by a conservative religious, political, and academic agenda.[7]

The fact that historical criticism serves conservative purposes is indeed a remarkable development. Initially, during the nineteenth and early twentieth centuries, biblical scholars found in historical criticism a method that liberated them from the religious and academic status quo. At that time, historical criticism was a subversive approach. This was particularly true in Germany, the center from which historical criticism emerged. It began with what we know today as source criticism and expanded into a full-blown method during the first part of the twentieth century, when historical criticism became the standard in many European and liberal US-American schools of theology. Yet, in the nineteenth century, scholars who applied historical method were welcomed neither by the church nor the established theological scene of the day. For instance, in the middle of the nineteenth century a highly influential and powerful theology professor in Berlin, Ernst W. Hengstenberg (1802–1869), made sure that proponents of historical criticism would not gain access to tenured faculty positions.[8] As a result, the historical critic Johann K. W. Vatke (1806–1882), later recognized as a key figure in the development of historical criticism, did not become a full professor as long as Hengstenberg and like-minded colleagues held influential faculty positions in Berlin. They prevented Vatke's promotion for decades, as they defended the Christian doctrinal position according to which the starting point for reading the Bible was "the atoning work of Christ."

Among these like-minded colleagues was Old Testament scholar, Franz Delitzsch (1813–1890). In 1853, he dismissed historical-critical exegesis. In the first edition of his renowned Genesis commentary he writes:

> If one reads J. Severin Vater's (3d ed., 1802–05) critical, arbitrary, exegetically spiritless commentary on the Pentateuch and Peter v. Bohlen's (1835) apparently learned but sloppy and extremely impudent interpretation of Genesis, one feels the pain about the depth of the decline from scriptural faith. . . . They all do not appreciate Holy Scripture as a book

7. For instance, Elisabeth Schüssler Fiorenza points out that "since 1947 no [SBL] presidential address has explicitly reflected on world politics, global crises, human sufferings, or movements for change"; see her SBL presidential address delivered on December 5, 1987, titled "The Ethics of Biblical Interpretation: Decentering Biblical Scholarship," in *Reading the Bible in the Global Village: Helsinki*, ed. Heikki Räisänen et al. (Atlanta: Society of Biblical Literature, 2000), 113.

8. See Rogerson, *Old Testament Criticism*, 85–90.

of divine revelation and are not interested in Christianity as a religion of reconciliation. Therefore, their indifference, which culminates in [August W.] Knobel's commentary and is deeply saddening, deprives Christianity of the inalienable prehistoric basis that is contained in Genesis.[9]

In later editions of his commentary, Delitzsch changed his position on historical criticism and included what he called "preparatory works of [Julius] Wellhausen, [Abraham] Kuenen and preferably [August] Dill- mann," but he also emphasized that "the spirit of this [commentary = 5th ed.; 1887] remained the same since 1852 [year of 1st ed.]."[10] From 1828 to 1869, then, the opponents of historical criticism prevailed. Only when the old school retired did historical critics gain ground. After Julius Wellhausen's *Prolegomena to the History of Israel* came out in 1878, ten years after Hengstenberg's reign in Berlin, the situation was reversed and historical criticism began to dominate the field of biblical studies. Many churches tried their best to prevent what they considered the worst, namely, the application of historical criticism to the Bible. In the United States several Protestant denominations tried to fire historical critics who taught at Christian seminaries. Among them is the famous case of Charles A. Briggs (1841–1913), who taught Hebrew and cognate languages at Union Theological Seminary in New York City, then a Presbyterian institution.[11] In 1892, the Presbyterian Church subjected this scholar to a presbytery trial for heresy. The denomination demanded that Briggs either refrain from applying his- torical methods to the Hebrew Bible or leave his post. Supported by Union's faculty, Briggs did not waiver but continued his work and kept his position. The Presbyterian denomination did not accept this situ- ation and cut its ties with the seminary, which has been nondenom- inational ever since. Many other such stories exist, illustrating that

9. Franz Delitzsch, *Die Genesis*, 2nd ed. (Leipzig: Dorffling & Franke, 1853), 590 (my translation).

10. Franz Delitzsch, *Neuer Commentar über die Genesis*, 5th ed. (Leipzig: Dorffling & Franke, 1887), iii.

11. On the trial, see Robert T. Handy, "The Trials of Charles Briggs (1881–1893)," in *A History of Union Theological Seminary in New York* (New York: Columbia University Press, 1987), 69–93. See also Charles A. Briggs, *The Case against Professor Briggs* (New York: Scribner, 1892–1893); Briggs, *Authority of Holy Scripture: Inaugural Address and Defense, 1891/1893* (New York: Arno, 1972); and Mark Stephen Massa, *Charles Augustus Briggs and the Crisis of Historical Criticism* (Minneapolis: Fortress Press, 1990). This kind of dispute continues even today. See, for instance, the court case between New Testament scholar Gerd Lüdermann and the University of Göttingen (Germany). Lüdermann's research on the historical Jesus and the doctrine of Christ's resurrection led the regional Protes- tant *Landeskirche von Niedersachsen* to withdraw Lüdermann's teaching authority. For detailed information, see www.gerdluedemann.de/, as well as Horst Hirschler, "Wir wollen kein Lehrver- fahren: Der hannoversche Landesbischof zum Streit um den Göttinger Theologieprofessor Gerd Lüdemann," *Das Sonntagsblatt*, February 23, 1995, available at http://wwwuser.gwdg.de/~glue- dem/ger/001003002.htm (accessed June 9, 2017). Also see Jennie Brokkman, "German Heretic Remains in a Chair," *The Times Higher Education Supplement*, January 1, 1999, 10.

academic integrity persevered over ecclesiastical intimidation. Scholars risked and sometimes lost their positions when they maintained that the Bible is historical literature like any other document of the past and is to be studied as such.

In the twentieth century, the historical-critical method became part of the standard curriculum in Protestant theological studies, and Catholic and Jewish academic institutions eventually accepted it as the standard for biblical interpretation. With the retirement of Ernst W. Hengstenberg, historical criticism rose to prominence, becoming the symbol for the success of the modern scientific worldview. Historical criticism made the reading of the Bible acceptable as a modern academic endeavor so that biblical research was recognized as a scientific activity. Even today, historical criticism is still very effective in encounters with fundamentalist Christians, and so publications on the history of biblical literature abound.

Opposition from the Margins

The situation has, however, begun to change. During the past decade, a sustained and strong opposition to historical criticism as an adequate method in biblical exegesis has come prominently from scholars marginalized by ethnicity, race, or continental location. Asian American, African American, and Hispanic diasporic scholars in the United States as well as African and Asian exegetes have started to articulate their concerns openly and forcefully. They view historical criticism as a Eurocentric tool that facilitates Western imperialistic practice and distances the academic field of biblical studies from the issues of our time and various locations. Accordingly, Asian American theologian, Russell Moy, asserts that "the historical-critical method of biblical scholarship is Eurocentric in its methods and ideology due to its historical roots. With the dominance of this method, its practitioners uncritically exalt its cultural worldview over others and regard its methods as normative and objective. Its exclusivity prevents an appreciation of non-Western hermeneutical approaches such as oral tradition."[12] Moy locates the formation of historical criticism in Europe, which cannot be denied, and then continues to limit the method's validity to the European cultural-philosophical context shaped by the modern scientific worldview. What is perceived as universal is in fact limited to a particular

12. Russel G. Moy, "Biculturalism, Race, and the Bible," *RelEd* 88 (1993): 424.

geopolitical location. Moy also reminds historical critics of the need to integrate non-Western approaches into their exegetical repertoire.

Other scholars, too, contend that historical criticism is a Western endeavor and thus belongs to a particular geographical context. To them, the method prevents researchers from making much-needed connections between biblical literature and the challenges of the present era. One of them is William H. Meyers, an exegete of African American descent, who questions the usefulness of historical criticism because it distances scholarly work from contemporary issues. He observes that "this method tends to lock the interpretative task in the past (e.g., in debates over authorial intent) while evading key contemporary issues like racism or intercultural dialogue. . . . One rarely finds any discussion of an African American interpretation of the Scriptures."[13] This situation has changed only slightly since Meyers made this comment. Even though major studies on African American interpretations of the Bible are now available,[14] many exegetical commentaries still stress historical meaning over and against cultural-contextual analysis, separating biblical meaning from contemporary questions.[15]

Scholars from African and Asian countries are among the most vocal critics of historical criticism. Some of them regard the method as a politically, religiously, and economically powerful tool of past and present imperialistic practices of industrialized nations. Although the influence of historical criticism on international politics and economics seems overstated, the connection between intellectual perspective and political practice needs to be taken seriously. After all, Christian missionary movements from Western countries have promoted politically and theologically conservative agendas, which have shaped the beliefs of many Christians in Africa, Asia, and Latin America. In fact,

13. William H. Meyers, "The Hermeneutical Dilemma of the African American Biblical Student," in *Stony the Road We Trod: African American Biblical Interpretation*, ed. Cain H. Felder (Minneapolis: Fortress Press, 1991), 41.
14. See, e.g., Vincent L. Wimbush, ed., *African Americans and the Bible* (New York: Continuum, 2001). For the related African context, see also Kurt Holter, *Yahweh in Africa: Essays on African and the Old Testament*, Bible and Theology in Africa (New York: Lang, 2000); and Gerald O. West and Musa W. Dube, eds., *The Bible in Africa: Transaction, Trajectories and Trends* (Leiden: Brill, 2001).
15. More recently the field of historical criticism has developed approaches that account for the relationship between a historian's social location and their historical analysis. Besides the works mentioned in footnote 3 above; see also Paul Hamilton, *Historicism*, 2nd ed. (New York: Routledge, 2003); Peter N. Stearns, Peter C. Seixas, and Samuel S. Wineburg, eds., *Knowing, Teaching, and Learning History: National and International Perspectives* (New York: New York University Press, 2000); John Kucich and Dianne F. Sadoff, *Victorian Afterlife: Postmodern Culture Rewrites the Nineteenth Century* (Minneapolis: University of Minnesota Press, 2000); and Keith Jenkins, ed., *The Postmodern History Reader* (New York: Routledge, 1997).

conservative positions in African, Asian, and Latin American Christian-ities haunt Western Christians today as they try to implement progres-sive religious policies. This situation became evident in the election of the first openly gay Episcopalian bishop in the United States.[16] The idea that historical criticism has contributed to the success of imperialistic practices and policies in the past and present is thus a claim not to be dismissed too quickly.

African feminist exegete, Musa W. Dube, rejects historical criticism outright, arguing that, as an imperialistic instrument of the West, it has left political and economic structures of exploitation and oppression in the world unchallenged. She writes that "to divorce biblical interpre-tation from current international relations, or to discuss it primarily as an ancient text, becomes another western ideological stance that hides its direct impact on the postcolonial world and maintains its imperial domination of Two-Third World countries."[17] Dube suggests that the Bible has profoundly shaped society, and so the Bible's formative role in the postcolonial world requires that scholars engage this body of lit-erature not just as historical material related to the ancient Near East or the early Christian and rabbinic eras. The Bible still affects today's world in manifold ways, and so it needs to be explicated with care and in detail. Dube also asserts that historical criticism enables Western scholars to ignore the Bible's relationship with political and economic structures of exploitation on the one hand and religious ideology on the other hand. The method has prevented Western interpreters from opposing colonialism, imperialism, and the systematic socioeconomic impoverishment of countries in Africa and elsewhere. In short, histori-cal criticism has fostered in Western Bible readers an acceptance of the societal status quo.

The situation has affected Western and non-Western Bible readers who have come into contact with Western Christian missionaries and their Bibles. In fact, Sri Lankan exegete Rasiah Sugirtharajah goes as far as to characterize historical criticism as a "legacy of colonial hermeneutics,"[18] which "effectively eclipsed allegorical, symbolic, fig-urative, and metaphorical ways of appropriating the text" intrinsic to the interpretation of indigenous Hindu sacred texts. "Indigenous reading practices" disappear when colonized Asian Christian scholars

16. See, e.g., Marc Lacey, "African Anglican Leaders Outraged Over Gay Bishop in U.S.," *New York Times*, November 4, 2003, A21.

17. Musa W. Dube, *Postcolonial Feminist Interpretation of the Bible* (St. Louis: Chalice, 2000), 20.

18. Rasiah S. Sugirtharajah, *The Bible and the Third World: Precolonial, Colonial and Postcolonial Encounters* (Cambridge: Cambridge University Press, 2001), 71–77.

learn to accept historical criticism, and so, to Sugirtharajah, their work illustrates "creative Asian mimicry."[19] Sugirtharajah also contends that even when Asian Christian scholars view historical criticism "as an effective weapon of decolonization,"[20] they have been successfully brainwashed. They employ the tools of the colonizers. For Sugirtharajah, then, historical criticism is not an approach well suited for Asian biblical studies.[21]

Kwok Pui-lan, a Chinese Asian feminist theologian originally from Hong Kong, also opposes historical criticism, suggesting that it was created by white, male, middle-class academics to whom this method belongs. In her view, people of other social locations need to rely on alternative approaches because "many Asian and indigenous Christians live in cultures that understand history and historiography in a totally different way. The Eurocentric positivist approach must not be taken as the sole norm for the historical quest. The Bible is too important to be subject to *only* one norm or model of interpretation."[22] Kwok does not want the Bible to be seen as a relic of the past, a document that exists solely to inform readers about ancient worlds. She thus suggests reading biblical literature in conversation with our experiences and the world, in dialogue with multiple religions, cultural practices, and beliefs. A strict historical-critical approach disallows such dialogical and imaginative work, which is needed in our religiously pluralistic world. In Kwok's view, the method of white, middle-class, academic males is too restrictive in a world in which so many people of different geographical, racial, ethnic, and religious contexts live together trying to make sense of the diverse, multicultural, and multireligious world.

Finally, the American Hispanic scholar, Fernando Segovia, describes clearly and matter-of-factly the problems inherent in historical criticism. He suggests that the method gives scholarly readers the illusion of executing an objective, universally valid, and value-neutral study of biblical literature, separated from the messiness and complexities of their respective social locations. The method helps them claim to be doing exegesis and not eisegesis, the latter being regarded as unacceptable. In the process revered teachers select small groups of future

19. Rasiah S. Sugirtharajah, *Asian Biblical Hermeneutics and Postcolonialism: Contesting the Interpretations* (Sheffield: Sheffield Academic, 1998), 11.
20. Ibid., 129.
21. For a critical reception of Sugirtharajah's position, see, e.g., Heikki Räisänen, "Biblical Critics in the Global Village," in *Challenges to Biblical Interpretation: Collected Essays 1991-2000*, Biblical Series 59 (Leiden: Brill, 2001), 283–309; repr. from Räisänen et al., *Reading the Bible in the Global Village*, 9–28.
22. Kwok Pui-lan, *Discovering the Bible in the Non-biblical World*, Bible and Liberation Series (Maryknoll, NY: Orbis, 1995), 86 (emphasis original).

experts as their students who continue the task of the historical project. Segovia characterizes this process as "highly hierarchical and
authoritative in character, with strong emphasis on academic pedigree
(who studied under whom) and school of thought (proper versus
improper approximations to the text)."[23] The approach deliberately
and forcefully excludes anybody who does not subscribe to the agenda
of historical criticism. Therefore Segovia, too, classifies historical criticism as "colonialist and imperialist."

> It emerged out of a Eurocentric setting, and, as such, it was and remained
> thoroughly Eurocentric at every level of discourse and inquiry. As a result,
> the construct unreflectively universalized its bracketed identity, expect-
> ing on the surface all readers everywhere to become ideal critics,
> informed and universal, while in actuality requiring all readers to inter-
> pret like Eurocentric critics. In fact, the entire discussion, from beginning
> to end and top to bottom, was characterized and governed by the funda-
> mental concerns, questions, and horizons of this particular group, uncrit-
> ically disguised as the fundamental questions, horizons, and concerns of
> the entire Christian world. To become the ideal critic, therefore, was to
> enter into a specific and contextualized discussion, a Eurocentric discus-
> sion.[24]

In light of this critique, it is not surprising that Segovia proposes an
alternative, namely, to connect biblical exegesis with cultural studies.[25]

Feminist Compliance with Androcentric Historiography

In contrast to these unambiguous challenges, Western feminist scholars of the Hebrew Bible do not exhibit an equally strong opposition
to historical criticism. In fact, many of them appear invested in this
method even when they acknowledge its inherent difficulties. For
instance, exegete Silvia Schroer of the University of Bern in Switzer-
land recognizes "traces of European-imperialistic theory" in historical

23. Fernando F. Segovia, "'And They Began to Speak in Other Tongues': Competing Modes of Discourse
in Contemporary Biblical Criticism," in *Reading From This Place*, vol. 1, *Social Location and Biblical
Interpretation in the United States*, ed. Fernando F. Segovia and Mary A. Tolbert (Minneapolis:
Fortress Press, 1995), 13. See also Mary A. Tolbert's commentary on the situation of graduate work
in the field of biblical studies, "Graduate Biblical Studies: Ethos and Discipline," *SBL Forum* (2003):
http://tinyurl.com/l2n794t.
24. Segovia, "They Began To Speak," 29–30.
25. See Fernando F. Segovia, "Cultural Studies and Contemporary Biblical Criticism: Ideological Criticism as Mode or Discourse," in *Reading from This Place*, vol. 2, *Social Location and Biblical Interpretation in Global Perspective*, ed. Fernando F. Segovia and Mary A. Tolbert (Minneapolis: Fortress Press,
1995), 1–17.

criticism, but she hopes to remedy past interpretative practice with what she calls "expanded historical research." By this assertion she means that historical critics need to disclose their hermeneutical interests and renegotiate their agenda for historicizing biblical literature. The renegotiated agenda includes addressing the history of interpretation, rewriting the history of women in the Yahweh-religion, reconceptualizing the development of monotheism, and reemphasizing the legal traditions of the Hebrew Bible.[26] This agenda is impressive but it remains firmly rooted in historical criticism. A sustained critique of this method and the integration of contextualized approaches are not considered as options.

The severity of the problem is obvious in a short essay by Old Testament exegete, Phyllis Bird. Ambivalent about characterizing her work as feminist, she distinguishes between two exegetical steps that have to be kept apart.[27] The first step requires "formulat[ing] the sense of the text in its ancient social and literary context."[28] According to Bird, an interpreter has to understand a biblical passage as the original author's effort to communicate a particular position or message to the ancient audience. This step is "descriptive" and "analytical" and "may not contain any clearly recognizable feminist message." Only in the second step may a feminist reader identify "signs of feminist orientation in readings of biblical texts."[29] This step is based on a "systemic analysis of gender relations . . . a *critique* of relationships, norms and expectations that limit or subordinate women's thought, action and expression."[30] It alone decides whether a feminist interpretation "rings true for women readers"[31] and "makes sense to men as well."[32] In feminist biblical exegesis, historical criticism is thus key, and so Bird asserts:

> I find no tension between historical criticism and feminist commitment between attempts to view the past on its own terms and a commitment to change the terms of participation and discourse generated by that past. I see no reason why an attempt to enter sympathetically into the

---

26. Silvia Schroer, "Bibelauslegung im europäischen Kontext," in *Hermeneutik, sozialgeschichtlich: Kontextualität in den Bibelwissenschaften aus der Sicht (latein)amerikanischer und europäischer Exegetinnen und Exegeten*, ed. Erhard S. Gerstenberger and Ulrich Schönborn, EUZ 1 (Münster: LIT, 1999), 126–30.
27. Phyllis A. Bird, "What Makes a Feminist Reading Feminist? A Qualified Answer," in *Escaping Eden: New Feminist Perspectives on the Bible*, ed. Harold C. Washington, Susan L. Graham, and Pamela L. Thimmes (New York: New York University Press, 1998), 124–31.
28. Ibid., 126.
29. Ibid., 128.
30. Ibid., 129 (emphasis original).
31. Ibid.
32. Ibid., 130.

minds or consciousnesses of historical persons and empathize with their feelings, motives and actions should exclude critique and ultimate rejection of those views. . . . Dismissal of historical criticism simply means that unexamined assumptions are read into the text. Historical criticism makes no claims concerning the normativity, or representativeness, of the ancient texts; in fact, it alerts readers to the dangers of such assumptions by considering the perspective, location and interests of the ancient author (including class, gender, religious party, etc.).[33]

Bird values historical criticism because it provides insight into the authorial contexts, alerts contemporary readers to potential projections of their assumptions onto ancient Israelite times, and creates exegetical distance. The method allows interpreters to give priority to the textual-historical meaning and only then to formulate a response. To feminist scholars like Bird, historical criticism is a tool suited for the feminist interpretative task.

The willingness among Western feminist Hebrew Bible scholars to rely on historical criticism is particularly obvious when they examine biblical stories and laws on rape. The problem is that historical readings, even when undertaken by feminist readers, seem not to promote feminist views but to endorse androcentric notions of rape and gender. The conviction that it is possible to describe the intentional meaning of a biblical passage independent of a reader's hermeneutical interest limits the interpretative task. Three examples illustrate the problem. One example relates to the rape of Dinah in Genesis 34, another to the rape laws in Deuteronomy 22:25–29, and yet another to the rapes of Bilhah and Zilpah in Genesis 29:31–30:24. It is a matter of feminist debate whether these texts can be classified as rape texts and how they might be read as androcentric literature.

In the case of Genesis 34, interpreters, feminist or not, have long debated whether the story favors Shechem—Dinah's rapist—or Dinah's brothers. Two interpreters, Danna Nolan Fewell and David Gunn, joined the debate years ago. Fewell and Gunn use mostly literary reading strategies to describe how the narrator tries to make the reader side with the rapist, but then, in an unexpected move, they leave the terrain of literary analysis and fortify their position with a historical assertion. They contend that Shechem deserves our sympathy because he "loves her [Dinah] and takes delight in her."[34] In their opinion,

---

33. Ibid., 128.
34. Danna Nolan Fewell and David M. Gunn, "Tipping the Balance: Sternberg's Reader and the Rape of Dinah," *JBL* 110 (1991): 210.

Shechem's sincerity is apparent in his marriage proposal, which, to Fewell and Gunn, was in Dinah's "best interests within the narrow limits of this society."[35] A reference to ancient customs serves to exonerate the rapist. The interpreters claim that the marriage proposal helped Dinah survive in a society that offered no other option for raped women but marriage to their rapist. Fewell and Gunn sense the difficulty of their position and acknowledge that "to advocate a woman marrying her rapist might itself seem to be a dangerous and androcentric advocacy," but, in the end, they suggest that "the story world" offers no "other liberating alternatives."[36] A reference to ancient Israelite society thus defends the action of the rapist and, even worse, justifies his marriage proposal. Fewell and Gunn call their reading "feminist," but it is clear something has gone terribly wrong in this interpretation when it is examined from the perspective of feminist theories dealing with rape.[37] From this perspective it is not a "feminist" position to approve of a rapist marrying the raped victim-survivor.[38] Promoting androcentric values, Fewell and Gunn's reading not only offers a badly argued historical position but also illustrates the dangers involved in justifying patriarchal habit with historical argumentation.

The rape laws of Deuteronomy 22:25–29 provide another example to demonstrate the difficulties of applying historical criticism to biblical rape stories. Old Testament professor, Carolyn Pressler, who has written extensively on Deuteronomic law,[39] rejects the possibility that rape laws existed in ancient Israel. She explains that "it is anachronistic to speak about the Deuteronomistic view of sexual laws."[40] Pressler rejects mixing contemporary assumptions with her historical reconstructive work because she considers a historian's task to merely describe "authorial intent." Pressler's writing reveals the conflict that she senses between her description of the historical task and her feminist convictions. On the one hand, she disallows bringing

---

35. Ibid.
36. Ibid.
37. See also Meir Sternberg's reply to Fewell and Gunn's interpretation in his "Biblical Poetics and Sexual Politics: From Reading to Counterreading," *JBL* 111 (1992): 463–88. For an extended discussion of this and other interpretations, see Susanne Scholz, *Rape Plots: A Feminist Cultural Study of Genesis 34*, StBibLit 13 (New York: Lang, 2000), 116–27.
38. In Peru, for instance, feminists fought vehemently against the legal situation in their country that approves of a rapist marrying the raped woman; see Susanne Scholz, "Was It Really Rape in Genesis 31? Biblical Scholarship as a Reflection of Cultural Assumptions," in Washington, Graham, and Thimmes, *Escaping Eden*, 182–98, esp. 195–97.
39. See, e.g., Carolyn Pressler, *The View of Women Found in Deuteronomic Family Law*, BZAW 216 (Berlin: de Gruyter, 1993).
40. Carolyn Pressler, "Sexual Violence and Deuteronomic Law," in *A Feminist Companion to Exodus and Deuteronomy*, ed. Athalya Brenner, FCB 6 (Sheffield: Sheffield Academic, 1994), 102–12.

contemporary terminology and concepts to the biblical text. On the other hand, she accepts the need to read with contemporary questions in mind. She states: "This is not to say that it is inappropriate to bring modem categories to the biblical texts. It is appropriate to ask how Deuteronomy views acts that we consider acts of sexual violence. . . . It is important to analyze and criticize these and any 'texts of terror.'"[41] Yet she also insists that "the offense [described in Deuteronomy 22:25–29] is not 'rape' according to the modern definitions of that term."[42] Pressler goes back and forth, but, when it is time to describe the legal situation, she follows almost exclusively the perspective of the "redactors." She explains that "the Deuteronomic laws regard female sexuality as the possession of the woman's father or husband. The father's claims are akin to property claims; the husband's claims are more extensive. *It follows* that the woman has no claims over her own sexuality; *she therefore cannot be sexually assaulted.*"[43]

Historical perspective traps this feminist reader here. The apparently historical description is no longer grounded in feminist analysis but presents the androcentric view of the ancient law as the norm. It is important to note that feminist scholars using historical-critical arguments often seem anxious when they explain the supposedly historical meaning of rape texts. Perhaps they worry about reinforcing androcentric values since, from a contemporary feminist perspective, a woman can, of course, be sexually assaulted even when a father owns her like property. So Pressler is careful at this point. She acknowledges that Deuteronomistic laws "negate women's will, deny women's right to sexual and physical integrity and erase women's personhood." But then she affirms explanations provided by decades-old scholarship about the historical "intention" of the biblical law.[44] Historical argumentation does not serve this feminist analysis well.

Our lack of historical data regarding ancient Israelite life, especially as it relates to rape, sometimes persuades feminist exegetes to ignore certain stories altogether since they are known for containing little historical information. An example is the story about the rapes of the enslaved women Bilhah and Zilpah, found in Genesis 29:31–30:24. The story has received little treatment in traditional literature, which usually remembers the story for its genealogical value and gives it

---

41. Ibid., 112.
42. Ibid., 103.
43. Ibid., 111 (emphasis added).
44. See Pressler, "Sexual Violence," 103n3, where she refers to the source of her arguments: David R. Mace, *Hebrew Marriage: A Sociological Study* (London: Epworth, 1953).

headings such as "The Birth and Naming of Jacob's Sons: Genesis 29:31–30:24,"[45] "The Birth of Jacob's Children (29:31–30:43),"[46] or, including the mothers' names, "Jacob's Four Sons by Leah (29:31–35)" and "Jacob's Children by Bilhah (30:1–8)."[47] Yet, besides an emphasis on genealogy, the story is no longer viewed as providing historical information about premonarchic times in ancient Israel, a period that, according to a large segment of current scholarship, cannot reliably be reconstructed on the basis of biblical literature.

This scholarly consensus has also affected feminist work. Feminist exegetes rarely discuss Genesis 29:31–30:24 although the passage includes four women who speak and act prominently. Feminist comments are usually limited to a historical reference on surrogate motherhood, as it appears here as well as in Genesis 16, the story of Hagar and Sarah. For instance, Susan Niditch explains that the custom of having children through another woman is reported in several ancient Near Eastern texts. And so Niditch justifies the exploitative treatment of Bilhah and Zilpah, the enslaved women of Leah and Rachel, when she writes that "surrogate motherhood allowed a barren woman to regulate her status in a world in which children were a woman's status and in which childlessness was regarded as a virtual sign of divine disfavor."[48] The custom of surrogate motherhood is accepted as a legitimate solution for infertile women of the ancient Near East. In fact, historical interrogation hinders feminist readers from considering this text as a story about class-privileged women replicating androcentric values, and so many feminist interpreters move on to other texts. Only Renita J. Weems characterizes the action of Leah and Rachel as "nothing less than reprehensible."[49]

The difficulty for feminist interpreters in identifying the procreative activities in Genesis 29:31–30:24 as rape appears clearly in the interpretation of feminist commentator, Elyse Goldstein. She writes from a literary-theological and not a historical perspective, but her explanations have the air of universality, as if what was told then makes sense

---

45. Claus Westermann, *Genesis 12–36*, trans. John J. Scullion, CC (Minneapolis: Fortress Press, 1984–1986), 469.
46. Nahum M. Sarna, *Genesis*, JPS Torah Commentary (Philadelphia: Jewish Publication Society, 1989), 206.
47. Victor P. Hamilton, *The Book of Genesis: Chapters 18–50*, NICOT (Grand Rapids: Eerdmans, 1995), 265, 269.
48. Susan Niditch, "Genesis," in *The Women's Bible Commentary*, ed. Carol A. Newsom and Sharon H. Ringe, 2nd ed. (Louisville: Westminster John Knox, 1998), 20.
49. Renita J. Weems, "Do You See What I See? Diversity in Interpretation," *Church & Society* 82 (1991): 34.

now. She writes: "God rewards Leah with fertility to make up for her troubles with her husband, and the women [Leah and Rachel] are now equalized. One [Rachel] gets a man's love; the other [Leah] gets a child's love. One woman [Rachel] gains status through her husband, the other woman [Leah] status through her children."[50]

In Goldstein's feminist commentary, which focuses almost exclusively on Leah and Rachel, the enslaved women are absent from the discussion. Yet they are forced into sexual intercourse with Jacob, the husband, when the slaveholding wives are desperate for children or husbandly *love*. Goldstein assumes that the androcentric values surrounding motherhood cause Leah and Rachel to compete with each other. After they accomplish their goals, all is well. The enslaved women, Bilhah and Zilpah, receive no consideration, and the power differential between socially privileged and exploited women remains unexplored. The historical conviction that ancient Israelite society respected women only as mothers prevents Goldstein as well as other interpreters[51] from reading Genesis 29:31–30:24 as a critique of women's divergent social positions in a patriarchal order and as a story about the repeated rapes of the enslaved women Bilhah and Zilpah. Instead, historical clichés about surrogate birthing customs and universalizing assumptions about love between husband and wife/wives prevail in this feminist commentary on Genesis 29:31–30:24. A powerful story about the co-optation of women into androcentric structure and class oppression turns into a story about two women becoming mothers.

Cultivating Alternative Ways of Reading Biblical Literature

So the problem is how to read the Bible in Western societies in which historical criticism, though initially subversive, has turned to supporting the political, cultural, and religious status quo, as put forward by postcolonial scholars but overlooked by many Western feminist

---

50. Elyse Goldstein, *ReVisions: Seeing Torah Through a Feminist Lens* (Woodstock, VT: Jewish Lights, 1998), 65. For the idea of God as the equalizer between the women, see also John Calvin, *Genesis*, trans. John King (Carlisle, PA: Banner of Truth Trust, 1992), 140.

51. For another example, see Esther Fuchs, *Sexual Politics in the Biblical Narrative: Reading the Hebrew Bible as a Woman*, JSOTSup 310 (Sheffield: Sheffield Academic, 2000), 158. Fuchs limits her analysis to Leah and Rachel and does not consider the dynamics of class as an integral element for understanding the dynamics between socially privileged and marginalized women. She also makes historical arguments supported largely by out-of-date anthropological scholarship; see the reference to an anthropological study of 1974 on 158n48. See further Susanne Scholz, "Gender, Class, and Androcentric Compliance in the Rapes of Enslaved Women in the Hebrew Bible," *Lectio difficilior* 1 (2004): http://tinyurl.com/n4njgrf.

historical critics. It seems to me that at the dawn of the twenty-first century biblical studies has to be brought up to speed with the Western culture of "Tandoori Reindeer," in which Norwegian-Indians prepare their tandoori with the meat of the land, reindeer, or in which American Jews celebrate Hanukah alongside Christmas. In Western secularized societies of Europe and North America, people live in a world in which East meets West and North encounters South, diasporic people become increasingly visible, and multireligious and polycultural sensibilities represent the hope for a future in which human rights and the planetary ecosystem will flourish.[52] Ours is a culture that lives with much freedom in religious, social, and cultural interaction and experimentation. For many, though not for all, syncretism is no longer a word but an everyday occurrence, if not in our towns, then on television, in film, or on the Internet.

In light of this multicultural dynamic in our lives, historical criticism seems obsolete. In biblical studies other approaches hold more promise for communicating the ongoing need for the academic study of the Bible than a method developed in confrontation with the experiences of the nineteenth century. In particular, two such methods stand out that take into account the questions, concerns, and developments of our time and place. One approach, which defines the study of the Bible in terms of cultural studies, envisions the field as a radically interdisciplinary project that cooperates with such fields as sociology, political science, history, and anthropology. This notion is not entirely new but needs to be pursued more actively and broadly in mainstream biblical research than is currently done. The interdisciplinary character of such work supports research that goes beyond the text-focused approach so dear to many scholars of biblical studies, and takes seriously the contextual and cultural histories and traditions of reading the Bible. Biblical analysis, defined accordingly, illuminates the material conditions of interpretations and helps explore how biblical meanings are constructed in a wide range of reading communities across time and space. This approach looks at the Bible as a document of abundant histories of interpretation in the East, West, South, and North, as a reflection of past and present cultures, political structures, and religions. Bible research turns into a multidisciplinary and multicultural

---

52. For the phrase "Tandoori Reindeer," see Craig S. Smith's report on the Muslim Norwegian comedian Shabana Rehman in "Where East Meets West Warily, She Makes Them Laugh," *New York Times*, November 14, 2003, A4.

endeavor that examines multiple geographies, histories, and sociologies of reading.

Some of this work is already underway. For instance, the *Global Bible Commentary*,[53] edited by Daniel Patte and others, is based on the insight that contextualized readings are the future for biblical studies and that different contexts yield different meanings, many largely unknown to Western Bible scholars and readers. The volume is text-focused, but commentators address the assigned biblical books from their own sociopolitical and religious situations. Another example of the kind of work that biblical scholars increasingly need to pursue in a multireligious world comes from Chinese Hebrew Bible scholar, Archie Lee. In a society that is mostly nonbiblical and non-Christian, Lee developed a paradigm for examining the Bible that values cross-cultural and cross-religious exchange. His work on Chinese and biblical creation myths, for instance, explores similarities and differences in the scriptural traditions prevalent in a Chinese Buddhist context.[54]

The work of Vincent Wimbush, New Testament professor and director of the Institute for Signifying Scriptures at the School of Religion of Claremont Graduate University,[55] also contributes to the study of the Bible as a culminating artifact of many cultures, histories, and peoples. The mission statement of the institute makes an important and—for the field of biblical studies—crucial claim, namely, that "interpretive meaning is less about the codified text, and more about the encoded meanings in cultural behaviors," especially in the context of "historically enslaved and colonized peoples of the world," such as African Americans. To politically, culturally, and religiously dominated Bible readers, "signifying Scriptures" has often meant appropriating texts in performance as an "alternative" mode of interpretation rather than as a limitation to investigations of the text itself or the world behind the text. The exploration of alternative approaches is thus a central aspect of the institute's work. Yet these and other projects are still on the margins of the academic field. They deserve sustained support from scholarly societies, such as the Society of Biblical Literature, or departments of religious and theological studies. All of this research contributes to an understanding of the Bible as a part of our syncretistic ways of life.

---

53. Daniel Patte et al., eds., *Global Bible Commentary* (Nashville: Abingdon, 2004).
54. Archie C. C. Lee, "The Chinese Creation Myth of Nu Kua and the Biblical Narrative in Genesis 1–11," *BibInt* 2 (1994): 312–24.
55. For more information on the institute, see http://www.signifyingscriptures.org/.

In contemporary Western societies brimming with multiple languages, cultures, and traditions, yet another direction needs to be developed. Within a societal context of tandoori reindeer, biblical studies would benefit from a focus on "ordinary" readers. The idea of taking seriously ordinary readers in the study of the Bible is most prominently developed, so far, by South African researchers.[56] They claim that an indigenization of the Bible has been underway among Christians for some time, but has gone unnoticed by researchers in biblical studies. South African scholars decided to remedy this situation and deliberately attend to laypeople's readings. In the process, their work has focused on the needs of their political, cultural, and religious context.[57]

Western biblical scholarship is far behind in this movement. One of the problems is, of course, that in Western secularized countries many people do not read the Bible, feeling alienated from the religious tradition of their ancestors. Still, many of them consider themselves on a spiritual quest, and so they are often part of what is commonly, and perhaps mistakenly, called the "New Age movement." The latter is an attempt by largely secularized people to bring religious-spiritual meaning to their lives, a concern shared with Christian fundamentalists. In postbiblical Western societies many of these ordinary readers come from the North American and Western European white, middle-class, and reasonably educated strata of society.

If biblical researchers want to reach those ordinary readers, I suggest they need to go beyond the exoteric, analytical approach of traditional biblical research and develop an experiential, inner understanding of the Bible so that people experience on a personal-individual and embodied level the Bible's possible contributions to the religious-spiritual quest. This turn toward an inner reading enables teachers and professional readers of the Bible to explain to ordinary readers of secularized Western societies that an understanding of the Bible is not only an academic, perhaps historically interesting, subject matter but also of significance to their lives. In a time in which the Bible plays a central role only to fundamentalist Christians and to Jews and Christians committed to their respective religious institutions, scholars cannot simply assume the importance of the Bible anymore. Rather, the field

56. See, e.g., Gerald O. West, *The Academy of the Poor: Towards a Dialogical Reading of the Bible* (Sheffield: Sheffield Academic, 1999).
57. See, e.g., Madipoane Masenya (ngwana' Mphahlele), "Their Hermeneutics Was Strange! Ours Is a Necessity! Rereading Vashti as African–South African Women," in *Her Master's Tools? Feminist and Postcolonial Engagements of Historical-Critical Discourse*, ed. Caroline Vander Stichele and Todd Penner (Atlanta: Society of Biblical Literature, 2005), 179–94.

has to articulate in its work that the study of this sacred text matters even today. In my view, this process of communicating the relevance of biblical studies is twofold. On the one hand, the Bible has to be studied deliberately as an artifact of diverse and manifold worlds, which informs about past and present cultures. On the other hand, scholars need to introduce ordinary readers of Western secularized societies to the Bible as a sacred text by capturing the attention of an audience that is already committed to Easternized approaches to the meaning of life.

The latter approach takes seriously a group of people that has little interest in the Bible but is already committed to spiritual-religious concerns.[58] It also recognizes that Western postbiblical societies sentimentalize, ignore, or are indifferent toward biblical literature and, at best, privatize, individualize, and socially marginalize its role. Sometimes, especially in the United States, Christian fundamentalists organize themselves politically in order to foster change, trying to reinstate the Bible's political centrality. A problem with this approach is, of course, that it remains stuck in literalist viewpoints. Another detriment is that the fundamentalist theological and political struggles confront an indifferent majority that favors the Western scientific worldview over biblical primacy. Among this majority are those people who are nevertheless quite interested in issues related to spirituality. They look for religious meaning beyond the institutionalized religious traditions of Christianity and Judaism. Does biblical studies have anything to offer to these "ordinary readers" of the Western secularized world?

Some academics suggest that an experientially based, inner reading practice is a positive answer. For instance, J. Kakichi Kadowaki, professor of philosophy at the University of Sophia, who is a Westerner and a Jesuit, aptly observes the detachment of biblical studies from embodied spiritual practice. He writes: "Most students of theology will agree that their academic biblical studies do little for their spiritual lives."[59] He explains that, after beginning to practice Zen, he also learned to read with the body and to appreciate the quest for inner meaning. He considers a Western disembodied approach to the Bible as a reason for feelings of alienation among many Western Christians. A solution,

---

58. Marie-Theres Wacker, Professor of the Old Testament and Theological Research on Women at the University of Münster (Germany), was among the first Hebrew Bible scholars of a Western country to articulate this dynamic so prevalent in Western societies. In December 1999, she organized a conference entitled "How to Read the Bible in a Postbiblical World" at the University of Münster. To my knowledge, the group of scholars did not develop a future agenda for pursuing research on the Bible in a postbiblical society such as Germany.

59. J. Kakichi Kadowaki, *Zen and the Bible*, trans. J. Rieck (Maryknoll, NY: Orbis, 2002), ix.

according to Kadowaki, is to combine both Zen and the Bible and to discover the inner meaning of the Bible, a meaning completely detached from historical or materially defined approaches.

The effort of regaining the "inner" or "esoteric" meaning of the Bible is not new but has a long tradition both in Christianity and Judaism. The mystic traditions of the kabbalists and the medieval Christians are probably among the most well-known examples. The Catholic tradition has been particularly rich in developing esoteric readings, such as the Prayer of the Heart, Christian meditation, or *lectio divina*, all of them interiorized forms of prayers and Bible meditation.[60] Others combine Eastern spiritual practices, such as Yoga, with the study of Western religious texts like the Bible. For instance, Jay G. Williams published a book titled *Yeshua Buddha: An Interpretation of New Testament Theology as Meaningful Myth*.[61] As the title indicates, Williams offers a reading of the Jesus story based on Eastern religious ideas. Each chapter of the book focuses on selected New Testament passages and relates them to Eastern teachings. Presented as the "Enlightened One," Jesus emerges as Buddha, not in a historical but in an existential and spiritual sense.

Another, much smaller, pamphlet-like publication by Albrecht Frenz relies on individual Bible passages to prove the compatibility of Christianity with the interior practice called Yoga. In *Yoga in Christianity*, Frenz shows that some of Yoga's basic tenets are also found in the Bible. For instance, the emphasis on developing an attitude of quietude and stillness, so prevalent in the Eastern traditions, appears in Exodus 14:14 and Isaiah 30:15, and this attitude is crucial for the notion of the Sabbath. Frenz is defensive at times—as, for instance, when he writes: "If the content is clear, then Christian Yoga cannot lead to Hinduism, but is and remains a Christian expression of life."[62] Nonetheless, Frenz recognizes the great overall benefit of the esoteric Eastern practice for the Christian tradition.

Yet another example is Joseph Leeming's *Yoga and the Bible*, first published in 1963.[63] Each of the eighteen chapters begins with a quotation from a New Testament passage, mostly from Matthew and John,

---

60. For more on these and related practices in the Catholic tradition, see Thomas P. Ryan, *Prayer of Heart and Body: Meditation and Yoga as Christian Spiritual Practice* (Mahwah, NJ: Paulist Press, 1995).
61. Jay G. Williams, *Yeshua Buddha: An Interpretation of New Testament Theology as Meaningful Myth* (Wheaton, IL: Theosophical Publishing House, 1978).
62. Albrecht Frenz, *Yoga in Christianity* (Madras: Christian Literature Society, 1986), 13.
63. Joseph Leeming, *Yoga and the Bible* (Punjab, India: Radha Soami Satsang Beas, 1978). For another publication in a similar vein, see Noelle Perez-Christiaens, *Le Christ et le Yoga* (Paris: Institut de Yoga B.K.S. Iyengar, 1980).

using these texts as clues for describing the nature of spiritual-religious growth. Leeming's study is based on the conviction that the teachings of the Yoga masters are "in essence" similar to the teachings of the New Testament. Since Leeming addresses a Western and Christian-oriented audience, he introduces the spiritual teachings of "past and present Masters" with the words of the "enlightened teacher" of the first century CE. For instance, the first chapter quotes Matthew 7:7–8 ("Ask, and it will be given you.") in order to elaborate on the age-old spiritual quest of humanity. Many of today's seekers do not find their needs satisfied by religious institutions such as the churches, Leeming presciently observes. Writing in 1963, he points out that those seeking spiritual enlightenment are searching elsewhere, including in the Eastern traditions. Yet Leeming also cautions seekers not to give up too quickly on their own religious tradition. They can find in Jesus Christ a teacher who will accompany them on their spiritual journey, once they come to appreciate his wisdom.

These and other works aim at recapturing spiritually meaningful interpretations of the Bible through the embodied experience of Eastern religious traditions. Whether or not the academic field is ready for this direction remains to be seen, but the need is clearly there. In short, both suggestions—researching biblical meanings as reflections of cultural, political, and religious contexts of readers, and teaching the Bible experientially as esoteric literature—represent new ways of reading and studying the Bible at the dawn of the twenty-first century. The former aligns itself with scholarly efforts underway, especially among subaltern scholars. The latter relates to the context of the postbiblical West, and might or might not be suited to other social locations. Both the exoteric and the esoteric approaches, complementing each other, offer alternatives to the historical-critical paradigm.

Conclusion: Toward a Holistic Hermeneutic of the Bible

Once, not so long ago, in the nineteenth century of Western societies such as Germany and the United States, historical criticism was a radical, even subversive method. Yet not long after that, in the twentieth century at many Western European universities and North American seminaries, the approach turned normative; it became a method of the political and religious status quo. Its success was its downfall, as it became the litmus test of academic legitimacy. This dynamic is particularly well described and understood by scholars who come from socially, ethnically, racially, and geographically marginalized locations. They tell the story about the failure of historical readings that have come to dominate and oppress their ancestors and contemporaries. For them, historical criticism signifies a method that has helped Westerners to colonize and exploit the world. Accordingly, they often reject this method and offer alternatives such as the cultural study of biblical literature.

The clarity of postcolonial scholars is unfortunately not always shared in Western feminist readings of the Bible. A brief discussion about feminist interpretations on rape stories illustrates the problem. Feminist historical treatment of these passages demonstrates the frequent inability to read against androcentric assumptions, often excusing or even justifying them. Unlike postcolonial interpreters, many Western feminist historians of the Bible align themselves with the status quo of malestream scholarship. Historical criticism does not enable them to read against the political, cultural, or religious grain, and so they sometimes find it difficult to read the biblical text from a socially progressive perspective. Consequently, their readings illustrate quite well the hermeneutical and ethical challenges to the historical method.

The question thus arises how Bible scholars are supposed to study biblical literature in a Western "tandoori reindeer" culture, especially since historical criticism has proved to fail on so many accounts. We need to cultivate alternative ways of reading to leave behind the historical-critical paradigm. I suggest relying on exoteric and esoteric approaches in our readings of biblical texts. The exoteric approach is analytical and examines the Bible's cultural, political, and religious meanings as part of the wide range of histories of biblical interpretation. The esoteric approach develops inner meanings of the Bible, so communicating the value of biblical texts to people who have often abandoned their Christian and Jewish lineages. Both approaches promise to connect biblical studies to the political, economic, social, and religious dynamics of this time and place. This alternative way leaves behind the narrow confines of historical criticism. It represents a holistic hermeneutic that, in my view, will give renewed vitality and exegetical drive to the reading of the Bible in the secularized societies of the West.

Indeed, the exoteric and esoteric approaches to the study of the Bible may well become what historical criticism once was in its early stage: new ways of reading. But even historical criticism holds a place in this holistic hermeneutic since historical interpretations provide insights into the assumptions and outlooks of people who have been reading the Bible in the past and present. Both approaches, the exoteric and the esoteric ones, aim for an integrated view of biblical literature as literature in and of the world as well as a sacred text of Judaism and Christianity. The result of this hermeneutical and methodological combination may well be as innovating and inspiring as tandoori reindeer.

The next chapter is focused on the development of an exoteric approach that goes beyond authorial meaning. It subscribes to the conviction that readers create biblical meanings, and it illustrates this fact with a study of ancient Near Eastern and biblical rape legislation. It will become clear that ancient rape laws are a promising opportunity for contemporary exegetes to debate the epistemological, hermeneutical, and methodological uncertainties and complexities involved in biblical studies. The interpretation of rape laws also communicates the urgent need for dialogue across the scholarly divides in biblical studies and elsewhere, to develop tandoori-reindeer ways of interpreting biblical texts.

5

———

"Back Then It Was Legal": The Epistemological Imbalance in Readings of Biblical and Ancient Near Eastern Rape Legislation

Even though the influential thinker of postmodernity, Jacques Derrida, passed away on October 8, 2004, the postmodern era is here to stay.[1] "Master narratives" do not convince anymore, and so they have to be asserted over and over again since their authority and power are gone, as is the consensus about history, identity, and core cultural values.[2] We are living under a new configuration of politics, culture, and economics, which is sometimes called "late capitalism."[3] In this new configuration transnational economies, based on the global reach of capitalism, dominate human life and organization almost everywhere.

Ours is the early stage of a new period that subsumes, assumes, and

1. For an extensive obituary, see "Jacques Derrida," *The Times of London*, October 11, 2004, https://www.thetimes.co.uk/article/jacques-derrida-w6hbt0t3g92.
2. Jean-François Lyotard, *The Postmodern Condition: A Report on Knowledge*, trans. Geoff Bennington and Brian Massumi (Minneapolis: University of Minnesota Press, 1984).
3. Frederic Jameson, *Postmodernism, or The Cultural Logic of Late Capitalism* (Durham, NC: Duke University Press, 1991).

extends the modern. This is the time *after* the modern age in which hybridity and the postcolonial flourish. We mix styles of different cultures and time periods, whether in the arts, literature, architecture, language, or food. We know there are many ways of doing things, an insight that fundamentalist movements resist worldwide, trying to suppress or ignore the drive toward multiplicity, diversity, and alternative ways of seeing and living life. Although most of humanity is excluded from the benefits of our era's advances due to incredible levels of global poverty, planet Earth has become a "global village" in which the nation-state is redefined, human networks of communication are mediated by technology, and ecological changes affect humans everywhere. We live in huge and complex networks of relations, interdependent on each other and this planet's ecology. Accordingly, most earthlings know that they could go somewhere else if they had the money or the opportunity, and more people are refugees now than ever before.[4] They leave home due to economic, political, or cultural devastation, and sometimes they succeed in making a better living elsewhere. Little remains stable. Ours, then, is a time of remarkable tensions between the raw forces of social, political, economic, and religious conservatism on the one hand and openness and the need, even sheer necessity, for change on the other hand.

In biblical studies the tensions between conservatism and change play out primarily on the level of textual interpretations grounded in empiricist-positivist[5] or postmodern epistemological assumptions. The former is characteristic of the modern Western worldview and assumes objectivity, value neutrality, and universality; it is primarily interested in the historical quest.[6] The latter recognizes the contextualized, particularized, and localized nature of all exegetical work,

---

4. See United Nations High Commissioner for Refugees, "Refugees by Numbers 2003," www.irr.org.uk/pdf/unher_2003.pdf (accessed on April 7, 2005): "At the start of 2003 the number of people 'of concern' to UNHCR was 20.6 million—roughly one out of every 300 person on earth—compared with 19.8 million a year earlier."

5. The term "empiricist-positivist epistemology" was coined by Elisabeth Schüssler Fiorenza, *Rhetoric and Ethic: The Politics of Biblical Studies* (Minneapolis: Fortress Press, 1999). She explains on p. 24: "The scientistic ethos of value-free detached inquiry insists that the biblical critic needs to stand outside the common circumstances of collective life and stresses the alien character of biblical materials. What makes biblical interpretation possible is radical detachment and emotional, intellectual, and political distancing. Disinterested and dispassionate scholarship enables biblical critics to enter the minds and world of historical people, to step out of their time, and to study history on its own terms, unencumbered by contemporary questions, values, and interests. A political detachment, objective literalism, and scientific value-neutrality are the rhetorical postures that seem to be dominant in the positivistic paradigm of biblical scholarship."

6. For a poignant of this approach, see Keith W. Whitelam, "Interested Parties: History and Ideology at the End of the Century," in *Reading from Right to Left: Essays on the Hebrew Bible in Honour of David J. A. Clines*, ed. J. Cheryl Exum and H. G. M. Williamson (Sheffield: Sheffield Academic, 2003), 402–22.

and emphasizes the readers' responsibilities in the meaning-making process. The trouble is that biblical interpreters are not always conscious of their epistemological assumptions, which makes them claim as fact what is only an assertion of "truth" according to modern conventions.[7] This chapter examines the particularities of this epistemological dynamic in the area of biblical and ancient Near Eastern rape laws. There, an imbalance prevails because many exegetes continue interpreting the ancient legal texts primarily within the modern paradigm. They define the task of reading ancient legislation as historical, and so they search for authorial meaning.[8] Contextualized readings based on a postmodern epistemology are rarely found.

Different epistemological assumptions lead to different views on ancient rape laws, a situation that has serious implications for people living in a global rape culture.[9] The empiricist-scientific epistemology erases rape from the analysis because it considers rape a contemporary category that does not fit the ancient legislation. It accepts androcentric meaning as historically accurate and rejects connections between interpretations and readers. The ancient laws become rules on marriage, adultery, or seduction. Yet when readers take seriously that we live, work, and interpret in a global rape culture, different meanings for the same laws emerge. They turn into rules on various rape situations when rape is understood as forced sexual intercourse without the consent of one of the partners—mostly of girls and women. Such a move often makes scholars nervous because they fear that suddenly "anything goes." This, however, is not the case. What is required is that readers acknowledge their interpretive interests and look critically at the social, political, economic, or religious implications of their readings. In the context of a global rape culture, it is crucial to uplift ancient rape legislation and to identify past and present strategies that continue obfuscating the prevalence of rape even today.

Accordingly, this essay is not an exercise in authorial meaning, and in fact it rejects such meaning as unattainable. It subscribes to

---

For the effort to integrate historical criticism with postmodern epistemological assumptions, see Gina Hens-Piazza, *The New Historicism* (Minneapolis: Fortress Press, 2002).

7. To most laypeople, the entire discussion on the epistemological divide in biblical studies is completely lost. A recent editorial in the *New York Times* by Nicholas D. Kristof illustrates many lay people's lack of basic knowledge in biblical studies; see Nicholas D. Kristof, "God and Sex," *New York Times*, October 23, 2004, A17.

8. The intentional fallacy was dismantled decades ago; see, e.g., William K. Wimsatt Jr. and Monroe C. Beardsley, "The Intentional Fallacy," in *20th Century Literary Criticism: A Reader*, ed. David Lodge (London: Longman, 1972), 334–45.

9. For more information on the global rape culture of our time, see Emilie Buchwald and Pamela R. Fletcher, eds., *Transforming a Rape Culture* (Minneapolis: Milkweed, 1995).

the conviction that readers are the ones creating textual meaning even when they claim to reiterate only positions of the original writers.[10] Interpreters who look for rape legislation in the ancient codes find it there, and readers who do not bring this interpretative interest to the texts raise other issues, depending on their assumptions. It is futile to argue over the appropriateness or insufficiency of each other's interpretations when the underlying issue is a difference in epistemology. If one subscribes to the principles of an empiricist-positivist epistemology, one will identify readings grounded in postmodern epistemology as biased, circular, or subjective. There is no middle ground for a compromise because it would come across as contrived, awkward, and false.

Three sections structure the investigation. The first section examines how empiricist-positivist readings present Deuteronomy 21:10–14 as a law on marriage and not on rape. The second section analyzes Deuteronomy 22:22–29, and shows that this biblical passage emerges as adultery laws within the modern paradigm of interpretation. The third section focuses on ancient Near Eastern legislation to demonstrate that the laws address the rapes of women, children, and certain kinds of animals when a contemporary reader, living in the global rape culture, searches for rape in the ancient legislative materials. A conclusion, acknowledging the current impasse between modern and postmodern epistemologies, suggests that currently this imbalance cannot be evened out.

A Case for Marriage? The Law of the Enemy Woman (Deuteronomy 21:10–14)

When scholars of an empiricist-positivist epistemology interpret the case of the enemy woman (Deut 21:10–14), they present this law as a ruling about marriage during or after war. Accordingly, the law is often characterized as a rule about marriage with a woman captured in war.[11] When the passage is discussed as part of the larger literary unit in Deuteronomy 21, exegetes sometimes classify it more generally: "Issues of Life and Death: Murder, Capital Offenses, and Inheritance"[12] regulating the "treatment of a woman taken as a captive in war and

---

10. Steven Mailloux, *Reception Histories: Rhetoric, Pragmatism, and American Cultural Politics* (Ithaca, NY: Cornell University Press, 1998).
11. See, accordingly, Duane L. Christensen, *Deuteronomy 21:10–34:12*, WBC 6B (Nashville: Thomas Nelson, 2002), 471; Jeffrey H. Tigay, *Deuteronomy*, JPS Torah Commentary (Philadelphia: Jewish Publication Society, 1996), 194.

subsequently married by her captor, or purchaser."[13] Empiricist-positivist epistemology advances androcentric ideology.

Since commentators do not usually elaborate on their hermeneutical perspectives, except perhaps to say that they rely on historical and literary methodologies, interpretations take on the aura of objectivity and inevitability. They claim to present *the* meaning of the law as it was understood in its original context, a position that usually softens the soldierly claim for the "enemy woman" and emphasizes the need for marriage as the law's noble intention. That the marriage is coerced does not become a problem. For instance, one interpreter, Duane L. Christensen, appreciates the law as advice on abstinence in premarital consensual relationships. He explains that the law stresses "the importance of a husband and wife sharing common spiritual values as the proper basis of a lasting union." He also suggests: "We would do well to follow the example here in deliberately delaying commitment in marriage for a period of time to assure that the decision to marry is not based primarily on physical lust."[14] By asserting the law of Deuteronomy 21:10–14 as morally and spiritually commendable, Christensen ignores not only its particularities—a soldier "desiring" an enemy woman—but also that the woman has no choice but to convert to the soldier's habits and religion. His interpretation mutates this rape law into a benign and even desirable ruling on marriage.

Ronald E. Clements, another exegete, also minimizes the coercion in the biblical law when he maintains: "Even when the marriage was to a woman who had been taken as a captive and turned into a slave, that marriage could never be reduced simply to a master/slave relationship."[15] To Clements, marriage rather than coercion is the important lesson, although he does not give a reason for the claim. Writing from an empiricist-positivist epistemology, the commentator assumes the omniscient stance of an objective, universal, and value-neutral observer who does not disclose his interpretative interests. Hermeneutical assumptions remain hidden, and a particular perspective appears

---

12. Ronald E. Clements, "The Book of Deuteronomy: Introduction, Commentary, and Reflections," *NIB* 2:443.

13. Ibid., 2:445. This law was probably never practiced. For instance, Harold C. Washington acknowledges that "there is reason to doubt that this law was extensively applied"; see his "'Lest He Die in the Battle and Another Man Take Her': Violence and the Construction of Gender in the Laws of Deuteronomy 20–22," in *Gender and Law in the Hebrew Bible and the Ancient Near East*, ed. Bernhard M. Levison, Victor H. Matthews, and Tikva Frymer-Kensiy, JSOTSup 262 (Sheffield: Sheffield Academic, 1998), 185–213.

14. Christensen, *Deuteronomy 21:10–34:12*, 475.

15. Clements, "Book of Deuteronomy," 448.

as objective information. In the case of Deuteronomy 21:10–14, it is the perspective of the male soldier.

To some interpreters who take for granted a modern epistemology, this law regulates a specific kind of marriage, in which a male soldier wants to marry an enemy woman when the war is over. This position is perhaps most extensively and comprehensively developed in Carolyn Pressler's study on women in Deuteronomic law.[16] Pressler asserts that Deuteronomy 21:10–14 does not regulate a rape situation during war—a position she claims dominated earlier scholarly treatments.[17] Instead, she explains that the law regulates the marriage between a male soldier and a foreign captive woman after the war. To Pressler, the law provides the legal means for marriage when "normal procedures for contracting marriage are impossible."[18] It also depicts a ritual necessary for the "former captive"[19] so that the soldier is legally qualified to marry her. Pressler stresses that the law refers only to this particular constellation and does not prohibit a "man from engaging in sexual relations with the woman without marrying her."[20]

As typical for readers grounded in an empiricist-scientific epistemology, this commentator does not disclose her interpretative interests. She proceeds as if reading from "nowhere," wanting to read the text as a "window to historical reality"[21] but only illuminating the perspective of the male soldier and the original legislators. In other words, her interpretation is grounded in the modern fallacy of objective literalism, scientific value neutrality, and apolitical detachment. Interestingly, Pressler also hints at the possibility that the law is a rape law. Firmly rooted in the reconstruction of authorial meaning, Pressler suggests that the law's drafters might have viewed the marriage as an imposition on the woman. It violated the woman "in some way," Pressler explains, and the original authors used the verb ʿinnâ in verse 14 to describe the violation.[22] In short, Pressler believes the original writers might have acknowledged that the woman does not consent to the marital act; they might have regarded the law as a regulation on rape.

---

16. Carolyn Pressler, *The View of Women Found in the Deuteronomic Family Laws* (Berlin: de Gruyter, 1993), 10–15.

17. Ibid., 11.

18. Ibid.; Cheryl B. Anderson, *Women, Ideology, and Violence: Critical Theory and the Construction of Gender in the Book of the Covenant and the Deuteronomic Law* (London: T&T Clark, 2004), 47.

19. Pressler, *View of Women*, 12.

20. Ibid., 43.

21. Schüssler Fiorenza, *Rhetoric and Ethic*, 43.

22. Pressler, *View of Women*, 22.

Another interpreter writes from a more tentatively argued empiricist-positivist framework and clearly defines Deuteronomy 21:10–14 as a rape law. In a study on violence in biblical narrative, Harold C. Washington maintains that readings are always located "somewhere" even if they presume to read from "nowhere." Accordingly, he attempts to connect contemporary lawsuits with biblical constructions of rape law when he states: "My aim . . . is to contribute to the genealogy of this peculiar legal subject who appears in the courts even today—the man who by 'virtue' of his violence confirms his control of a feminine subject. . . . My interest is not in the juristic application of these laws in ancient Israel. . . . Instead I am concerned with the discursive capacity of these laws to construct gender."[23] This is not a historical reconstruction of the legal practice on rape cases in ancient Israel, but a more broadly conceived study on the historical discourse of gender as it emerges from the ancient laws. Washington, writing from a "poststructuralist view of gender as a discursive product,"[24] examines the ancient laws as "foundational texts of Western culture . . . [that] authenticate the role of violence in the cultural construction of gender up to the present day."[25]

The interpretation covers several legal texts in the Hebrew Bible, but it also investigates Deuteronomy 21:10–14. According to Washington, this law has the following purpose: "The primary effect of the law is to assure a man's prerogative to abduct a woman through violence, keep her indefinitely if he wishes, or discard her if she is deemed unsatisfactory."[26] Unlike other interpreters, Washington recognizes the violence to which the woman is exposed in the situation described by the law. He names clearly that she is the object of the soldier's action, and he emphasizes the effect of the law on the woman's ability to be in control. Washington is even clearer about the effect of this law when he asserts: "The fact that the man must wait for a month before penetrating the woman . . . does not make the sexual relationship something other than rape. . . . Only in the most masculinist of readings does the month-long waiting period give a satisfactory veneer of peaceful domesticity to a sequence of defeat, bereavement, and rape."[27] To Washington, the law is unambiguously about rape. Other readings are

---

23. Washington, "Lest He Die in the Battle," 186.
24. Ibid., 192.
25. Ibid., 187.
26. Ibid., 207.
27. Ibid., 205.

"masculinist," and so Washington charges them with favoring the soldier's perspective.

Yet despite this clear language and the interpretative focus on gender as a "discursive product," Washington locates the legal meaning of Deuteronomy 21:10–14 primarily within the ancient text. The law is the agent, and so Washington writes: "By authorizing the violent seizure of women, this law takes the male-against female predation of warfare out of the battlefield and brings it to the home."[28] The law creates the meaning as if it advanced male violence in the home, ignored the women's perspective, authorized androcentric bias, and were not the basis for a reader's opposition to androcentric policy. In other words, when Washington addresses the particularities of Deuteronomy 21:10–14, he succumbs to an empiricist-scientific epistemology in which the reader is not in charge. Nevertheless, Washington's reading is a rare example for exposing androcentric bias in other interpretations. It recognizes the need for writing from the woman's perspective, and it illustrates the potential for multiple meanings of biblical law. In contrast to other interpreters, Washington does not promote Deuteronomy 21:10–14 as a marriage law but applies the contemporary term of rape. He claims postmodern assumptions even though he falls back to empiricist-scientific convictions. His reading thus struggles with the epistemological imbalance prevalent in interpretations of biblical rape legislation.

The Death Penalty for Adultery? The Legislation in Deuteronomy 22:22–29

The epistemological imbalance also appears in studies on a set of legislation found in Deuteronomy 22:22–29. The debate about the meaning of these laws is contested, but most scholarly interpreters, searching for authorial intent, distance themselves from characterizing these laws as rape legislation. Reconstructing the views of the ancient legislators, interpreters rely on androcentric assumptions that, according to them, prevailed in those days. Predictably, the legal meaning they reconstruct emerges as undisputed and fixed. Deuteronomy 22:22–29 contains four rulings that modern-scientific interpreters often characterize as cases on adultery. The verses are part of a larger section on what interpreters call "family and sex laws,"[29] "Marital and

---

28. Ibid., 207.

Sexual Misconduct,"[30] "Miscellaneous Laws, relating chiefly to Civil and Domestic Life,"[31] and "a subset of the general law of adultery preceding them in Deuteronomy 22:22."[32] In the history of interpretation the four rulings are rarely, if ever, regarded as rape legislation.

The first case appears in verse 22. There a man and a wife of another man receive the death penalty after they are found "lying" together. The question is if their "lying" is consensual, an ambiguity that the literature does not emphasize. Many interpreters assume that the law addresses consensual sex, and so they characterize it as a rule on adultery. For instance, Jeffrey H. Tigay titles his interpretation on the law "Adultery with a Married Woman."[33] He relates the law to a ritual procedure, described in Numbers 5:11–31, when a husband suspects his wife's adultery. Tigay also relates the Deuteronomic law to Leviticus 20:10, which orders capital punishment for adulterous behavior. Similarly, another interpreter, Tikva Frymer-Kensky, follows Tigay's lead and characterizes Deuteronomy 22:22 as a law against adultery.[34]

Yet the situation is not that simple. The prose in Deuteronomy 22:22 is terse, and it does not provide conclusive information on the precise nature of the relationship between the man and the woman. Focusing on the punishment and not on the description of the crime, it does not specify whether the "lying" is consensual or forced. It also elaborates only on the consequences of his lying with her. Does the woman consent? It is possible to conjecture that the man threatened or forced her, but the focus is on the penalty. Both the woman and the man are to be killed. Why do both receive the penalty? Most interpreters believe that the punishment indicates the guilt of the woman. To them, she consented and thus receives the appropriate penalty as an adulterer. Yet it is also possible to argue that the penalty does not indicate her guilt but androcentric jealousy that blames the woman regardless of her consent.

A comparison with ancient Near Eastern laws in cases of assumed adultery shows that sex between a man and a married woman does

---

29. Alexander Rofé, "Family and Sex Laws in Deuteronomy and the Book of Covenant," *Henoch* 9 (1987): 131–59.

30. Tigay, *Deuteronomy*, 204; Christensen, *Deuteronomy 21:10–34:12*, 510.

31. G. R. Driver, *A Critical and Exegetical Commentary on Deuteronomy* (Edinburgh: T&T Clark, 1895), 244.

32. Washington, "Lest He Die in the Battle," 208.

33. Tigay, *Deuteronomy*, 206.

34. Tikva Frymer-Kensky, "Deuteronomy," in *Women's Bible Commentary*, ed. Carol A. Newsom and Sharon H. Ringe, 2nd ed. (Louisville: Westminster John Knox, 1998), 63; Angelika Engelmann, "Deuteronomium: Recht und Gerechtigkeit für Frauen im Gesetz," in *Kompendium Feministische Bibelauslegung*, ed. Luise Schottroff und Marie-Theres Wacker, 2nd ed. (Gütersloh: Kaiser, 1999), 73; Anderson, *Women, Ideology, and Violence*, 43–44.

not always merit the death penalty. Several laws prescribe a range of penalties, leaving it to the husband to determine the severity of the penalty. For instance, Middle Assyrian Law (MAL) 15 stipulates:

> If a seignior has caught another seignior with his wife, when they have prosecuted him (and) convicted him, they shall put both of them to death, with no liability attaching to him. If, upon catching (him), he has brought him either into the presence of the king or into the presence of the judges, when they have prosecuted him (and) convicted him, if the woman's husband puts his wife to death, he shall also put the seignior to death, but if he cuts off his wife's nose, he shall turn the seignior into a eunuch and they shall mutilate his whole face. However, if he lets his wife go free, they shall let the seignior go free.[35]

Like the Deuteronomic law, this law focuses only on the moment when a husband finds his wife with another man. The emphasis is on the postdiscovery phase. Similarly, MAL 15 does not specify the nature of the crime or the consent of the woman. Yet unlike the biblical parallel, MAL 15 authorizes the husband to determine the form of the penalty ranging from the death penalty for both, cutting off the woman's nose and the other man's testicles, or no penalty at all. A similar case appears in §129 of the Code of Hammurabi, which also contains various penalty options that range from drowning to leniency. It, too, emphasizes the postdiscovery phase, not detailing whether the woman consented. The scholarly literature classifies this law as one on adultery, although it does not name the actual crime.

> If the wife of a seignior has been caught while lying with another man, they shall bind them and throw them into the water. If the husband of the woman wishes to spare his wife, then the king in turn may spare his subject.[36]

Again, the emphasis is on the penalties, and the law offers the husband the option to spare his wife and consequently the other man. In other words, ancient Near Eastern laws do not exclusively prescribe the death penalty for cases that scholars usually view as laws on adultery. Unlike Deuteronomy 22:22, they offer several penalty options. The biblical law is thus more limited in its punishment options, and it also

---

35. James B. Pritchard, ed., *Ancient Near Eastern Texts Relating to the Old Testament* (Princeton: Princeton University Press, 1969), 181. For another more recent translation, see Martha T. Roth, ed., *Law Collections from Mesopotamia and Asia Minor* (Atlanta: Scholars Press, 1995).
36. Pritchard, *Ancient Near Eastern Texts*, 171.

orders much harsher punishment than comparable ancient Near Eastern laws.[37] Yet none of the biblical or ancient Near Eastern laws identifies itself as a law on adultery, leaving the question of consent to the readers. Possibly, then, Deuteronomy 22:22 is a rape case in which androcentric jealousy condemns a woman as guilty regardless of her consent.[38]

The second case in Deuteronomy 22:23–24 supports the notion that verse 22 is a rape case, although the scholarly literature considers these verses sometimes as a mere case on seduction. In verses 23–24, the law orders the death penalty for both an engaged young woman and a man who has sex with her in town. The law explains that he "met" her in town, and it finds both guilty because nobody heard her cry for help.[39] Many interpreters explain that this law assumes her consent, and so they, too, classify it as a law on adultery. Tigay, for instance, titles his interpretation of this and the next unit as "Adultery with an Engaged Virgin (vv. 23–27)."[40] Alexander Rofé elaborates on verses 23–24 in a section on ancient legislation on adultery,[41] and Christensen talks about "the law of the seduction of a betrothed woman."[42] Only some commentators characterize this case as rape legislation[43] because, to them, the law does not exclude that the woman called for help, as it merely states that nobody heard her. This law thus describes a potential situation of rape in which a man forces a woman to have sex with him. As in the previous case of verse 22, the law prescribes the death penalty to both the woman and the man, although the penalty does not clearly mention the woman's consent. It is androcentric ideology that sees no need in listening to a woman's viewpoint. Androcentric ideologies distrust her word and action, and readers following this

---

37. According to some scholars, the harsh punishment is due to the fact that, different from ancient Near Eastern law, biblical law considers all crimes as transgressions against God, the lawgiver; see, e.g., Moshe Greenberg, "Some Postulates of Biblical Criminal Law," in *A Song of Power and the Power of Song: Essays on the Book of Deuteronomy*, ed. Duane L. Christensen, Sources for Biblical and Theological Study Old Testament Series 2 (Winona Lake, IN: Eisenbrauns, 2993), 283–300.

38. All forms of punishment mentioned in these laws are at best unreasonable from a contemporary Western perspective on rape. First, only the rapist and not the victim-survivor should receive a penalty. Second, the Universal Declaration of Human Rights gives everyone the right to life in its article 3, which, for instance, the organization of Amnesty International interprets as a rejection of the death penalty in its article 2. It is, however, highly unlikely that any of the biblical or ancient Near Eastern penalties were practiced because their status as practiced law is questionable.

39. See also Middle Assyrian Law 55 and §197 of the Hittite Laws, and the discussion of these laws below.

40. Tigay, *Deuteronomy*, 207.

41. Rofé, "Family and Sex Laws," 147.

42. Christensen, *Deuteronomy*, 51.

43. Engelmann, "Deuteronomium," 74.

ideology do not look for ambiguity. Consequently, they do not entertain a woman's innocence, and the interpretation history gives witness to the widespread disregard for her perspective.

The third case, in verses 25–27, depicts a clear-cut situation of rape, even for androcentric sensibilities. Here a woman is raped "in the open country." According to the law, her innocence is undisputed because nobody was able to hear her cry for help. Androcentric ideology, which relies on outside witnesses rather than a woman's word, does not need to hear anything else. The rapist is declared guilty, and, as usual, interpreters comply. It has to be stressed that this and the previous law in verses 23–24 use important vocabulary to describe the sexual violation. The verb "to rape" (piel; 'innâ) appears in verse 24, and in verse 25 the man "seizes" or "catches" the woman. These verbs convey her unwillingness and his active effort of getting her.[44] The verbs also appear in ancient Near Eastern rape legislation where they emphasize the force of the attack.[45] Accordingly, these laws are about rape, although androcentric bias is clearly present. Many readers, accepting this fact, follow what they think is the law. Empiricist-scientific assumptions make interpreters ignore that it depends on them, as readers, whether the law emerges as rape legislation in androcentric disguise, or whether the law refers to consensual but socially unacceptable acts of sexual intimacy.

The androcentric perspective, mostly taken for granted in the scholarly literature, is at its most horrendous in the last part of the Deuteronomic rape legislation (vv. 28–29). This fourth case describes the rape of a single young woman and stipulates that her father has to receive financial compensation, a solution that is also found in the Code of Hammurabi §156 and MAL 55. The biblical law commands that the rapist marry the young woman "because he raped her" (v. 29). Again, Deuteronomic law is considerably harsher than ancient Near Eastern law, specifically §156 of the Code of Hammurabi, which allows the raped woman to marry whomever she wants. The biblical law is also more restrictive than MAL 55, giving the father of the raped woman

44. Against the view of Frymer-Kensky, "Deuteronomy," 93, who maintains that in this context the verb means "illicit sex," that is "sex with someone with whom one has no right to have sex." Frymer-Kensky's position is also supported by Mayer I. Gruber, "A re-examination of the Charges against Shechem Son of Hamor," *Beit Mikra* 157 (1999): 119–27; Washington, "Lest He Die in the Battle," 208–12. For a recent study of these and related verbs, see Sandie Gravett, "Reading 'Rape' in the Hebrew Bible: A Consideration of Language." *JSOT* 28 (2004): 279–99.

45. Sophie Lafont, *Femmes, Droit et Justice dans l'Antiquité orientale: Contribution á l'étude du droit penal au Porche-Orient ancient* (Göttingen: Vandenhoeck & Ruprecht, 1999), 138. For an opposing view, see Anthony Phillips, "Another Look at Adultery," *JSOT* 20 (1981): 3–25.

several options; only one option allows the father to marry his daughter to the rapist. In biblical law codes only Exodus 22:16, a case of premarital consensual sex between a young woman and her lover, mentions the father's options. There the father is authorized to order or to refuse a wedding between the two, or to demand financial compensation.[46]

Deuteronomy 22:28–29 is unquestionably androcentric, emphasizing the interests of the father, and interpreters of a modern-scientific mind-set accept the androcentric bias. As Washington remarks correctly: "The laws do not interdict sexual violence; rather they stipulate the terms under which a man may commit rape."[47] The problem is that interpreters, following this stipulation, do not question the legal bias that promotes male sexual violence. They subscribe to empiricist-positivist assumptions and perpetuate as objective, value neutral, and universal a concern that represents only one possible reading. They do not analyze as rhetorical constructs what may never have regulated ancient people's "real" lives. After all, these laws were probably never used for legal practice in ancient Israel and the Near East.[48] Whether these regulations are discussed in the context of adultery, seduction, or rape is therefore up to the readers, and it is a limitation of the modern-scientific mind-set to ignore rape as an explanation for these cases of sexual violence.

"If a Man . . .": Rape Laws in Ancient Near Eastern Codes

Scholars of ancient Near Eastern rape laws do not show much, if any, appreciation for the notion that all exegetical work is contextualized, particularized, and localized, and that readers are central in the process of "meaning-making." Instead, they, too, assume objectivity,

---

46. Against Frymer-Kensky, who considers Exod 22:16 as a "comparable law" to Deut 22:28–29; see Tikva Frymer-Kensky, "Law and Philosophy: The Case of Sex in the Bible," *Semeia* 45 (1989): 93. Her arguments stand in a long tradition of premishnaic readers; see Robert J. V. Hiebert, "Deuteronomy 22:28–29 and Its Premishnaic Interpretations," *CBQ* 56 (1994): 203–20. Anderson also considers the act in Exod 22:16 as consensual when she uses the term "seduction"; see Anderson, *Women, Ideology, and Violence*, 40.
47. Washington "Lest He Die in the Battle," 211.
48. See the comment by Henry McKeating, "Sanctions against Adultery in Ancient Israelite Society, with Some Reflections on Methodology in the Study of Old Testament Ethics," *JSOT* 11 (1979): 70: "What I am suggesting, to put it another way, is that the ethics of the Old Testament and the ethics of ancient Israelite society do not necessarily coincide, and the latter may not be represented altogether accurately by the former. Old Testament ethics is a theological construction, a set of rules, ideals and principles theologically motivated throughout and in large part religiously sanctioned. Were the principles by which real Israelites actually lived quite so closely determined by religious faith? It may be that they were, but we cannot without further ado assume so."

value neutrality, and universality of all exegetical work. They classify as sex offenses, adultery, or laws about marriage what are rape laws according to an interpretation located in a global rape culture. Interestingly, older studies are sometimes more open toward the characterization of these cases. Yet the earlier studies, too, do not consistently define the laws as rape legislation.[49] For instance, written in 1966, an influential article by J. J. Finkelstein, "Sex Offenses in Sumerian Laws," differentiates between "coercive" and "consentive" Sumerian laws, and only a chart defines the "coercive" laws as rape laws.[50] Mostly, however, Finkelstein uses the term "adultery." He provides only indirectly a rationale for his terminological preference when he comments on the meaning of a text called "A Trial at Nippur (3N T403 T340)." The first line of the Sumerian law reads:

> Lugalmelam, son of Nanna'aramugi seized Ku(?)-Ninšubur, slave-girl of Kuguzana, brought her into the KI-LAM building, and deflowered her.[51]

The key question here is: What happened between the man called Lugalmelam and the enslaved young woman called Ku(?)-Ninšubur? Finkelstein allows for the possibility that the woman was raped but then dismisses it as socially "immaterial" for Mesopotamian law. He also suggests that rape, seduction, and consensual sex be interchangeable offenses against the slave owner. Here is his comment:

> From the juridical point of view it may be worth mentioning that the trial does not discuss the question of whether the slave-girl was raped or was a willing partner in the offense. This is unquestionably to be explained by the fact that in the eyes of Mesopotamian law, consent in such cases is immaterial. Hence, her sexual violation, whether by rape, seduction, or even by her own solicitation, is exclusively considered as a tortuous invasion against her owner, for which he may seek redress.[52]

In other words, Finkelstein claims to read from the perspective of the presumed original writers ("the eyes of Mesopotamian law") when he characterizes the slave owner as the violated person who "may seek redress." Identifying with the ancient lawgivers, he takes his choice for granted and considers it irrelevant whether the woman was raped,

---

49. Ernst Neufeld, *The Hittite Laws* (London: Luzac, 951), 194.
50. Jacob J. Finkelstein, "Sex Offenses in Sumerian Laws," *JAOS* 86 (1966): 355–72.
51. Ibid., 359. The choice of translating the Sumerian verb into English as "to deflower" reflects an inherently androcentric perspective.
52. Finkelstein, "Sex Offenses," 360.

seduced, or participating in consensual sex. To him, the law protects the slave owner, and from this perspective Finkelstein develops the law's meaning. He does not acknowledge that this is what he is doing, which enables him to mention the possibility of rape but then to dismiss it as an interpretative option. He reads from the perceived status quo of Mesopotamian society that favors the male owner or husband. As a result, it does not occur to Finkelstein to consider the law from another perspective. Hence, most of his article examines legal cases on "adultery" as perceived by the supposed status quo of ancient society even though the title promises a study on "sex offenses."

The influence of Finkelstein's analysis should not be underestimated for it continues to inform current work. For instance, in the article "Adultery in Ancient Law," Raymond Westbrook refers to MAL 12 as an illustration for vocabulary that is sometimes used to make a point about the rights of a husband when his adulterous wife is discovered "*in flagranti delicto*."[53] To make his point, Westbrook quotes the law to explain the legality of punishing an adulterous woman. Yet a connection between MAL 12 and vocabulary on adultery is awkward because this law is a recognized rape law. Perhaps, to Westbrook, the difference between rape and adultery is irrelevant since he asserts that according to ancient law "adultery forms part of a complex of interrelated scholarly problems discussing social offenses such as seduction and rape."[54] Assuming an empiricist-positivist epistemology, Westbrook does not disclose his hermeneutical perspective, which makes his study appear to be an objective treatment of ancient law. He posits as a fact that adultery and rape are linked, but he fails to discuss the rationale for this relationship.[55]

Yet to readers who acknowledge reading in a global rape culture, ancient Near Eastern law codes address rape as a distinct problem, which is part of a long history "abundantly documented in the legal codes from the Sumerian to the Roman period."[56] Unfortunately, during the past century, not a single scholarly publication examines in

---

53. Raymond Westbrook, "Adultery in Ancient Law," *RB* 97 (1990): 562.
54. Ibid. In this very context, Westbrook refers to the study of Finkelstein in 548n26.
55. The 1995 translation of ancient Near Eastern rape laws, edited by Martha Roth, exhibits a similar reliance on Finkelstein's work. The index "Selected Legal Topics and Key Words" lists the category "sexual offenses" under which the following terms appear: "adultery and fornication, consent, defloration, flirtatious behavior, incest, procuring, promiscuity, rape and sexual assault, seduction, sodomy." Why these various terms are part of the category "sexual offenses" is clear only when one studies the history of scholarship. Still, it is hard to believe that adultery, consent, and flirtatious behavior appear as "sexual offenses" in the index of a 1995 publication; see Roth, *Law Collections*," 282.
56. Lafont, *Femmes, Droit et Justice*, 133.

depth ancient Near Eastern rape laws. For instance, the multivolume *Reallexikon der Assyriologie und Vorderasiatischen Archäologie* has yet to publish a single entry on rape.[57] Following is therefore a discussion of selected laws in the Codex of Ur-Nammu, the Laws of Eshnunna, the Code of Hammurabi, the Middle Assyrian Laws, and the Hittite Laws. They are read as legislation on rape.

The Codex of Ur-Nammu from Sippar

The fragmentary tablet contains two laws on rape in §§6 and 8. According to Fatma Yildiz, the first paragraph reads as follows:

> If a man
> the wife of a young man in service (*gurus*)
> whose marriage has not yet been consummated,
> using violence
> deflowers her,
> that male they shall slay.[58]

The particular legal situation remains grammatically unclear in this translation because it stays close to the Sumerian original. A smoother translation rearranges the syntax: "If a man uses violence against the wife of a young man, who has not been deflowered, and deflowers her, this man shall be killed."[59] The ancient law describes a situation that other law codes also mention. A man "uses violence" against a woman who is in the process of getting married but has not yet had sex with her fiancé. The law orders the death penalty for a rapist who attacks a woman of this status. It is important to note that the Sumerian text relies on two verbs to communicate the action of rape, which are rendered into English as "to use violence" and "to deflower." Accordingly, the woman does not consent or volunteer to sexual activity. She is raped.

The Codex of Ur-Nammu from Sippar contains a second law, §8, about another situation of sexual violence. There a man rapes an enslaved woman.

---

57. Erich Ebeling and Bruno Meissner, eds., *Reallexikon der Assyriologie und Vorderasiatischen Archäologie* (Berlin: de Gruyter, 1928–).
58. Fatma Yildiz, "A Tablet of Codex Ur-Nammu from Sippar," *Orientalia* 50 (1981): 96.
59. In the original French: "Si un homme a fait violence á l'éspouse d'un jeune homme, qui n'était pas déflorée, et l'a déflorée, ces homme sera tué"; see Lafont, *Femmes, Droit et Justice*, 467. My translation of the French.

> If a slave-girl
> who is a virgin
> a man deflowers
> with violence,
> he shall pay 5 shekels of silver.[60]

In contrast to §6, about a case with a young and engaged woman, this law does not prescribe the death penalty. When a man "deflowers with violence" an enslaved young woman, he has to pay only a monetary fee. It is unclear to whom the fee is paid, and usually commentators maintain that the money goes to the slave owner. They also assert that the penalty represents the value of an average enslaved woman who is of less value to her owner than a married woman.[61] Moreover, they assert that the rape of an enslaved woman does not raise paternity issues in contrast to the first law about an engaged virgin. Yet interpreters do not usually point out that the laws do not value a woman's perspective whether she is enslaved or free. Instead, they focus on the damages accrued to a husband or a slave owner. The rape of a married young woman requires a more severe penalty than the rape of an enslaved woman, clearly an offensive expression of classism.[62] Yet at the same time, both laws refer to a situation of rape, and it is due to the modern-scientific epistemology, enmeshed with androcentric bias, that the scholarly literature has not emphasized this point.

The Laws of Eshnunna

The laws of Eshnunna contain two rape cases that are similar to §§6 and 8 of the Codex of Ur Nammu. They read as follows:

> 26. If a man gives bride-money for a(nother) man's daughter, but another man seizes her forcibly without asking the permission of her father and her mother and deprives her of her virginity, it is a capital offence and he shall die.

> 31. If a man deprives another man's slave-girl of her virginity, he shall pay one-third of a mina of silver; the slave-girl remains the property of her owner.[63]

---

60. Yildiz "A Tablet of Codex," 96–97.
61. For a discussion of the rape of enslaved women, see Lafont, *Femmes, Droit et Justice*, 144–45.
62. For an extensive discussion of classism in combination with androcentric cooptation of women in the Hebrew Bible, see Susanne Scholz, "Gender, Class, and Androcentric Compliance in the Rapes of Enslaved Women," *lectio difficilior: European Electronic Journal for Feminist Exegesis* 1 (2004): http://tinyurl.com/lwgehrw.

In the first case a man rapes an engaged woman, and in the second case he rapes an enslaved woman. In the first situation he receives the death penalty for the "capital offense," and in the second situation he is asked to make a payment. Class discrimination leads to discrimination in the extent of the penalty.

The Code of Hammurabi

Several laws of the Code of Hammurabi relate to forced sexual intercourse, but the scholarly literature acknowledges only the law of §130 as a rape law. It reads:

> If a seignior found the (betrothed) wife of a(nother) seignior, who had no intercourse with a male and was still living in her father's house, and he has lain in her bosom and they have caught him, that seignior shall be put to death, while that woman shall go free.[64]

The law of §130 is similar to §6 of the Codex of Ur-Nammu from Sippar and §26 of the Laws of Eshnunna, but it also adds two pieces of information. First, the woman is still living with her parents, and second, the law emphasizes that she is not to be punished. Only the rapist receives the death penalty. This is an obvious rape law, even recognized as such by Finkelstein: "This case too is an act of rape."[65]

Sometimes, however, scholars avoid the term "rape," especially when they speculate about the rationale of ancient Near Eastern marriage laws. For instance, Westbrook refers to §130 of the Code of Hammurabi as being similar to §26 of the Laws of Eshnunna. To Westbrook, both laws explain what happens under the conditions of an "inchoate marriage,"[66] which is defined by "a lapse of time between conclusion of the marriage contract and the act of marriage."[67] To Westbrook, §130 of the Code of Hammurabi is part of the marriage laws, and so his book on Old Babylonian marriage legislation does not discuss rape despite references to this and similar laws.

Westbrook is not alone in this treatment of ancient Near Eastern

63. Pritchard, *Ancient Near Eastern Texts*, 162.
64. Ibid, 171.
65. Finkelstein, "Sex Offenses," 356.
66. Raymond Westbrook, *Old Babylonian Marriage Law* (Horn, Austria: Berger, 1988), 30. The terminology of "inchoate marriage" appeared initially in the early decades of the twentieth century; see Benno Landsberger, "Jungfräulichkeit: Ein Beitrag zum Thema 'Beilager und Eheschliessung,'" in *Symbolae Iuridicae et Historicae: Martiono David Dedicatae*, ed. J. A. Ankum, Robert Feenstra, and William F. Leemans (Leiden: Brill, 1968), 2:41–103.
67. Westbrook, *Old Babylonian Marriage Law*, 32.

rape legislation. Much of the scholarly literature has not identified rape as an issue. In fact, as they do in studies on biblical legislation, scholars often treat ancient Near Eastern rape laws as cases on marriage and adultery. For instance, Eckart Otto supports the view that §130 of the Code of Hammurabi describes marital procedures.[68] Walter Kornfeld mentions "the case of a rape of a young engaged girl" in his study on adultery, but he refrains from further comments.[69] Similarly, Benno Landsberger's translation and commentary mentions the relevant rape terminology in German (i.e., the verbs *vergewaltigen* and the old-fashioned *notzüchtigen*, and the nouns *Vergewaltiger* and *Notzucht*), but he discusses the laws within the larger topic on virginity.[70] Androcentric bias and modern-scientific epistemology merge to a potent combination, eliminating interpretative alternatives that unambiguously classify these laws as rape legislation.

Yet when this potent combination is dismantled and interpretative interests are disclosed, the Code of Hammurabi holds additional rape laws, more specifically laws on incestuous rape. They are §§154, 155, and 156, and the first one reads like this:

> If a seignior has had intercourse with his daughter, they shall make that seignior leave the city.

If interpreters mention this law at all, they discuss it as a case on incest. Yet it is certainly also relevant as a rape law. The law of §154 refers to the problematic constellation in which a father rapes his daughter, a constellation that biblical laws do not address.[71] The law does not prescribe the death penalty for this crime because, as scholars often explain, the rape does not threaten another man's paternal rights or legal authority. He is the man in charge and only required to leave town.

The next law, §155, describes another situation of incest.

> If a seignior chose a bride for his son and his son had intercourse with her, but later he himself has lain in her bosom and they have caught him, they shall bind that seignior and throw him into the water.

---

68. Eckart Otto, "Rechtssytematik im altbabylonischen Codex Ešnunna und im alatisraelitischen Bundesbuch," *Ugarit-Forschungen* 19 (1987): 184–85. For a discussion on Egyptian texts about adultery, see C. J. Eyre, "Crime and Adultery in Ancient Egypt," *JEA* 70 (1984): 92–105.
69. Walter Kornfeld, "Ladultère dans l'orient antique," *RB* 57 (1950): 98. My translation from the French original. Other examples are Rafael Yaron, "The Rejected Bridegroom (LE 25)," *Orientalis* 34 (1965): 23–29.
70. Landsberger, "Jungfräulichkeit," 53, 56, 63–64.
71. See the omission in Lev 18:6–30.

In this case the father has sexual intercourse with the lover of his son. Is it imaginable that the bride consented? The law stipulates that the father has to be drowned if he is caught in the act of raping his son's bride. Does this mean that he would go free if he were not caught? The law does not address this possibility, and only mentions what happens if he is caught. The position of the young woman is not considered. Does she go free and marry the rapist's son?

Another incest law, §156, focuses on the bride of a father's son.

> If a seignior chose a bride for his son and his son did not have intercourse with her, but the himself has lain in her bosom, he shall pay to her one-half mina of silver and he shall make good to her whatever she brought from her father's house in order that the man of her choice may marry her.

This law presents a situation in which a bride did not yet have sex with the man whose father rapes her. Accordingly, the father is only required to pay a fine, and she is free to marry whomever she wishes to marry, a surprising offer since other laws order a marriage between the woman and the first man who had sex with her whether or not the sex was violent.[72] This case, too, does not mention whether the bride consented. It is a potential rape law that grants the woman decision-making power.[73]

The Middle Assyrian Laws

Another set of ancient Near Eastern legislation addresses cases of rape. The Middle Assyrian Laws describe four such scenarios, all of which refer to explicit situations of a man raping a woman. In §§12, 16, and 23, the woman is married, and in §55 she is young, single, and lives in the parental home.

> 12. If, as a seignior's wife passed along the street, a(nother) seignior has seized her, saying to her, "Let me lie with you," since she would not consent (and) kept defending herself, but he has taken her by force (and) lain with her, whether they found him on the seignior's wife or witnesses have charged him that he lay with the woman, they shall put the seignior to death, with no blame attaching to the woman.[74]

---

72. See, e.g., §156 of the Code of Hammurabi, MAL 55, or Deut 22:28–29, as discussed above.
73. Harry A. Hoffner, "Incest, Sodomy and Bestiality in the Ancient Near East," in *Orient and Occident: Essays Presented to Cyrus H. Gordon on the Occasion of His Sixty-Fifth Birthday*, ed. Harry A. Hoffner (Neukirchen-Vluyn: Neukirchener Verlag, 1973), 81–90.

This law presents an undisputable rape scene. A married woman is attacked by a man in the street. She resists, but he succeeds in raping her. It is the classic rape scenario, and the Akkadian terminology is unambiguous. The phrase *emuqa sabiitu* is usually translated with "to take by force."[75]

The punishment for the rapist is the same as in other ancient Near Eastern laws. He receives the death penalty only if—and this is the androcentric limitation of this particular law—other people or witnesses charge the rapist with the crime. The charge depends on others because the woman is not accepted as an accuser. Still, the very existence of the law demonstrates that rape was perceived as a problem even if this law was never legislatively practiced or served the Middle Assyrian Empire for other purposes.[76]

Another law presents a rape case next to one on adultery. In MAL 16, the first case refers to a married woman who invites a man to have sex with her. The second case mentions a man who forces a woman to have sex with him, possibly a situation of acquaintance rape. In the second situation the husband has the authority to decide the fate of the other man, but it remains unclear whether the woman is handed over to her husband's authority or she is innocent. The second case, in MAL 16, reads:

> If he [a seignior] has lain with her [another seignior's wife] by force, when they have prosecuted him (and) convicted him, his punishment shall be like that of the seignior's wife.[77]

The hermeneutical problem is, of course, that the law mentions adultery, rape, and the various penalties in one long law. Additionally, the husband appears as the injured party but not the raped wife, an androcentric bias that Western laws have overcome only in recent decades.

Yet another law portrays a rape of a married woman. The second part of MAL 23 refers to a situation in which a wife is invited to the house of another woman where she is raped by a man who is already there. She is declared innocent if she decides to press charges. The other woman and the rapist receive the death penalty. If, however, the

---

74. Pritchard, *Ancient Near Eastern Texts*, 181. See also Roth, *Law Collections*, lists MAL 9 as a rape law in the index, but the meaning of this law is vague and not included here.
75. Lafont, *Femmes, Droit et Justice*, 137.
76. Raymond Westbrook, "Biblical and Cuneiform Law Codes," *RB* 92, no. 2 (1985): 247–64. An early publication supports the notion of rape being a problem in the ancient Near East; see G. R. Driver and John C. Miles, *The Assyrian Laws* (Oxford: Clarendon, 1935).
77. Pritchard, *Ancient Near Eastern Texts*, 181.

raped woman does not press charges, her husband has the authority to penalize her. In either case the other woman and the rapist receive the death penalty. The section reads as follows:

> However, if the seignior's wife did not know (the situation), but the woman who brought her into her house brought the man to her under pressure and he has lain with her, if when she left the house she has declared that she was ravished, they shall let the woman go free, since she is guiltless; they shall put the adulterer and procuress to death. However, if the woman has not (so) declared, the seignior shall inflict on his wife such punishment as he sees fit (and) they shall put the adulterer and the procuress to death.[78]

In contrast to the rape laws of MAL 12, 16, and 23, according to which the woman is married, MAL 55 refers to a rape of a single young woman who lives with her parents.

> In the case of a seignior's daughter, a virgin who was living in her father's house, whose [father] had not been asked (for her in marriage), whose hymen had not been opened since she was not married, and no one had a claim against her father's house, if a seignior took the virgin by force and ravished her, either in the midst of the city or in the open country or at night in the street or in a granary or at a city festival, the father of the virgin shall take the wife of the virgin's ravisher and give her to be ravished; he shall not return her to her husband (but) take her; the father may give his daughter who was ravished to her ravisher in marriage. If he has no wife, the ravisher shall give the (extra) third in silver to her father as the value of a virgin (and) her ravisher shall marry her (and) not cast her off. If the father does not (so) wish, he shall receive the (extra) third for the virgin in silver (and) give his daughter to whom he wishes.[79]

This law is significant for several reasons. It states unambiguously the rape of a young and single woman.[80] It also acknowledges that a rape may take place anywhere, "in the midst of the city or in the open country or at night in the street or in a granary or at a city festival." In other words, the charge of rape does not depend on the presence of other people.[81] Yet the range of penalties reflects an ingrained androcentric

---

78. Ibid., 182.
79. Ibid., 185.
80. Against Driver and Miles, *Assyrian Laws*, 52–53, who, on the basis of a grammatical ambiguity, argue for the possibility that §55 describes either a rape or consensual sex and is followed by the law of §56 in which "the girl is the prime mover."
81. Other laws have different views about this matter; see §197 of the Hittite Laws and its discussion below.

perspective. No matter what the penalty is, the girl's father authorizes it. He has three basic options. He may seek revenge according to "vicarious punishment"[82] and rape the rapist's wife and afterward marry his daughter to the rapist. Alternatively, the father may accept money if the rapist does not have a wife, and then he may marry his daughter to the rapist. Finally, he may choose none of the prior options, but accept money and marry his daughter to whomever he wishes to marry her. Cruel androcentrism rules while women are imagined as the recipients of male violence and authority.

Interpreters note the stark contrast in the penalty choices here and in the other three rape laws. For instance, G. R. Driver and John Miles explain that the penalty is more lenient in §55 than in the other cases because the woman is single. "The draftsman" of these laws "never lost" this distinction because they "always stated definitely at the outset whether the woman is unmarried or married."[83] The interpreters conclude from this consistent distinction that a "sexual offence" with an unmarried woman was "a comparatively trivial offence" in Assyrian law. However, the problem is that these interpreters do not clearly object to this understanding of the law. Steeped in modern scientific epistemology, the interpreters hand off this androcentric explanation as acceptable, and thus they perpetuate androcentric views on women and rape. They read from an empiricist-scientific paradigm, content to pass on as objective categories what are androcentric biases toward women's relations to male power.

The Hittite Laws

The Hittite Laws, too, contain several texts on rape. Scholars recognize only one of them and usually classify the others as laws on adultery, incest, and bestiality. The undisputed rape law, §197, is reminiscent of Deuteronomy 22:29. It reads:

> If a man seizes a woman in the mountain, it is the man's crime and he will be killed. But if he seizes her in (her) house, it is the woman's crime and the woman shall be killed. If the husband finds them, he may kill them, there shall be no punishment for him.[84]

---

82. Guillaume Cardascia, *Les Lois Assyriennes* (Paris: Cerf, 1969), 252.
83. Driver and Miles, *A Critical and Exegetical Commentary on Deuteronomy*, 37; Cardascia, *Les Lois Assyriennes*, 249.
84. Pritchard, *Ancient Near Eastern Texts*, 196.

The law describes two situations.[85] In the first case a rapist attacks a woman outside an inhabited area, "in the mountain," a location that assumes a woman's unsuccessful opposition to the attack. In the second case the attack takes place in a house, perhaps even in "her" house. In the first scenario, the rapist receives the death penalty, whereas in the second scenario the death penalty is given only to the woman.[86] If, however, the husband discovers the couple, he has the right to kill both of them. Some commentators maintain that this option is part of a third situation that continues in §198 and is similar to other ancient Near Eastern laws such as MAL 15 or §129 of the Code of Hammurabi.[87] In this case the husband discovers the couple and has the opportunity to decide on the fate of his wife and the other man, either sparing their lives or ordering their death.

It is important to note that the Hittite term "woman" refers to a woman of any status, whether she is young and single, married, widowed, free, or enslaved,[88] even when the law includes the option that a woman's husband may kill the attacker and the woman. The terminological inclusiveness indicates that rape is not only a crime when a woman is married or in the process of getting married. According to §197, the rape is punished under all circumstances when it takes place outside a town. The other part of the law is more problematic since it prescribes punishment for both the woman and the man when the attack takes place in a house. The penalty seems to assume consensual sex, although the man might have forced the woman into the house. Thus this law, too, reflects an androcentric worldview that privileges men over women.

Several other Hittite laws are not usually classified as rape laws, but they should be seen as such when rape is defined (according to the American Heritage Dictionary), as "the crime of using force or the threat of force to compel a person to submit to sexual intercourse" and the term "person" is expanded to include other creatures than humans only. The laws mention two cases on incest and four cases on bestiality. §§189 and 190 are the incest laws:

---

85. Neufeld, Hittite Laws, 194; Jost Grothus, Die Rechtsordnung der Hethiter (Wiesbaden: Otto Harrassowitz, 1973), 35.
86. For a similar law with a different assessment on the significance of the location, see MAL 5 and Deut 22:23–24 and the discussions above.
87. Richard Haase, "Bemerkungen zu einigen Paragraphen der hethitischen Gesetze (§§197/98, 95, 35, 37)," Hethitica 56 (1994): 7–10.
88. Ibid., 7.

189. If a man violates his own mother, it is a capital crime. If a man violates his daughter, it is a capital crime. If a man violates his son, it is a capital crime.

190. If a man violates his stepmother, there shall be no punishment. (But) if his father is living, it is a capital crime.

The law of §189 describes three cases, two of which are unmistakable cases of incestuous rape. The first case mentions a son raping his mother. The second and third cases refer to a daughter and a son being raped by their father. Importantly, the punishment is not specified, and the law does not make the penalty dependent on the father's so-called property rights. All three cases are called "capital crimes." In the law of §190, a stepson violates his stepmother, which appears to be a crime only when the father is alive. If the father is dead, the son is not punished for raping his stepmother. Enveloped in androcentric bias, this law does not consider the position of the stepmother and focuses only on the son or the father.

The Hittite codes also include four laws on bestiality that, according to animal advocates, could be considered as possible rape legislation. They are §§187, 188, 199, and 200. Animals are unable to consent, and if they could, one would not know, as explained by animal rights people.[89] In fact, Harry A. Hoffner identifies an eighteenth-century legal decision that declares a female donkey as "a victim of [sexual] violence."[90] So perhaps it is in the realm of the possible to discuss the following laws as rape legislation:

187. If a man does evil with a head of cattle, it is a capital crime and he shall be killed. They bring him to the king's court. Whether the king orders him killed, or whether the king spares his life, he must not appeal to the king.

198. If a man does evil with a sheep, it is a capital crime and he shall be killed. They bring him to the king's court. Whether the king orders him killed, or whether the king spares his life, he must not appeal to the king.

199. If anyone does evil with a pig, (or) a dog, he shall die. They will bring them to the gate of the palace and the king may order them killed, the king may spare their lives; but he must not appeal to the king....

89. Carol J. Adams, "Bestiality," in *Encyclopedia of Rape*, ed. Merril D. Smith (Westport, CT: Greenwood, 2004), 22–23.
90. Hoffner, "Incest, Sodomy and Bestiality," 83n13.

200 (A). If a man does evil with a horse or a mule, there shall be no punishment. He must not appeal to the king nor shall he become a case for the priest.[91]

The four laws illustrate that, strangely, sexual acts with cows, sheep, pigs, and dogs are punished with the death penalty whereas sexual acts with horses or mules remain penalty free. This distinction leads to two questions. Why did these laws become necessary in the first place, and why do the laws treat the rape of horses and mules differently from other animals? The first question cannot be answered conclusively, of course. Did the laws become necessary because bestiality was such an enormous problem in ancient Near Eastern societies that it required laws to "regulate" such practices? Did the legislators attempt to recognize an owner's property rights? Or are these laws only scribal fantasies? We do not know. The second question about the different treatment of horses and mules has received attempts at answers. For instance, Ernst Neufeld expresses his surprise about the distinction. He suggests that cows, sheep, pigs, and dogs were regarded as sacred in "the cult of animals." Since horses and mules were "late comers" in the geographical area of the Hittite Empire, they were excluded from animal cults and exempted from the laws.[92] Another commentator, Hoffner, refrains from any hypothesis and simply acknowledges his inability to give a reasonable explanation for the distinction.[93] In any case, the laws provide a glimpse into the violent pattern of male sexual fantasy or practice. They are disturbing, whether or not they are viewed as legislation on rape.

It is important to note that the incest and bestiality laws share a crucial grammatical characteristic. They use the same Hittite verb, katta waištai, to communicate the action performed by the man. Different translations of the verbal phrase provide different meanings. The translation given above is found in the renowned edition by James B. Pritchard, which offers two translations of the verbs. In the law on incest the English verb is rendered as "to violate" and in the law on bestiality the same verb is translated as "to do evil." Other translations use the same English term for the Hittite verb. Neufeld translates the verb with "to sin." The bestiality law of §187 thus reads:

91. Pritchard, *Ancient Near Eastern Texts*, 196–97.
92. Neufeld, *Hittite Laws*, 188.
93. Hoffner, "Incest, Sodom and Bestiality," 82.

If a man sins with a cow, (it is) an abomination, he shall die.

Similarly, the incest law in §189 is translated:

> [If a man] sins with his mother, (it is) an abomination. If a [man] sins with
> a daughter, (it is) an abomination. If a man sins with a son, (it is) an abom-
> ination.

Neufeld explains that the verb *katta waištai* means literally "sin
together (sexually)"[94] and "denotes indecent exposure or carnal knowledge and is an idiomatic description of sexual intercourse."[95] In other
words, the verb depicts the same action in the incest and bestiality
laws. The translation in Martha Roth's edition of ancient laws is
explicit when it reads §187 as: "If a man has sexual relations with
a cow . . . ," and §189: "If a man has sexual relations with his own
mother. . . ."[96] The verb is the same, and so readers must decide
whether it implies physical and psychological violation or a moral
transgression of normative behavior in Hittite culture. Does the verb
connote sexual violence, an "evil" deed, or "sinful" behavior in general? These actions are characterized as *hurkel*, a Hittite noun for a
sexual act that, according to Hoffner, does *not* refer to a crime involving "a sexual combination which is condemned by social mores"[97] but
more generally is used for a "forbidden sexual combination, incest."[98]
In other words, the act is something that is "forbidden." Was the forbidden deed an act of rape? It depends on a reader to make this
decision.

The difficulty about the meaning of these laws relates to the limited
number of existing Hittite Laws. Yet clearly the laws on incest and
bestiality describe situations of sexual harm for humans and animals.
Whether the legislators themselves identified these acts as "rape" is
not a question we can answer, nor does the answer matter much, especially since we do not even know if these laws were ever used legislatively.[99] What matters is that ancient Near Eastern codes contain an
impressive number of rape laws. Whether fantasy or reality, they indicate that rape was an issue in the ancient Near East.

In short, scholarship on ancient Near Eastern rape legislation

94. Neufeld, *Hittite Laws*, 53.
95. Ibid., 188.
96. Roth, *Law Collections*, 236.
97. Hoffner, "Incest, Sodomy and Bestiality," 83.
98. Ibid., 84.
99. Westbrook, "Biblical and Cuneiform Law Codes." See also footnote 48 of this essay.

would greatly benefit from the epistemological insights of postmodern theory. If all interpretations are always "located somewhere," the study of biblical and ancient Near Eastern laws reveals more about the hermeneutical interests of readers than the authorial meaning of ancient lawgivers. Yet many scholars seem undeterred by the epistemological advances of the last decades, and so much work remains to be done. Clearly an epistemological imbalance prevails, and bridging conversations are not in sight.

Toward a Conclusion, Not a Resolution

The purpose of this essay has been threefold. It brings attention to the current epistemological imbalance in interpretations on rape law. It invites scholars to acknowledge that interpretative differences are based on epistemological differences, and it reminds scholars in the field of ancient law that authorial meaning, too, is coming from "somewhere." The scholarly opposition to this threefold purpose is strong. Generally, many empiricist-positivist interpreters insist on placing the meaning of biblical and ancient Near Eastern texts into the safe distance of ancient history. They avoid the debate about the ongoing cultural, historical, political, or religious significance of their interpretations. Instead, they continue reading from "nowhere," which makes their explanations vulnerable to androcentric bias, alienating readers aware of the global rape culture. They also disregard why the next generation should limit the scholarly work to authorial intent when it only reproduces historically fixed meaning disconnected from contemporary life on earth. We face, then, a serious epistemological imbalance in the study and teaching of biblical law.

If the position of empiricist-positivist scholars is that "back then rape was legal" because it was mostly understood as marital, adulterous, or seductive behavior by men who were legally in charge and able to do as they pleased, it is pedagogically irresponsible to transmit such a history to students without critical commentary. Yet the pedagogical impetus is entirely absent from research on ancient rape laws. The postmodern notion of the contextualized nature of all exegetical work would easily solve these problems. What is required is a vibrant and fresh debate on these matters.

Yet if a discussion does not take place, the terrain will be left to the increasingly dominant discourse of the Christian Right, which insists on the literal meaning of the Bible, a notion that is closely aligned with scientific objectivist hermeneutics.[100] In my view, ancient rape laws represent a promising opportunity for people of the twenty-first century CE to debate the hermeneutical uncertainties and complexities of sacred texts like the Bible. It also enables us to relate the epistemological imbalance in studies on ancient rape legislation to the larger arena in which we live, and to communicate the urgent need for dialogue across the hermeneutical, religious, cultural, and political divide in biblical scholarship and elsewhere.[101] Certainly, the scholarly opposition to recognizing the contextualized nature of all (biblical) exegesis is deeply ingrained, and the following chapter explores it further. It scrutinizes the long-lasting roots of the German white male denial and rejection of exegetical context-specificity, with a focus on the highly influential twentieth-century Old Testament scholar, Gerhard von Rad.

100. Other scholars also see this connection between the Christian Right and the modern worldview; see, e.g., Schüssler Fiorenza, *Rhetoric and Ethic*, 42: "In spite of their critical posture, academic biblical studies are thus akin to fundamentalism insofar as they insist that scholars are able to produce a single scientific, true, reliable, and nonideological reading of the Bible. Scholars can achieve scientific certainty as long as they silence their own interests and abstract from their own sociopolitical situation."
101. I owe the idea of connecting the epistemological imbalance in ancient rape law with the current (US) sociopolitical and religious divide to Charles Nelson, professor emeritus at Tufts University, Boston, MA, during a conversation on November 6, 2004.

6

Lederhosen Hermeneutics: Toward a Feminist Sociology of German White Male Old Testament Interpretations

Bible scholars working beyond Western white male European and North American social locations have long asserted a context-specific hermeneutics. For instance, Chinese Hebrew Bible scholar Archie Chi Chung Lee, points to "the shift of focus in biblical hermeneutics from the deliberate hiding of the identity of the interpreter to the much anticipated exposure of the reading subject."[1] Articulating context-specific biblical hermeneutics in English-speaking publications since 1985,[2] Lee, like other like-minded interpreters, contends that biblical readings are always located "somewhere."[3] When he encounters biblical readings, he asks: "Whose story is it? Who is telling it? For whose benefit is it told? Who stands to gain and who will suffer as a result of

---

1. Archie C. C. Lee, "The Bible and Contextual Reading: Encountering Communities, Encountering Texts—A Response," *Union Seminary Quarterly Review* 56, no. 1–2 (2002): 78.
2. See, e.g., Archie C. C. Lee, "Doing Theology in Chinese Context: The David-Bathsheba Story and the Parable of Nathan," *East Asia Journal of Theology* 3, no. 2 (1985): 243–57.
3. See, e.g., the highly influential volumes by Fernando F. Segovia and Mary Ann Tolbert, eds., *Reading from This Place*, vol. 1, *Social Location and Biblical Interpretation in the United States* (Minneapolis: Fortress Press, 1995), and *Reading from This Place*, vol. 2, *Social Location and Biblical Interpretation in Global Perspective* (Minneapolis: Fortress Press, 2000).

the narrating? What other stories are being suppressed? Are there any other silent voices? In brief, what are the power dynamics inherited in the inscribing of the text? How do we characterize the community in struggles?"[4]

Lee, located in the Chinese-Asian religiously pluralistic setting of Hong Kong, interprets the Bible with a "cross-cultural method." He "assume[s] that readers, who are shaped by their own cultural and social texts, have always interpreted the Bible in an interactive process that accommodates the multiplicity of texts."[5] Lee explains that such a cross-cultural approach correlates "other" texts with the Bible and so "highlights the interactive reading process in the understanding of the biblical text." This approach recognizes that "these other texts are part of the textuality that makes up our life contexts, shapes our political existence, models our social vision, and enriches our religiosity."[6] In fact, to Chinese Christian Bible readers, the "other" texts are primary, "indigenous," and turn the Bible into "a newcomer to the already very rich textual and commentarial traditions in the Asian context."[7] More importantly, Lee also asserts that "only with such kind of open recognition of one's tradition, together with one's acceptance of one's identity as a believer in the Christian faith, can one be regarded as having integrity and as being dignified as a Chinese Christian."[8]

The hermeneutical insight into the contextuality of all biblical interpretation has, however, not much affected German white male scholarship on the Hebrew Bible. In its dominant expression, such scholarship insists on promoting the historical-critical paradigm, defined as objective, universal, and value-neutral text analysis. Accordingly, it does not usually consider itself to be shaped by its sociopolitical, theo-cultural, and historical-economic context. In fact, it is probably fair to say that many German white male Bible scholars pride themselves on avoiding the "traps" of context specificity. To them, scientifically valid scholarship must be context-independent, and so they work hard on keeping it this way.

This essay challenges this position by suggesting that the very absence of context specificity must be recognized as the hallmark of

---

4. Lee, "The Bible and Contextual Reading," 79.
5. Archie C. C. Lee, "Mothers Bewailing: Reading Lamentations," in *Her Master's Tools? Feminist and Postcolonial Engagements of Historical-Critical Discourse*, ed. Caroline Vander Stichele and Todd Penner (Atlanta: Society of Biblical Literature, 2005), 195.
6. Ibid., 209.
7. Ibid.
8. Archie C. C. Lee, "The Names of God and Bible Translation: Engaging the Chinese Term Question in the Context of Scriptural Interpretation," *Journal of Theologies and Cultures in Asia* 5 (2006): 15.

German white male scholarship on the Old Testament. It is its very essence, going back to the Nazi era from 1933 to 1945. During that time period German right-wing ideology endorsed the incorporation of a German-specific hermeneutics, including in biblical studies.[9] Some scholars, among them Gerhard von Rad, were theology professors during that time and sought to escape the Nazi hermeneutics by rejecting any context specificity in their work. Their context-free hermeneutics constituted an intellectual form of resistance that was, however, not openly articulated, perhaps impossible during the Nazi regime. Interestingly, their resistance hermeneutics became most popular in postwar Germany, where it still shapes much of German white male exegesis today. This development was further enhanced due to the incorporation of the modern-epistemological principles of objectivity, universality, and value neutrality—the uncontested standards of Western scholarship since the eighteenth century—into the resistance hermeneutics. It made for a powerful interpretation model because it rejected the contextualizing Nazi hermeneutics and proclaimed its loyalty to modern-epistemological principles. Perhaps unsurprisingly, context-free Bible research has been the norm in German white male exegesis ever since.

Differently stated, the refusal to recognize social location as a key factor in today's German white male exegesis suggests that its practitioners are stuck in a historical-ideological paradigm originally advanced in resistance to Nazi ideology. What is needed, therefore, is a recovery of the cultural-historical connection that made German white male exegetes refuse their context specificity. Several recently published studies, especially on Gerhard von Rad, have started to investigate this connection. Indirectly, then, they support this essay's thesis that a hermeneutics is, in fact, a lederhosen hermeneutics, a quintessentially German white male reading of the Old Testament, when it asserts *not* to be socially located but to merely advance the epistemological principles of the Enlightenment. Such a hermeneutics, developed during the heyday of Nazi ideology and successfully opposing the

---

9. For a detailed analysis, see Cornelia Weber, *Altes Testament und völkische Frage: Der biblische Volksbegriff in der alttestamentlichen Wissenschaft der nationalsozialistischen Zeit, dargestellt am Beispiel von Johannes Hempel* (Tübingen: Mohr Siebeck, 2000). See also Susannah Heschel, "Theologen für Hitler: Walter Grundmann und das Institut zur Erforschung und Beseitigung des jüdischen Einflusses auf das deutsche kirchliche Leben," in *Christlicher Antijudaismus und Antisemitismus: Theologische und kirchliche Programme Deutscher Christen*, ed. Leonore Siegele-Wenschkewitz (Frankfurt am Main: Haag Herchen, 1994), 125–70; Peter von der Osten-Sacken, ed., *Das mißbrauchte Evangelium: Studien zu Theologie und Praxis der Thüringer Deutschen Christen* (Berlin: Institut Kirche und Judentum, 2002).

Nazi hermeneutics, fosters historical-critical detachment from contextualized readings of the Bible. Perhaps for that very reason this kind of hermeneutics still enjoys widespread popularity in German Hebrew Bible studies and elsewhere. This essay focuses on this dynamic, first, by taking a closer look at von Rad's work as it has been appraised since the 1970s, and second, by discussing the implications of the German white male hermeneutics that redefines its hermeneutical ethnocentrism as a universally obligatory paradigm.

Gerhard von Rad's Lederhosen Hermeneutics

Von Rad is widely acknowledged as one of the most influential Old Testament scholars of the twentieth century. In 1972, Werner H. Schmidt published an article titled "Old Testament Theology *before and after* Gerhard von Rad"[10] In 1973, Rolf Rendtorff agreed that von Rad's work constituted a major break, primarily due to his "profound methodological reorientation" (*die grundlegende methodische Neuorientierung*) of the discipline of Old Testament studies. In 1978, James L. Crenshaw also stated that von Rad's "influence has been keenly felt throughout the entire discipline of Old Testament studies. It would be difficult to find an Old Testament scholar anywhere who is not indebted to Gerhard von Rad in one way or another."[11]

All of them recognize the extraordinary significance of von Rad's work, but Rendtorff further specifies the moment of von Rad's "decisive methodological breakthrough." In his view, it occurred with the 1938 publication of *The Form Critical Problem of the Hexateuch*. To Rendtorff, von Rad articulated his ideas initially in 1938 but developed them fully "after the profound break [*tiefen Einschnitt*] of the Second World War." Thus "the years from 1946 to 1953 constituted his most productive writing period in his career."[12] Rendtorff explains: "During these years he produced numerous studies with profound methodological considerations, in which he reflected upon and evaluated his works of earlier years methodologically and so developed the foundation for his scholarship forthcoming in the next decades."[13] In short, not only has

10. Werner H. Schmidt, "'Theologie des Alten Testaments' vor und nach Gerhard von Rad," *Verkündigung und Forschung* (1972): 1–25 (emphasis added to title in text).
11. James L. Crenshaw, *Gerhard von Rad*, Makers of the Modern Theological Mind (Waco: Word, 1978), 15.
12. Rolf Rendtorff, "Die alttestamentlichen Überlieferungen als Grundthema der Lebensarbeit Gerhard von Rads," in *Gerhard von Rad: Seine Bedeutung für die Theologie: Drei Reden von H. W. Wolff, R. Rendtorff, W. Pannenberg* (Münich: Kaiser, 1973), 27.
13. Ibid.

von Rad's research been recognized as most influential for the post-Holocaust generations of German white male scholars, but he is also seen as laying the foundation for his work during the pinnacle of the Nazi era, in 1938.

The latter insight, however, remains underdeveloped in studies that discuss von Rad's work. They began to appear shortly after his death in 1971. Published between the 1970s and 1980s, these studies do not focus on the fact that von Rad conceived his scholarly agenda during the Nazi era. For instance, in 1978, James L. Crenshaw portrayed von Rad's contributions to the field in 189 pages, but he mentions possible connections between the Nazi era and von Rad's early work only in passing. Crenshaw refers to von Rad's invitation to teach at the University in Jena in 1934,

> where national socialism flourished. Accepting the challenge, perhaps because of his genuine love for the Hebrew tradition, von Rad soon found that an Old Testament scholar was not welcome in such an environment. He reminded everyone of the Jewish problem by the very fact that he taught the language and literature of ancient Israel. His classes virtually empty, von Rad went in search of hearers, and the following years saw him engaging in seemingly endless illegal church discussions with those who had not surrendered to the anti-Semitism of the day. . . . His contributions to the church were quickly recognized, and led to an offer to become the senior pastor at a Hamburg church. Choosing to remain at Jena, where the task of confronting anti-Semitism was more pronounced, von Rad worked diligently and published prolifically. During these years many popular works in defense of the Old Testament appeared, such as *The Old Testament—God's Word for the Germans!* and *Moses.* But from this period also came the epoch-making programmatic essay, "The Form Critical Problem of the Hexateuch."[14]

In other words, Crenshaw hints at the difficulties von Rad experienced in these years but then insinuates that von Rad's scholarly work was not connected to these struggles. According to Crenshaw, von Rad taught against the Nazi propaganda *but* his crucial study on the Hexateuch was disconnected from it. Crenshaw's insertion of "but" suggests that von Rad's teaching against the Nazi propaganda represented the more practical aspect of his work that was *apart* from his "real" research. In fairness, Crenshaw also notes that "von Rad's theology is an attempt to bring together the two Testaments, a concern

14. Crenshaw, *Gerhard von Rad*, 20–21.

that cannot be entirely divorced from the struggle with national socialism and its disdain for everything Jewish."[15] Yet no further comments
detail the significance of von Rad's social location for his reconceptualization of the field.

Other discussions on von Rad's work are similarly terse. For
instance, in 1973, Hans-Walter Wolff describes von Rad's time as a prisoner of war in the spring of 1945 and mentions the scholar's efforts to
teach the book of Genesis to a small group of fellow imprisoned clergy
members, theology students, and deacons. Wolff ruminates:

> It is obvious that he did not only try out a historical critical but also an
> empirical critical method, without declaring the latter as the dominant
> one. Von Rad's great Genesis commentary thus went even through these
> kinds of tests of fire, a manuscript that already began to develop in Jena
> and today has sold more than 50,000 copies in the German language alone,
> not to mention the numerous translations, and probably is the most
> widely distributed and read Old Testament commentary in history.[16]

Wolff recognizes that von Rad's social location as a professor at a pro-
Nazi faculty of the University of Jena and his status as a prisoner of
war must have exerted some effect on his scholarship. Wolff, however, does not outline *how* this context might have shaped von Rad's
hermeneutical or methodological work, and so he depicts von Rad's
work as entirely disconnected from his Nazi context.

This disconnect can also be observed in Rudolf Smend's renowned
study published in 1989, in which he ponders briefly the extent to
which von Rad's work is shaped by his encounter with the *Deutschkirch-
ler* (early German Christians prior to the Nazi era) in the 1920s when
von Rad served as an assistant pastor in Bavaria. Smend raises the
question of whether perhaps von Rad's early publications, especially
his dissertation in which he articulates his ideas about the Deuteronomistic people of God for the first time, might have been written in
opposition to the early right-wing encounters.[17] Smend also sketches
von Rad's intellectual battles during the Nazi era when von Rad "lec-
tured tirelessly for years and everywhere" (*jahraus jahrein, landauf
landab*) to students, during church meetings, as part of unofficial adult
education programs, and to congregations on topics such as "The Old

15. Ibid., 35.
16. Hans-Walter Wolff, "Gerhard von Rad als Exeget," in *Gerhard von Rad*, 16. My translation from the
original German.
17. Rudolf Smend, "Gerhard von Rad," chap. in *Deutsche Alttestamentler in drei Jahrhunderten* (Göttingen: Vandenhoeck & Ruprecht, 1989), 236.

Testament—God's Word to the Germans" (1937), "The Ongoing Significance of the Old Testament" (1937), "Questions about Interpreting the
Old Testament" (1938), and "Why Does the Church Teach the Old Testament?" (1939).[18]
 Smend recognizes that von Rad's work gained depth and credibility
due to these settings. Smend also explains that von Rad's work
defended the historical-critical study of the Old Testament not only
against German Christian theologians, such as Emanuel Hirsch, but
also against leading theologians of the Confessing Church, such as the
Old Testament scholar Wilhelm Visher, who were appalled by von
Rad's critique. Von Rad challenged their work by proclaiming that
"nowadays" biblical scholars "were obligated to work with the formative results of historical, source, and *religionsgeschichtliche* criticism"
because these results "could simply never again be ignored."[19] These
comments suggest that von Rad was heavily invested in his social location. Yet, in the end, Smend does not further investigate the Nazi era's
ramifications on von Rad's research, as if von Rad's work developed
undisturbed by the very disturbing circumstances in which he articulated it.
 More recent studies have begun to make connections between von
Rad's scholarship and his social location.[20] One of them comes from
Bernhard M. Levinson and Douglas Dance.[21] They maintain that von
Rad's work on Deuteronomy, starting with his dissertation in 1929
and culminating in his commentary on Deuteronomy in 1964, "comes
closer to eisegesis than exegesis" and "says less about Deuteronomy
than it says about the situation in which he wrote."[22] Levinson and
Dance place von Rad's work squarely into "the historical situation in
which he wrote during the formative part of his career: Germany,
under the National Socialist dictatorship from 1933–1945."[23]
 To them, von Rad was not only confronted with the early debates

18. Ibid., 237.
19. Ibid.
20. There are still a majority of reviews who do not make this connection. Even when they refer to
von Rad's life, they rarely develop deep connections to his work; see, e.g., Konrad von Rabenau,
"Als Student bei Gerhard von Rad in Jena 1943-1945," in *Das Alte Testament und die Kultur der Moderne*, ed. Manfred Oeming, Konrad Schmid, and Michael Welker (Münster: LIT, 2004), 7–12; Rudolf
Smend, "Gerhard von Rad," in *Das Alte Testament*, ed. Oeming, Schmid, and Welker, 13–24.
21. Bernhard M. Levinson and Douglas Dance, "The Metamorphosis of Law into Gospel: Gerhard von
Rad's Attempt to Reclaim the Old Testament for the Church," in *Recht und Ethik im Alten Testament:
Beiträge des Symposiums "Das Alte Testament und die Kultur der Moderne" anlässlich des 100. Geburtstags
Gerhard von Rads (1901-1971) Heidelberg, 18.-21. Oktober 2001*, ed. Eckart Otto and Bernard M. Levinson
(Münster: LIT, 2004), 82–110.
22. Ibid., 85.
23. Ibid.

on German Nazi ideology as a Lutheran minister in the mid- to late 1920s. Since 1934, he also held a professorship at the University of Jena which "stood at the forefront of the attempt to create the ideal Nationalist Socialist University."[24] There he encountered daily debates about National Socialist and German Christian ideology in the administrative university structure, faculty appointments, the theological curriculum, student research, and language requirements. He was also involved in Gerhard Kittel's influential project *Theologisches Wörterbuch zum Neuen Testament*; Kittel was "a prominent support of National Socialism."[25] Von Rad's "early and apparently brief membership in the Sturmabteilung (SA)"[26] might have even helped him get the position at the University of Jena, but it also indicates his initial involvement in Nazi ideology. When this ideology put pressure on his discipline and his university courses lacked student enrollment because they dealt with the Old Testament, his social location directly affected his scholarship. Levison and Dance assert: "What von Rad wrote about Deuteronomy must be understood in that specific historical context."[27]

So how did he write about Deuteronomy? Von Rad approached this biblical book not as law but as sermon, as the gospel of the Old Testament. Since Nazi German Christians pursued a "neo-Marcionite assault" on the Old Testament, von Rad defended it as "a testament of Christ,"[28] "rehabilitating" it to "a foundational Christian text preaching salvation." In his interpretation Deuteronomy is about "kerygma" rather than "Jewish legalism."[29] This position enabled him to oppose the efforts by his colleagues who marginalized, even eliminated, the comprehensive study of the Old Testament for being too Jewish. Thus von Rad, as a "committed Christian Old Testament scholar" and sympathizer with the Confessing Church, stood "outside the mainstream in the Faculty of Theology at Jena."[30] He designed his theological arguments to reclaim the Old Testament "as a vital witness of Christ for the Church"[31] and as establishing Christianity as "the legitimate heir of the Old Testament."[32] His theological solution proclaimed the Old Testament as Christian literature and placed the book of

24. Ibid., 91.
25. Ibid., 95.
26. Ibid.
27. Ibid., 85.
28. Ibid., 87.
29. Ibid.
30. Ibid., 101.
31. Ibid., 102–3.
32. Ibid., 103.

Deuteronomy at the heart of God's promise for salvation to the Church resting in Christ.

According to Levinson and Dance, he accomplished this feat by shifting his argument from "theological to exegetical."[33] He characterized Deuteronomy and later also Chronicles as sermonizing literature "created by traveling Levites."[34] This view allowed him to "rescue the Old Testament from the realm of dead Jewish letter into the familiar and superior oral sermon tradition" of the Protestant church.[35] To von Rad, Deuteronomy (and also Chronicles) does not constitute "narrow legalism" but "sermonic exhortations."[36] Not law but God's mercy and salvation stand at the center of his approach to the Old Testament, already articulated in his dissertation, *Das Gottesvolk im Deuteronomium*.[37] The same trend emerges in his groundbreaking 1938 work, *Das formgeschichtliche Problem des Hexateuch*.[38] Levinson and Dance explain in some detail:

> Von Rad's 1938 work, *Das formgeschichtliche Problem des Hexateuch*, also had little to say about law. While it discusses Deuteronomy 5–11 as a hortatory allocution or sermon, the legal section of Deuteronomy (Deuteronomy 12–26) is not analyzed in this way. It suggests that Deuteronomy's law code arises from a covenant ceremony whereby the law is read publicly. Only with *Deuteronomium Studien* does von Rad turn his attention meaningfully to the legal corpus of Deuteronomy. This work was written in the winter of 1945/1946, when he was appointed to Göttingen. Von Rad extends the approach that he had developed for his analysis of Chronicles and applies it to the laws of making this move, however von Rad shows surprisingly little interest in making any intellectual connection between *Deuteronomium Studien* and his own previous treatment of Deuteronomy, *Das formgeschichtliche Problem des Hexateuch*. In fact, the first edition of *Deuteronomien Studien* (1947) contains just one brief reference to that work. Only in his second edition (1948) did von Rad attempt to rectify this omission. He expanded the second edition to incorporate the theory of Deuteronomy's origin as a cultic renewal festival, as in *Das formgeschichtliche Problem des Hexateuch*. He also reinforced the idea of Deuteronomy's connection with Levitical preachers, as in the earlier work on Chronicles.[39]

33. Ibid.
34. Ibid., 104.
35. Ibid.
36. Ibid.
37. Gerhard von Rad, *Das Gottesvolk im Deuteronomium*, BWANT 47 (Stuttgart: Kohlhammer, 1929).
38. Gerhard von Rad, *Das formgeschichtliche Problem des Hexateuch*, BWANT 78 (Stuttgart: Kohlhammer, 1938).
39. Levinson and Dance, "The Metamorphosis of Law into Gospel," 106.

In short, Levinson and Dance observe that von Rad highlighted the sermonic sections in Deuteronomy. He considered them as the core legal components, as independently developed from the Levitical preachers, and he stressed that "Gospel subsumed Law,"[40] an apologetic position directly conversant with the neo-Marcionite position of the German Christian colleagues at the University of Jena. Accordingly, Levinson and Dance urge us to understand his scholarship within his social location:

> At every key point, the language that von Rad employs to defend Deuteronomy resonates with issues that engaged him personally, academically, and theologically. Von Rad's professional life and scholarly accomplishments provide poignant testimony to that period. Through his scholarship, von Rad took a stand.[41]

Levinson's and Dance's reading, then, squarely locates von Rad's work within the Nazi era. In their view, his work is ultimately trapped by this context because von Rad "constrained" himself by "the antithetical categories that he constructed." Von Rad insisted throughout his career that Deuteronomy could never be seen as law because it is "the last defense against an increasing legalization." Deuteronomy is "kerygmatic proclamation" and "properly 'Christian' rather than 'Jewish.'"[42] This hermeneutical constraint makes it impossible for von Rad to "allow the text to speak for itself" or to consider the possibility that Deuteronomy was law or even "both law and grace."[43] Thus von Rad should be viewed as "a victim of the historical context in which he found himself."[44] This assessment links von Rad's exegesis directly within the Nazi era.

Another recently published study shows von Rad's "concern about the inalienable connection between the Old and the New Testaments developed during the theological disputes of the 1930s that tried to define the value and significance of the Old Testament for the Church."[45] The author, Susanne Böhm, describes the various positions

---

40. Ibid., 109.
41. Ibid.
42. Susannah Heschel states unambiguously: "Like other members of the Confessing Church, von Rad came to defend the significance of the Old Testament for Christians. He did so by rejecting its Jewishness: Deuteronomy, the major focus of his scholarship, was a proto-gospel, a kerygma, and not a law book, he argued." See Susannah Heschel, *The Aryan Jesus: Christian Theologians and the Bible in Nazi Germany* (Princeton: Princeton University Press, 2008), 216.
43. All of these quotes are from ibid., 110.
44. Ibid.
45. Susanne Böhm, "Gerhard von Rad in Jena," in *Das Alte Testament—ein Geschichtsbuch?! Geschichtss-*

regarding the Old Testament at the time and against which von Rad took his stance. One position was powerfully articulated by German Christians who diminished the value of the Old Testament. They maintained that the New Testament alone guides Christians and that the Christian faith has to fit the German race and be rearticulated within Teutonic religious and historical traditions. Accordingly, they classified the Old Testament as *wesensfremd* (in the sense of: "alien to the Teutonic people") and replaced it with Teutonic fairy tales and myths.[46]

A second position is affiliated with a countermovement that was closely aligned with Karl Barth and his dialectic theology. It emphasized the christological character of the Old Testament. The most distinguished scholar of this position, Wilhelm Vischer, read biblical literature as a witness to Christ. He also dared to structure his analysis according to the Jewish canon, and he even integrated rabbinic literature into his work. His scholarly boldness encouraged ministers of the Confessing Church to preach from the Old Testament and to counter effectively the anti-Old Testament rejection of pro-Nazi theological and ecclesiological voices. Yet Vischer attacked historical-critical exegesis because, in his view, it "missed the forward looking intention of biblical texts and lost itself in historiographical possibilities."[47] Another similarly located position comes from a neo-Lutheran conservative perspective in the work of Wilhelm Lütgert. He was aligned with the Confessing Church but did not become a member. In a book entitled *Schöpfung und Offenbarung* (Creation and revelation), Lütgert uplifted the creator God over against the redeemer God, and so attempted to salvage the Old Testament for the Christian faith.[48]

A third position, represented by the systematic theologian and church historian Emanuel Hirsch, viewed the Old Testament as a "religion of the Law" (*Gesetzesreligion*) that is similar to other non-Christian religion. Yet Hirsch also regarded the Old Testament and Jewish religion as unique because it represents a classic paradigm. He articulated with distinct clarity what it means to believe in a God of the law and rejected christological appropriations of the Old Testament. He

chreibung oder Geschichtsüberlieferung im antiken Israel, ed. Uwe Becker und Jürgen van Oorschot (Leipzig: Evangelische Verlagsanstalt, 2005), 202.
46. Ibid., 209.
47. Ibid., 210–11. For a comprehensive analysis of Visher's work, see Brigitte Schroven, *Theologie des Alten Testaments zwischen Anpassung und Widerspruch: Christologische Auslegung zwischen den Weltkriegen* (Neukirchen-Vluyn: Neukirchener Verlag, 1995), esp. 173–234.
48. Böhm, "Gerhard von Rad in Jena," 212–13.

characterized the New Testament as the "religion of the Gospel" that alone is necessary for the Christian faith.[49]

According to Böhm, von Rad's work must be understood in direct conversation with these three positions. They helped shape his hermeneutics, and he challenged all of them, most prominently in a 1938 essay titled "Fragen der Schriftauslegung im Alten Testament" (Questions about scriptural interpretation of the Old Testament). Combining various features, his hermeneutics adhered to a christological approach but grounded it in source-critical investigations that place each source within its specific historical situation. Böhm, following Manfred Oeming's work,[50] also observes that von Rad's theological convictions have long been identified as characteristic for his biblical hermeneutics. He combined four hermeneutical models into one overarching framework: (1) the history of promise model, (2) the history of tradition model, (3) salvation history, and (4) the history of salvation. Importantly, von Rad began articulating these models in the historical-political and theological context of the Nazi era. They allowed him to reject the Nazi contextualizing hermeneutics while indirectly conversing with it. Yet he never discussed his hermeneutics as constituting his exegetical response to the historical-ideological and political context in which he developed it. Consequently, his students and the students of his students have taken for granted his apparently contextless hermeneutics. Like their teacher, they have rarely reflected on their contexts and usually dismissed any contextualizing hermeneutics as academically inappropriate and even unscholarly.

Ethnocentrism as Universality: Toward a German Post-Holocaust, Postcolonial, and Feminist White Male Hermeneutics of the Hebrew Bible

I am writing these reflections as a diasporic German feminist scholar of the Hebrew Bible who was theologically raised in the "homeland," also credentialed there, but who has lived and taught in the United States since 1990. Today's technological advances and means of transportation make it easy to stay in continuous communication across the Atlantic Ocean; family and collegial connections as well as conference opportunities ensure that I stay in touch with my native

---

49. Ibid., 213–14.
50. Ibid., 215. See Manfred Oeming, *Gesamtbiblische Theologien der Gegenwart: Das Verhältnis von AT und NT in der hermeneutischen Diskussion seit Gerhard von Rad* (Stuttgart: Kohlhammer, 1985).

country. Yet my diasporic life on the North American continent, the many trips back and forth and to elsewhere, as well as a semester's stay at the Chinese University of Hong Kong have contributed to my conviction that German Old Testament studies has always been contextual even when it proclaims itself as universal, objective, and value neutral. To be sure, German *feminist* Bible scholars have long acknowledged their social locations, perhaps most notably articulated by German feminist scholar of the New Testament Luise Schottroff.[51] Yet mainstream German white male exegetes still refrain from context-specific references.[52] They believe their scholarly accomplishments to be independent of ethnocentric characteristics and view them as objective, impartial, and factual scholarship.

Sometimes exceptions seem to exist. For instance, Manfred Oeming, who teaches at the University in Heidelberg, where von Rad once taught decades ago, seems to move into a hermeneutical direction that embraces a reader-centered hermeneutics. He suggests that "we must relativise our passion for objectivity."[53] He even gives room to the notion that context plays a role in the meaning-making process. In his view, "context is determined by three aspects: *the idiosyncrasy of the interpreter, the idiosyncrasy of the text, and the purpose of the exegesis.*"[54] Hence, in Oeming's view, "not every method is suited for every interpreter; the degree of education as well as other aspects will determine whether an academic approach or a meditative, pragmatic approach to the text is more appropriate."[55] Oeming places the decision with "the exegete," who "must develop a careful sense of which method may be appropriate for which situation. This requires experience, sensitivity,

---

51. See, e.g., Luise Schottroff, *Lydia's Impatient Sisters: A Feminist Social History of Early Christianity*, trans. Barbara Rumscheidt and Martin Rumscheidt (Louisville: Westminter John Knox, 1995).
52. There are two exceptions: Erhard S. Gerstenberger, and to a certain extent also Rolf Rendtorff when he discusses hermeneutical issues related to the Jewish-Christian dialogue and the Hebrew Bible. See, e.g., "Erhard S. Gerstenberger (1932)," in *Alttestamentliche Wissenschaft in Selbstdarstellungen*, ed. Sebastian Grätz und Bernd U. Schipper (Göttingen: Vandenhock & Ruprecht, 2007), 141–52; Rolf Rendtorff, *Kontinuität im Widerspruch: Autobiographische Reflexionen* (Göttingen: Vandenhoeck & Ruprecht, 2007), esp. 77–99, 144–56. Gerstenberger regrets the disregard for social location among German Bible scholars when he states on 147: "Lateinamerikanische Exegese beginnt oft mit einer Analyse des eigenen Standortes. Sehr logisch! Denn wenn man eingesehen hat, wie weit die Ergebnisse der Interpretation vom eingenommenen und vorgegebenen Blickwinkel abhängen, dann muss man ehrlicherweise dem 'Vorverständnis' des Exegeten/der Exegetin eine bedeutende (natürlich nicht: absolut bestimmende) Rolle zubilligen. Wer ist dazu im alten Europa bereit?"
53. Manfred Oeming, *Contemporary Biblical Hermeneutics: An Introduction*, trans. Joachim F. Vette (Aldershot: Ashgate, 2006), 146.
54. Ibid., 145 (emphasis original).
55. Ibid.

an awareness of one's audience as well as a good measure of plain common sense."[56]

Although Oeming recognizes the significance of context, he places final authority with "educated readers" who choose methodological approaches according to their assessment of contextual needs. This paternalistic notion is quite different from the hermeneutics advanced by Archie Lee and like-minded Bible scholars. With Oeming we again encounter a hermeneutical model that does not take into account the dynamic interplay between readers and their contexts. This model does not analyze critically the notion of contextuality for German white male Bible scholars, and it does not let go of the supremacy of textual or even authorial meaning. The last point becomes especially apparent in an extensive discussion of the current plethora of biblical methods and the difficulties of establishing fixed, objective, and unilateral biblical meaning. Oeming ends the discussion with this proclamation: "Whenever the Bible comes into play, we will experience a hermeneutical transformation as the interpreted text becomes the interpreter. Scripture illuminates our existence."[57] To Oeming, when all is said and done, the text becomes the agent, the supreme authority, and the meaning maker. He returns to the safety net of his exegetical tradition, which places authority neither in readers nor in their contexts but in *sola Scriptura*, in the biblical texts. Without explaining how biblical texts can in fact illuminate readers' lives without the readers serving as the agents of textual meaning(s), Oeming maintains that, rather than its readers, the Bible speaks to us. This is a return to a traditional dogmatic position, which is however not openly acknowledged. Oeming's proposal must therefore be regarded as not more than a wink at the notion that context matters in biblical hermeneutics.[58]

Admittedly, Oeming's work is only *one* example of a recent German white male approach to the Hebrew Bible. Yet he holds a prominent professorship at a Protestant theological department in Germany. His ambiguous rejection of a contextualized hermeneutics upholds a

---

56. Ibid.
57. Ibid., 147.
58. See also Oeming's entirely inadequate discussion on feminist exegesis. For instance, he incorrectly attributes the book, *Texts of Terror*, to Elisabeth Schüssler Fiorenza, demonstrating his inadequate knowledge of the field of feminist biblical studies; see ibid., 106. He is also surprisingly polemical when he states: "What value can a creative, alternative, feminist re-writing of supposed biblical 'texts of terror' have for understanding the Bible? Can understanding be developed from this premise? This is hardly possible. This approach does not interpret the Bible; instead, war is declared on it. What refers to itself as a 'reading' of the Bible is in truth defamation and slander!" See ibid., 112. The scholarly quality of such polemic is certainly questionable.

tradition that views modernist hermeneutical principles as divorced from context and readers. As we have seen, von Rad uses these principles to resist one of the most theo-politically treacherous ideologies in German history. It is a truism that von Rad is not the first Bible scholar to rely on a modern hermeneutics. It predates him, as historical criticism rose to prominence in the nineteenth century.[59] Nevertheless, von Rad's obedience to a modern hermeneutics as a (conscious or unconscious) strategy for rejecting Nazi ideology makes his students and students of his students follow his path without any questions asked. Hence, they have rarely recognized the contextuality of their own exegetical work and refuted any serious attempt to contextualize it. Oeming's work must be understood as being part of this tradition. The question then is this: What would German white male scholarship of the Hebrew Bible look like if it took into account its post-Holocaust as well as class- and gender-privileged position, its social location, on the national and international level?

This is a difficult question, and ready answers do not (yet) exist. Moreover, when the topic requires reflecting on the German context for biblical exegesis, the fear of the German nationalistic past makes some Bible scholars immediately hesitant.[60] We have little guidance and experience in dealing with German-specific social locations in a nonfascist way, and so some worry that a context-specific perspective might strengthen right-wing propaganda in contemporary German society. Will the focus on national identity backfire and serve an agenda that shapes contemporary right-wing groups in Germany and in other European countries?[61] After all, we do not have a "positive" role model on how to move toward a German post-Holocaust white male hermeneutics that challenges structures of domination, such as ethnocentrism, colonialism, and sexism.

59. See, e.g., Hans-Joachim Kraus, *Geschichte der historisch-kritischen Erforschung des Alten Testaments von der Reformation bis zur Gegenwart*, 3rd ed. (Neukirchen-Vluyn: Neukirchener Verlag, 1982); John W. Rogerson, *Old Testament Criticism in the Nineteenth Century: England and Germany* (Philadelphia: Fortress Press, 1985); Ronald E. Clements, *One Hundred Years of Old Testament Interpretation* (Philadelphia: Westminster Press, 1976).
60. See, e.g., Elisabeth Schüssler Fiorenza, "Resident Alien: Dazugehören und doch fremd bleiben," in *Zwischen-Räume: Deutsche feministische Theologinnen im Ausland*, ed. Katharina von Kellenbach und Susanne Scholz (Münster: LIT, 2000), 69–83.
61. See, e.g., Reimar Paul, "Nazis aufm Bauernhof: Ein Anwesen in der Lüneburger Heide ist seit Jahren rechter Treffpunkt," *Neues Deutschland*, December 18, 2009, http://www.neues-deutschland.de/artikel/161397.nazis-aufm-bauernhof.html; Heribert Prantl, "Rechtsaußen, rechts draußen: Neonazis in Deutschland," *Süddeutsche Zeitung*, December 22, 2008, http://tinyurl.com/kotl4r2; "Rechtsextremismus: Zahl der Neonazis in Deutschland steigt an," *Süddeutsche Zeitung*, April 16, 2008, http://www.welt.de/politik/article1906787/Zahl_der_Neonazis_in_Deutschland_steigt_an.html.

Still, I want to suggest that the development of five research areas would provide considerable insight into the correlation between German white male Bible scholarship and political, economic, and social power structures in the past and the present. First, such work would need to investigate the historical, sociopolitical, and theo-cultural impact of German white male Bible scholarship on colonialism worldwide. Already in 1978, Edward W. Said indicated that academic disciplines affiliated with biblical studies, such as Egyptology, Ethnology, African Studies, or *Altorientalistik* provided the intellectual-academic framework in support of colonialism in Africa, Asia, and Latin America.[62] Extensive archival work in the respective missionary libraries and the libraries of the relevant academic institutes would be necessary to understand how German white male Bible scholarship helped promote assumptions and attitudes of Western colonial superiority.[63] Such research should also include a systematic account of the curricular developments of biblical studies in seminaries and universities in the formerly colonized countries since German white male biblical studies so successfully shaped the biblical studies curriculum everywhere. In this regard it would also be important to know more about the institutional connections between international doctoral students and their German white male *Doktorväter*. Are there letters kept anywhere that would give evidence about ongoing scholarly conversations in which former international students sought advice from their mentors, perhaps about building "respectable" theological departments in their countries? Some of this information is probably lost to history, but it is also possible that few scholars have searched for it in a systematic way. In my view, this kind of research could make a significant contribution to ongoing postcolonial research in general and the correlation between colonialism and German white male Bible scholarship in particular.

Second, another research area that would explore the relationship of German white male Bible scholarship to past and present political, economic, and social power structures should focus on German institutions in which such work played a major role during the past 150

---

62. Edward W. Said, *Orientalism* (New York: Pantheon, 1978).
63. See, e.g., Eric Ames, Marcia Klotz, and Lora Wildenthal, eds., *Germany's Colonial Pasts* (Lincoln: University of Nebraska Press, 2005); Heike Möhle, *Branntwein, Bibeln und Bananen: Der deutsche Kolonialismus in Afrika: eine Spurensuche* (Hamburg: Libertäre Assoziation, 1999); Volker M. Langbehn, ed., *German Colonialism, Visual Culture, and Modern Memory* (New York: Routledge, 2010); Michael Perraudin and Jürgen Zimmerer, eds., *German Colonialism and National Identity* (New York: Routledge, 2010).

years. Such research would provide evidence for the largely exclusionary character of German white male Bible research in academic and ecclesial discourse and practice. For instance, such work could investigate the notion of paganism and "otherness" and ask how German white male Bible scholarship has advanced exclusionary and supersessionist concepts about those "other" groups. Some of this work has already been done, especially as it relates to Judaism and gender, but much remains still unexplored. Largely thanks to feminist theological research, the issue of gender and women has been broadly examined. For instance, a feminist-scholarly anthology contains important information on feminist initiatives in German churches and universities of the past thirty years and characterizes those initiatives as mostly successful.[64] And even Manfred Oeming declares that "the feminine (feminist) perspective has gained some recognition: in some regional German churches it appears even in ordination exams; in some theology departments adjunct positions in feminist theology have become permanent and even professorships have been established for it."[65] Still most German white male Bible scholars do not bring their work into conversation with gender issues and "otherness," a situation that is certainly true for Bible scholars of other nationalities as well, and most German theology departments exist without any institutionalized pressure to include feminist and "other" research in the curriculum or in new hires. Thus it would be important to analyze the institutionalized reasons with which exclusion rather than inclusion persists in research agendas, personnel policies, and the curriculum.[66]

---

64. Gisela Matthiae et al., eds., *Feministische Theologie: Initiativen, Kirche, Universitäten: eine Erfolgs-geschichte* (Gütersloh: Gütersloher Verlagshaus, 2008).

65. Manfred Oeming, "Theologie des Alten Testaments aus der Perspektive von Frauen—was ist das und wozu soll das nützen," in *Theologie des Alten Testaments aus der Perspektive von Frauen*, ed. Manfred Oeming (Münster: LIT, 2003), 11. Again, the fact that Oeming uses the adjective "feminine" and "feminist" interchangeably indicates his cursory reading of the field.

66. The uproar about the first Bible translation in inclusive German, the *Bibel in gerechter Sprache* (*BigS*), illustrates the utter persistence of androcentric, sexist, and modern hermeneutical assumptions in many academic, journalistic, and ecclesial institutions in Germany. For a discussion on the *BigS* in English, see Susanne Scholz, "The *Bibel in gerechter Sprache* (*BigS*): The Secular Press, *Kirchenherren*, and Theology Professors React To a New German Inclusive Bible Translation," *SBL Forum* (April 2008): http://tinyurl.com/myemrds; Luzia Sutter Rehmann, "What Is the *Bibel in gerechter Sprache*? Assumptions, Process, and Goals of a New German Bible Translation," trans. and ed. Sussane Scholz, *SBL Forum* (April 2008): http://tinyurl.com/kgw3eph; Wolfgang Stegemann, "Translation or Interpretation: Intense Controversy about the New German Translation of the Bible," trans. and ed. Susanne Scholz, *SBL Forum* (April 2008): http://tinyurl.com/nxgrqnc; Irmtraud Fischer, "Why the Agitation? The Status of the *Bibel in gerechter Sprache* in Academia and the Churches," trans. and ed. Susanne Scholz, *SBL Forum* (April 2008): http://tinyurl.com/lw6hgt6; Marie-Theres Wacker, "The New Inclusive Bible Translation in the Context of (Post)modern Germany," trans. and ed. Susanne Scholz, *SBL Forum* (April 2008): http://tinyurl.com/kphg7fr.

Third, the correlation between German white male Bible scholarship and past and present societal power structures also requires further examination, namely, how biblical historicity has reinforced the a-contextualizing hermeneutics deeply linked to the sociopolitical, economic, and theo-cultural dynamics in society. For instance, James Pasto describes the connections between W. M. L. de Wette's reconstruction of biblical history and his social location in early nineteenth-century Germany. De Wette developed a "disjunctive model"[67] that classifies Judaism as a post-Babylonian development, distinguishing it from preexilic Israel/Hebraism, because "de Wette was writing his Biblical past as a metaphor for his German Protestant present" and "thus transformed a unified Israelite-Judean past into *dualistic Hebraic and Judaic pasts* in order to inscribe and authorize his German Protestant present."[68] In other words, de Wette's "post-exilic 'Judaism' was a metaphor for his 'negative' Germany and his Biblical past was a field of representation on which he sought to inscribe his German political present."[69]

The distinction between Hebrews and Jews enabled de Wette to align German Protestants with the Hebrews and to avoid affiliating them with Judaism, although, as Pasto quickly points out, liberal Protestant scholars like de Wette "opposed racial identities and repressive measures against Jews in Germany."[70] Yet "the separation between Hebrews and Jews in a Biblical past . . . serves to link Christians to Hebrews in an identity present"[71] and distinguishes "between a pristine Israel and a degenerate Judaism" that, "along with the fulfillment of the former in Jesus, became central to the ideology and identity of later German Liberal Protestants."[72] Pasto's provocative and timely call for the careful study about the "politics"[73] of biblical scholarship is long overdue. Yet even more recent publications, such as *A Farewell to the Yahwist? The Composition of the Pentateuch in Recent European Interpretation*,[74] do not address questions about social location or the politics of biblical historiography. These studies do not mind that the

67. James Pasto, "When the End Is the Beginning? Or When the Biblical Past Is the Political Present: Some Thoughts on Ancient Israel, 'Post-exilic Judaism,' and the Politics of Biblical Scholarship," *SJOT* 12, no. 2 (1998): 171.
68. Ibid., 165. Emphasis original.
69. Ibid., 171.
70. Ibid., 173.
71. Ibid.
72. Ibid.
73. Ibid., 201.
74. Thomas B. Dozeman and Konrad Schmid, eds., *A Farewell to the Yahwist? The Composition of the Pentateuch in Recent European Interpretation* (Atlanta: Society of Biblical Literature, 2006).

Old Testament historiographical debate is almost entirely populated by white male scholars from Germany and other northern European countries as well as from the United States. The absence of "other" scholars invites the question: Does the focus on biblical historiography not reinforce the field's dominant modern hermeneutics that divorces itself from questions about social location? The answer to this question is still open, and no systematic study is available that would examine how the focus on biblical historicity reinforces the a-contextualizing hermeneutics among German white male scholars.[75] In short, the development of these three research areas might offer a comprehensive understanding of the contributions of German white male Bible scholarship to past and present power structures. The three research areas might explain why this a-contextualized hermeneutics has sustained and advanced structures of domination such as colonialism, androcentrism, and other forms of oppression, while the a-contextualized hermeneutics also helped in resisting the Nazi ideology during the 1930s and 1940s in Germany.

The Quest for a Lederhosen Hermeneutics: Concluding Comments

So it is becoming clearer why it is so difficult for German white male Hebrew Bible scholars to develop context-specific interpretations. Not only have they communicated successfully within their national academic institutions the absolute necessity of an acontextualized approach, but they have also made their case around the globe. They convinced everybody else that academic scholarship on the Old Testament requires adhering to the modern hermeneutical principles of objectivity, universality, and value neutrality. Trained in this kind of *Wissenschaft*,[76] biblical scholars anywhere are thus often willing to submit to the paradigm originally developed by German scholars, whether or not it fits their contexts. The *Wissenschaft* approach is required to become a legitimately credentialed researcher because it "still dominates biblical scholarship."[77] Even today the *Wissenschaft* approach is

---

75. See the discussions in Keith W. Whitelam, *The Invention of Ancient Israel: The Silencing of Palestinian History* (New York: Routledge, 1996); Diane Banks, *Writing the History of Israel* (New York: T&T Clark, 2006).
76. The editors, Mary F. Foskett and Jeffrey Kah-Jin Kuan, make that point in the foreword of their anthology, *Ways of Being, Ways of Reading: Asian American Biblical Interpretation* (St. Louis: Chalice, 2006), xii.
77. Ibid.

still considered as academically the most rigorous and irrefutable approach to biblical literature even despite its disregard for readerly questions and concerns. In fact, its very aloofness and disconnect gives it its authority, power, and mystique. It has successfully circumvented the fact that the scientific study of the Hebrew Bible has been grounded in the German historical, political, and intellectual context. Said differently, the very denial of contextuality signifies its German male white context, selling its epistemological ethnocentrism as universality, when it is in fact a *Lederhosen* hermeneutics only.

The question is, of course, why it has been necessary to classify, even deny and reject, context specificity for German white male Bible scholarship. How has this a-contextual hermeneutics been able to uphold structures of domination? As indicated in the previous discussion, in the twentieth century the a-contextual hermeneutics helped resist Nazi ideology, as illustrated in von Rad's work. The problem is that this modern hermeneutics is still largely employed without awareness of its inherent context specificity. To start understanding these dynamics, three research areas were suggested to begin demystifying German white male Bible hermeneutics as universal and contextless and also to begin developing what is here called a *Lederhosen* hermeneutics. This hermeneutics is a hybrid, a mixture, that relies on a double logic. It is a "hermeneutics of hyphenation"[78] based on the effort of German white male Bible scholars to come to terms with relating biblical literature to an "alien" culture and society, the German one, during the past two hundred years or so.

That the insistence of context-free exegesis is not limited to the German biblical context is obvious. The next chapter discusses the ongoing effort of the US-American Christian Right to carry out its politically and religiously conservative vision of gender, family, and sexuality, and all of that with the help of Eve and Adam in Genesis 2–3.

---

78. For an elaboration of biblical hermeneutics as hybrid, mixed, and double, see Sze-kar Wan, "Betwixt and Between: Toward a Hermeneutics of Hyphenation," in Foskett and Kuan, *Ways of Being, Ways of Reading*, esp. 150–51.

7

The Forbidden Fruit for the New Eve: The Christian Right's Adaptation to the (Post)modern World

Postsecularism, Gender, and Interreligious Dialogue in Europe: Introductory Comments

In Europe, the so-called Enlightenment project has been "threefold." It aimed for "the radical separation between the realm of Faith and that of Reason; entrusting the ruling of the public sphere exclusively to the dictates of the realm of Reason; and the promotion of liberty and equality for all."[1] Yet social-religious dynamics are changing the Enlightenment project in Europe. For instance, Michel Rosenfeld observes that religion has become "derelativized" and "deprivatized, and as a corollary secularism falls off its modernist pedestal and becomes yet one more religion or purely subjective postmodern ideology."[2] In other words, it appears that in Europe, "reason loses its modernist grip" and "religion (moved from within) finds more room to project its truth

---

1. Michel Rosenfeld, "Introduction: Can Constitutionalism, Secularism and Religion Be Reconciled in an Era of Globalization and Religious Revival?," *Cardozo Law Review* 30 (2009): 2333.
2. Ibid., 2336.

as absolute and exclusive, while secularism viewed from the outside becomes more susceptible to being cast as yet one more (false) religion."[3] Secular values and convictions have lost their power. They are viewed as a belief system, similar to religious values and convictions. Consequently, religion leaves the private realm and stakes its claim in public life.

This dynamic has real-life consequences in Europe. A filmmaker is murdered on the street, Muslim writers are threatened with murder for their fiction, newspaper cartoons create unexpected fury,[4] and Europeans find themselves at odds when they try to explain the reasonableness of their secular positions. Does the majority have the right to impose its views on the minority, and does the minority have the right to ignore the values of the land? One scholar, José Casanova, points to the heart of the matter when he writes:

> What makes the intolerant tyranny of the secular, liberal majority justifiable in principle is not just the democratic principle of majority rule, but rather the secularist teleological assumption built into theories of modernization that one set of norms is reactionary, fundamentalist, and antimodern, while the other set is progressive, liberal and modem.[5]

The problem is that the "secular alternative" has come to sound as exclusionary and intolerant as its religious equivalent. In postsecular European societies Enlightenment principles do not have the final say anymore because a Muslim minority rejects being confined to the realm of "MTD," that is, moralistic therapeutic deism. Instead, it has become clear that both religious and secular arguments are part of public discourse today.

Since the 1960s, sociopolitical and cultural transformations have been brought about by progressive grassroots and the anti-Vietnam movements in the United States. Black power, women's rights, gay rights, and even the eco-justice movements have made racism, sexism, homophobia, and ecological exploitation key issues in Western consciousness. Joined by philosophical, scientific, and epistemological inquiries into the nature of knowledge, the discourse has moved from modern to postmodern principles of knowing. Thus today's Europeans

---

3. Ibid.
4. Lauren Fulton, "Europe's Immigrant Problem: Integrating Minority Populations," *Harvard International Review* 31, no. 3 (2009): 28–33.
5. José Casanova, "Immigration and the New Religious Pluralism: A European Union/United States Comparison," in *Democracy and the New Religious Pluralism*, ed. Thomas Banchoff (New York: Oxford University Press, 2007), 65.

recognize diversity, globalization, and the shifting sociocultural and socioeconomic paradigms as a given to human life on earth. Since Western European countries, after the devastation of the Second World War, have oriented themselves toward the United States, they have become open to the new sociocultural developments coming from the West.[6] Religion has come to be seen as part of the past problems in Europe, as something to be left behind when society aims for secular and rational cooperation with the world.[7] Yet these comprehensive transformations have not eliminated all religious discourse and practice,[8] and so the question has become: "How should liberal, tolerant Europeans protect their values, even as they protect the rights of less liberal minorities in their midst?"[9] When religious minorities reject secular values and, in fact, promote fundamentalist religious positions, European societies are confronted with a public reemergence of religion that they believed had been overcome.

This development bewilders secularized Europeans because it exposes "a series of unresolved issues which—for decades, if not centuries—have been placed in the realm of the private."[10] One of these unresolved issues is the fact that secularism does not convince everybody to detach themselves from religion. Another issue is the fear that a reemergence of public religion might lead to new religious strife, which haunted generations of Europeans in the past. Today's secularized Europeans wonder why the principle of "live and let live" does not offer an acceptable solution to everybody. They worry that the Enlightenment principles have been compromised because no acceptable answer can be found to the question: "Who will give way to whom in these very difficult issues?"[11] In the meantime, the majority rules prohibit a Muslim minority by law from publicly practicing their religion as they see fit. The legal battles over headscarves, minarets, and

---

6. Susanne Scholz, "Going West: Zur Situation deutscher Theologinnen," in *Zwischenräume: Deutsche feministische Theologinnen im Ausland*, ed. Katharina von Kellenbach and Susanne Scholz (Münster: LIT, 2000), 55–67.

7. Peter Berger, Grace Davie, and Effie Forkas, *Religious America, Secular Europe? A Theme and Variations* (Aldershot: Ashgate, 2008), 120.

8. Sam Harris, *The End of Faith: Religion, Terror, and the Future of Reason* (New York: Norton, 2004); see also Harvey G. Cox, *The Secular City: Secularization and Urbanization in Theological Perspective* (New York: Macmillan, 1965).

9. See, e.g., "In Knots over Headscarves," *Economist*, September 19, 2009, 64; Robert Marquand, "No Burqas in France? Ruling Party Moves to Ban Veils in Public," *Christian Science Monitor*, December 23, 2009, http://tinyurl.com/ko3uko6; Ruben Seth Fogel, "Headscarves in German Public Schools: Religious Minorities are Welcome in Germany, Unless God Forbid They are Religious," *New York Law School Review* 51 (2007): 620–53.

10. Berger, Davie, and Forkas, *Religious America, Secular Europe*, 105.

11. Ibid.

immigration policies are only the tip of the iceberg of the profound sociopolitical, economic, and cultural-intellectual changes taking place in European countries today.

These changes also affect Christian discourse in Europe. For instance, Pope Benedict XVI chastises multicultural tolerance as the cause of social rootlessness, urges Europeans to stand firm on Christian values, and then reasserts traditional family roles and women's child-rearing responsibilities as key principles of a European identity. His social position aligns with fundamentalist Muslim views and the Christian Right in the United States. To all of them, only a society anchored in religion provides prosperity and stability in contrast to societies that favor multicultural and secular values, including socially progressive views on gender.[12]

It should not come as a surprise that gender and women's roles have thus become a focal point in recent political discourse. Gender is contested territory because of the long-standing patriarchal religious traditions in Western countries.[13] This essay provides an account of the ongoing presence of these views as they shape Christian conservatism today. The discussion illuminates the profound impact Christian conservatism has had on Western countries for centuries and the challenges it still poses. If nothing changes, the Christian Right will represent the dominant Christian discourse, a prospect that secularized Europeans will find disturbing, but it will perhaps also encourage them to support the development of progressive religious discourse. Thus an understanding of the hermeneutical assumptions and strategies, as currently advanced by the US-American Christian Right, provides insights into the European situation. It teaches how to engage religious discourse effectively without committing two opposing but interrelated hermeneutical fallacies. One is the "secular fallacy," which rejects religious discourse as irrational and irrelevant. The other is the "fundamentalist fallacy," which accepts the Christian Right's position as the only Christian belief system, as if alternative Christian and other religious positions did not exist.

The following analysis elaborates on this dynamic. It outlines key considerations about the Christian Right's discourse on gender, family, and sexuality, as they have emerged from selected publications from the Christian Right. Another section shows that the secular and fundamentalist fallacies are interrelated, a point that reactions to inclusive

12. Ibid., 108.
13. Ibid., 120.

146

Bible translations exemplify. Reviews from the secular and academic press of the first German inclusive Bible translation, *Bibel in gerechter Sprache* (*BigS*), and the Christian Right's debate on "gender-neutral" Bible translations document that the secular and fundamentalist fallacies are indeed interrelated. Both cannot see beyond a literalist-scientific paradigm, and thus both reject religiously progressive alternatives.[14] A final section exposes literalist hermeneutical arguments as part of the scientific-empiricist epistemology, shaping the Western intellectual and scientific worldview since the so-called Enlightenment. It demonstrates the continuing difficulties of secular and religiously conservative constituencies in Western countries to develop an intellectual understanding of religion, based on postmodern views, that does not continue to endorse structures of domination, especially as they relate to gender, family, and sexuality.

The Christian Right's Responses to (Post)modern Discourse and Practice on Gender, Family, and Sexuality

The Christian Right is an inherently US-American phenomenon with its own particular history in the American sociopolitical and religious infrastructure that reaches back to the late nineteenth- and early twentieth-century battles over Darwin's theory of evolution. A religiously, politically, socially, and economically powerful movement, it is organized from the grassroots level up. Since the 1990s it has been one of the most visible and prominent movements in the United States. This holds true even after the presidential election of President Obama in 2008 because, on the grassroots level, Christian conservative organizations remain deeply entrenched within local politics despite some claims of an increasing introspection among the Christian Right's organizations.[15] The Christian Right's responses to (post)modern challenges to gender, family, and sexuality are not only well articulated but also well distributed within the many media outlets of US society, so much so that Christian Right's views are usually identified as "the" Christian position on gender, family, and sexuality. Many people, especially if

14. Elisabeth Schüssler Fiorenza, *The Power of the Word: Scripture and the Rhetoric of Empire* (Minneapolis: Fortress Press, 2007), 239–66.
15. See, e.g., Americans United for Separation of Church and State, "Is the 'Righteous Right' Dead? Hardly, Say Church-State Experts," *Church and State* 60, no. 4 (2007): 11–14. Also see "Religious Right Power in Washington Is Greatly Diminished, Says Americans United," November 5, 2008, https://au.org/media/press-releases/religious-right-power-in-washington-is-greatly-diminished-says-americans-united (accessed June 8, 2017).

they are secular or only loosely affiliated with Christian or other religious organizations, assume that the Christian Right's theological positions represent mainstream Christian doctrine and practice.

Since the Christian Right is firmly anchored in traditional Christian doctrine, its insistence on a public voice in the United States contributes to illuminating the European interreligious situation. It exemplifies that also within Christianity the urge to be a public agent in political, social, cultural, and economic life plays a major role today. The marginalization of religion to the private realm—a consequence of the secularizing paradigm in Europe—is thus an unacceptable position not only to Islam but also to the Christian Right. Due to secularization, Christian organizations in Europe have largely accepted privatized functions. Yet Islamic fundamentalist communities in European countries have challenged this arrangement, similar to the Christian Right in the United States. An understanding of the Christian Right's discourse is thus helpful to the European context because it illustrates the general tendency among today's conservative-fundamentalist religious communities to seek visibility and influence in politics, culture, and society in general.

It is also crucial to recognize that the Christian Right's success in defining its message as *the* Christian position makes it difficult in the United States to communicate politically, socially, and religiously progressive ideas about religion, gender, family, and sexuality without engaging the Christian Right's discourse. The problem is a narrowly conceptualized hermeneutical framework in which the Christian Right successfully dominates the interpretation of Christian texts and traditions on the one hand and a Christian understanding of gender, family, and sexuality on the other. Thus ideas about religion, gender, family, and sexuality remain stuck in a Christian discourse that has contributed to sociopolitical and cultural-theological conservatism for centuries.

Upholding the Bible: The Christian Right's Struggle against the Gender Revolution

Three major positions characterize the Christian Right's discourse on gender and the Bible within the context of conservative American Christianity.[16] All three positions assume that the Bible is the "actual"

---

16. Susanne Scholz, "The Christian Right's Discourse on Gender and the Bible," *JFSR* 21 (2005): 83-104; Scholz, "Bible Truth, Mega Churches, and the Christian Right in the USA," in *Theologie von Frauen*

or "inspired word of God," but they differ on the significance of gender in biblical literature. First, probably the most influential and politically powerful position is called "complementarianism;" sometimes it is also identified as "hierarchicalism" or "traditionalism."[17] Complementarians maintain that women and men are equal according to the biblical record but have different tasks in church and society. Second, another position is called "egalitarianism," and in evangelical circles followers of this position are considered to be "feminists."[18] They reject the complementarian notion of "equal but different" because to them the Bible supports women's equal participation in church and society. They also struggle against being silenced or excluded from the larger evangelical community, in which the complementarian position dominates. Third, yet another position contributes to the Christian Right's discourse on gender, and this view is held by Christian theologians who affiliate neither with the complementarians nor the egalitarians. This "moderate evangelical" group engages Christian conservative, mainstream, and even progressive Bible research, and mainstream publishers such as Paulist Press and Eerdmans Publishing Company print their work.

A central feature of the Christian Right's discourse on gender, family, and sexuality is the sincere commitment with which proponents relate their Bible readings to contemporary gender practices in American church and society. They consider a discussion about biblical gender depictions not merely as an academic exercise but as a matter directly related to today's societal and ecclesiastical life. To them, the Bible connects to today's world because the Bible is the single and most authoritative guide to evangelical Christian faith. To be sure, distinctions can and need to be made among the complementarians, egalitarians, and moderate evangelicals, but overall they agree that they present biblical, and not their personal or scholarly, views on gender,

---

für Frauen? Chancen und Probleme der Rückbindung feministischer Theologie an die Praxis: Beiträge zum Internationalen Kongress anlässlich des zwanzigjährigen Gründungsjubiläums der Europäischen Gesellschaft für theologische Forschung von Frauen (ESWTR), ed. Irmtraud Fischer (Münster: LIT, 2007), 202–26.

17. Complementarians are "uncomfortable" with the label "'traditionalist" and outright reject the label "hierarchicalist" because it does not connote "mutual interdependence"; see, e.g., John Piper and Wayne A. Grudem, eds., *Recovering Biblical Manhood and Womanhood: A Response to Evangelical Feminism* (Wheaton: Crossway, 1991), xiv. For a rejection of the term "complementarian'" and a reference to "traditionalist," see Rebecca Merrill Groothuis, *Good News for Women: A Biblical Picture of Gender Equality* (Grand Rapids: Baker, 1997), 15. See also Groothuis, *Women Caught in the Conflict: The Culture War between Traditionalism and Feminism* (Grand Rapids: Baker, 1994).

18. Sometimes they are also called "biblical feminists"; see Jack Cottrell, *Gender Roles and the Bible: Creation, the Fall, and Redemption* (Joplin, MO: College Press, 1994), 18–20. For an extensive discussion of egalitarian biblical feminism, see Jack Cottrell, *Feminism and the Bible: An Introduction to Feminism for Christians* (Joplin, MO: College Press, 1992), 239–338.

family, and sexuality. All of them share a sincere commitment to the Bible, a passionate struggle over the value of patriarchal gender roles, a lack of engagement with mainstream scholarship, and an attachment to gender essentialism. To them, the Bible should be the foundation for gender practice in today's society because they believe that Christians should relate biblical teachings to today's society and live by them.

Accordingly, theologians of the Christian Right assert that biblical teachings help readers understand "God's good design" of "God-given" gender identities.[19] One complementarian, Alexander Strauch, explains:

> I emphasize the Scriptures because the answer to this debate (about gender) is found in God's Word, not in books of sociology or anthropology. . . . It is essential that Christians hear clearly the voice of Cod through the Word of God in order to counteract secular society's pervasive influence.[20]

The Bible supersedes contemporary convictions and customs, because, as Jack Cottrell claims, the Bible is "the inspired and inerrant Word of God and . . . the final authority on all matters."[21] To Bible readers of the Christian Right, it is crucial to reconcile the sacred text with a culture that is not Bible-centered but increasingly diverse in terms of religious, cultural, and gender practices.

The Christian Right's effort to correlate the Bible with modern life is more than a century old. What is new is the attack on contemporary gender practices packaged into traditional, that is, androcentric, theological rhetoric[22] that takes full advantage of contemporary media and marketing tools. Its opposition to the "gender revolution," which goes back to the 1960s, is a radical departure from biblical, apostolic Christianity, and so the movement speaks in essentializing and dualistic categories of biblical "manhood" and "womanhood." The aim to define women's and gender roles is based on a divinely sanctioned order.

19. John Piper and Wayne A. Grudem, eds., *Recovering Biblical Manhood and Womanhood: A Response to Evangelical Feminism* (Wheaton: Crossway, 1991), 33.

20. Alexander Strauch, *Men and Women, Equal Yet Different: A Brief Study of the Biblical Passages on Gender* (Littleton, CO: Lewis & Roth, 1999), 3–4.

21. Cottrell, *Feminism and the Bible*, 21.

22. The official position of the Roman Catholic Church shares this position; see "Letter to the Bishops on the Collaboration of Men and Women in the Church and the World," Vatican website, May 31, 2004, http://tinyurl.com/lw7c4h2.

The New Eve: Teaching Women to Be Good Wives and Mothers

The Christian Right's strategy to advance traditional theology with savvy marketing tools is apparent in a popularly marketed book entitled *The New Eve: Choosing God's Best for Your Life*.[23] In fact, this book caught my attention when I was browsing the Christianity section in one of the big bookstore chains in New York City in 2008. Written by Robert Lewis, with Jeremy Howard, and published by B&H Publishing Group, formerly known as Broadman & Holman, an evangelical publishing house that grounds its vision in "biblical authority,"[24] the volume was listed with an Amazon.com sales rank of 51,727 on April 12, 2009, certainly not an entirely reliable comparison tool. Still, feminist Christian classics ranked considerably lower in April 2009. For instance, Elisabeth Schüssler Fiorenza's *In Memory of Her* ranked 627,970, Phyllis Trible's *Texts of Terror* was at 211,496, and Mary Daly's *Beyond God the Father: Toward a Philosophy of Women's Liberation* made it to 262,657.

What is remarkable about this book is its comprehensive offline and online media packaging. The book was launched with a website, which contains interview videos of the author and video clips for each chapter; a CD comes with the book.[25] Previously, Robert Lewis had developed a small media empire on men's ministry and had written books, such as *Raising a Modern Day Knight* or *Rocking the Roles: Building a Win-Win Marriage*, all of them available with DVDs and website order forms.[26] Lewis's community-building strategies called "Men's Fraternity" have been replicated in many church ministries, and numerous testimonials attest to the apparent success of his instructions.[27] In *The New Eve*, Lewis explains that women asked him to write a book on "authentic biblical womanhood" because they noticed "so many positive changes in the men in their lives" after the men had read Lewis's books. Lewis complied and conceptualized *The New Eve* as a "counterpart" to his "teachings on authentic biblical manhood . . . in the context of the modern world."[28]

---

23. Robert Lewis, *The New Eve: Choosing God's Best for Your Life* (Nashville: B&H, 2008).
24. See the website of B&H Academic, http://bhpublishinggroup.com/academic/ (accessed on April 27, 2010).
25. See http://bhpublishinggroup.com/neweve/ (accessed on April 27, 2010; see the Wayback Machine at http://archive.org/web/web.php to access the publisher's book website that does not exist anymore as of June 9, 2017).
26. See, e.g., *Raising a Modern-Day Knight*, http://www.rmdk.com/online-training-program.
27. See Men's Fraternity, http://www.mensfraternity.com.
28. See *The New Eve* website, http://tinyurl.com/kehccos.

In *The New Eve*, Lewis explains that contemporary Western women face many challenges regarding their careers and families. Although women can have it all, few are happy, and many face "a painful life of regret"[29] after they made the wrong choice. Five issues confuse today's women, according to Lewis: one issue relates to the changed definitions of "femininity," another to the emphasis on having a career, yet another to their relationships with men, one to the refusal of becoming mothers, and finally one to "the maze of unlimited choices."[30] Lewis relates women's situation to a Christian traditional paradigm that distinguishes between Eve and Mary, the "old" Eve and the "new" Eve. This is a "scriptural pattern," Lewis asserts, that envisions "biblical womanhood like that of Adam and Jesus."[31] Lewis defines biblical manhood as following the models of Adam and Jesus. Thus, when he searches for a similar paradigm for women, he asks himself: "If Jesus is the second Adam, is there a second Eve? Almost as soon as I asked that question, I had my answer. *Mary*. This special woman presents herself in such a way as to be considered Eve's righteous twin. Any serious reader of Scripture can't help but notice this."[32] Like classic Christian doctrine, then, Lewis emphasizes two biblical women, Eve and Mary, and renames Mary as the "new Eve." They serve as models for today's women.

To Lewis, the biblical "old" or "first" Eve represents a type of woman who enjoys "immense freedoms and opportunities" but makes "the wrong choices that squandered her potential." As in classic Christian theology, Eve is a negative role model. She takes the forbidden fruit, which Lewis parallels with women who focus on their careers only and do not devote their full attention to husbands and children. They are falling prey to the temptation of the "old" Eve and ignore "God's command" in Genesis 1:28 ("Be fruitful and multiply."). To them, "motherhood is no longer automatic or even a top priority."[33]

Lewis advises that Christian women make a better choice, one that adheres to the principles of Mary, "the New Eve," who "knows how to navigate our modem world and its endless opportunities."[34] The new Eve "makes the right choices" because she grounds her life in the Bible. Her life is not committed to establishing a career

29. Robert Lewis, *The New Eve*, xxi.
30. Ibid., 27–39.
31. Ibid., 75.
32. Ibid.
33. Ibid., 37.
34. Ibid.

and having professional success. Instead, it is defined by ten phases. It begins with being a single adult, then moves to "single and engaged," "newly married and no children," "married with preschoolers," "married with grade-schoolers," "married and younger adult children," "married and empty nester," "mother-in-law and grandparent," "late-in-life widow," and finally it ends in being a "glorified saint."[35] A woman's "core calling" is to nurture a "deep companionship" with her husband, raise and launch healthy children," and "advance God's kingdom."[36] A new Eve's life is characterized by being wife and mother.

It is impressive and, in fact, irritating that this traditional patriarchal theological perspective has gained considerable popularity in Christian Right circles. Countless similar publications exist. For instance, Carolyn McCulley published a book titled *Radical Womanhood: Feminine Faith in a Feminist World*, in which she explains "how feminism came about, how it influenced my thinking, and why femininity as defined by the Bible wasn't a throwback to some horrible era."[37] To her, a woman's life has to be grounded in the Bible, which means that her life is defined by marriage, having and raising children, listening to her husband, and sitting "at the feet of Jesus in order to receive from Him."[38] The message is very similar in other publications, such as Elyse Fitzpatrick's *Helper by Design: God's Perfect Plan for Women in Marriage*[39] or Nancy Leigh DeMoss's *Lies Women Believe and the Truth That Sets Them Free.*[40] These books illustrate the tendency in the Christian Right's movement to engage media and marketing tools to effectively communicate conventional androcentric messages to women. It is "reactionary" Christian theology that responds to the (post)modern world in a technologically advanced and attractive packaging format. Other examples abound, such as the teachings of Beth Moore and her Living Proof Ministries, which targets women audiences and increasingly also men.[41] In other words, gender is an important issue to the Christian Right and helps the movement to reinforce androcentric gender roles as a "defense" against (post)modern developments.

35. Ibid., 93.
36. Ibid., 171.
37. Carolyn McCulley, *Radical Womanhood: Feminine Faith in a Feminist World* (Chicago: Moody Press, 2008), 28.
38. Ibid., 199.
39. Elyse Fitzpatrick, *Helper by Design: God's Perfect Plan for Women in Marriage* (Chicago: Moody Press, 2003).
40. Nancy Leigh DeMoss, *Lies Women Believe and the Truth That Sets Them Free* (Chicago: Moody Press, 2001).
41. Living Proof Ministries, http://www.lproof.org/; http://livingproohninistries.blogspot.com/2009/01/drive-thru-bible.html (accessed on April 27, 2010).

The relative success of the Christian Right's theological perspective is deeply grounded in the sociopolitical developments that have fostered multicultural and secular ways of life. The Christian Right also fights the Enlightenment position that relegates religion to the private realm. Similar to fundamentalist Muslim communities in Europe, the US movement asserts public influence on sociocultural issues, especially but not exclusively on gender. They reject multicultural and secular ways of life because they want to bring back religious convictions into a secularized society. In turn, secularized constituencies resist religious claims toward public power. A circular pattern of assertion and resistance locks the discourse into an ongoing cycle. Neither group understands the limited hermeneutical framework within which it operates. The debate on inclusive Bible translations illustrates this dynamic, and so the next section focuses on it.

The Bible as "Men's" Words: The Challenge of Inclusive Bible Translations

The hermeneutical tensions between the fundamentalist and secular fallacies found an outlet in the debate on inclusive Bible translations. It shows that the insistence on a literal-scientific hermeneutics is shared by both Christian conservative and secular commentators when they are confronted with an alternative hermeneutical model that advances a progressive sociopolitical and cultural agenda. The first inclusive German Bible translation, *Bibel in gerechter Sprache* (literally "Bible in just language")[42] indicates that the problem is not limited to the Christian Right's insistence on a "literal" Bible translation but also characterizes secular responses.

In October 2006, when the *Bibel in gerechter Sprache* (*BigS*) was published, a major theological-intellectual upheaval erupted in Germany. The *BigS*, as this translation is called, provoked strong, even shrill,

---

42. Ulrike Bail et al., eds., *Bibel in gerechter Sprache*, 3rd ed. (Gütersloh: Gütersloher Verlagshaus, 2006); see also Susanne Scholz, "The *Bibel in gerechter Sprache* (*BigS*): The Secular Press, *Kirchenherren*, and Theology Professors React to a New German Inclusive Bible Translation," *SBL Forum* (April 2008): http://tinyurl.com/myemrds; Irmtraud Fischer, "Why the Agitation? The Status of the *Bibel in gerechter Sprache* in Academia and the Churches," trans. and ed. Susanne Scholz, *SBL Forum* (April 2008): http://tinyurl.com/lw6hgt6; Wolfgang Stegemann, "Translation or Interpretation: Intense Controversy about the New German Translation of the Bible," trans. and ed. Susanne Scholz, *SBL Forum* (April 2008): http://tinyurl.com/nxgrqnc; Luzia Sutter Rehmann, "What Is the *Bibel in gerechter Sprache*? Assumptions, Process, and Goals of a New German Bible Translation," trans. and ed. Sussane Scholz, *SBL Forum* (April 2008): http://tinyurl.com/kgw3eph; Marie-Theres Wacker, "The New Inclusive Bible Translation in the Context of (Post)modern Germany," trans. and ed. Susanne Scholz, *SBL Forum* (April 2008): http://tinyurl.com/kphg7fr.

reactions in daily, weekly, and other newspapers and magazines, as well as in academic and ecclesiastical journals. Certainly, the *BigS* has also found many supporters and is already in its fourth edition, but in post-Christian Germany, a theological publication—no less a Bible translation—has rarely, if ever, produced such sweeping reactions from the secular media and the church.

Interestingly, the new inclusive Bible translation has stimulated manifold responses from journalists who do not usually engage theological issues, much less biblical scholarship. German-speaking countries are, as is well known, secular, and religion is viewed as an outdated area of intellectual discourse, although its social contributions are valued and even cherished. Yet the new translation has changed this perception—if only for a relatively brief moment. Columns and reviews of renowned and local daily and weekly papers alike express great skepticism of the *BigS*, which reflects a deep-seated androcentric bias prevalent in German-speaking countries even today. Examples abound in secular and popular media discussions. In April 2006, several months prior to the release of the Bible translation, Robert Leicht questioned the legitimacy of the project in the weekly newspaper *Die Zeit*. He maintained that the translation allegedly confuses the distinction between translation and interpretation. This confusion creates a "real danger" because, so Leicht, the *BigS* misrepresents the *Urtext*.[43]

This naive hermeneutical view of the translation process is not an exception. Other reviewers, such as Heike Schmoll, also charged that the *BigS* overturns Luther's principle that advises to follow the meaning of the original text. Schmoll argued that the new translation "does not allow the text to speak for itself" and "reverses the principle into its absurd opposite."[44] Some reviewers, such as Edgar S. Hasse, tried a different path and ridiculed specific translation decisions that aim for inclusivity. For instance, Hasse did not want to believe that female and male shepherds came to see the newborn Christ child in the manger. Other commentators made cynical remarks about God receiving feminine names, such as *Die Ewige* (the Eternal), whereas "the devil remains always male."[45] The weekly *Der Spiegel* published an article in the very week during which the Bible's release was celebrated by editors,

---

43. Robert Leicht, "Kein Wort sie wollen lassen stahn," *Die Zeit*, June 4, 2006, http://www.zeit.de/1989/52/das-wort-sie-sollen-lassen-stahn.
44. Heike Schmoll, "Befreit zur religiösen Mündigkeit," *Frankfurter Allgemeine*, October 30, 2006, 1.
45. Edgar S. Hasse, "Weihnachten mit den 'Hirtinnen,'" *Die Welt*, December 3, 2006, https://www.welt.de/print-welt/article699817/Weihnachten-mit-den-Hirtinnen.html; see also Elisabeth Gössman et al., *Der Teufel blieb männlich* (Neukirchen-Vluyn: Neukirchener Verlag, 2007).

translators, and supporters. The author, Matthias Schulz, wondered if "modernists are messing up the Sacred Scriptures" when "female and male shepherds hurry to the manger" and "male and female neighbors"[46] surround Jesus in his childhood.[47] Simplistic hermeneutical assumptions and outright hostility made for a rather unpleasant debate. Yet, for the first time, the general German-speaking public confronted the extent of theological discriminatory patterns—a positive effect in a contest in which the secular fallacy was taken for granted and considered to be superior to religious discourse of any kind.

Predictably, various church bodies and Christian theologians also reacted to the historic publication. Perhaps equally expected is the forcefulness of the attack on the Bible's editors, translators, and even grassroots supporters. Many critics used a harsh and vengeful tone that dismissed the project as theologically invalid and flimsy.[48] A retired bishop and translator of a well-known New Testament translation, Ulrich Wilckens, even went so far as to accuse the editors and translators of "heresy" and a "simply wrong translation."[49] Other theology professors asserted that this Bible translation "goes behind the ideas of the Protestant Reformers . . . serving theological and political interests"[50] of the translators only. Still others contended that the *BigS* hits rock bottom in the modern history of Bible interpretation.[51] And systematic theologian Ingolf U. Dalferth declared the translation

---

46. For other reviews in the popular press, see also "Umstrittene Übersetzung: Die Schlange hatte mehr drauf," *Der Spiegel*, October 25, 2006, http://tinyurl.com/kkxp5g9; "Nicht zum Gebrauch im Gottesdienst geeignet," June 5, 2007, http://www.faz.net/aktuell/politik/bibel-in-gerechter-sprache-nicht-zum-gebrauch-im-gottesdienst-geeignet-1433739.html; Ursula Persak, "In Gottes Namen: Eine Neuübersetzung der Bibel berücksichtigte Erkenntnisse der Geschlechterforschung," *Nürnberger Nachrichten*, May 1, 2007, www.nn-online.de; Katharina Eckstein, "Die Bibel aus dem Gleichstellungsbüro," *Kölner Stadt-Anzeiger*, June 6, 2007, www.ksta.de; Uwe Birnstein, "Sagen Sie mal, Hirtin: Interviews mit Personen der Bibel," *Sonntagsblatt Bayern*, December 23, 2007, www.son tagsblatt-bayem.de. All websites were last accessed on April 27, 2010.
47. Matthias Schulz, "Wortsalat im Garten Eden," *Der Spiegel*, October 30, 2006, 190 (http://tinyurl.com/le5z9ws).
48. For a comprehensive collection of academic and ecclesial statements on the inclusive Bible, see "Kontroverse um die 'Bibel in gerechter Sprache,'" *epd-Dokumentation*, April 24, 2007, 4–83; "Bibel in gerechter Sprache (2): 'Sola scriptura'—Zur Aktualität des Protestantischen Erbes," *epd-Dokumentation*, May 29, 2007, 4–40; "Bibel in gerechter Sprache (3): Tradition erneuem—Glauben starken," *epd-Dokumentation*, July 24, 2007, 4–37.
49. Ulrich Wilckens, "Theologisches Gutachten zur 'Bibel in gerechter Sprache,'" *epd-Dokumentation*, April 24, 2007, 30; see also Luise Schottroff, "Stellungnahme zum theologischen Gutachten von Ulrich Wilckens zur Bibel in gerechter Sprache," *epd-Dokumentation*, July 24, 2007, 34–37.
50. Ingolf U. Dalferth and Jens Schröter, *Bibel in gerechter Sprache: Kritik eines misslungenen Versuchs* (Tübingen: Mohr Siebeck, 2007), 19; see also Jens Schröter, "Kritische Anmerkungen zur 'Bibel in gerechter Sprache'," *epd-Dokumentation*, April 24, 2007, 18–20.
51. Ulrich H. J. Kortner, "Bibel oder nicht Bibel: Das ist hier die Frage! Zur Kritik der 'Bibel in gerechter Sprache,'" *epd-Dokumentation*, April 24, 2007, 23.

"theologically bankrupt" and "philologically, historically, and theologically useless."[52]

This extremely heated, even intellectually violent, debate should not surprise if one understands the implications of the two fallacies mentioned above. The secular fallacy accepts the Christian Right's narrow definition of what is the hermeneutically "correct" approach to theological discourse, particularly when the topic is related to gender, family, and sexuality. It is a hermeneutics that Elisabeth Schüssler Fiorenza defines as "undemocratic"[53] for its deep embeddedness in imperialistic epistemology. Such an epistemology refutes the insights of a postmodern hermeneutics that affirms the multiplicity, indeterminacy, and infinity of all interpretations.

Similar to the secularized and academic press in Germany, the Christian Right in the United States also opposes inclusive Bible translations. Its adherents reject what they call "gender neutral" Bible translations, especially after the British publisher Hodder & Stoughton released the NIVI, an inclusive edition of the New International Version, in 1996. The outrage was so large in US-American Christian Right circles that the American publisher, Zondervan, decided to postpone the publication of this edition in the United States. In fact, the NIVI has yet to be published. Detailed descriptions of the ensuing outrage exist. For instance, D. A. Carson, a complementarian, provides a fair description of the heated responses from other complementarian and egalitarian Christians.[54] He asserts that the inclusive-translation debate is not new and has occupied translators for centuries. His example from the first printed English New Testament translation by William Tyndale, published in 1526, is a case in point. Carson shows that Tyndale selected the word "children" when he translated the Greek noun *huioi* (sons) in Matthew 5:9: "Blessed are the peacemakers, for they shall be called the children of God," although the Greek noun is "sons." Carson also refers to individual complementarian assessments of the NIV with the NIVI to illustrate their concerns and contestations. One of them is Wayne Grudem, who objects to changing singular pronouns to plural to eliminate gender specificity, as in John 14:23: "If anyone loves me, he will obey my teaching. My Father will love him and we will come to him and

52. Ingolf U. Dalferth, "Der Ewige und die Ewige: Die 'Bibel in gerechter Sprache'—weder richtig noch gerecht, sondern konfus," *Neue Zürcher Zeitung*, November 18, 2006, http://tinyurl.com/l27eedo.
53. Elisabeth Schüssler Fiorenza, *Democratizing Biblical Studies: Toward an Emancipatory Educational Space* (Louisville: Westminster John Knox, 2009).
54. D. A. Carson, *The Inclusive Language Debate: A Plea for Realism* (Grand Rapids: Baker, 1998), 15–38, 183–92.

make our home with him" (NIV). The NIVI replaces the singular masculine with plural pronouns: "Those who love me will obey my teaching. My Father will love them, and we will come to them and make our home with them."

Grudem is concerned that the NIVI loses the individual person and speaks of Father and Son dwelling among a group of people.[55] Reviewing this and other discussions on the NIVI, Carson concludes that passions run high and "some people . . . are extraordinarily self-disciplined and gracious, and many . . . are between the extremes."[56] But he wonders: "Where do we go from here?"[57] At the end of his book he offers this response:

> Inclusive language has not swept everything in front of it away. . . . Yet so far as I can see, the move toward inclusive language in the English-speaking world has not yet come close to cresting. . . . As far as I can read the situation, the times they are a-changing and the English language with them.[58]

Such a statement is quite unusual for someone of the Christian Right, which has tried hard to incorporate "traditional," that is, androcentric, theology into contemporary faith perspectives.

Others have been less sympathetic in recognizing the merits of inclusive Bible translations, classifying "the current attack upon the received linguistic structure of Christianity" as "an antagonistic religious discourse."[59] In fact, according to Robert W. Jenson, "the current crisis" compares to the "gnostic crisis of the second and third centuries and the crisis of vulgar Enlightenment at the hinge of the eighteenth and nineteenth centuries."[60] In his view, proponents of inclusive Bible translations follow the "gnostic spirit" when they believe that "we have continuously . . . [to] make up language in which to speak of God." Instead, Jenson claims, "Christianity" knows that "we are given language that is immune to our manipulating."[61] Jenson's statement shows that he assumes a literalist-naturalizing translation theory that refutes human involvement in the biblical meaning-making process. It adheres

55. Ibid., 31–32.
56. Ibid., 37.
57. Ibid., 38.
58. Ibid., 192.
59. Robert W. Jenson, "The Father, He . . . ," in *Speaking the Christian God: The Holy Trinity and the Challenge of Feminism*, ed. Alvin F. Kimel (Grand Rapids: Eerdmans, 1992), 92.
60. Ibid., 96.
61. Ibid., 109.

to a literalist-scientific hermeneutics because it rejects the notion of a human-involved process in the creation of textual meanings.

The same hermeneutical stance appears in a detailed treatise against inclusive Bible translations written by complementarians Vern S. Poythress and Wayne A. Grudem.[62] The two writers present a history of what they call "gender-neutral" Bible translations. This book discusses a wide array of issues. It affirms the need to believe in the inerrancy of Scripture; it outlines how translations should be done; it provides details for "permissible changes in translating gender-related terms" and "unacceptable changes that eliminate references to men"; and it discusses the "generic 'He'" and the "feminist opposition to the generic 'He.'" Yet like Jenson, Poythress and Grudem also claim that "profound spiritual issues" are involved in the translation disputes when they maintain:

> On one side stands feminism and egalitarianism, promoting its own way of salvation and distorting the truth, insisting that there should be no gender-based differences between status, prominence, or authority of one person and another. On the other side stands the teaching of the Bible that God affirms both the honor of all human beings and the God-ordained differences among them, including differences in men's and women's roles in marriage.[63]

They think they are on the side of God, charging that inclusive translators put their own ideas first. They do not acknowledge that all translations are interpretations, which exposes their work as being grounded in a literalist-scientific epistemology. Their modernist-fundamentalist stance conveniently ignores the various developments in translation studies, such as Vermeer's *skopos* theory of translation (i.e., what is the purpose of translation), systems theories of translation (i.e., what is the position of the translated literature in the historical and literary systems of the target culture), or the cultural and ideological turns in translation theories (i.e., what are the interactions between translation and culture; how does culture influence and constrain translation; and what are the larger issues of context, history, and convention).[64] As a result, both secular and Christian conservative positions are locked within their respective fallacies. The secular fallacy rejects religious

---

62. Vern S. Poythress and Wayne A. Grudem, *The Gender-Neutral Bible Controversy: Muting the Masculinity of God's Words* (Nashville: B&H, 2000).
63. Ibid., 141–42.
64. Jeremy Munday, *Introducing Translation Studies: Theories and Applications*, 2nd ed. (New York: Routledge, 2008).

discourse as arbitrary and irrelevant. The fundamentalist fallacy presents itself as the only "true" Christian belief system. Alternative Christian and other religious positions remain on the public margins of this loud and sociopolitically conservative debate.

Literalist-Scientific Hermeneutics as Part of the Scientific-Empiricist Epistemology: The Challenge of Progressive Interreligious Dialogue

Usually, alternative Christian and other religious positions remain on the margins of interreligious dialogue when such dialogue gains any significant publicity, as the scandal about Pope Benedict's comments on Islam indicates.[65] Then interreligious participants do not acknowledge that their religious assumptions are steeped in literalist-scientific hermeneutics that seeks to identify "a single, one-dimensional meaning"[66] and to hold on to theological positivism. Their hermeneutics is not based on the idea that all meaning is "contextual-cultural" and "transactional."[67] They are not interested in investigating and dismantling structures of oppression, be they of a religious, political, economic, or cultural nature. Yet this has to change because, as Fernando F. Segovia argues perceptively in a study on postcolonial biblical studies: "The past dominance of the West in the formulation and direction of Christianity will gradually but inexorably yield to a much more decentered and diversified formation."[68]

The emergence of the literalist-scientific hermeneutics in Western Christianity has been part and parcel of the "imperial/colonial formations" since the fifteenth century in Europe, in conjunction with "the climax of Western expansionism and diaspora from the early nineteenth century through the third quarter of the twentieth century."[69] To Segovia, this process has "come full circle" today because what began in the late fifteenth century with a dispersion from Europe outward, leading to a massive European diaspora of global proportions, has yielded in the late twentieth century to a dispersion from outside

65. Philip Blond and Adrian Pabst, "Benedict's Post-secular Vision," *New York Times*, November 29, 2006, http://tinyurl.com/kvonuyu.
66. Schüssler Fiorenza, *Power of the Word*, 49.
67. Ibid., 49, 50.
68. Fernando F. Segovia, "Interpreting beyond Borders: Postcolonial Studies and Diasporatic Studies in Biblical Criticism," in *Interpreting beyond Borders*, ed. Fernando F. Segovia (Sheffield: Sheffield Academic, 2000), 22.
69. Ibid., 23.

the West into the West, leading to a massive non-Western diaspora of global proportions within the West itself, above all in North America (Canada and the United States) but also in Europe.[70] Segovia thus maintains that the Western hermeneutical model will give way to one in which "the real reader" is central, "the flesh-and-blood reader, always positioned (the question of social location) and interested (the question of social agenda)."[71] The still dominant literalist-scientific hermeneutics will have to move to "a constructive contextual democratic practice," a practice that "investigate[s] and lift[s] into consciousness" how religious texts and doctrines inscribe empire and how empire reinscribes itself into religious teachings.[72]

This vision is certainly removed from the hermeneutical realities described above. When the Christian Right refers to the Bible, it presupposes that biblical truth "can be positively established and proven. Thus it stresse[s] verbal inspiration and calls for Christians to accept without question the Bible as the direct, inerrant Word of G*d. This emphasis on verbal inerrancy affirms that the Bible and its interpretation transcend ideology and particularity."[73] In this respect, then, Christian fundamentalism assumes the scientific-empiricist epistemology, promoting objectivity, universality, and value neutrality as central hermeneutical principles. This "positivist paradigm of knowledge" gives primacy to facts, to "evidence, data, and empirical inquiry."[74] Its rhetorical power is strong because Western minds are used to subscribing to this kind of thinking in general. Thus, theological rhetoric that regards its faith convictions as being grounded in objectivity, universality, and value neutrality builds on an unconsciously held scientific-empiricist epistemology characteristic of the Western worldview. The literal meaning of religious convictions or texts makes sense to people because the transactional process involved in the meaning-making efforts is not questioned and remains unconscious.[75] Consequently, an alternative epistemology has to work hard to make the hermeneutical process of literalist meanings visible before it can make a convincing case for alternative meanings.

This dynamic also explains why secular and fundamentalist fallacies are interrelated and feed on each other's concerns. The hermeneutical

70. Ibid., 19.
71. Ibid., 30.
72. Schüssler Fiorenza, *Power of the Word*, 51.
73. Schüssler Fiorenza, *Democratizing Biblical Studies*, 66.
74. Schüssler Fiorenza, *Power of the Word*, 68.
75. Schüssler Fiorenza, *Democratizing Biblical Studies*, 50.

alternative, as, for instance, characteristic of the inclusive German Bible translation, has no rhetorical space in this dynamic that requires unquestioned loyalty to the scientific-empiricist epistemology. Compromises cannot be established because the epistemological assumptions cannot be reconciled. While the scientific-empiricist epistemology upholds objectivity, universality, and value neutrality, the postmodern epistemology is based on multiplicity, indeterminacy, and the infinity of interpretative meaning. There is no middle ground, although in recent years proposals have been advanced commenting on the end of postmodernity.

Called the era of post-postmodernism, the new intellectual period is defined by a pragmatic, ethically oriented epistemology that builds on postmodern principles of knowing. Sometimes it is classified as "critical realism," "performatism," and "digimodernism." It is the intellectual impetus coming *after* postmodernism. Critical realism, insisting on the possibility of truth, is traced outside the hermeneutical tradition and defines a stance initially developing from "a sustained and rigorous critique of positivism in the natural sciences."[76] Raoul Eshelman coined the term *performatism*, as he views art as not open-ended and ambiguous but unified and aesthetically closed in the act of performance.[77] Alan Kirby introduced the concept of "digimodernism" as the new twenty-first-century paradigm. He contends that digimodernism does not displace postmodernism because postmodernism is just "another stage within modernity."[78] In his view, digimodernism is the shallow, unoriginal, bankrupt, uninspired, insubstantial, and "lingering residue of its predecessor," postmodernism.[79]

Another proposal for the time after postmodernism comes from Nicolas Bourriaud, who explains:

> If, at the beginning of this century, it is important to "rethink the modern" which thus means moving beyond the historical period defined by the postmodern, it is necessary first to tackle globalization, understood in its economic, political, and cultural aspects. Still more important, it is necessary to grapple with a blindingly obvious fact: if twentieth century modernism was a purely Western cultural phenomenon, later picked up and inflected by artists the world over, today there remains the task of

---

76. Garry Potter and José López, eds., *After Postmodernism: Introduction to Critical Realism* (London: Athlone, 2001), 8.
77. Raoul Eshelman, *Performatism, or the End of Postmodernism* (Aurora, CO: Davies Group, 2008).
78. Alan Kirby, *Digimodernism: How New Technologies Dismantle the Postmodern and Reconfigure Our Culture* (London: Continuum 2009), 3.
79. Ibid., 49.

envisaging its global equivalent, that is, the task of inventing innovative modes of thought and artistic practices that would this time be directly informed by Africa, Latin America, or Asia and would integrate ways of thinking and acting current in, say, Nunavut, Lagos, or Bulgaria. This time around, to have an impact, African tradition won't have to influence new Dadaists in a future Zurich, nor will Japanese print art have to rely on inspiring tomorrows Manets. Today's artists, whatever latitudes they live in, have the task of envisaging what would be the first truly worldwide culture. But there is a paradox bound up with this historic mission, which will have to be undertaken not in the wake of, but in resistance against, that political pressure to conform known as globalization. In order for this emergent culture, born of differences and singularities, to come into being, instead of conforming to the ongoing standardization, it will have to develop a specific imagination, relying on a logic unlike that which presides over capitalist globalization.[80]

Bourriaud proposes that the era after postmodernism includes "the first truly world-wide culture"; it does not imitate "capitalist globalization" but opposes it. He charges us to invent "a common world" and to build "practically and theoretically a global space of exchange," and that its establishment requires "a space of horizontal negotiations without an arbiter," "a counter-movement," and "a new exodus."[81]

Interestingly, none of these works on post-postmodernism reflect on the state of religion and what effect religious movements and identities have on the era after postmodernism. Yet their suggestions and proposals fit nicely with the critique of literalist-scientific hermeneutics and the scientific-empiricist epistemology taken for granted by the Christian Right and secularists. Especially, Bourriaud's proposal to create a global culture that does not conform to capitalist globalization should find approval among many religious organizations and progressive theological thinkers. In addition, the dramatic increase of Christians in the Southern Hemisphere makes Bourriaud's comment appear reasonable and indeed sensible. The past mixing of people from the north moving to the south and today's people from the south going to the north contributes to the uniformity in culture. The tendency of capitalist globalization to make everything the same, whether it is located in New York, Taipei, or Johannesburg, is indeed a threat. Resistance must therefore be part of developing a "truly" worldwide culture that recognizes the locality and specificity of each place,

80. Nicolas Bourriaud, *The Radicant* (New York: Lukas & Sternberg 2009), 17.
81. Ibid., 188.

without succumbing to parochialism or the dominant market paradigm. It seems obvious that the study of religion and theology as "constructive-contextual democratic practice" should be part of this alternative that resists participating in capitalist globalization.[82] When viewed in this intellectual context of post-postmodernism, the debate between secular and fundamentalist constituents seems old-fashioned, quaint, and out of date.

The (Post)modern Impotence toward Secular and Religious Fundamentalism: Concluding Comments

Discussions on the relationship between interreligious hermeneutics and issues on gender, family, and sexuality within the European context benefit from understanding how this relationship is currently defined by the Christian Right in the United States. As one of the most visible and prominent movements in the United States since the 1990s, this religiously, politically, socially, and economically powerful movement recognizes and resists (post)modern challenges by communicating in accessible and well-distributed literatures its views on gender, family, and sexuality from decidedly patriarchal and theologically conservative perspective. Yet the influence of the Christian Right goes far beyond the US-American context because of its active missionary programs shaping Christian thought and practice worldwide. Its hermeneutics is literalist while it claims universality, objectivity, and value neutrality in opposition to (post)modern challenges, and it tries to creatively solve the epistemological tensions by subscribing to patriarchal gender roles. Yet, simultaneously, the Christian Right adapts its biblical interpretations to contemporary sociocultural and political debate and aims to advance the universal truth of God. In other words, the Christian Right engages with the sociopolitical, economic, and cultural-intellectual developments of our time. It must thus be understood as a direct response to the (post)modern conditions in Western societies.

Considering their politically powerful stance, one should not be surprised that proponents of both the secular and fundamentalist fallacies challenge alternative exegetical positions. Those who vehemently reject religion or subscribe forcefully to it make it difficult, perhaps even impossible, for those articulating progressive theological and

---

82. Schüssler Fiorenza, *Power of the Word*, 51.

religious viewpoints. Accordingly, the task of those supporting exegetical alternatives is to understand these dynamics and communicate them directly, clearly, and effectively. If they fail, the future of progressive biblical studies looks grim. It is thus high time to constructively reflect upon the hermeneutical-epistemological challenges of progressively articulated academic studies of the Bible in Europe and elsewhere. The next chapter explores some of the political-exegetical options available to (feminist) biblical exegetes who recognize working in today's post-postmodern era.

8

Tell Me How You Read This Story and I Will Tell You Who You Are: Post-Postmodernity, Radicant Exegesis, and a Feminist Sociology of Biblical Hermeneutics

The Post-9/11 Era and Biblical Exegesis: An Introduction

More than ten years ago, the postmodern age ended with the collapse of the Twin Towers in New York City. Yet postmodernity's ending began already in 1989 when Jacques Derrida had turned to writing on "ethico-political issues," when Emmanuel Levinas had garnered much attention with his religious-philosophical writings, "when Beckett died" on December 22, 1989, and for sure when the Berlin Wall fell, "suggesting the final triumph of capitalism."[1] The globally recognized event of 9/11 sealed the deal. Some scholars leave little doubt about the decisiveness of the event. For instance, David Bennett, a professor

---

1. Josh Toth and Neil Brooks, "Introduction: A Wake and Renewed?," in *The Mourning After: Attending the Wake of Postmodernism*, ed. Neil Brooks and Josh Toth (Amsterdam: Rodopi, 2007), 2.

of English and cultural theory at the University of Melbourne, states firmly:

> The terrorist attacks on the twin symbols of American economic and military hegemony, however, had consigned postmodern value-relativism and irony to the historical waste bin, revivifying for Americans the dichotomies between "beauty" and "evil," "art" and "barbarism," which underpin the Western cultural tradition now under attack from "Osama bin Laden and his cronies, the ones who banned secular music from Afghanistan."[2]

The ashes of the twin towers indicated to Americans and the world at large that something enormous had happened. Since then, people have been less willing to agree that "anything goes," and they have yearned for the binaries of good and evil, war and peace, and "us versus them." Some scholars have thus called the 9/11 era "a 'new dark age of dogma' in which religious, economic, political and nationalist fundamentalisms have been rapidly expanding their 'empires' and pursuing their grand narratives of global history."[3]

Ours is the "post-postmodern" era in which religion has gained new prominence,[4] making it a postsecular culture that is sociopolitically conservative and in a "schizoid double bind."[5] Curator and art critic, Nicolas Bourriaud, calls it the era of "altermodernity," which he defines as a mode of thought and life that resists the neocolonial and Eurocentric forces of the global economic infrastructure.[6] To Bourriaud, we live in "a new modernity . . . combat[ing] everything in postmodern thought that in practice supports the trend toward standardization inherent in globalization. It is a matter of identifying what is valuable and extracting it from the binary and hierarchical schemes of yesterday's modernism as well as from regressive fundamentalism of all sorts."[7]

---

2. David Bennett, "Checking the Post: Music, Postmodernism or Post-postmodernism," *New Formations* 66 (Spring 2009): 7.
3. They make this point in a description of Stuart Sim's work; see Toth and Brooks, "Introduction," 10.
4. See, e.g., Tony Carroll, SJ, "Secularization in Recent Social Theory," *Communio Viatorum* 44, no. 2 (2002): 250–65; John A. McClure, "Post-Secular Culture: The Return of Religion in Contemporary Theory and Literature," *Cross Currents* (Fall 1997): 332–47.
5. Rose Braidotti, "A Critical Cartography of Feminist Post-Postmodernism," *Australian Feminist Studies* 20. no. 47 (July 2005): 177.
6. Nicolas Bourriaud, *The Radicant* (New York: Lukas & Sternberg, 2009), 19, 37, 39, 40, 93. For an interpretation of Bourriaud's notion of altermodernity, see Michael Larson, "Altermodernity and the Ethics of Translation," *Peninsula: A Journal of Relational Politics* 1, no. 1 (2011): http://tinyurl.com/l57chan.
7. Bourriaud, *The Radicant*, 27.

And regressive it has been. An important book presents various views on our situation during the past decade. Published in 2010 and entitled *Academic Repression: Reflections from the Academic Industrial Complex*,[8] the volume includes thirty-three articles that analyze the deepening corporate alignment of universities and colleges in the United States. One of the contributors is Henry Giroux, a professor at McMaster University who describes the increasing affiliation of universities with corporate power and military values.[9] Giroux presents a chilling account of the United States that, in his view, "establishes itself as a punitive power, eager to dismantle all vestiges of the social state, militarize public space, and eliminate those institutional spheres and rights that enable dialogue, debate, and dissent."[10] In fact, so bad is the situation according to Giroux that he sees both democracy and "the legacy of higher education's faith in academic freedom and commitment to democracy" fading in the United States since 9/11.[11] In his view, "higher education has become part of a market-driven and militarized culture imposing upon academics and students new modes of discipline that close down the spaces to think critically, while undermining substantive dialogue and restricting students from thinking outside of established expectations."[12] The goal of this educational process, so Giroux, is "to produce dutiful subjects willing to sacrifice their sense of agency for a militaristic sense of order and unquestioning respect for authority."[13] He provocatively sums up the situation in contemporary academia when he contends that this "blueprint for conformity . . . is a recipe for a type of thoughtlessness that . . . lies at the heart of totalitarian regimes."[14] Such is the post-9/11 condition in the United States and perhaps also elsewhere.

One may wonder: And what does that have to do with biblical exegesis and hermeneutics, with gender, feminism, and sexuality? I believe: everything. If it is true that readers, grounded in their social locations, create (biblical) meanings, then it matters in what kind of sociopolitical, theo-cultural, and economic contexts we find ourselves when we

8. Anthony J. Nocella, Steven Best, and Peter McLaren, eds., *Academic Repression: Reflections from the Academic Industrial Complex* (Oakland: AK Press, 2010).
9. Henry Giroux, "Higher Education after September 11th: The Crisis of Academic Freedom and Democracy," in Nocella, Best, and McLaren, *Academic Repression*, 92–111.
10. Ibid., 92.
11. Ibid., 93. For an account of the erosion of civil liberties and rights in the United States since 9/11, see Jonathan Turley, "10 Reasons the U.S. Is No Longer the Land of the Free," *Washington Post*, January 13, 2012, http://tinyurl.com/n2epthh.
12. Giroux, "Higher Education," 109.
13. Ibid.
14. Ibid.

interpret the Bible. Many agree with R. S. Sugirtharajah's statement that the days are gone when exegetes openly endorse an objectivist, universalizing, and value-neutral hermeneutics. Sugirtharajah even points out that such a hermeneutics was illusionary all along. He explains: "To imagine . . . an age in which scholarship was ideologically free and unrelated to political concerns or the personal proclivities of scholars is to assume a golden age of dispassionate judgment that never existed. That scholars were detached and their reading a noble activity is not true."[15] Instead, it is crucial to articulate the sociopolitical, economic, and religious conditions in which one reads the text. All meanings are, after all, socially located.

Sugirtharajah's assertion seems quite hopeful in light of the fact that the hermeneutical quest for historical origins and the basic tenets of the empiricist-scientific epistemology shape most biblical studies curricula and publications.[16] In my view, the scholarly situation merits a less optimistic assessment. Many exegetes settle for familiar territories and establish historically conceptualized meanings. They also prefer interpretative security by staying with recognized scholarly authorities and conventions. Coveted advanced academic degrees, tenured or tenure-track teaching positions, and academic recognition further keep in place the empiricist-scientific epistemology. Usually, though not always, the quest for the hermeneutical status quo successfully marginalizes feminist, gender, and "other" voices that aim for alternative biblical meanings positioned in the post-9/11 world.[17]

Ultimately, however, Sugirtharajah is right: exegetical arguments that affirm modernist methodological and epistemological assumptions prove dissatisfying for readers in the post-postmodern world. After all, the impact of 9/11 is such that it demands a new "system of thought" that makes "connections between disparate cultures without denying each one's singularity."[18] What biblical research needs is hermeneutical openness to "engage in productive dialogue with a variety of different contexts"[19] because in the post-9/11 era identities are

---

15. R. S. Sugirtharajah, "The End of Biblical Studies," in *Toward a New Heaven and a New Earth: Essays in Honor of Elisabeth Schüssler Fiorenza*, ed. Fernando F. Segovia (Maryknoll, NY: Orbis, 2003), 134.
16. For a critical engagement of the curricular situation, see Elisabeth Schüssler Fiorenza and Kent Harold Richards, eds., *Transforming Graduate Biblical Education: Ethos and Discipline* (Atlanta: Society of Biblical Literature, 2010).
17. For a discussion on historical criticism as the dominant methodology in biblical studies, see Todd Penner and Davina C. Lopez, "Homelessness as a Way Home: A Methodological Reflection and Proposal," in *Holy Land As Homeland? Models for Constructing the Historic Landscapes of Jesus*, ed. Keith W. Whitelam (Sheffield: Sheffield Phoenix, 2011), 151–76.
18. Bourriaud, *The Radicant*, 40.
19. Ibid., 106.

not "located, registered, nailed to a locus of enunciation, locked into the tradition in which he or she was born."[20] The same holds true for textual identities. They too are shaped by global and continuous migrations because this is an era of the "wanderer."[21] If the field of biblical studies wants to take into account these shifting intellectual, sociological, and political dynamics, it has to be built on the notions of hermeneutical fluidity, multiplicity, and "creolization." Such post-9/11 hermeneutical convictions are also necessary when the topic is gender. They help us develop a hermeneutical stance that moves out of the binary impasse so prevalent today. It serves as the foundation for radicant exegesis, recognizing the shifting and wandering qualities of all identities, including gender.

Radicant Exegesis and the Transmission of Gender Identities

In the post-9/11 world two interrelated hermeneutical fallacies prevail. They are the "fundamentalist fallacy" and the "secular fallacy."[22] The fundamentalist fallacy is based on a literalist-historical hermeneutic that Elisabeth Schüssler Fiorenza calls "biblicist fundamentalism."[23] It shapes much of the public discourse on the Bible and prevails in the politics of the Christian Right. The other fallacy is the secular one, limiting the study of the Bible mainly to historical and literary analysis. It is sometimes characterized as the "Critical-Scientific-Modern Paradigm."[24] In biblical studies, both approaches are often combined to varying degrees, as if a compromise were the solution to the current epistemological impasse. Yet the interesting point is this: both hermeneutical paradigms, appearing to be each other's opponent, share the same epistemological conviction. Both pursue the quest for "origins," history, the roots of it all, historical beginnings, the essence, and the foundation of the Bible. Hence, both take for granted the modern empiricist-scientific epistemology, and so both seek to establish "a single, one-dimensional meaning" of the text. In short, both promote theological positivism.[25]

20. Ibid., 34.
21. Ibid., 22.
22. Susanne Scholz, "The Forbidden Fruit for the New Eve: The Christian Right's Adaptation to the (Post)modern World," in *Interreligious Hermeneutics in Pluralistic Europe: Between Texts and People*, ed. David Cheetham et al. (Amsterdam: Rodopi, 2011), 292.
23. Elisabeth Schüssler Fiorenza, *The Power of the Word: Scripture and the Rhetoric of Empire* (Minneapolis: Fortress Press, 2007), 49.
24. Elisabeth Schüssler Fiorenza, *Democratizing Biblical Studies: Toward an Emancipatory Educational Space* (Louisville: Westminster John Knox, 2009), 67–71.
25. Schüssler Fiorenza, *Power of the Word*, 49.

Yet, according to Bourriaud, the quest for historical origins is an endeavor of the pre-9/11 era that engulfed the intellectual sensibilities of modernity, while those of us living in *this* century need to articulate "our own century's modernity."[26] Bourriaud classifies this period as "altermodernity," the moment in time that stands "in opposition to all radicalism, dismissing both the bad solution of re-enrooting in identities as well as the standardization of imagination decreed by economic globalization."[27] This, then, is the time of the *radicant*, a botanical term. It describes plants "taking root on, or above, the ground; rooting from the stem, as the trumpet creeper and the ivy."[28] The term *radicant* captures what is going on today because a radicant is "an organism that grows its roots and adds new ones as it advances."[29] In other words, the term *radicant* recognizes that our era is permeated by wandering people who have roots and previously lived somewhere else. Thus, today, many people live not in one but in several places. They move from here to there and all the way back again, which Bourriaud takes as the characteristic of the post-9/11 era. He writes about being radicant:

> To be radicant means setting one's roots in motion, staging them in heterogeneous contexts and formats, denying them the power to completely define one's identity, translating ideas, transcoding images, transplanting behaviors, exchanging rather than imposing. What if twenty-first-century culture were invented with those works that set themselves the task of effacing their origin in favor of a multitude of simultaneous or successive enrootings? This process of obliteration is part of the condition of the wanderer.[30]

The position of the radicant, the wanderer, or the migrant takes seriously the fact that almost 200 million people, and growing, find themselves "living in more or less voluntary exile."[31] Refugees, professional nomads, and irregular workers are everywhere[32] and "increasingly commonplace," as are an "unprecedented circulation of goods and services" and "the formation of transnational political entities,"[33] the latter also known as corporations. The post-9/11 era, then, is an era of the

26. Bourriaud, *The Radicant*, 22.
27. See the advertisement for the book at the publisher's website at http://tinyurl.com/ld6qq9q.
28. See *Encyclo.co.uk English Encyclopedia*, s.v. "Radicant," http://tinyurl.com/k5c6k8o.
29. Bourriaud, *The Radicant*, 22.
30. Ibid.
31. Ibid., 21.
32. Khalid Koser, *International Migration: A Very Short Introduction* (Oxford: Oxford University Press, 2007).
33. Bourriaud, *The Radicant*, 21.

global mobilization of people, things, and transnational entities, not to mention the global web of data infrastructures.

In short, Bourriaud reminds those of us interested in identity issues that "the question of identity is most pressing for immigrant communities in the most globalized countries." He observes perceptively that wandering people, migrants, wanderers from culture to culture and land to land suffer because of their roots, their pre-immigrant identities to which they are often holding on.[34] That is why second and third generations find life in a new land so much easier than the migrating generation. They do not so vividly remember their roots, the "mythologized 'origin' against an integrating and homogenizing 'soil.'"[35] They mix and match multiple identities and develop new roots, adapting to the new soil more easily than their parents or grandparents. Bourriaud proposes that what is needed on the theoretical level is not "set[ting] one fixed root against another"[36] but an appreciation of multiple locations, various influences, shifting preferences not played out against each other but nurtured by "a multitude of simultaneous or successive enrootings."[37] Moving, shifting, and multiple locations, influences, and preferences are the characteristics of our age, the era of altermodernity or post-postmodernity. In "radicantity" we "engage in productive dialogue with a variety of different contexts,"[38] not seeking exclusive origins, histories, or roots, because in this era people develop portable identities that "become more important than their local reality."[39]

Bourriaud makes another important observation. He suggests that a radicant perspective stands in opposition to commercialization and marketability. It is a stance that resists the globalizing forces of capitalist consumption and "economic standardization."[40] It neither adapts to the status quo nor resigns itself to neoliberal and corporate structures of hierarchy and infrastructures. Rather, the stance of altermodernity fosters a "form of wandering, an ethics of precariousness, and a heterochronic vision of history."[41] Altermodernity signifies a position of resistance within a world of exodus, diaspora, and exile.

Bourriaud's conceptualization of the post-9/11 world has much to teach us in biblical studies. It suggests taking seriously the post-9/11

34. Ibid.
35. Ibid.
36. Ibid.
37. Ibid., 22.
38. Ibid., 106.
39. Ibid., 32.
40. Ibid., 185.
41. Ibid., 184.

world because we, too, have seen "the satellite dishes in ethnic ghettos" and the immigrant "customs that do not adapt to the host country."[42] Some of us know from personal experience the stresses and joys of bi- or even multilocality and their implications for our lives and work. Most importantly, biblical literature is "essentially" migration literature. It tells stories of people displaced from their "original" homes, wandering in the world and escaping famines and oppressive empires. In other words, tales of migration are at the heart of what we call the Bible.[43] The challenge is how to read its stories and poems in our era of global wandering and how we as biblical scholars "define and inhabit a globalized culture, against the standardization presupposed by globalization."[44]

The challenge also pertains to gender identities and their fluid performances practiced in many shades of color, form, experience, tradition, and expression. Gender identities are certainly never fully reachable and always negotiated in the local while conversant with the global and vice versa. They need to be understood as part of this wandering, the "counter-movement," the "new exodus . . . amid the constant unrest caused by economic globalization."[45] Our gendered traveling toward "a common world, or realizing, practically, and theoretically, a global space of exchange," becomes "a space of horizontal negotiations" that "will give rise to a new common intelligibility."[46] This is Bourriaud's hope for the future.

In other words, the quest for origins does not satisfy anymore. Times have changed and the historical impetus complies with the neocolonial status quo. Instead, biblical scholars need to assume the stance of the radicant that aligns itself with those who practice an ethics of resistance to "the official representations of the world."[47] In my view, the

---

42. Ibid., 21.
43. See, e.g., John Ahn, "The Bible and the Immigrant Experience," *Insights* 124, no. 2 (2009): 13–17; M. Daniel Carroll R., "The Bible, the Church, and Human Rights in Contemporary Debates about Hispanic Immigration in the United States," *Journal of Latin American Theology* 2, no. 1 (2007): 161–84; Emilio G. Chávez, "Welcoming the Foreigner: A Biblical Theology," *Josephinum Journal of Theology* 11 (2004): 226–34; Wim Hoekstra, "Migrants, the Church and the Bible," in *New Direction in Missions and Evangelization*, vol. 3, *Faith and culture*, ed. Henry Rowold (Manly, Australia: Catholic Institute of Sydney, 1988), 114–28; Joan M. Maruskin, "The Bible: the Ultimate Migration Handbook," *Church & Society* 95, no. 6 (2005): 77–90; Jean-Pierre Ruiz, *Reading from the Edges: The Bible and People on the Move* (Maryknoll, NY: Orbis, 2011); Lindy Scott, "Mi Casa Es Tu Casa: A Biblical Perspective on the Current Immigration Situation," *Journal of Latin American Theology* 1, no. 2 (2006): 122–41.
44. Bourriaud, *The Radicant*, 188.
45. Ibid.
46. Ibid.
47. Ibid., 186. See also Susanne Scholz, "Occupy Academic Bible Teaching: The Architecture of Educational Power and the Biblical Studies Curriculum," in *Teaching the Bible in a Liberal Arts Classroom*, ed. Jane S. Webster and Glenn S. Holland (Sheffield: Sheffield Academic, 2012), 28–43.

radicant is a comfortable place for feminist scholars. It is an alternative space, on the margins, one that invites the dismantling of power and control mechanisms prevalent in gender hierarchies relentlessly executed in the world.

At the Heart of the Phallogocentric Symbolic Order: The Study of Biblical Rape Discourse as Part of Radicant Exegesis

So if the goal is no longer the quest for history but the strengthening of the countermovement to the forces of economic globalization, standardization, and commercialism, it becomes paramount for biblical scholars to contribute to the building of an ethics of resistance and the fostering of productive dialogue. Such a task can be accomplished when biblical exegetes critically investigate the constructions of gender identities in the history of biblical interpretation. Many gender-oriented topics come to mind, and one of them is rape. Unquestionably, rape remains one of the major gender issues of our time. Rape is often defined as "a type of sexual assault usually involving sexual intercourse or other forms of sexual penetration carried out against a person without that person's consent. The act may be carried out by physical force, coercion, abuse of authority, or against a person who is incapable of giving valid consent, such as one who is unconscious, incapacitated, has an intellectual disability or is below the legal age of consent."[48] In today's world, rape abounds, and feminist theorists speak of a global rape culture.[49] It is a culture "in which sexual assault, rape, and violence is common and in which prevalent attitudes, norms, practices, and media normalize, excuse, tolerate, or even condone sexual assault and rape."[50]

Hardly a day goes by without a report of rape in the news. In Libya, the leader of the country, Col. Muammar el-Qaddafi authorized the rape of Libyan women, according to a *New York Times* report in June 2011.[51] In New York City, two police officers were acquitted of rape in

48. *Wikipedia*, s.v., "Rape," available at http://en.wikipedia.org/wiki/Rape (accessed June 9, 2017).
49. Emilie Buchwald, Pamela Fletcher, and Marth Roth, *Transforming a Rape Culture*, 2nd ed. (Minneapolis: Milkweed, 2005).
50. Women and Gender Advocacy Center at Colorado State University, "What is a Rape Suportive Culture?," available at http://www.wgac.colostate.edu/what-is-rape-supportive-culture (accessed June 9, 2017).
51. Kareem Fahim, "Wartime Rape Unsettle and Divide Libyans," *New York Times*, June 19, 2011, http://tinyurl.com/m5nhgmm. For the newly expanded legal definition of rape in US-American law, see Charlie Savage, "U.S. to Expand Its Definition of Rape in Statistics," *New York Times*, January 6, 2012, http://tinyurl.com/lah8dsu.

May 2011.[52] In the US-American military, one of every three service-women experience sexual assault.[53] In Congo, women, girls, and also some men have been gang-raped for more than a decade, especially in the war-torn parts of the country.[54] And during the 1994 Rwanda geno-cide, rape was ordered as a military strategy even by a female minister of the then government.[55] There are the "everyday" allegations of rape, such as the case of the International Monetary Fund chief Dominique Strauss-Kahn, who was accused of sexual assault by a housekeeper in New York City.[56] The list of cases is endless.

However, the list of scholars who have dealt with rape as a hermeneutically central issue for biblical exegesis is short despite the long history of interpretation. In fact, it is quite amazing to ruminate on the fact that the topic of rape and sexual violence in the Bible has come to our attention only since the 1970s. In other words, rape is a central topic for radicant exegesis because, first, it affects countless women, children, and men in today's world, especially when they are vulnerable refugees and immigrants. Second, the topic is central because it goes to the heart of the phallogocentric symbolic order that remains unabashedly powerful in the post-9/11 era. Third, the sys-tematic analysis of interpretations on biblical rape texts documents that, at best, biblical scholarship has been complicit with these struc-tures. When we expose the phallogocentric symbolic order assumed in biblical interpretations, we begin to offer rhetorical, symbolic, and hermeneutical alternatives, or as Elisabeth Schüssler Fiorenza states, we become part of creating "a radical democratic religious imaginary and pedagogical praxis of transformation."[57] We learn to question the globalized rape culture and join the countermovement of altermoder-nity. We come to resist hegemonic practices of the phallogocentric order.

52. John Eligon, "Two New York City Police Officers Acquitted of Rape," *New York Times*, May 26, 2011, http://www.nytimes.com/2011/05/27/nyregion/two-new-york-city-police-officers-acquitted-of-rape.html?scp=3&sq=rape &st=cse.
53. Lawrence J. Korb, "Welfare of Military Women Letter," *New York Times*, June 23, 2011, http://www.nytimes.com/2011/06/24/opinion/l24kristof.html?scp=1&sq=rape military&st=cse.
54. Jeffrey Gettleman, "Mass Rapes in Congo reveals U.N. Weakness," *New York Times*, October 3, 2010, http://www.nytimes.com/2010/10/04/world/africa/04congo.html?ref=congothedemocra-ticrepublicof.
55. Marlise Simons, "Life Sentences in Rwanda Genocide Case," *New York Times*, June 24, 2011, http://www.nytimes.com/2011/06/25/world/africa/25rwanda.html?scp=3&sq=rape military&st=cse.
56. John Eligon, "The Strauss-Kahn Case: Sizing Up a Legal Clash's Many Facets," *New York Times*, June 5, 2011, http://www.nytimes.com/2011/06/06/nyregion/the-strauss-kahn-case-sizing-up-a-legal-clashs-many-facets.html?ref=dominiquestrausskahn.
57. Schüssler Fiorenza, *Power of the Word*, 241.

As is widely known, the Bible contains numerous texts on rape. Among them are the stories of Hagar and Sarah (Genesis 29–30), Sarah and Rebecca (Genesis 12; 20; 26), Lot's daughters (Genesis 19), Dinah (Genesis 34), Ms. Potiphar (Genesis 39), Delilah (Judges 13–16), the concubine and the daughters of Shiloh (Judges 19–21), Bathsheba (2 Samuel 13), and Abigail (1 Kings 1). Other rape texts are part of the legal codes (e.g., Deuteronomy 22), and there are poems in the prophetic literature that mention rape in metaphoric speech (e.g., Jer 13:22; 20:7; Ezek 16:6–8, 36–42). The latter represent some of the most misogynist and pornographic poems in the Hebrew Bible. The wisdom literature also includes references to rape when it is read in the sociocultural contexts of sexual violence. For instance, several lamentation psalms, such as Psalms 6 and 55, can be understood as describing the emotional experiences of those having lived through sexual violence. Then there is the metaphor of sexual violence against Job in Job 30:11, in which God metaphorically opens "his" pants ("loosening his rope") and rapes the man, an image that scholars have classified as intolerable and blasphemous.[58]

Some of these texts are famous whereas others are rarely mentioned. Yet even the famous ones are not necessarily recognized as rape stories. For instance, the thrice-told narrative of the "wife-sister motif" in Genesis 12 (parallels in Genesis 20; 26) is generally known but not usually read as a tale about a rape threat. For fear of death, Abraham introduces his wife as his sister to the Egyptian pharaoh. In the first version of the story (Genesis 12) the king learns about the deceit only after terrible plagues hit his house. In the second version (Genesis 20) another ruler, King Abimelech, has a dream that reveals to him the relationship between Sarah and Abraham. In the third version (Genesis 26) King Abimelech accidentally looks out of the window when wife and husband, in this case Rebekah and Isaac, "caress" each other. All three narratives imagine the patriarch's wife as the potential sexual object of the imperial ruler.[59]

Another story—the tale of Samson and Delilah (Judges 16)—is renowned, but rarely presented as one about rape. The French opera *Samson et Dalila*, composed by Camille Saint-Saens and first produced in 1877,[60] illustrates this view. Samson appears as a tragic hero who falls

58. For a discussion of this passage in the commentary literature, see Susanne Scholz, *Sacred Witness: Rape in the Hebrew Bible* (Minneapolis: Fortress Press, 2010), 204–5.
59. For an additional analysis of these narratives, see ibid., 84–93.
60. For two studies on the appropriation of the Hebrew Bible in music, see, e.g., Helen Leneman, *The*

in love with Delilah. She is portrayed more ambiguously, and the opera tackles the question of whether "she really love[s] him."[61] Like many scholarly interpretations, the opera disregards an ambiguity in Judges 16:5, where the Philistines advise Delilah: "Coax him, and find out what makes his strength so great, and how we may overpower ['innâ; possibly "to rape"] him, so that we may bind him in order to subdue ['innâ] him; and we will each give you eleven hundred pieces of silver." The question is what it means that the Philistines want to "overpower" and "subdue" him (see also Judg 16:6, 19). Suffice it to say that the linguistic ambiguity makes it possible to classify this text as a rape account of a male.[62]

Other biblical texts, excavated by feminist scholars in the 1970s and 1980s, are well-known rape narratives. For instance, the stories of the unnamed woman and the women of Shiloh (Judges 19–21) are recognized as perhaps the most horrific tales about gang rape in the Hebrew Bible.[63] An unnamed woman runs away from her husband and later, when she and her husband are on their way back home, she is gang-raped by hostile men in the town. It is a tale of rape in so-called peacetime, depicting gruesomely the fate of many migrating women in foreign lands. The story mentions that her husband cuts her body into twelve pieces and sends them to the twelve tribes of Israel. They get so outraged that they go to war with the Benjaminites, which results in the sex-trafficking of the women of Shiloh. Androcentric commentators, euphemistically calling this act "marriage,"[64] disregard that the women were taken against their will.

In other biblical narratives, references to rape and sexual violence are contested even among feminist readers. A prominent example is the story of Dinah in Genesis 34. The novelist Anita Diamant has significantly contributed to the interpretive dispute. In her novel *The Red Tent*, she presents Genesis 34 as a love story gone awry.[65] Imagining the Genesis stories of Leah, Rachel, and Dinah from the women's perspectives, Diamant makes Dinah's fate a central event in the family

Story of Ruth in Opera and Oratorio (Sheffield: Sheffield Academic, 2007); Leneman, *The Stories of Saul and David in Music* (Sheffield: Sheffield Phoenix, 2010).

61. Herbert Kupferberg, "Song of Samson," *Metropolitan Opera Stagebill*, February 1998, 16.

62. For more details, see Scholz, *Sacred Witness*, 173–75.

63. See, e.g., Carol Meyers, Toni Craven, and Ross S. Kraemer, eds., *Women in Scripture: A Dictionary of Named and Unnamed Women in the Hebrew Bible, the Apocryphal/Deuterocanonical Books, and the New Testament* (Grand Rapids: Eerdmans, 2000), 248.

64. Ibid., 135–55. See also, e.g., Susan Niditch, *Judges: A Commentary*, OTL (Louisville: Westminster John Knox, 2008).

65. Anita Diamant, *The Red Tent* (New York: Picador, 1997). See also, e.g., Ita Sheres, *Dinah's Rebellion: A Biblical Parable for Our Time* (New York: Crossroad, 1990).

account. It portrays Dinah and Shechem as being in love with each other whereas the brothers are xenophobic murderers who ignore their sister's wish. Diamant's retelling stands in a long exegetical tradition that characterizes rape as love, sides with the rapist, and condemns the brothers for their vengeful actions.[66]

Other narratives have not always been recognized as rape stories, even by feminist interpreters. Such is the case of Hagar (Genesis 16; 21) who, as an enslaved woman, cannot say no to her masters. For instance, Delores Williams does not state that Hagar is a rape victim survivor, although she refers to Hagar as "a sexual victim exploited by members of a family prominent and more powerful than she."[67] Her interpretation emphasizes Hagar's story as a "survival" story because Hagar, like "a black mother," cares for "the survival needs of children or family."[68] Complex connections about gender, ethnicity, and class run deep in Genesis 16 and 21, and so the implications of the sociopolitical, economic, and religious structures of domination are prominent in feminist and womanist interpretations.[69] Yet even they do not always address the significance of sexual violence in this or in other biblical texts (see, e.g., Gen 29:31–30:24 or 1 Kgs 1:1–4).

In general, feminist readings of biblical rape texts need to be viewed as part of radicant exegesis because they recognize that biblical texts mean different things to different people, as the history of interpretation clearly illustrates. A single, universal, and objective textual meaning does not exist, as biblical (like other) meanings are multiple, shifting, and contextual. Thus reading within global rape cultures, feminist interpreters classify as biblical rape texts what others characterize as prose and poetry about marriage, love, or divine scorn for neglectful worship practices.[70] To the latter, the classification of biblical texts as references to rape is anachronistic, debatable, or even plain wrong,[71] whereas to the former meanings are readerly creations, even when they are based on historical or linguist methods.[72]

---

66. For a detailed analysis of this interpretation history, see Susanne Scholz, *Rape Plots: A Feminist-Cultural Study of Genesis 34* (New York: Lang, 2000).
67. Delores Williams, "Hagar in African American Biblical Appropriation," in *Hagar, Sarah, and Their Children: Jewish, Christian, and Muslim Perspectives*, ed. Phyllis Trible and Letty M. Russell (Louisville: Westminster John Knox, 2006), 173.
68. Ibid.
69. For more on Genesis 16 and 21, see Scholz, *Sacred Witness*, 55–63.
70. See, e.g., Yael Shemesh, "Rape Is Rape: The Story of Dinah and Shechem (Genesis 34)," *ZAW* 119, no. 1 (2007): 2–21; Alexander Izuchukwu Abasili, "Was It Rape? The David and Bathsheba Pericope Re-examined," *VT* 61 (2011): 1–15.
71. See, e.g., Ellen van Wolde, "Does *'innâ* Denote Rape? A Semantic Analysis of a Controversial Word," *VT* 52 (2002): 528–44.

Those of us who wander within multiple identities and shifting locations approach the Bible as a powerful opportunity to resist servile resignation into the inevitability of rape. How we speak about such texts matters even when habits of conformity and fear of repercussion make it difficult in the post-9/11 era to consistently and persistently dismantle rape-prone rhetoric. Yet such an exegetical stance is much needed because it challenges the contemporary phallogocentric symbolic order. A radicant exegetical commitment ensures an unflinching look at suffering, pain, and injustice in the world in which rape is a daily occurrence. Unsurprisingly, the results of such work are not popular, not much talked about, and not prominently featured anywhere. Yet they are grounded in three hermeneutical principles that help in shaping a radicant exegetical stance, whether it locates itself in contemporary rape cultures or in some other urgent ethical-political issue of the world.[73] The first hermeneutical principle posits that all sacred texts, including the Bible, are inherently flexible, elastic, and ambiguous. The second hermeneutical principle affirms that every translation is an interpretation. The third hermeneutical principle maintains that readers, grounded in social locations, create (biblical) meanings.

These hermeneutical principles develop in readers the understanding that biblical meanings are not static, fixed, or immovable but shifting, moving, and permeable creations. They help readers to recognize that biblical interpretations are access points to examining who we are. Rather than telling us what the Bible says, they are sources for critical interrogations about the world.[74] They inform about readerly positions on society, culture, politics, economics, and religion. We learn from them who we were in the past, who we are in the present, and perhaps they even teach us what needs to be done in the future.

So what are we to do when some exegetes interpret biblical texts as prose and poetry about love and marriage, or as divine chastisement, while others read the same texts as rape literature? According to Bourriaud, in the altermodern era we cannot claim that interpretations are right or wrong. Rather, different contexts produce "a multitude of simultaneous or successive enrootings,"[75] and so

---

72. See, e.g., Choi Hee and Katheryn Pfisterer Darr, eds., *Engaging the Bible: Critical Readings from Contemporary Women* (Minneapolis: Fortress Press, 2006).

73. For other important issues, see, e.g., Randall C. Bailey, Tat-siong Benny Liew, and Fernando F. Segovia, eds., *They Were All Together in One Place? Toward Minority Biblical Criticism* (Atlanta: Society of Biblical Literature, 2009); David Cheetham et al., eds., *Interreligious Hermeneutics in Pluralistic Europe: Between Texts and People* (Amsterdam: Rodopi, 2011).

74. For an early articulation of this notion, see, e.g., Vincent L. Wimbush, "Reading Texts Through Worlds, Worlds Through Texts," *Semeia* 62 (1993): 129–40.

interpretations provide sociological insights into the world. Said differently, biblical interpretations demonstrate how past and present interpreters have defined biblical rape literature as texts about marriage and love. They illustrate that biblical meanings have contributed to rape-prone ideas and behavior in various ways: first, they comply with the phallogocentric order in the name of history, linguistics, or anthropology; second, they disconnect their readings from contemporary cultures of rape; and third, they accept modern claims of universality, objectivity, and value neutrality.

Another of Bourriaud's observations is important. He proposes to develop an ethics of resistance to neoliberal and corporate structures of hierarchies and infrastructures. In his opinion, altermodernity promotes an ethics that is aware of wandering, precarious, and heterochronic perspectives of the world. I suggest that a biblical hermeneutic of rape align itself with these qualities of the altermodern age. It will then not just be another expression of the modern quest for historical singularity of meaning,[76] but also promote an interrogatory stance that challenges the phallogocentric symbolic order and contributes to ending the powerful functioning of phallogocentrism in the world. Or put differently, we need to develop ethical-political standards because, as Todd Penner points out so perceptively, "[t]his debate about who interprets the Bible and how it is interpreted is ultimately a political engagement *on both sides.*"[77]

Ethical Genealogies of Biblical Interpretation, or Toward a Feminist Sociology of Biblical Hermeneutics

In our era of altermodernity, then, much depends on "the demystification of the political dimensions of religious rhetoric."[78] At stake is how biblical scholars position themselves in the sociopolitical struggles over power, control, and money. Do they stand "as part of the oligarchy or in resistance to such powers"?[79] Bourriaud is clear on this point. He promotes a stance of resistance in opposition to neoliberal and corporate forces of conformity, hierarchy, and domination.

---

75. Bourriaud, *The Radicant*, 22.
76. For this position, see Todd Penner and Lilian Cates, "Textually Violating Dinah: Literary Readings, Colonizing Interpretations, and the Pleasure of the Text," *Bible and Critical Theory* 3, no. 3 (2007): http://www.bibleandcriticaltheory.com/.
77. Todd Penner, "Is Boer among the Prophets? Transforming the Legacy of Marxian Critique," in *Secularism and Biblical Studies*, ed. Roland Boer (London: Equinox, 2010), 75.
78. Ibid.
79. Ibid., 78.

To align ourselves with this stance, I suggest we develop sociological genealogies of biblical interpretations that analyze how biblical readings advance ethical-political resistance to the status quo. When we do such genealogical-sociological work, little doubt remains of how to evaluate biblical meanings today. Let me illustrate this point with a brief analysis of three interpretations on Hosea 2:2–23 (in Hebrew 2:4–25) to exemplify that biblical meanings are multiple, shifting, and dynamic, always standing within particular hermeneutical contexts.[80]

One commentator who famously shaped the meaning of Hosea 2:2–23 is Hans-Walter Wolff. His commentary on Hosea, published in 1974, is still placed on the reference shelves of theological libraries. Wolff's interpretation cemented a reading of the poem that is widely assumed. Claiming to ground the poem's meaning in ancient Israel, Wolff advances a historical and linguistic interpretation which emphasizes that Israel, abandoning God for its worship of Canaanite deities, is scorned in this "parable of the unfaithful wife."[81] Wolff reads firmly in solidarity with the divine voice of the poem. He regards the text as a polemic "against the introduction of Canaanite mythology into Israel" in which "God seeks a variety of paths by which to lead her back."[82] According to Wolff, the poem is "an unprecedented modernism that Hosea so consistently utilizes the Canaanite mythologoumenon of divine marriage."[83] Yet Wolff leaves unaddressed the fact that the poem is the first in the chronological line of the so-called marriage metaphors that classify God as husband and Israel as wife. Instead, Wolff isolates the poem in Hosea as an "unprecedented modernism" from a terrifying lineage of poems that imagines sexual violence against the metaphorical wife.

Wolff structures his interpretation according to the poem's two parts. Wolff explains that the first strophe (vv. 2–17) "is concerned with the question of how Yahweh deals with unfaithful Israel."[84] The cuckolded divinity, so Wolff, tries repeatedly to bring Israel back because "he refuses to accept as final the divorce his wife both desired and initiated."[85] Predictably, Wolff sides with the "husband" who

80. For another example of this kind of feminist analysis, see Susanne Scholz, "A 'Third-Kind' of Feminist Reading: Toward a Feminist Sociology of Biblical Hermeneutics," *Currents of Biblical Research* 9, no. 4 (October 2010): 1–22.

81. Hans-Walter Wolff, *Hosea: A Commentary on the Book of the Prophet Hosea*, trans. Gary Stansell, ed. Paul D. Hanson (Philadelphia: Fortress Press, 1974), 44.

82. Ibid.

83. Ibid.

84. Ibid.

85. Ibid.

"suffers in his love for Israel," and so Wolff ignores that the husband threatens his wife with severe physical and psychological violence. Wolff also focuses on the anti-ecumenical attitude he finds in the poem, although he wrote at a time when interfaith relations flourished. Yet instead of criticizing centuries of Christian and Western hostility toward other religions, Wolff uses highly pejorative terms, such as "pagan worship," in an apparently neutral way. In short, Wolff finds the husband's threats justifiable, the charges appropriate, and the violence justified, whether directed against the metaphorical adulterous wife or the historically defined Israel. And despite all of these obvious biases in his reading, Wolff believes to objectively reconstruct Israelite history.

In the second strophe (vv. 18–25), Wolff moves on to another theological point. He maintains that God offers Israel a "new covenant"[86] as an expression of God's saving grace. This is a classic Protestant-Lutheran notion, and it permeates Wolff's reading of verses 18–25. It stresses that God alone brings about the new covenantal relationship. Most importantly, to Wolff, the new covenant is "not the restoration of the old covenant"[87] but based in "a new marriage" and "in nuptial love."[88] This reading stands in the long supersessionist tradition of Christian theology, and so Wolff believes that "Hosea 2:18-25 can help the people of the New Covenant to grasp more fully in faith and hope the gift of life as they stand in God's presence and in the world."[89] In other words, this Old Testament commentator, claiming to ground his interpretation in historical criticism and linguistics, promotes an anti-Jewish Christian theology that substitutes Israel with the followers of Jesus. Historical assertions blend with an androcentric and Christocentric theological position that creates a theo-culturally dangerous meaning of the Old Testament poem. Importantly, this meaning shapes interpretations to this day, as any online search easily illustrates.[90]

This biblical meaning is, however, not the only available one. Another interpretation presents an entirely different reading of the prophetic text. It is located within the feminist intellectual movement and appears in the *Women's Bible Commentary*.[91] The author is Gale A.

---

86. Ibid., 55.
87. Ibid.
88. Ibid.
89. Ibid.
90. See, e.g., the online Bible Study site *Bible.org*, "Hosea: An Exegetical Commentary," http://tinyurl.com/lorulr9.
91. Gale A. Yee, "Hosea," in *Women's Bible Commentary*, ed. Carol. A. Newsom and Sharon H. Ringe, 2nd ed. (Louisville: Westminster John Knox, 1998), 207–15.

Yee, who covers some of the basics on the book of Hosea and then states: "Hosea's distinctive metaphor for the Yahweh-Israel relationship was one of husband and wife."[92] Focused on the so-called marriage metaphor, this interpretation assumes that adultery plays a central role in the poem's meaning. Yee locates the poem's significance in the patrilineal and patrilocal kinship structure and the honor-shame value system of Israelite society. As such, Yee's argument is historical and anthropological, reinforcing traditional perspectives about ancient Israel.[93] Perhaps due to the relative brevity of this one-chapter commentary, the initial part of Yee's interpretation is shaped by declarative statements about Israelite practices, rules, and regulations of marriage and adultery. For instance, Yee explains that "marriage arrangements . . . were patrilocal. A wife was brought to live with her husband in the household of her father-in-law."[94] Such a general statement is, of course, unable to account for potential shifts in Israelite social life during several hundreds of years. It also does not allow for any exceptions in social practice, despite some objections from scholars, such as Athalya Brenner, who observes that we do not know much about marriage and other social customs in Israelite times.[95] Still, in contrast to Wolff, Yee highlights the gendered aspects of the poem and so features a very different meaning, which centers on the marriage metaphor, as the title suggests: "God as Faithful Husband, Israel as Faithless Wife."[96] In short, this feminist reading takes seriously the gender dynamics of the text by highlighting the impact of the "marriage metaphor" that depicts the wife as "the primary offender in an adulterous affair."[97]

The feminist hermeneutical stance alters the meaning of Hosea 2:2–25 in dramatic ways. The poem does not emerge as symbolic prophetic speech that articulates the covenantal relationship between God and Israel, as Wolff's commentary maintains. Rather, Yee focuses on the gender assumptions of a marriage in which husband and wife are in a battering relationship. Yee defines this dynamic and its "theological problems for present-day women"[98] as central to the poem's

92. Ibid., 209.
93. Yee's later work elaborates on the historical background, see Gale A. Yee, *Poor Banished Children of Eve: Woman as Evil in the Hebrew Bible* (Minneapolis: Fortress Press, 2003).
94. Ibid.
95. Athalya Brenner, "Some Reflections on Violence against Women and the Image of the Hebrew Bible," in *On the Cutting Edge: The Study of Women in Biblical Worlds: Essays in Honor of Elisabeth Schüssler Fiorenza*, ed. Jane Schaberg, Alice Bach, and Esther Fuchs (New York: Continuum, 2004), 71.
96. Ibid., 211.
97. Ibid.
98. Ibid.

meaning, detecting a "three-part strategy" with which the divine husband curbs "his 'wife's' actions" and controls her sexuality.[99] First, the
husband isolates his wife from the outside world so that she becomes
dependent on him (2:7b–8). Second, he punishes her physically and
psychologically (2:9), which the poem describes with sexually graphic
terminology. Third, the husband promises his wife love and tenderness
to further control her (2:14). Yee finds this strategy "the most insidious
one, because the implications of such a strategy for actual battered
wives tend to be ignored, as the reader becomes caught up in the joyous reconciliation between Yahweh and Israel."[100] Yee also contends
that as beautiful or profound as this metaphor may be, it "is very problematic for women," as "studies have shown that many wives remain
in abusive relationships because periods of mistreatment are often followed by intervals of kindness and generosity."[101]

To Yee, then, the poem depicts a strategy, commonly used by battering husbands, that reinforces a battered wife's dependence. The problem is aggravated by the fact that the poem identifies God with the
husband. Yee explains: "This metaphor makes its theological point at
the expense of real women and children who were and still are victims
of sexual violence."[102] In other words, the hermeneutical danger consists in the possibility that some readers may justify husband battering
because God, the husband, punishes Israel, the wife, for her presumed
transgressions. Yee cautions against the uncritical appropriation of the
metaphor when she writes: "Moreover, the imaging of God as male/
husband becomes difficult when one forgets the metaphor God is *like* a
husband and insists literally that God *is* a husband and therefore always
male."[103]

The identification of God as a husband and the husband as God
is indeed dangerous and unacceptable. To Yee, the metaphor is not
"appropriate in describing the divine-human relationship for the modern reader."[104] She proposes the use of alternative metaphors for God,
such as in Hosea 11 or the expression, "the Wisdom of God, Woman
Wisdom as the tree of life."[105] In classic feminist fashion, then, Yee
advises abandoning harmful androcentric metaphors and replacing

99. Ibid.
100. Ibid., 212.
101. Ibid.
102. Ibid.
103. Ibid.
104. Ibid.
105. Ibid., 214.

them with women-centered images, as popularized by feminists since the 1970s.

Yet a third interpretation illustrates that a genealogical tracing of biblical meanings helps in understanding how interpreters view the world. Published in the *Global Bible Commentary* in 2004, this third interpretation is part of the increasing effort to contextualize biblical meanings in the Southern Hemisphere and to make "explicit the context and concerns from which the scholar reads the Bible."[106] The author, Tânia Mara Vieira Sampaio, examines Hosea 2:2–23 in conversation with Brazilian women who earn a living as prostitutes. She explains that to these women, living in great poverty, prostitution "is a means of survival and a practice of resistance."[107] Like Yee, Sampaio reads the poem from the perspective of the wife, but she concentrates on the issue of prostitution. She observes that, to the prophet, prostitution was not problematic as a social institution. Rather, Hosea criticized how prostitution was used in Israelite society. After a brief reference to the poem's presumed historical context, Sampaio elaborates on prostitution, its effects on the relationship between wives and husbands, and the hegemonic power dynamics in politics, economics, and religion that are part of the phenomenon of prostitution. Sampaio repeatedly underscores that the poem does not target "people's unfaithfulness"[108] but needs to be understood as "a broader critique of the social order, including a critique of a use of power comparable to prostitution by certain segments of the population, and in particular by the priests."[109] Sampaio thus proposes to regard prostitution as a characteristic of the sociopolitical interactions of the society's elite. She explains: "Prostitution marks the life of priests and political leaders because they expropriate the life of men, women, and children and interfere with the household rules of solidarity (*hesed*)."[110] In short, to Sampaio, the poem criticizes male political and religious leaders who, like prostitutes, destroy the lives of the people for money and power.

In Sampaio's interpretation, then, the biblical woman and the female prostitutes in São Paulo, Brazil, are vital to unlocking the poem's meaning. She states: "Keeping in mind the women from the Barrios of São Paulo, we seek to renew the reading of Hosea by reconsidering its

---

106. Daniel Patte, introduction to *Global Bible Commentary*, ed. Daniel Patte (Nashville: Abingdon, 2004), xxiii.
107. Tânia Mara Vieira Sampaio, "Hosea," in *Global Bible Commentary*, ed. Patte, 263.
108. Ibid.
109. Ibid.
110. Ibid., 268.

central theme, prostitution."[111] Hence, Sampaio rejects viewing prostitution as a universal metaphor to be filled with a reader's personal views, and instead she proposes to regard it as an "actual aspect of Israel's way of life."[112] Interpreted accordingly, the poem challenges sociopolitical and economic structures of injustice, oppression, and hierarchies in ancient Israel, but it does *not* criticize the wife. The poem's envisioned transformation is not limited to the relationship of wife and husband; it targets society as a whole.

Similar to Wolff, the twofold structure of Hosea 2:2–23 reinforces Sampaio's hermeneutical goal. The wife is not to be blamed for prostituting herself because she provides the necessities for her family's survival, similar to the women in São Paulo. The husband is, however, implicated in her dire situation because he does not help her to support the family. Consequently, readers should not hold the woman responsible or demand her repentance prior to the renewal of the relationship with her husband. Instead, so Sampaio, the poem presupposes that a renewal of the spousal relationship requires a change of the societal structures of domination toward equality and justice. The poem expresses this insight in Hosea 2:6, in which the wife refers to the husband as her "man" who is no longer her "Baal." Renewal occurs, so Sampaio, when the relationship becomes mutually wanted and the wife recognizes her husband as "the man with whom I freely associate myself," an association established "through a covenantal agreement between the woman and the man."[113] This voluntary and egalitarian relationship becomes possible only when the woman gains financial independence. Sampaio explains: "This new relationship is between the woman who, in her condition of prostitution, has been empowered to be a full partner in this covenant and the man who is also free to enter this covenant by resisting the existing social structures."[114] In other words, Sampaio attributes a positive aspect to the woman's work as a prostitute.

Importantly, the new relationship is not limited to the level of individuals. Instead, it is based on a transformation of all other sociopolitical relationships. To Sampaio, Hosea 3:3–4 depicts this necessary shift of power in society.[115] It ensures that prostitution ceases to exist, as it proliferates only during times of oppression and injustice. Sampaio

111. Ibid., 264.
112. Ibid., 266.
113. Ibid., 267.
114. Ibid.
115. Ibid., 268.

also demands that misogynist interpretations have to be relinquished because they fail to understand that the prophet critiques the hegemony of power exercised by political and religious leaders. Sampaio's interpretation combines historical references with contemporary cultural observations, merging into an innovative contextualized meaning of the poem. A focus on prostitution links the sociopolitical critique to the hegemonic structures of domination in society. This interpretation, then, demystifies the sociopolitical dimensions of biblical rhetoric and demands resistance to the exploitative status quo.

In summary, the genealogical tracing of three interpretations on Hosea 2:2–23 illustrates that biblical meanings provide access to views about "the world" that are multiple, shifting, and dynamic. They depend on the context in which they are produced, and they endorse or contest the sociopolitical, cultural, economic, and religious status quo. They illustrate that one simple, historical, and fixed meaning is unavailable. The genealogical tracing of the selected interpretations depicts the shifting, multiple, and "wandering" meanings that give insight into the hermeneutics of biblical interpreters and their views about the world.

Radicant Exegesis as a Practice of Coming to Know Ourselves in the Era of Altermodernity? Concluding Comments

As José Cabezón and Sheila Greeve Davaney state, many contemporary scholars do not subscribe to fixed, stable, and unchanging identities anymore but recognize the shifting, moving, and dynamic qualities of their interpretations.[116] The notion of fragmentary, transitory, and plural senses of identity is widespread, and the expectation of a detached and neutral observer has become obsolete. In this era of altermodernity, "unbound from an essentialist notion of roots and a pre-given endpoint,"[117] the focus is on the "subject" doing the research and the inextricable link between biblical meanings and readers.

This essay maintains that radicant exegesis develops such a sociologically defined task for biblical hermeneutics. It suggests that we need to examine biblical interpretations as illustrations of the moving, shifting, and multiple locations, influences, and preferences that are at work when people read biblical literature. As

---

116. José Cabezón and Sheila Greeve Davaney, introduction to *Identity and the Politics of Scholarship in the Study of Religion* (New York: Routledge, 2004), 4.
117. Larson, "Altermodernity and the Ethics of Translation," 3.

part of the post-postmodern age, biblical exegesis ought not to seek for exclusive origins or histories of the biblical world anymore. Rather, it needs to contribute to an ethics of resistance to—what Bourriaud calls—the globalizing forces of capitalist consumption and economic standardization. Radicant exegesis, sociologically understood, fosters such a stance. It offers a venue for understanding the world through the prism of biblical meanings.

When the focus is on gender and the phallogocentric symbolic order, the topic of rape proves critical, as this violent gender practice continues to shape hegemonic domination in the world. A feminist sociology of biblical hermeneutics takes account of these practices by tracing the genealogy of phallogocentrism in biblical interpretations, such as in Hosea 2:2–23. At stake is whether biblical meanings challenge or affirm the neocolonial status quo and how biblical interpreters have contributed to an ethics of gender that resists or contributes to phallogocentric and globalizing structures of hierarchy and domination.

As the case of Hosea 2:2–23 demonstrates, interpreters have developed very different biblical meanings. Wolff proposes the historical relationship between God and Israel as the central message. Writing in the early 1970s, he was oblivious of any gender discriminatory language, and he even advanced harsh anti-ecumenical views about Canaanite religion and Jewish-Christian theological relations. Yet he believes to present an objective account that depicts the historical meaning of this biblical poem. In contrast, Yee articulates a meaning of the poem that highlights the issue of adultery and the battering qualities in the relationship between divine husband and his wife, Israel. Grounded in a feminist hermeneutics, Yee's reading does not let go of historical explanations about the poem's references to Israel. Still her interpretation centers on the sexually violent imagery as the issue of contemporary feminist concern. The third interpretation by Sampaio moves the poem's meaning even further away from a phallogocentric interpretation. Presenting prostitution as the central topic, Sampaio emphasizes the interlocking systems of oppression as the key to her reading. Accordingly, the prophet envisions the transformation not only of the spousal relationship but also of society as a whole.

The three interpretations illustrate the larger sociological dynamics at play as they have developed in biblical hermeneutics: a history-focused, modern hermeneutic gives way to a gender-sensitive yet still modern hermeneutic, culminating in a postcolonial and gendered hermeneutic. These sociological developments are not linear, as these and other hermeneutical dynamics exist in a heterochronic fashion. The point is to recognize the different biblical meanings as part of a colorful and variously formed mosaic shaping the interpretation history of Hosea 2:2–23. Placed and analyzed together, the various readings teach about past and present discourses in which interpreters stand and within which they view the world. For instance, we need to discuss why Wolff is so oblivious to the poem's gendered discourse while Yee and Sampaio make it their unambiguous starting point. In other words, when we investigate the history of biblical interpretations we come to understand the biblical hermeneutics of the interpreters and their views about the world. The analysis helps us to determine whether their interpretations foster "a new common intelligibility,"[118] whether they contribute to the "countermovement" against neoliberal hierarchies and structures of domination, or whether their interpretations endorse "the official representations of the world."[119] The analysis exposes the politics of biblical meanings that readers advance even today.

In sum, radicant exegesis enables us to see the sociological contexts within which we articulate this or that biblical meaning. Our hermeneutical choices become plainly visible as embodied choices that serve particular power arrangements in the world. By placing various biblical meanings in conversation with each other, we understand that biblical meanings are subject to negotiation and part of the context in which they are created. They are identity makers and shapers, and there is no other way to give meanings to biblical texts in our post-postmodern era. Yet the recent history of feminist biblical studies demonstrates that feminist exegetes have found all kinds of paths to develop feminist meanings prior to the post-postmodern era. The next chapter presents the feminist exegetical discoveries since the 1970s.

---

118. Bourriaud, *The Radicant*, 188.
119. Ibid., 186.

PART III

The Politics of Hermeneutical and Cultural Alternatives

9

———

Discovering a Largely Unknown Past for a Vibrant Present: Feminist Hebrew Bible Studies in North America

The rise of feminist biblical studies in North America has been an ocean wave flooding the malestream world of biblical scholarship. Early on, feminist biblical scholars believed themselves to be the first to examine Christian and Jewish sacred texts with a feminist epistemology. They knew little about the accomplishments of previous generations of feminists and even less about the suffragists who opposed the use of the Bible in the justification of North American women's secondary status.[1] Only by chance did second-wave feminists discover the first feminist commentary on the Bible, published in the 1890s by US-American suffragist, Elizabeth Cady Stanton, and her editorial team.[2] Reading *The*

---

1. For a survey on American women reading the Bible in the eighteenth and nineteenth centuries, see Carolyn De Swarte Gifford, "American Women and the Bible: The Nature of Woman as a Hermeneutical Issue," in *Feminist Perspectives on Biblical Scholarship*, ed. Adela Yarbro Collins (Chico, CA: Scholars Press, 1985), 11–33.
2. Elizabeth Cady Stanton, ed., *The Woman's Bible* (Boston: Northeastern University Press, 1993). For a history on the leading suffragist in the United States, see, e.g., Kathi Kern, *Mrs. Stanton's Bible* (Ithaca, NY: Cornell University Press, 2001), 7: "In 1974, the Seattle-based Coalition Task Force on Women and Religion published its edition of *The Woman's Bible*, a reprint made from two volumes that Jane T. Walker of Tacoma, Washington, had inherited from her suffragist mother. . . . Having

Women's Bible, second-wave feminists learned about the nineteenth-century feminist engagement with religion and the Bible. Similarly, feminist biblical scholars at the end of the twentieth century were inspired by the larger civil rights and social movements of liberation and justice of their own time. Initially, they focused on gender and soon connected their theories with other forms of oppression, such as race, class, and the globalizing structures of empire.

Several feminist Bible scholars of the pioneering generation reminisced about the impact of larger social movements on feminist biblical scholarship. Kathleen M. O'Connor, Old Testament professor at Columbia Theological Seminary, refers to the "troubling disruption" feminist thought brought to biblical studies, stirring up "vital energy" for the well-being of people and the globe.[3] She states: "Feminist ideas broke in upon us all as a troubling disruption of the way things were and as an exhilarating revelation of how they might be. . . . They stirred up vital energy to work for the well-being of future generations, and ultimately for the earth itself."[4] Similarly, Phyllis Bird acknowledges the far-reaching effects of the women's movement on women and men and its critique of the interpretation history and discriminatory stereotypes when she explains:

> The women's movement of the seventies and eighties has affected us all, male and female. We have been led in directions we never planned to go, and we have arrived at places we could not have imagined when we began our journeys. . . . It was an exciting time of discovery as we explored a largely unknown past, attempting to disentangle it from an interpretive legacy of narrow and oppressive stereotypes.[5]

Also Elisabeth Schüssler Fiorenza makes comprehensive connections between the social justice movements of the civil rights era and the emergence of feminist studies as a new intellectual force, bursting forth in every academic field, deconstructing androcentric knowledge, and envisioning "an inclusive feminist comprehension of the world, human life, and history." She observes:

enjoyed *The Woman's Bible* herself, Walker wrote to the Coalition Task Force, she was 'glad to share it with my sister women.'"

3. Kathleen M. O'Connor, "The Feminist Movement Meets the Old Testament: One Woman's Perspective," in *Engaging the Bible in a Gendered World: An Introduction to Feminist Biblical Interpretation in Honor of Katharine Doob Sakenfeld*, ed. Linda Day and Carolyn Pressler (Louisville: Westminster John Knox, 2006), 3.
4. O'Connor, "Feminist Movement Meets the Old Testament," 3.
5. Phyllis A. Bird, preface to *Missing Persons and Mistaken Identities: Women and Gender in Ancient Israel* (Minneapolis: Fortress Press, 1997), 3–4.

The resurgence of the women's movement in the 1960s not only revived women's political struggle for civil rights and equal access to academic institutions but also brought forth feminist studies as a new intellectual discipline. In all areas of scientific and intellectual knowledge there now exist courses and research projects that seek to expand our knowledge of women's cultural and historical contributions as well as to challenge the silence about us in historiography, literature, sociology, and all the human sciences. Such feminist scholarship is compensatory as well as revolutionary. It has inaugurated a scientific revolution that engenders a scholarly paradigm shift from an androcentric—male-centered—world view and perspective to an inclusive feminist comprehension of the world, human life, and history.[6]

This essay describes major developmental phases of feminist biblical studies in North America since the 1970s, beginning with sections outlining its inception; moving to the 1980s, when feminist biblical studies expanded and deepened its institutional connections and scholarly perspectives; and surveying the 1990s when the field moved toward intersectional hermeneutical approaches, and also mentioning the current phase in the early twenty-first century, when feminist biblical scholars work on fostering global intersectionality and dialogical relationships.[7] The essay then discusses the implications of economic neoliberalism on expanded concepts of feminist biblical hermeneutics, and eventually elaborates on three challenges for the current development of the field. The conclusion stresses the need to resist fragmentation and disengagement in large part due to the global neoliberal economic structures affecting academic work in religious and theological studies in particular and the humanities in general.

Discovering "Women" as a Category of Biblical Interpretation in the 1970s

Once women's right to vote was established in Canada in 1919 and in the United States in 1920, the heyday of women's activism declined. Books on women and the Bible were still published, but they lacked the political zeal and intellectual fervor of nineteenth-century

6. Elisabeth Schüssler Fiorenza, *Bread Not Stone: The Challenge of Feminist Biblical Interpretation* (Boston: Beacon, 1984), 2.
7. For a slightly different mapping of the phases in feminist biblical studies, see Pamela J. Milne, "Toward Feminist Companionship: The Future of Feminist Biblical Studies and Feminism," in *A Feminist Companion to Reading the Bible: Approaches, Methods, and Strategies*, ed. Athalya Brenner and Carole Fontaine (Sheffield: Sheffield Academic, 1997), 39–60.

suffragists.[8] It did not help that very few women were admitted into the ranks of biblical scholarship from the 1920s to the 1950s. Those who became professors remained at the margins of the scholarly discourse, as a cursory look at the membership roster of the Society of Biblical Literature (SBL) illustrates.[9] This situation only changed with the emergence of the feminist movement in general and the early publications of Mary Daly in particular,[10] all of which radicalized feminists of various religious traditions in North America. Judith Plaskow firmly makes this connection when she states: "The history of feminist biblical scholarship in the 1970s in the United States cannot be separated from the larger history of the feminist movement."[11]

Also important was a 1971 meeting in Atlanta during the gathering of two major professional societies, the American Academy of Religion (AAR) and the SBL. The meeting's goal was to establish "a women's caucus in the field and to demand that program time be allotted to papers and panels on women and religion."[12] Rita Gross, a professor of comparative religion, remembers:

> That meeting, which occurred in November in Atlanta, was probably the single most generative event of the feminist transformation of religious studies. Before the meeting, isolated, relatively young and unestablished scholars struggled to define what it meant to study women and religion and to demonstrate why it was so important to do so. After the meeting, a strong network of like-minded individuals had been established, and we had begun to make our presence and our agenda known to the AAR and the SBL.[13]

At this meeting the AAR/SBL Women's Caucus was founded and two chairs were elected: Carol Christ, who became renowned for her work

---

8. For more details, see Susanne Scholz, *Introducing the Women's Bible* (London: T&T Clark, 2007), 19–23.
9. See Dorothy C. Bass, "Women's Studies and Biblical Studies," *JSOT* 22 (February 1982): 6–12, esp. 9: "Similar growth between 1910 and 1920 brought women's membership to twenty-four in a total of 231, better than ten per cent. . . . After 1920, however, the figures began to slip. In 1930, women were at approximately eight per cent; in 1940, about six per cent; and in 1950, five per cent. Figures are missing for 1960, but by 1970 women were only three and one-half per cent of SBL members."
10. Mary Daly, *The Church and the Second Sex* (New York: Knopf, 1968); Mary Daly, *Beyond God the Father: Toward a Philosophy of Women's Liberation* (Boston: Beacon, 1973).
11. Judith Plaskow, "Movement and Emerging Scholarship: Feminist Biblical Scholarship in the 1970s in the United States," in *Feminist Biblical Studies in the Twentieth Century: Scholarship and Movement*, ed. Elisabeth Schüssler Fiorenza, The Bible and Women: An Encyclopedia of Exegesis and Cultural History 10 (Stuttgart: Kohlhammer, 2014), 28.
12. Rita Gross, *Feminism and Religion: An Introduction* (Boston: Beacon, 1996), 46.
13. Ibid., 47.

on goddess religions, and Elisabeth Schüssler Fiorenza, who served as the first woman president of the SBL in 1987.[14]

The creation of a feminist infrastructure at the scholarly level helped to gather momentum on the feminist hermeneutical level. In 1973, Phyllis Trible published a widely read article titled "Depatriarchalizing in Biblical Interpretation,"[15] in which she acknowledges a "terrible dilemma"[16] presented by the movement: to choose between "the God of the fathers or the God of sisterhood."[17] Trible considers this choice to be a false dichotomy. To her, the Bible is not irredeemably patriarchal,[18] and so she asserts: "The Women's Movement errs when it dismisses the Bible as inconsequential or condemns it as enslaving. In rejecting Scripture women ironically accept male chauvinistic interpretations and thereby capitulate to the very view they are protesting."[19] Hence, Trible declares that "the Hebrew Scriptures and Women's Liberation do meet and . . . their encounter need not be hostile."[20] She also warns that feminist Bible readers are "unfaithful readers" if they do not apply "the depatriarchalizing principle and recover it in those texts and themes where it is present, and . . . accent it in our translation."[21] Otherwise they "neglect biblical passages which break with patriarchy"[22] and permit "interpretations to freeze in a patriarchal box of our own construction."[23]

Other feminist scholars also produced pioneering work. In 1974, Rosemary Radford Ruether, at the time professor at Garret-Evangelical Seminary, edited a highly influential anthology titled *Religion and Sexism: Images of Women in the Jewish and Christian Traditions*.[24] The volume

14. By 2017, only eight women scholars have served as SBL presidents: Phyllis Trible in 1994, Adele Berlin in 2000, Carolyn Osiek in 2005, Katherine Doob Sakenfeld in 2007, Carol Newsom in 2011, Carol Meyers in 2013, Athalya Brenner in 2015, and Beverly Roberts Gaventa in 2017. Patrick Gray calls the SBL "an exclusive fraternity" and finds this "not a wholly inappropriate term" despite the service of several women presidents since its founding in 1880; see Patrick Gray, "Presidential Addresses of the Society of Biblical Literature: A Quasquicentennial Review," *JBL* 125, no. 1 (2006): 167–77, esp. 167.
15. Phyllis Trible, "Depatriarchalizing in Biblical Interpretation," *JAAR* 41, no. 1 (1973): 30–48.
16. Ibid., 30.
17. Ibid., 31.
18. Ibid.
19. Ibid.
20. Ibid., 47.
21. Trible's proposal created important inner-feminist biblical critique; see, e.g., Nancy Fuchs-Kreimer, "Feminism and Scripture Interpretation: A Contemporary Jewish Critique," *Journal of Ecumenical Studies* 20 (1988): 539–41; Elisabeth Schüssler Fiorenza, *But She Said: Feminist Practices of Biblical Interpretation* (Boston: Beacon, 1992), 21–24.
22. Trible, "Depatriarchalizing," 48.
23. Ibid.
24. Rosemary Radford Ruether, ed., *Religion and Sexism: Images of Women in the Jewish and Christian Traditions* (New York: Simon & Schuster, 1974).

includes an article on the Hebrew Bible by Phyllis Bird,[25] who presents a reading of Genesis 1–3 that assesses the biblical creation narratives from a feminist perspective. Grounded in historical criticism, Bird suggests that the first story portrays humanity—female and male—with its biological functions as divinely created in the image of God. The second narrative stresses psychosocial rather than biological functions of women and men in ancient Israelite society. Bird's interpretation highlights gender with the aim of challenging essentialized meanings attributed to the biblical creation texts in Western society. At the end of the 1970s, then, the feminist study of the Hebrew Bible in North America had burst onto the scholarly scene.

The Expansion of Sexual Politics and Gender in Feminist Biblical Perspectives during the 1980s

In the 1980s, feminist biblical scholars expanded and deepened the study of the Bible in relation to women, gender, and sexuality. One publication, "The Effects of Women's Studies on Biblical Studies," illustrates the energies that began to manifest in the field. The volume contains the papers from a panel discussion that had taken place during the 1980s centennial celebration at the annual meeting of the SBL. In 1982, the papers appeared in the British publication *Journal for the Study of the Old Testament*[26] and not in the SBL-sponsored *Journal of Biblical Literature*. Pamela J. Milne points out that it must have been "surely an embarrassment to the SBL"[27] when it became obvious that the SBL had missed the mark. The editor of the volume, Phyllis Trible, hints at this when she acknowledges:

> From the beginning, all of us involved in this session, speakers and listeners, knew that we were not celebrating a centennial. In the SBL, as in society at large, women have little, if anything, to celebrate.[28]

During this second phase, the nearly exclusive research focus was on women and gender. Already in 1982, Katherine Doob Sakenfeld recognized "the cultural and functional inseparability of racism, sexism, and

---

25. Phyllis Bird, "Images of the Women in the Old Testament," in Ruether, *Religion and Sexism*, 41–88. For yet another influential early feminist interpretation, see Phyllis Trible, "Eve and Adam: Genesis 2–3 Reread," *Andover Newton Quarterly* (March 1973): 251–58.

26. Phyllis Trible, ed., "The Effects of Women's Studies on Biblical Studies," *JSOT* 22 (February 1982): 3–71.

27. Milne, "Toward Feminist Companionship," 42.

28. Ibid., 3.

classism,"[29] and saw these issues addressed "on the theological front" but not in biblical studies, where "the literature dealing with these three 'isms' remains on three separate tracks."[30] She accepted that "we Bible specialists have more work to do in this area"[31] and in analyzing the intersectionality of gender and other social categories.

In 1987, Toinette M. Eugene, an ethicist and womanist scholar, responded to these discussions by articulating the parameters of a womanist biblical hermeneutics. She explained that due to women of color's "doubly and triply oppressed" status in patriarchal society, it does not suffice to identify patriarchal oppression with androcentrism alone. Rather, sexism must be understood as part of other oppressive ideologies, such as racism, militarism, or imperialism, because "the structures of oppression are all intrinsically linked."[32] She thus advises that a feminist biblical hermeneutics needs "to articulate an alternative liberating vision and praxis for all oppressed people by utilizing the paradigm of women's experiences of survival and salvation in the struggle against patriarchal oppression and degradation."[33] Yet Eugene's general proposal for the inclusion of other forms of social analysis did not find full articulation in the 1980s, when many feminist biblical scholars continued focusing on gender and androcentrism only. Accordingly, Nyasha Junior remarks:

A brief survey of key works in that field [i.e., feminist biblical studies] attests to the lack of substantive impact that womanist approaches have had on the discipline of biblical studies. The volume edited by Adela Yarbro Collins, *Feminist Perspectives on Biblical Scholarship* (1985), does not include an article on black feminist or womanist thought. In Letty Russell's edited volume, *Feminist Interpretation of the Bible* (1985), Cannon, an ethicist, contributes an article on black feminist consciousness. In addition, Cannon writes "Womanist Interpretation and Preaching in the Black Church," in Elisabeth Schüssler Fiorenza's *Searching the Scriptures* (1993). In the seventeen volumes of the Feminist Companion to the Bible series, edited by Athalya Brenner, only one article has an explicitly womanist approach. Brenner's overview volume, *A Feminist Companion to Reading the*

---

29. Katharine Doob Sakenfeld, "Old Testament Perspectives: Methodological Issues," *JSOT* 22 (1982): 13–20 (here 19).
30. Ibid., 19.
31. Ibid.
32. Toinette M. Eugene, "A Hermeneutical Challenge for Womanists: The Interrelation between the Text and Our Experience," in *Perspectives on Feminist Hermeneutics*, ed. Gayle G. Koontz and Willard Swartley (Elkhart, IN: Institute for Mennonite Studies, 1987), 20. For a general discussion of womanist theology, see, e.g., Delores S. Williams, "The Color of Feminism: Or Speaking the Black Woman's Tongue," *Journal of Religious Thought* 43, no. 1 (Spring-Summer 1986): 42–58.
33. Eugene, "A Hermeneutical Challenge for Womanists," 25.

Bible (1997), does not include an article on womanist biblical interpretation. In the nine volumes of the Feminist Companion to the New Testament and Early Christian Writings series, edited by Amy-Jill Levine, there are no articles from a womanist perspective. Moreover, to date there is no full-length monograph on womanist biblical interpretation or edited volume utilizing womanizing approaches.[34]

The omission of race, class, and geopolitical dynamics as analytical categories in much of the pioneering work in feminist biblical studies is obvious today, and so many feminist scholars from around the world have come to embrace intersectional, postcolonial, and dialogical hermeneutics. Yet in the 1980s, North American feminist biblical scholars were mainly white women working in departments of religious studies and schools of theology. They aimed to establish themselves in academic institutions and in a discipline that defines exegetical work as objective, universal, and value neutral, and they were surrounded and embedded in white, kyriarchal contexts mostly hermeneutically hostile toward feminism of any kind. Thus the exegetical focus on women and gender was usually already a huge challenge to the mostly white, male, and senior academic colleagues who populated schools and departments. The feminist hermeneutical stance challenged the dominant modernist notion of objectivity, disinterestedness, and the possibility of extracting the original meaning of the biblical text. From the beginning, thus, feminist exegetes have understood their projects as analyzing multi-axial power relations in which gender, sexuality, race, ethnicity, nationality, age, physical abilities, and other ideological-theological stances play central roles, although much of the early work was limited to women and gender.

Two feminist biblical publications stand out in this period because they fueled the feminist research agenda for years to come. These books reframe epistemological, hermeneutical, and methodological priorities and lend scholarly legitimacy to women and gender research in biblical studies. Elisabeth Schüssler Fiorenza's *In Memory of Her* is one of the books.[35] The author explains in the introduction to the tenth edition that she "set out to explore the problem of women's historical agency in ancient Christianity in light of the theological and historical

34. For a constructive critique of this situation, see, e.g., Nyasha Junior, "Womanist Biblical Interpretation," in *Engaging the Bible in a Gendered World: An Introduction to Feminist Biblical Interpretation in Honor of Katharine Doob Sakenfeld*, ed. Linda Day and Carolyn Pressler (Louisville: Westminster John Knox, 2006), 44.
35. Elisabeth Schüssler Fiorenza, *In Memory of Her: A Feminist Theological Reconstruction of Christian Origins*, 10th anniversary ed. (New York: Crossroad, 2002).

questions raised by the feminist movements in society and church and to do so in terms of critical biblical studies."[36] To Schüssler Fiorenza, Christian women and men of the first century attempted to practice "the call to coequal discipleship" with various levels of success. At the time, she worried whether "feminists might label the book as 'male scholarship,' whereas my colleagues in biblical studies might not take it seriously."[37] Yet her concerns were unfounded, as the book was quickly recognized as a milestone accomplishment. For instance, in 1984, the feminist ethicist Beverly W. Harrison asserted: "In *Memory of Her* is, I believe, the most fulsome proposal we yet possess for a feminist hermeneutics that addresses the full circle of human interpretation."[38]

The other work that galvanized feminist biblical studies comes from Phyllis Trible. Her 1984 volume, *Texts of Terror*,[39] presents four biblical women: Hagar, Tamar, an unnamed woman, and the daughter of Jephthah. Informed by a feminist hermeneutic and rhetorical criticism, Trible selected these "ancient tales of terror" because, as she explains, they "speak all too frighteningly of the present."[40] She acknowledges that her study was possible only because of her earlier and more joyous work of 1978, *God and the Rhetoric of Sexuality*.[41] Both volumes unearth stories about women and gender in the Hebrew Bible that have been neglected in Christian and Jewish communities. Trible's project jolted scholars and lay readers alike into a newfound awareness of these biblical texts and their tremendous significance for discussions on women and gender with hints toward other forms of oppression, such as nationality and class.[42]

Informed by a feminist hermeneutic, Trible reads the selected narratives in *Texts of Terror* as "stories of outrage on behalf of their female victims in order to recover a neglected history, to remember a past that the present embodies, and to pray that these terrors shall not come to pass again."[43] Trible's method of rhetorical criticism emphasizes the literary form of the biblical texts. Her interpretations also hint at other

36. Ibid., xiv.
37. Ibid.
38. Beverly W. Harrison, review of *In Memory of Her*, by Elisabeth Schüssler Fiorenza, *Horizons* 11, no. 1 (Spring 1984): 150.
39. Phyllis Trible, *Texts of Terror: Literary-Feminist Readings of Biblical Narratives* (Philadelphia: Fortress Press, 1984).
40. Ibid., xiii.
41. Phyllis Trible, *God and the Rhetoric of Sexuality* (Philadelphia: Fortress Press, 1978).
42. See, e.g., ibid., 27.
43. Trible, *Texts of Terror*, 3.

forms of oppression, such as nationality and class.[44] In 1986, Claudia Camp praises the work with the following words:

> Trible's groundbreaking literary-critical method operates on the principle that storytelling speaks for itself and, indeed, her subtle application of the method coupled with her own evocative prose prove the dictum true. One emerges from the book fainting with horror and, on reflection, amazed that one's consciousness has been thus raised not by polemic against either biblical or contemporary patriarchy, but simply by a close reading of the texts themselves.[45]

Many important studies of the 1980s explore the complexities of female characters, topics, and references in biblical literature, history, and tradition. In Hebrew Bible studies they include the works of Phyllis Bird, Peggy L. Day, J. Cheryl Exum, Tikva Frymer-Kensky, Esther Fuchs, Alice L. Laffey, Carol Meyers, Katharine Doob Sakenfeld, Elisabeth Schüngel-Straumann, and Renita J. Weems;[46] in early Christian literature they include the studies by Bernadette Brooten, Mary Rose D'Angelo, Jane Schaberg, Sandra M. Schneiders, Luise Schottroff, Mary Ann Tolbert, and Antoinette Wire.[47] The studies of these and other scholars expand and deepen feminist research beyond anything ever written before. Yet it needs to be remembered that for institutional, hermeneutical, and sociopolitical reasons, feminist interpreters do not usually attend to other intersectional dynamics in this period, and so these publications practice a politics of omission despite their tremendously innovative and pioneering accomplishments.

Toward a Differentiation of Feminist, Womanist, and *Mujerista* Exegesis in the 1990s

Feminist exegesis expanded in the 1990s when voices of "otherness" became increasingly vocal. For the first time, African American women

44. See, e.g., ibid., 27.
45. Claudia V. Camp, review of *Texts of Terror: Literary-Feminist Readings of Biblical Narratives*, by Phyllis Trible, *JAAR* 54, no. 1 (1986): 160.
46. Renita J. Weems, *Just A Sister Away* (New York: Grand Central Publishing, 1988); Carol Meyers, *Discovering Eve: Ancient Israelite Women in Context* (New York: Oxford University Press, 1988); Alice L. Laffey, *An Introduction to the Old Testament: A Feminist Perspective* (Philadelphia: Fortress Press, 1988); Peggy L. Day, ed., *Gender and Difference in Ancient Israel* (Minneapolis: Fortress Press, 1989).
47. Bernadette Brooten, *Women Leaders in the Ancient Synagogue* (Chico, CA: Scholars Press, 1982); and Mary Ann Tolbert, *The Bible and Feminist Hermeneutics* (Chico, CA: Scholars Press, 1983); Sandra M. Schneiders, *Women and the Word* (Mahwah, NJ: Paulist Press, 1986); Jane Schaberg, *The Illegitimacy of Jesus: A Feminist Theological Interpretation of the Infancy Narratives* (San Francisco: Harper & Row, 1987).

scholars join interpreters from South Africa and other African countries.[48] All of them criticize white feminist biblical discourse for
neglecting race. They prefer the term *womanism* for Christian black
women scholarship, based on Alice Walker's definition coming "from
womanish. . . . A black feminist or feminist of color. From the black
expression of mothers to female children, 'You acting womanish,' like
a woman. Usually referring to outrageous, audacious, courageous or
willful behavior."[49]

Womanist theologians assert that racism is as urgent as sexism and
demand that feminist biblical scholarship investigate both gender and
race. They want biblical interpretations to focus "on *all* historically
marginalized persons, women and men, who have been victimized by
patriarchal dominance."[50] They advise white feminists to deal with
racist assumptions[51] because "black women seek to redeem life from
patriarchal *and* racist death."[52] Womanists also criticize the binary distinction of female and male, urging feminist biblical scholars to seek
the transformation of sociopolitical and cultural-religious structures
of oppression based on sexism, classism, sexuality,[53] and geopolitics.[54]

48. See, e.g., Madipoane J. Masenya, "African Womanist Hermeneutics: A Suppressed Voice from
South Africa Speaks," *JFSR* 11, no. 1 (1995): 149–55; Maxine Howell, "Towards a Womanist Pneuma-
tological Pedagogy: Reading and Re-reading the Bible from British Black Women's Perspectives,"
Black Theology 7, no. 1 (2009), 86–99. For an example of a womanist interpretation on a specific biblical text, see, e.g., Ncumisa Manona, "The Presence of Women in Parables: An Afrocentric Womanist Perspective," *Scriptura* 81 (2002): 408-21; Raquel A. St. Clair, *Call and Consequences: A Womanist
Reading of Mark* (Minneapolis: Fortress Press, 2008).

49. See Alice Walker, *In Search of Our Mothers' Gardens: Womanist Prose* (San Diego: Harcourt Brace
Jovanovich, 1983), xi. See also the reference to Walker's definition in Delores S. Williams, "Womanist Theology: Black Women's Voices," in *Black Theology: A Documentary History*, vol. 2, *1980-1992*,
ed. James H. Cone and Gayraud S. Wilmore (Maryknoll, NY: Orbis, 1993), 265; Williams' essay was
first published in 1987.

50. Clarice J. Martin, "Womanist Interpretation of the New Testament: The Quest for Holistic and
Inclusive Translation and Interpretation," *JFSR* 6, no. 2 (1990): 53. For a brief historical survey of
biblical womanist scholarship, see also Michael Joseph Brown, "The Womanization of Blackness,"
in *Blackening of the Bible: The Aims of African American Biblical Scholarship* (Harrisburg, PA: Trinity
Press International, 2004), 89–119.

51. See also the challenge by Asian feminist theologian Kwok Pui-lan, "Racism and Ethnocentrism in
Feminist Biblical Interpretation," in *Searching the Scriptures: A Feminist Introduction*, ed. Elisabeth
Schüssler Fiorenza (New York: Crossroad, 1993), 101–16.

52. Mukti Barton, "The Skin of Miriam Became as White as Snow: The Bible, Western Feminism and
Colour Politics," *Feminist Theology* 27 (May 2001): 80 (emphasis added). See also Koala Jones-War-
saw, "Toward a Feminist Hermeneutic: Reading of Judges 19–21," *Journal of the Interdenominational
Theological Center* 22, no. 1 (1994): 30. For a survey discussion, see Clarice J. Martin, "Womanist Biblical Interpretation," in *Dictionary of Biblical Interpretation*, ed. John H. Hayes (Nashville: Abingdon,
1999), 655–58.

53. See, e.g., Renee L. Hill, "Who Are We for Each Other? Sexism, Sexuality and Womanist Theology,"
in Cone and Wilmore, *1980-1992*, 345–51.

54. For early and influential publications, see Sheila Briggs, "Can an Enslaved God Liberate?
Hermeneutical Reflections on Philippians 2:6–11," *Semeia* 47 (1989): 137–53; Clarice J. Martin,
"Womanist Interpretations of the New Testament: The Quest for Holistic and Inclusive Transla-
tion and Interpretation," *JFSR* 6, no. 2 (1990): 4–61; Renita J. Weems, "The Hebrew Women Are Not

Otherwise, feminist scholarship would be "like patriarchal scholarship," "seeking its own perpetuation," and be "doomed."[55]

More recently, some black feminist/womanist biblical scholars discuss their ambivalence at being characterized as "womanist." Wilda C. M. Gafney explains that her "primary self-designation" is "a black feminist," a self-definition that reclaims the term *feminism* "from the pale hands of those who infected it with racism and classism."[56] She also acknowledges that in contexts dominated by racism and classism, she prefers the term *womanist* "to avoid being coopted by white feminists."[57] Sometimes she considers "a hybridized identifier, fem/womanist" most appropriate because it describes "the intersection of feminist and womanist practices."[58] New Testament scholar, Gay L. Byron, elaborates on the complexities of being classified as a "womanist Bible scholar." In a discussion on "my own brand of womanist biblical hermeneutics,"[59] she suggests taking seriously the transnational context of black feminism in the United States and developing "a more sustained focus on the common themes that U.S. Black feminists share with women of African descent throughout the world."[60] She also advises feminist Bible scholars, particularly in the field of New Testament, "to listen to the voices of those who adhere to 'different' faiths, hail from 'other' cultures, and live in 'distant' lands as we reformulate the methodologies that might lead to a more representative form of global feminist biblical interpretation."[61]

We need to keep in mind that the number of womanist *biblical* scholars has been relatively small. In 2001, only forty-five African American scholars held doctoral degrees in biblical studies. Eleven of them were women, eight of whom specialized in Hebrew Bible and three in New

Like the Egyptian Women: The Ideology of Race, Gender and Sexual Reproduction in Exodus 1," *Semeia* 59 (1992): 25–34.

55. Renita J. Weems, "Womanist Reflections on Biblical Hermeneutics," in *Black Theology: A Documentary History*, vol. 2, *1980-1992*, ed. Cone and Wilmore, 217. More recently, see Raquel St. Clair, "Womanist Biblical Interpretation," in *True to Our Native Land: An African American New Testament Commentary*, ed. Brian K. Blount (Minneapolis: Fortress Press, 2007), 54–62.

56. Wilda C. M. Gafney, "A Black Feminist Approach to Biblical Studies," *Encounter* 67, no. 4 (Autumn 2006): 397.

57. Ibid.

58. Ibid.

59. Gay L. Byron, "The Challenge of 'Blackness' for Rearticulating the Meaning of Global Feminist New Testament Interpretation," in *Feminist New Testament Studies: Global and Future Perspectives*, ed. Kathleen O'Brien Wicker, Althea Spencer Miller, Musa W. Dube (New York: Palgrave Macmillan, 2005), 97.

60. Ibid.

61. Ibid., 95. For another call toward multimethodological, multireligious, and multiperspectival hermeneutics, see, e.g., Cheryl B. Anderson, *Ancient Laws and Contemporary Controversies: The Need for Inclusive Biblical Interpretation* (New York: Oxford University Press, 2009).

Testament. As a consequence, many womanist *theologians* have published womanist Bible interpretations.[62] They have taken seriously Jacquelyn Grant's 1978 criticism that the black church and theologians "treat Black women as if they were invisible creatures" although "Black women represent more than 50% of the Black community and more than 70% of the Black Church."[63] Even in 2013, the situation is still dire. For instance, Junior states:

> Given the very few numbers of African American and other women of color in biblical studies, womanist biblical interpretation will have a limited impact in the field of biblical studies as long as "womanist" refers to an individual scholar instead of to her work. . . . As long as womanist work remains work that is to a considerable degree "of black women, by black women, and for black women" . . . it will remain on the margins of biblical scholarship.[64]

In the North American context, women's diverse social locations are also highlighted by *mujerista* theologians. The term *mujerista* derives from the Spanish word for woman, *mujer*. They stress that Hispanic women's contexts need to shape their Bible interpretations. For instance, Ada María Isasi-Díaz, a trained Christian ethicist, proposes to ground biblical interpretations in the lives of Hispanic women so that the Bible serves as their direct support system. She also recommends that Hispanic women "analyze and test their lives against those sections of the Bible which are life-giving for them."[65] Yet, to date, a book on *mujerista* biblical interpretation published by a *mujerista* scholar with a doctoral degree in biblical studies does not exist.[66]

62. See, e.g., Kelly Brown Douglas, who acknowledges: "I am a theologian and not a biblical scholar. . . . It is important for me to approach this timely issue as a theologian and not a biblical scholar." See her article entitled "Marginalized People, Liberating Perspectives: A Womanist Approach to Biblical Interpretation," *Anglican Theological Review* 83, no. 1 (2001): 41. For a historical survey on the significance of the Bible in African American communities, see Vincent L. Wimbush, "The Bible and African Americans: An Outline of an Interpretative History," in *Stony the Road We Trod: African American Biblical Interpretation*, ed. Cain Hope Felder (Minneapolis: Fortress Press, 1991), 81–97. For early womanist theological work, see Delores S. Williams, *Sisters in the Wilderness: The Challenge of Womanist God-Talk* (Maryknoll, NY: Orbis, 1993); Katie Geneva Cannon, *Katie's Canon: Womanism and the Soul of the Black Community* (New York: Continuum, 1995). See also Katie Geneva Cannon, "The Emergence of Black Feminist Consciousness," in *Feminist Interpretation of the Bible*, ed. Letty M. Russell (Philadelphia: Westminster Press, 1985), 30–40.
63. Jacquelyn Grant, "Black Theology and the Black Woman," in *Black Theology: A Documentary History*, vol. 1, *1966-1979*, ed. James H. Cone and Gayraud S. Wilmore (Maryknoll, NY: Orbis, 1993), 433.
64. Nyasha Junior, "Womanist Interpretation," in *The Oxford Encyclopedia of Biblical Interpretation*, ed. Steven L. McKenzie (New York: Oxford University Press, 2013), 455.
65. Ada María Isasi-Díaz, "The Bible and *Mujerista* Theology," in *Lift Every Voice: Constructing Christian Theologies from the Underside*, ed. Susan Brooks Thistlethwaite and Mary Potter Engel (Maryknoll, NY: Orbis, 1998), 274. See also, e.g., Isasi-Díaz, *En la Lucha: In the Struggle; A Hispanic Women's Liberation Theology* (Minneapolis: Fortress Press, 1993).

Despite the concerns articulated by womanist and *mujerista* theologians, many explicitly feminist publications focus mostly on androcentrism.[67] The various editions of the *Women's Bible Commentary*, edited by Carol A. Newsom and Sharon H. Ringe,[68] contain interpretations on every biblical book of the Christian canon with a focus on women and gender, and the second and third editions also include discussions on the Apocrypha. The editors explain that "women have read the Bible for countless generations" but "we have not always been self-conscious about reading as women."[69] They explain that the title of the commentary refers to women in the plural because the editors and contributors recognized the need for intersectional feminist readings even when individual interpretations do not always make such intersectional connections visible. In 2012, they also state that the third edition of the volume features North American feminist scholarship as a "pragmatic decision"[70] to deal with the growing plurality in women's interpretations of the Bible. The commentary is currently the best known and academically most rigorous one-volume publication on all biblical books of the Christian canon focused on women and gender. Its significance in the history of feminist biblical studies in North America cannot be overemphasized.

Yet there are others. One of them is the Jewish feminist Torah commentary of 2008 titled *The Torah: A Women's Commentary* and edited by Tamara Cohn Eshkenazi and Andrea L. Weiss, featuring multiple Jewish feminist voices and approaches to the first five books of the Bible.[71]

---

66. Yet articles do exist; see, e.g., Fernando F. Segovia, "Mujerista Theology: Biblical Interpretation and Political Theology," *Feminist Theology: The Journal of the Britain and Ireland School of Feminist Theology* 20 (2011): 1–7.

67. See, e.g., Sharon Pace Jeansonne, *The Women of Genesis: From Sarah to Potiphar's Wife* (Minneapolis: Fortress Press, 1990); Tikva Frymer-Kensky, *In the Wake of the Goddesses: Women, Culture, and the Biblical Pagan Myth* (New York: Free Press, 1992); Danna Nolan Fewell and David M. Gunn, *Gender, Power and Promise: The Subject of the Bible's First Story* (Nashville: Abingdon, 1993); Claudia V. Camp and Carole R. Fontaine, eds., *Women, War, and Metaphor: Language and Society in the Study of the Hebrew Bible*, Semeia 61 (Atlanta: Scholars Press, 1993); Ilona N. Rashkow, *Taboo or Not Taboo: Sexuality and Family in the Hebrew Bible* (Minneapolis: Fortress Press, 2000); Claudia V. Camp, *Wise, Strange and Holy: The Strange Woman and the Making of the Bible* (Sheffield: Sheffield Academic, 2000); Joan L. Mitchell, *Beyond Fear and Silence: A Feminist-Literary Reading of Mark* (London: Continuum, 2001); Dorothy Lee, *Flesh and Glory: Symbol, Gender, and Theology in the Gospel of John* (New York: Crossroad, 2002); Christina Grenholm and Daniel Patte, eds., *Gender, Tradition and Romans: Share Ground, Uncertain Borders* (London: T&T Clark, 2005).

68. Carol A. Newsom and Sharon H. Ringe, eds., *Women's Bible Commentary* (Louisville: Westminster John Knox, 1992); 2nd ed., 1998; 3rd ed., ed. Carol A. Newsom, Sharon H. Ringe, and Jacqueline E. Lapsley, 2012.

69. Carol A. Newsom and Sharon H. Ringe, "Introduction to the First Edition," in *Women's Bible Commentary*, 2nd ed., ed. Newsom and Ringe, xix.

70. Carol A. Newsom, Sharon H. Ringe, and Jacqueline E. Lapsley, "Introduction to the Twentieth-Anniversary Edition," in *Women's Bible Commentary*, ed. Newsom, Ringe, and Lapsley, 3rd ed., xxii.

Another commentary comes originally from the German context and was published in translation in 2013 as *Feminist Biblical Interpretation: A Compendium of Critical Commentary on the Books of the Bible and Related Literature*, edited by Luise Schottroff and Marie-Theres Wacker.[72] Another highly influential publication has been the nineteen-volume *Feminist Companion Series* to the Hebrew Bible, edited by Athalya Brenner.[73] Although this series was neither edited nor originally published in North America, numerous though certainly not all contributors to the first series (1993–2001) and the second series (1998–2002) worked and lived in North America. The articles explore biblical texts, characters, and topics with historical, literary, and cultural methods, and they represent the diverse range of scholarship on women and gender. Some essays come from explicitly feminist perspectives, while others remain moderately neutral about their sociopolitical stance. Although attention to intersectional hermeneutics is minimal, the nineteen volumes have made the extent of research on women and gender in biblical studies more accessible than many other anthologies.[74]

In short, the third phase in feminist biblical studies embraces the clarion call toward including minoritized voices in history, society,

71. Tamara Cohn Eshkenazi and Andrea L. Weiss, eds., *The Torah: A Women's Commentary* (New York: WRJ/URJ Press, 2008).

72. Luise Schottroff and Marie-Theres Wacker, eds., *Feminist Biblical Interpretation: A Compendium of Critical Commentary on the Books of the Bible and Related Literature*, trans. Lisa E. Dahill et al. (Grand Rapids: Eerdmans, 2012). See also the original German publication: Luise Schottroff and Marie-Theres Wacker, eds., *Kompendium: Feministische Bibelauslegung* (Munich: Kaiser, 1998). For a panel discussion on this translated commentary in the North American context, see Susanne Scholz, ed., "Feminist Commentary upon Feminist Commentary: A Report from the Feminist Biblical Trenches," *Lectio difficilior: European Electronic Journal for Feminist Exegesis* (2014): http://tinyurl.com/k6zkxhe.

73. The first series was edited by Athalya Brenner from 1993 to 2001 (with the exception of one coedited volume) and published by Sheffield Academic Press: *A Feminist Companion to Genesis* (1993); *A Feminist Companion to Judges* (1993); *A Feminist Companion to the Song of Songs* (1993); *A Feminist Companion to Ruth* (1993); *A Feminist Companion to Samuel and Kings* (1994); *A Feminist Companion to Wisdom Literature* (1995); *A Feminist Companion to the Esther, Judith and Susannah* (1995); *A Feminist Companion to the Latter Prophets* (1995); *A Feminist Companion to the Hebrew Bible in the New Testament* (1996); Athalya Brenner and Carole Fontaine, eds., *A Feminist Companion to Reading the Bible* (2001). The second series was also published by Athalya Brenner from 1998 to 2002 (with the exception of one coedited volume) and published with Sheffield Academic Press: *Genesis* (1998); Athalya Brenner and Carole Fontaine, eds., *Wisdom and Psalms* (1998); *Judges* (1999); *Ruth and Esther* (1999); *Samuel and Kings* (2000); *Exodus and Deuteronomy* (1998); *The Song of Songs* (2000); *Prophets and Daniel* (2002). The editor of the New Testament series is Amy-Jill Levine, who has published a growing series since 2000 with T&T Clark. The current publisher of Brenner's edited volumes is Bloomsbury T&T Clark.

74. For other anthologies, see, e.g., Linda Day and Carolyn Pressler, eds., *Engaging the Bible in a Gendered World*; Alice Bach, ed., *Women in the Hebrew Bible: A Reader* (New York: Routledge, 1999); Harold C. Washington, Susan Lochrie Graham, and Pamela Thimmes, eds., *Escaping Eden: New Feminist Perspectives on the Bible* (New York: New York University Press, 1999); Victor H. Matthews, Bernard M. Levinson, and Tikva Frymer-Kensky, eds., *Gender and Law in the Hebrew Bible and the Ancient Near East* (Sheffield: Sheffield Academic, 1998).

and religion. Yet, in practice, feminist biblical studies often focus on women and gender at every conceivable level of scholarly discourse and activity—from teaching courses at undergraduate and graduate schools of religious and theological studies to doctoral research projects and scholarly publications. At the same time, the field also moves toward the methodological development of cultural studies.[75] Institutional obstacles persist for feminist work in institutions of higher education even after twenty years of feminist scholarly work, and the institutionalization of a feminist infrastructure in biblical studies continues to depend largely on individual efforts. Thus the call for a biblical feminist hermeneutics that "empower[s] women to forge strategic bonds with other women—not just with women who share their same demographic profile, but women of differing religious, ethnic, political, class, and geographical identities and locations"[76] is an ongoing challenge to Bible scholars of all persuasions—feminist, womanist, *mujerista*, and other progressively inclined exegesis. Nevertheless, feminist exegesis has contributed to the general understanding that the study of biblical literature benefits from examinations grounded in social categories such as gender, race, class, sexual orientation, disability, geopolitical domination, and the dismantling of the "rhetoric of empire."[77] Yet the feminist endeavor is precarious in biblical studies because its academic infrastructure is far from securely established, and most feminist biblical scholars function on the margins of the scholarly and institutional establishment.

Endorsing Women, Faith, Queer Sexualities, or Economic Neoliberalism?

In all of these years, much of feminist biblical studies developed in relative isolation from feminist theories and the field of women's studies and what later expanded into gender studies.[78] Pamela Milne explains

---

75. See, e.g., J. Cheryl Exum, *Plotted, Shot, and Painted: Cultural Representations of Biblical Women* (Sheffield: Sheffield Academic, 1996); J. Cheryl Exum, ed., *Beyond the Biblical Horizon: The Bible and the Arts* (Leiden: Brill, 1999); Kristen E. Kvam and Linda S. Schearing, eds., *Eve and Adam: Jewish, Christian, and Muslim Readings on Genesis and Gender* (Bloomington: Indiana University Press, 1999); Susanne Scholz, *Rape Plots: A Feminist Cultural Study of Genesis 34* (New York: Lang, 2000); Yvonne Sherwood, *A Biblical Text and Its Afterlives: The Survival of Jonah in Western Culture* (Cambridge: Cambridge University Press, 2000).
76. Byron, "The Challenge of 'Blackness'," 96.
77. For this terminology, see Elisabeth Schüssler Fiorenza, *The Power of the Word: Scripture and the Rhetoric of Empire* (Minneapolis: Fortress Press, 2007).
78. Phyllis Trible, ed., "Effects of Women's Studies on Biblical Studies," *JSOT* special issue, 7, no. 22 (1982): 3–71; Jo Ann Hackett, "Women's Studies and the Hebrew Bible," in *The Future of Biblical*

that the disconnect between feminist biblical studies and women's and gender studies is related to the fact that feminist Bible scholars have felt primarily accountable to the academic discipline in which they had earned their doctoral degrees and in which they were hired to teach at institutions of higher learning.[79] Often, feminist exegetes have developed their work without considering the general feminist agendas, as articulated by the feminist movement and secular feminist theorists, despite some calls to do so since the early stages of feminist biblical exegesis.[80] To Milne, mainstream feminist discourse has mainly ignored feminist biblical scholarship.

There are other reasons for the disconnection. According to Milne, feminist biblical scholars have not usually articulated the relationship between their feminist and theological convictions, and in fact they often defend the Bible as a women-friendly authority.[81] Sometimes, they even reinforce the androcentric status quo, advance neoliberal feminist recuperations of the Bible, ignore or dismiss feminist theories, and reauthorize the "fathers" of the field. Esther Fuchs eloquently articulates this problem.[82] In her view, a neoliberal trend has emerged in feminist biblical studies since the 1990s. It has enabled feminist Bible scholars to conceptualize exegetical work by merely adding "women" to the existing field of biblical studies. This add-on approach advances a reformist and gradualist agenda, adheres to the notion of inevitable progress in social change and advancement, and does not question existing epistemologies and binary dualisms. Fuchs explains that this neoliberal compliance relies on an essentialist view of gender, as if fixed and unchanging traits shape women's identities formed by

Studies: The Hebrew Scriptures, ed. Richard Elliott Friedman and H. G. M. Williamson (Atlanta: Scholars Press, 1987), 141–64; Richard Coggins, "The Contribution of Women's Studies to Old Testament Studies: A Male Reaction," *Theology* 91, no. 739 (1988): 5–16; Peggy L. Day, "Biblical Studies and Women's Studies," in *Religious Studies: Issues, Prospects, Proposals*, ed. Klaus K. Klostermaier and Larry W. Hurtado (Atlanta: Scholars Press, 1991), 197–209; Tikva Frymer-Kensky, "The Bible and Women's Studies," in *Feminist Perspectives on Jewish Studies*, ed. Lynn Davidman and Shelly Tenenbaum (New Haven: Yale University Press, 1994), 16–39.

79. Pamela J. Milne, "Toward Feminist Companionship: The Future of Feminist Biblical Studies and Feminism," in *A Feminist Companion to Reading the Bible: Approaches, Methods, and Strategies*, ed. Athalya Brenner and Carole Fontaine (Sheffield: Sheffield Academic, 1997), 44.

80. Antoinette Clark Wire, "Theological and Biblical Perspective: Liberation for Women Calls for a Liberated World," *Church and Society* 76, no. 3 (1986): 7–17.

81. Trible, "Effects of Women's Studies"; Trible, "Feminist Hermeneutics and Biblical Studies," *Christian Century*, February 3–10, 1982, 116–18; Elisabeth Schüssler Fiorenza, "Feminist Theology and New Testament Interpretation," *JSOT* 22 (1982): 32–46; Mary Ann Tolbert, "Defining the Problem: The Bible and Feminist Hermeneutics," *Semeia* 28 (1983): 113–26.

82. Esther Fuchs, "Reclaiming the Hebrew Bible for Women: The Neoliberal Turn in Contemporary Feminist Scholarship," *JFSR* 24, no. 2 (2008): 45–65.

women's experiences that are self-evident and universally valid for women anywhere and at any time.

In addition, this kind of feminist biblical work, which Fuchs identifies in such books as Ilana Pardes's *Countertraditions in the Bible* (1992), Susan Ackerman's *Warrior, Dancer, Seductress, Queen: Women in Judges and Biblical Israel* (1998), and Tikva Frymer-Kensky's *The Bible and Women's Studies* (2006), rarely refers to feminist genealogies of knowledge, rarely acknowledges its indebtedness to feminist mothers, and rarely mentions methodological or theoretical departure from feminist predecessors. Fuchs states: "Contemporary neoliberal theories seek to introduce a commonsense, natural, and straightforward reading of the Bible, where women appear as real individuals, as universal typologies, or as sources of antipatriarchal thinking. This approach is positivist and essentialist."[83] It ignores what Fuchs characterizes as the "foundational proposition in feminist theory": "that 'woman' is a construct, much as the definitions of gender and sex are culturally determined, [and] that all three are implicated in historical processes and transformations."[84] In short, according to Fuchs, key feminist Bible scholars are more loyal to male-dominated conventional approaches than to feminist theories, and so they reinscribe "conventional hegemonic methodologies"[85] and the disciplinary status quo of biblical studies.

Other scholars highlight other factors as contributing to the ambiguity, hesitation, and even rejection of feminist goals in feminist biblical exegesis. Pamela Milne observes an increasing professionalization and depoliticization of feminist Bible work since the 1970s.[86] Feminist interpreters, trained by professional biblical scholars in seminaries and universities and aiming for recognition and acceptance in academic institutions of higher learning and in professional biblical scholarly organizations such as the SBL, have been co-opted into supporting the status quo. For them to be offered academic positions, their work has to comply with the standards of the field. They have to get reference letters for employment, tenure, and promotion, as well as collegial support for their publications. Hence, Milne argues, feminist scholars usually rely on "traditional methods of analysis to investigate non-traditional questions (i.e., questions of relevance and interest to women and about women) from feminist perspectives" to change "the way individuals

83. Ibid., 63.
84. Ibid., 65.
85. Ibid.
86. Milne, "Toward Feminist Companionship," 53.

interpreted biblical texts about women."[87] Such work is highly technical and, as dominantly practiced in biblical studies, focuses on biblical
texts as the primary resource for reconstructing ancient Israelite history and women's roles in biblical stories and poems.

For this reason, feminist biblical scholars do not usually study
women readers and their attitudes to the Bible. As employment opportunities have sharply decreased since the early 1990s, a wide acceptance of the professional and depoliticized standards in academia in
general and biblical studies in particular dominates.[88] This is how Milne
articulates the feminist conundrum:

> At a time when few teaching positions are available, and when depart-
> ments of religion and religious studies are being "down-sized" or elim-
> inated in favour of more "essential" disciplines, women—who have
> entered the discipline in record numbers over the last decade—find them-
> selves shut out by economic factors that compound the problem of sexist
> bias that has traditionally been a systemic barrier to women in this field.
> Personally, I do not think the economic argument is unrelated to the prob-
> lem of sexist bias. The devaluing of the field that we can now observe at
> many institutions may well be linked to the fact that what was once a vir-
> tually all-male discipline is now no longer so.[89]

Milne thus worries about the long-term viability of feminist scholarship in biblical studies, primarily owing to the gradual disappearance
of teaching positions.

Teresa J. Hornsby offers an even more disconcerting view of the status of biblical scholarship engaged with feminist, gender, and sexuality issues. She argues that the development from a women-centric
focus to a more broadly conceptualized gender and queer agenda is
not indicative of a subversive positioning of feminist biblical studies, as
for instance suggested by Deryn Guest.[90] Rather, according to Hornsby,
both women-centric and queer approaches in biblical studies need to
be understood as accommodating the forces in the economic-capital-
ist globalized world in which we live, since "sexuality and gender are
constructed in collusion with capitalistic power."[91] Therefore, Hornsby
claims, as capitalism changes and shifts, sexual and gender norms will

---

87. Ibid.
88. See, e.g., Susanne Scholz, "Occupy Academic Bible Teaching: The Architecture of Educational Power and the Biblical Studies Curriculum," in *Teaching the Bible in the Liberal Arts Classroom*, ed. Jane S. Webster and Glenn S. Holland (Sheffield: Sheffield Phoenix, 2012), 28–43.
89. Milne, "Toward Feminist Companionship," 43.
90. Deryn Guest, *Beyond Feminist Biblical Studies* (Sheffield: Sheffield Phoenix, 2012).
91. Teresa J. Hornsby, "Capitalism, Masochism, and Biblical Interpretations," in *Bible Trouble: Queer*

too. She bases her analysis on three assumptions, namely, that "power produces sexual normatives," "the dominant form that this power takes in Western Euro cultures is neoliberal capitalism," and "Christianity (indeed, organized religion) is an arm of power that aids in this production."[92] Accordingly, calls for changes in feminist, gender, and queer biblical scholarship, as well as in other areas of culture and society, are linked to the shift from a "closed, centrally powerful, and industrial" economic system to one that is "open, globally diverse, and electronically based."[93] Consequently, for Hornsby, theoretical inclusions of nonheteronormative and queer sexualities in culture, theology, and biblical interpretation are not deconstructive moves for overcoming worldwide oppression but "capitalism's use of Christian theology to construct the types of sexual/economic subjects it needs."[94] And what capitalism needs are bodies willing to submit and to enjoy masochistic positions in the societal-economic interplay of power. To Hornsby, feminist, gender, and queer biblical exegesis assists in this process even if this help is provided unintentionally; such is the power of the neoliberal capitalist system over every body and thing.

Hornsby illustrates these dynamics in cultural and exegetical feminist and nonfeminist approaches to the passion narratives of Christ and to Pauline theology, arguing that "the end product is an extraordinarily submissive body—a body that connects suffering with hope and humiliation with empowerment."[95] Since the dynamics in capitalism produce, reproduce, and sustain this kind of masochistic positioning for all people—no longer only for those performing as women as the position of the victim is increasingly masculinized—heteronormative expectations lessen and sociocultural space for queer desire increases. In other words, queering the Bible does not challenge neoliberalism, because "queer sexualities are manufactured and serve power just as much as a sanctioned sexuality."[96] Since capitalism needs people with "more open, fluid, ambivalent sexual identities," willing to suffer for this elastic and promised space, calls for feminist, gender, and queer readings of the Bible (and culture) accommodate this need. In Hornsby's assessment, then, resistance to neoliberalism is

---

Reading at the Boundaries of Biblical Scholarship, ed. Teresa J. Hornsby and Ken Stone (Atlanta: Society of Biblical Literature Atlanta, 2011), 137.

92. Ibid.
93. Ibid.
94. Ibid., 141–42.
95. Ibid., 149.
96. Ibid., 153.

an illusion because the feminist agenda is always already part of economic neoliberalism.

Hornsby's dystopian explanation takes on almost totalitarian proportions without any alternative options. Borrowing from Foucault without explicitly saying so, her discussion is a cautionary note about the difficulties of resisting the cultural, sociopolitical, economic, and religious dynamics of one's time. The jury is still out on whether feminist biblical scholarship can be reduced to helping those performing as women become fully integrated into a socioeconomic system dependent on a large and continuous supply of willing consumers who buy and comply. In comparison, Milne's suggestion that feminist biblical scholars connect their work directly to the social, political, legal, and economic goals of the feminist movement seems harmless.[97] Nevertheless, Milne's proposal to relate biblical exegesis to feminist theories and practices may be a better option than falling into resigned inaction because, according to Hornsby, resistance is futile.

Fostering Global Intersectionality and Dialogical Relationships in the Twenty-First Century

It should not be surprising that feminist Bible scholars wonder about the next step. After almost every biblical woman character has been identified, every scholarly method applied, and practically every biblical text analyzed for its gender ideology,[98] the question is, what remains to be done if we do not want to merely give in to the neoliberal status quo? Perhaps this is one of the reasons why feminist biblical scholars are currently in the process of surveying and assessing the field. For instance, Athalya Brenner poses the following questions when she reflects on the future of the field:

> *Quo vadis*, feminist biblical scholarship? . . . What is beckoning? Where do you want to go? Is the Master's House still the house you long to possess, only that you would like to become its legitimate(d) masters and mistresses instead of marginal(ized) lodgers? Would you like to move it (houses can be moved now from one location to another)? . . . Will an act of exchanging places within the accepted power paradigms be the object

---

97. Milne, "Toward Feminist Companionship," 59. She also offers important ideas about bringing feminist biblical studies into active conversation with feminist theories; see Pamela J. Milne, "Doing Feminist Biblical Criticism in a Women's Studies Context," *Atlantis* 35, no. 2 (2011): 128–38.

98. Carol Meyers, Toni Craven, and Ross S. Kramer, eds., *Women in Scripture: A Dictionary of Named and Unnamed Women in the Hebrew Bible, the Apocryphal/Deuterocanonical Books, and the New Testament* (Boston: Houghton Mifflin, 2000).

of desire? Are new structures of dominance, a shift in majority/minority balances, being implemented? Are you, we, aspiring to conquistador positions in the names of the proverbial "oppressed"? Should we not simply demolish the house instead of merely deconstructing it and its inhabitants, in order to build a completely new one instead? And if so, who will get right of occupation in the new house, and on what terms? . . . The contenders are many and the audiences are dwindling, as we are becoming more and more radicalized. Whose scholarship will matter, say, twenty-five years hence?[99]

Brenner wonders about the existing power hierarchies, as feminist Bible scholars adapt to the status quo or even change it. It is a reflection on the in-house situation of feminist Bible studies at the dawn of the twenty-first century.

Yet Brenner's concerns do not address the larger intellectual and societal developments, in contrast to Milne, who considers the political and social implications of biblical exegesis for women in the past and the present. Others, such as Guest, recommend that feminist biblical scholarship "tool up and become even more expansively theory-rich, able to bring the critical studies of masculinities, queer studies, trans studies, intersex studies, and lesbian and gay studies into negotiation with feminist theory without necessarily privileging what have been, to date, stalwart feminist positions."[100] Still others observe that feminist biblical exegetes need to be committed to intersectional hermeneutics and take seriously connections between sexism, racism, classism, homophobia, and geopolitics.

It also seems clear that in the early years of the second millennium CE, North American feminist biblical research is dealing with several new challenges. One challenge is related to the function of feminist biblical scholarship within the institutional boundaries of higher education. Another challenge comes from the Christian Right, which has taken on the issue of women and gender in numerous publications widely distributed to lay audiences. Yet another challenge—probably the most intellectually productive—pushes feminist studies toward investigations of "otherness" of all sorts, such as queer, ethnicity and race, and postcolonial studies.

First, North American feminist biblical scholarship has primarily

---

99. Athalya Brenner, "Epilogue: Babies and Bathwater on the Road," in *Her Master's Tools? Feminist and Postcolonial Engagements of Historical-Critical Discourse*, ed. Caroline Vander Stichele and Todd Penner (Atlanta: Society of Biblical Literature, 2005), 338.

100. Guest, *Beyond Feminist Biblical Studies*, 150.

developed within institutions of higher education and has become part of undergraduate and graduate departments of religious and theological studies and seminaries. This development means that feminist biblical scholars must not only earn the usual academic credentials and comply with established standards of tenure and promotion, but they also have to adapt to the dominant academic discourse and scholarly norms in teaching and research projects. Fuchs elaborates on the implications of these dynamics for feminist biblical work within the discipline of biblical studies when she writes:

> Though feminist scholarship has decidedly made serious inroads into biblical studies, the academic process of evaluation that decides who receives a grant and who gets published and where is still largely in male hands. Feminist students must get the approval of malestream professors, and even feminist professors continue to depend on malestream colleagues and administrators for approval and advancement. That male scholars continue to control the means of production of feminist knowledge means that this knowledge has been interpreted largely as yet another ingredient to be added to and stirred into the pot of biblical studies. The current co-optation of feminist studies makes it impossible to use it as a means of transforming the entire field of biblical studies into an ethically committed and institutionally independent field that valued both social action and scholarship.[101]

Scholars of the dominant status quo evaluate publications, grants, and the development of feminist knowledge. The feminist call to action—one of the initial drives of feminist scholarship in the 1970s—has all too often become secondary, and the impetus towards sociopolitical, economic, and cultural transformation been neglected. Perhaps unsurprisingly, then, feminist biblical research has turned into increasingly specialized, depoliticized, and co-opted projects that comply with dominant standards, norms, and expectations. As Caroline Vander Stichele and Todd Penner observe, the guild of biblical studies "maintains a strong line of male-identified scholarly assessment and production"[102] and "the difference that is tolerated does not challenge the phallocentric and colonial structures of the guild" but rather contributes to "solidify its hold."[103] Feminist biblical scholarship, like other

---

101. Esther Fuchs, "Points of Resonance," in *On the Cutting Edge: The Study of Women in Biblical Worlds*, ed. Jane Schaberg, Alice Bach, and Esther Fuchs (New York: Continuum, 2004), 12. See also her work titled *Sexual Politics in the Biblical Narrative: Reading the Hebrew Bible as a Woman* (Sheffield: Sheffield Academic, 2000).
102. Vander Stichele and Penner, *Contextualizing Gender*, 169.
103. Ibid., 170.

marginalized discourses by the "excluded other," functions as a "fetish" and "is granted access to the formal structure as a beneficent gesture."[104]

As a result, in North American institutions of higher education, feminist biblical research often serves as an add-on to the existing academic content management and distribution systems, and feminist biblical scholars must adapt to dominant academic expectations, the evaluation procedures of publishers, and the waning feminist sensibilities of their students. Moreover, as Milne notes, the emergence of feminist biblical studies and the inclusion of "others" into the field of biblical studies have concurrently led to "the devaluing of the field that we can now observe at many institutions." She insists that this development "may well be linked to the fact that what was once a virtually all-male discipline is no longer so."[105] Hector Avalos goes even further. He states that "the SBL is the agent of a dying profession" because it lacks teaching positions at credible academic institutions.[106] In this situation of gradually disappearing teaching positions, the "long-term viability" of feminist biblical scholarship is at stake, because innovation is "endangered or at least impeded."[107] Because of the survival mode in the humanities, the impetus toward maintaining the status quo discourages bold proposals for epistemological and hermeneutical change, including those from feminist biblical scholars.[108] At their best, then, feminist biblical scholars contribute to developing, promoting, and cultivating textual interpretations as "site[s] of struggle"[109] focused on issues that are "our own in this present world."[110] In other words, the ongoing marginalization of feminist biblical work in institutions of higher education has dampened the powerful energies that were set free in the 1970s.

Second, the Christian Right and its plethora of publications on women, gender, and the Bible also present considerable challenges to

---

104. Ibid., 169.
105. Milne, "Toward Feminist Companionship," 43.
106. Hector Avalos, *The End of Biblical Studies* (Amherst, NY: Prometheus, 2007), 316.
107. Milne, "Toward Feminist Companionship," 43.
108. See, e.g., Marc Bousquet, *How the University Works: Higher Education and the Low-Wage Nation* (New York: New York University Press, 2008).
109. Schüssler Fiorenza, *Power of the Word*, 254.
110. Vander Stichele and Penner, *Contextualizing Gender*, 173. For books that take seriously contemporary issues of the world today, see, e.g., Anne F. Elvey, *An Ecological Feminist Reading of the Gospel of Luke: A Gestational Paradigm* (Lewiston, NY: Mellen, 2005); Deryn Guest, *When Deborah Met Jael: Lesbian Biblical Hermeneutics* (London: SCM, 2005); Carole R. Fontaine, *With Eyes of Flesh: The Bible, Gender and Human Rights* (Sheffield: Sheffield Phoenix, 2008); Susanne Scholz, *Sacred Witness: Rape in the Hebrew Bible* (Minneapolis: Fortress Press, 2010).

North American feminist biblical studies, although it remains largely unacknowledged on either side. Beginning in the 1990s and then forcefully propelled into the public during the new millennium, proponents of conservative-fundamentalist Christianity have published books and anthologies on gender and the Bible. Defining themselves as complementarians, they have taken on writers and theologians within their own religious context and contested egalitarian positions about women and men in church and society. The mostly male and white authors are often powerful leaders in evangelical organizations, particularly the Council of Biblical Manhood and Womanhood.[111]

What is striking about the complementarian Christian Right's discourse on gender and the Bible is its disregard for feminist biblical scholarship as it has emerged in academia since the 1970s. Although many complementarian authors are seminary professors, such as John Piper and Wayne A. Grudem, their books do not engage academic feminist and nonfeminist biblical scholarship even when they discuss biblical passages such as Genesis 1–3, Ephesians 5:21–33, Colossians 3:18–19, or 1 Timothy 2:11–15.

As a result of the Christian Right's conservative sociopolitical and theological discourse, feminist exegetes continue combating the most basic and persistent androcentric views on women, gender, and the Bible that they have been deconstructing for more than forty years. The emergence of evangelical publications, such as *The IVP Women's Bible Commentary*, edited by Catherine Clark Kroeger and Mary Evans,[112] contributes to the confusion about the nature, goals, and positions of feminist biblical scholarship. Many lay readers do not distinguish between a women's commentary emerging from an evangelical-theological context and feminist biblical books published within the academic field of biblical studies and descending from the feminist movement of the 1970s. Thus evangelical-conservative books on women, gender, and the Bible remain within the boundaries of a sociotheologically conservative hermeneutics.[113]

---

111. See the online presence of the CBMW at http://www.cbmw.org. For an analysis of the complementarians, see Susanne Scholz, "The Christian Right's Discourse on Gender and the Bible," *JFSR* 21, no. 1 (2005): 81–100. See also Karen Strand Winslow's chapter titled "Recovering Redemption for Women: Feminist Exegesis in North American Evangelism," in *Feminist Interpretation of the Hebrew Bible in Retrospect*, vol. 2, *Social Location*, ed. Susanne Scholz (Sheffield: Sheffield Phoenix, 2014), 269–89.

112. Catherine Clark Kroeger and Mary J. Evans, eds., *The IVP Women's Bible Commentary* (Downers Grove, IL: InterVarsity Press, 2002).

113. See, e.g., recent publications by theologically conservative publishing houses: Stephen J. Binz, *Women of the Gospels: Friends and Disciples of Jesus* (Grand Rapids: Brazos, 2011); Binz, *Women of the Torah: Matriarchs and Heroes of Israel* (Grand Rapids: Brazos, 2011); Robin Gallaher Branch, *Jeroboam's*

Third, investigations on "otherness" related to queer studies, ethnicity and race, and postcolonialism constitute an intellectually very productive turn in feminist biblical studies. Publications such as the *Queer Bible Commentary* and other anthologies and monographs on queer biblical interpretations[114] have urged feminist biblical scholars to open up to LGBTQI issues. For instance, Guest observes the prevalence of a "heteropatriarchal framework" in feminist biblical studies that sheds light on women in the Bible but does not explicitly consider lesbian hermeneutical concerns. She writes:

> Feminists and womanists have done sterling work; shedding light on the role and status of scriptural women, asking new questions, modifying and challenging existing methodologies, raising issues not traditionally incorporated within historical critical exegesis. However, almost the entirety of this work has taken place within a heterocentric frame of reference; one that assumes the heterosexuality of the scriptural women themselves; one that appears to presuppose a heterosexual academic community, since lesbian-related concerns and issues have hardly been given a sentence until very recently. . . . Yet, for all this good work, the framework of enquiry has remained predominantly heterocentric.[115]

Guest grants a few exceptions in feminist biblical studies,[116] but overall she charges that female homoeroticism has been pushed into a space of "invisibility" due to the dominant "heteropatriarchal framework"[117] of academia and society. Also, Ken Stone encourages connections between feminist and queer biblical studies because "feminism, too, is

Wife: The Enduring Contributions of the Old Testament's Least-Known Women (Peabody, MA: Hendrickson, 2009); Lynn H. Cohick, *Women in the World of the Earliest Christians: Illuminating Ancient Ways of Life* (Grand Rapids: Baker Academic, 2009); Tammi J. Schneider, *Mothers of Promise: Women in the Book of Genesis* (Grand Rapids: Baker Academic, 2008).

114. Deryn Guest, Robert E. Goss, Mona West, and Thomas Bohache, eds., *The Queer Bible Commentary* (London: SMC, 2006); Robert E. Goss and Mona West, eds., *Take Back the Word: A Queer Reading of the Bible* (Cleveland: Pilgrim, 2000). See also Guest, *When Deborah Met Jael*; Theodore W. Jennings, *Jacob's Wound: Homoerotic Narrative in the Literature of Ancient Israel* (New York: Continuum, 2005); Jennings, *The Man Jesus Loved: Homoerotic Narratives from the New Testament* (Cleveland: Pilgrim, 2003); Robert E. Goss, *Queering Christ: Beyond Jesus Acted Up* (Cleveland: Pilgrim, 2002); Ken Stone, *Queer Commentary and the Hebrew Bible* (Cleveland: Pilgrim, 2001); Ken Stone, *Practicing Safer Texts: Food, Sex and Bible in Queer Perspective* (London: T&T Clark, 2005); Stephen D. Moore, *God's Beauty Parlor: And Other Queer Spaces in and Around the Bible* (Stanford: Stanford University Press, 2001); Daniel A. Helminiak, *What the Bible Really Says about Homosexuality* (Tajique, NM: Alamo Square Press, 2000); Stephen D. Moore, *God's Gym: Divine Male Bodies of the Bible* (New York: Routledge, 1996); Bernadette J. Brooten, *Love between Women: Early Christian Responses to Female Homoeroticism* (Chicago: University of Chicago Press, 1996); Nancy Wilson, *Our Tribe: Queer Folks, God, Jesus, and the Bible* (San Francisco: HarperSanFrancisco, 1995).

115. Guest, *When Deborah Met Jael*, 107.
116. Ibid., 108.
117. Ibid., 112.

devoted to the critical analysis of sex and gender."[118] To him, a critical gender analysis should not be limited to "biblical representations of women" but extend "to biblical representations of men and of 'masculinity.'"[119] In a way, then, queer biblical studies advances the work in feminist biblical studies as it "problematize[s] normative approaches to sexuality" and deconstructs "such dichotomies as 'homosexual/heterosexual' and 'male/female.'"[120] In short, the goal of LGBTQI exegesis is to disrupt "sex-gender-sexuality norms and academic conventions, playful and at times purposefully irreverent"[121] and to expand feminist research beyond the analysis of "woman" or "women."

Similarly, the emergence of studies on race and ethnicity has opened up feminist exegesis to perspectives from Asian American feminists and feminist scholars from minoritized North American communities.[122] Key in such explorations has been the hermeneutical insight that flesh-and-blood readers are central to the exegetical task of contextualizing biblical meanings in today's world.[123] Combined with postcolonial sensibilities, Mai-Anh Le Tran presents Lot's wife, Ruth, and the Vietnamese figure Tô Thị as female characters "that liberate rather than dominate."[124] Also Gale A. Yee problematizes the methodological, hermeneutical, and political soundness of ethnic/racial identity of biblical readers. She wonders what defines "my Asian Americanness, and how does this identity affect my biblical interpretation?"[125] In addition, postcolonial feminist studies on the Bible have emerged not only from North America but from other contexts as well.[126] A current goal of

---

118. Stone, *Queer Commentary*, 25.

119. Ibid., 26.

120. Ibid., 27.

121. Guest et al., *Queer Bible Commentary*, xiii.

122. See, e.g., Mary F. Foskett and Jeffrey Kah-Jin Kuan, eds., *Ways of Being, Ways of Reading: Asian American Biblical Interpretation* (St. Louis: Chalice, 2006); Randall C. Bailey, Tat-siong Benny Liew and Fernando F. Segovia, eds., *They Were All Together in One Place? Toward Minority Biblical Criticism* (Atlanta: SBL Press, 2009).

123. For the significance of the flesh-and-blood readers, see the very influential volumes by Fernando F. Segovia and Mary Ann Tolbert, eds., *Reading from This Place*, vol. 1, *Social Location and Biblical Interpretation in the United States*; vol. 2, *Social Location and Biblical Interpretation in Global Perspective* (Minneapolis: Fortress Press, 1995). For a more recent elaboration, see, e.g., Fernando F. Segovia, "Cultural Criticism: Expanding the Scope of Biblical Criticism," in *The Future of the Biblical Past*, ed. Roland Boer and Fernando F. Segovia, Semeia Studies (Atlanta: Society of Biblical Literature, 2012), 307–37.

124. Mai-Anh Le Tran, "Lot's Wife, Ruth, and Tô Thị: Gender and Racial Representation in a Theological Feast of Stories," in Foskett and Kuan, *Ways of Being, Ways of Reading*, 125.

125. This and the following quotes are from Gale A. Yee, "Yin/Yang Is Not Me: An Exploration into an Asian American Biblical Hermeneutics," in Foskett and Kuan, *Ways of Being, Ways of Reading*, 156.

126. For publications from the North American context, see, e.g., Joseph A. Marchal, *The Politics of Heaven: Women, Gender, and Empire in the Study of Paul* (Minneapolis: Fortress Press, 2008); Hee An Choi and Katheryn Pfisterer Darr, eds., *Engaging the Bible: Critical Readings from Contemporary Women* (Minneapolis: Fortress Press, 2006); Vander Stichele and Penner, *Her Master's Tools?* For studies

feminist biblical studies thus is to bring feminist scholars of different social locations and hermeneutical and methodological assumptions together to find common ground in the academic study of biblical literature, history, and tradition.[127]

Quilting Feminist Biblical Meanings: Concluding Comments

Yet again and again, some feminist scholars charge that second-waves feminist aims for equality and women's rights have been co-opted by the status quo. They are less optimistic about the future of feminism in general and feminist biblical studies in particular.[128] They fear that feminist calls to action have become secondary; that the impetus toward sociopolitical, economic, and cultural transformation is neglected; and loyalty to conventionally defined hermeneutical and methodological principles overshadows feminist exegesis. Perhaps unsurprisingly, then, twenty-first-century feminist biblical research often engages in depoliticized and technical projects that comply with dominant standards, norms, and expectations.

It is thus safe to state that feminist biblical scholars diverge on the future directions for feminist biblical studies. Fuchs suggests that feminist exegetes respect difference and "desire . . . solidarity and alliance across difference."[129] Because of the diverse array of feminist biblical scholarship, this suggestion is timely. Fuchs also advises that feminist biblical scholarship engage the "very heart of Biblical Studies and the theories that currently shape it" and work "for epistemological transformation," a key goal of feminist theory in general.[130] In Fuchs's view, feminist biblical scholars face the urgent task of "rethinking and

---

from other contexts, see, e.g., Seong Hee Kim, *Mark, Women and Empire: A Korean Postcolonial Perspective* (Sheffield: Sheffield Phoenix, 2010); Jean Kyoung Kim, *Woman and Nation: An Intercontextual Reading of the Gospel of John from a Postcolonial/Feminist Perspective* (Leiden: Brill, 2004); Musa W. Dube Shomanah, *Postcolonial Feminist Interpretation of the Bible* (St. Louis: Chalice, 2000). See also Phyllis A Bird, ed., *Reading the Bible as Women: Perspectives from Africa, Asia, and Latin America* (Atlanta: Scholars Press, 1997).

127. See, e.g., Dora Mbuwayesango and Susanne Scholz, "Dialogical Beginnings: A Conversation on the Future of Feminist Biblical Studies," *JFSR* 25, no. 2 (2009): 93–103. See also the ensuing nine responses on 103–43. For an integration of different voices into a single-voiced scholarly account, see, e.g., Barbara E. Reid, *Taking Up the Cross: New Testament Interpretations through Latina and Feminist Eyes* (Minneapolis: Fortress Press, 2007).

128. J. Cheryl Exum, "Where Have All the Feminists Gone? Reflections on the Impact of Feminist Biblical Exegesis on the Scholarly Community and Women's Lives," *Lectio difficilior: European Electronic Journal for Feminist Exegesis* (2010): http://tinyurl.com/jwnnbyz.

129. Esther Fuchs, "Biblical Feminisms: Knowledge, Theory and Politics in the Study of Women in the Hebrew Bible," *BibInt* 16 (2008): 224.

130. Ibid., 225.

re-inventing existing framework for the production and dissemination of knowledge."[131]

Another perspective on the future of feminist biblical studies comes from Schüssler Fiorenza. She states:

> The present institutional locations of feminist biblical discourses in the academy, organized religion, and the media are not able to promote justice, equality, and well-being for all as long as they remain beholden to said locations. While feminists have made great strides in recent times, they still lack sufficient strength to sustain scholarship that criticizes the dominant malestream ethos of the academy, church, synagogue, mosque, temple, and media. In addition, the increasing separation of academic feminism from social feminist movements has tended to steer feminist biblical studies more toward the interests of the academy and publishing houses than toward transglobal feminist movements for change.[132]

She does not consider academia alone as a viable context to work toward sociopolitical, economic, cultural, and theological transformation of society. In fact, she sees many social institutions as upholders of structures of domination. Thus only alliances with global feminist movements for change will enable feminist biblical scholars to work toward the elimination of gender, racial, class, and other forms of injustice. To Schüssler Fiorenza, feminist biblical scholarship "must be informed by a hunger and thirst for justice" so that feminist readings resemble "a critical quilting of meaning" and articulate a "holistic biblical vision of well-being for all."[133]

It seems obvious in the age of global neoliberalism and its omnipresent structures of domination that alliances beyond the narrow confines of one's immediate affiliation are essential. Progressive academics, religious leaders, political groups, and social networks need to resist the lure and rewards of what postcolonial theorists call the empire. We need to articulate theoretical and practical alternatives so that the next generation will be able to continue on. The establishment of institutions that foster "emancipatory" alternatives remains foremost on the agenda of North American feminist biblical studies at the dawn of the twenty-first century. With ecological, economic, and migratory challenges already present, this vision of feminist biblical

---

131. Ibid., 221.
132. Elisabeth Schüssler Fiorenza, "Reaffirming Feminist/Womanist Biblical Scholarship," *Encounter* 67, no. 4 (2006): 370.
133. Ibid., 372.

interpretation seems like a good starting point for the conversation to go far beyond the North American location.

The next chapter investigates some of the difficulties this call for emancipatory alternatives encounters when biblical interpretations are investigated for their complicities with cultural assumptions about rape, as in the particular case of Genesis 34. It demonstrates that biblical exegetes find it difficult to escape the cultural assumptions of their time and place. They frequently side with the rapist and thus often sideline the ethical implications of their readings. This exegetical situation illustrates that the ethical and political alliance of those readings is highly problematic, as many feminist biblical exegetes have long observed, because interpreters do not critically interrogate some key assumptions of rape culture.

10

Was It Really Rape in Genesis 34? Biblical Scholarship as a Reflection of Cultural Assumptions

In recent years biblical scholars have begun to examine critically the impact of the Bible on Western culture. For example, J. Cheryl Exum states that "perhaps no other document has been so instrumental as the Bible in shaping Western culture and influencing ideas about the place of women and about the relationship of the sexes."[1] Vincent L. Wimbush maintains that the Bible has "profoundly affected the imagination of Western culture."[2] A group of scholars calling themselves "The Bible and Culture Collective" argue that "the Bible has exerted more cultural influence on the West than any other single document."[3] These and other scholars claim that the Bible has shaped culture and vice versa.

This growing demand to investigate the Bible as "cultural heritage"[4]

1. J. Cheryl Exum, "Feminist Criticism: Whose Interests Are Being Served?," in *Judges and Method: New Approaches in Biblical Studies*, ed. Gale A. Yee (Minneapolis: Fortress Press, 1995), 66.
2. Vincent L. Wimbush, "Biblical-Historical Study as Liberation: Toward an Afro-Christian Hermeneutic," *Journal of Religious Thought* 42, no. 2 (1985–1986): 15.
3. The Bible and Culture Collective, *The Postmodern Bible* (New Haven: Yale University Press, 1995), 1.
4. Wim Beuken and Seán Freyne, eds., *The Bible as Cultural Heritage*, Concilium l (Maryknoll, NY: Orbis, 1995).

has already led to numerous publications with varied subject matters and methodological approaches. Some studies examine biblical interpretations of different historical and social perspectives to demonstrate the interpretative diversity available.[5] Others juxtapose biblical themes and characters with cultural sources, such as film, art, literature, and music.[6] Several works analyze how different communities located within and without the United States interpret the Bible.[7] *The New Interpreter's Bible* acknowledges the emergence of biblical cultural studies. The first volume includes several introductory essays that describe reading strategies of Bible readers from marginalized social locations. The essays discuss particularly the approaches of women, African Americans, Hispanics, and Native Americans.[8]

The analysis of readers has thus become crucial in biblical cultural studies. Fernando F. Segovia stresses this methodological turn when he writes: "This new development posits . . . a very different construct, the flesh-and-blood reader: always positioned and interested; socially and historically conditioned and unable to transcend such conditions. . . . It is a development that I would describe in terms of 'cultural studies'—a joint critical study of texts and readers, perspectives and ideologies."[9] Rejecting objective, value-free and universally valid reconstructions of the biblical past, cultural critics assume that no one reads from the vantage point of neutrality or impartiality. Thus George Aichele and Gary A. Phillips maintain that "meaning can no longer be thought of as an objective relation between text and extratextual reality, but instead it arises from the subjective, or ideological, juxtaposing of text with text *on behalf of* specific readers in specific historical/material

---

5. Theophus H. Smith, *Conjuring Culture: Biblical Formations of Black America* (New York: Oxford University Press, 1994); Brian K. Blount, *Cultural Interpretation: Reorienting New Testament Criticism* (Minneapolis: Fortress Press, 1995); Stephen Breck Reid, *Listening In: A Multicultural Reading of the Psalms* (Nashville: Abingdon, 1997).

6. Bernard Brandon Scott, *Hollywood Dreams and Biblical Stories* (Minneapolis: Fortress Press, 1994); J. Cheryl Exum, *Plotted, Shot, and Painted: Cultural Representations of Biblical Women*, JSOTSup 215 (Sheffield: Sheffield Academic, 1996); Alice Bach, *Women, Seduction, and Betrayal in Biblical Narrative* (Cambridge: Cambridge University Press, 1997).

7. Fernando F. Segovia and Mary Ann Tolbert, eds., *Reading from This Place*, vol. 1, *Social Location and Biblical Interpretation in the United States*; *Reading from This Place*, vol. 2, *Social Location and Biblical Interpretation in Global Perspective* (Minneapolis: Fortress Press, 1995); Bible and Culture Collective, *Postmodern Bible*.

8. *NIB* 1:150–87.

9. Fernando F. Segovia, "'And They Began to Speak in Other Tongues': Competing Modes of Discourse in Contemporary Biblical Criticism," in Segovia and Tolbert, *Social Location and Biblical Interpretation in the United States*, 28–29.

situations."[10] And so "readers become as important as texts"[11] in the investigation of the relationship between the Bible and culture.

The methodological implications of this development are significant. Whereas earlier interpretative paradigms, such as historical criticism, assumed a neutral and disinterested reader who put aside their presuppositions during the process of interpretation, biblical cultural criticism posits that interpretation is always perspectival. A cultural critic acknowledges assumptions and, in fact, constructs the interpretation accordingly. This understanding of the interpretive process has consequences for the meaning of exegesis. Segovia claims that "all exegesis is ultimately *eisegesis*."[12] Edward L. Greenstein stresses a similar point: "To engage in Biblical Criticism means we must exercise our beliefs."[13] Also Exum explains: "To think that interpretations can be neutral or objective would be to assume that meaning resides in the text. My position . . . is that meaning resides in the interaction between reader and text."[14] Hence, biblical cultural critics uncover and examine the various interests and positions of the readers and discuss the findings in relation to the broader culture. Biblical cultural studies offers the opportunity to understand the contribution of biblical scholarship to culture and, indeed, to the world.

Focusing on the readers and their interpretations, cultural critics describe how interpreters use biblical texts to support cultural, political, economic, and societal developments. Different critics emphasize different aspects in this critical work. For Segovia, biblical cultural criticism begins a process of liberation and decolonization. For Brian K. Blount, culturally diverse readings of selected biblical texts show that the final, definitive interpretation of a text will always be unattainable. For Exum, the various "cultural afterlives" of women pose the question of whether contemporary readers can avoid the gender bias present in biblical texts and in the history of interpretations. For Alice Bach, biblical cultural studies give women analytical guidance to extricate themselves from "the androcentric logic of the roots of Western culture."[15]

---

10. George Aichele and Gary A. Phillips, "Introduction: Exegesis, Eisegesis, Intergesis," *Semeia* 69/70 (1995): 15.

11. Segovia, "Other Tongues," 32.

12. Fernando F. Segovia, "Cultural Studies and Contemporary Biblical Criticism: Ideological Criticism as Mode of Discourse," in Segovia and Tolbert, *Social Location and Biblical Interpretation in Global Perspective*, 16.

13. Edward L. Greenstein, "Theory and Argument in Biblical Criticism," in *Essays on Biblical Method and Translation*, BJS 92 (Atlanta: Scholars Press, 1989), 68.

14. Exum, *Plotted*, 90.

15. Segovia, "Cultural Studies," 16; Blount, *Cultural Interpretation*, 184; Exum, *Plotted*, 9; Bach, *Women*, 1.

Biblical cultural studies are not restricted to the historical examination of biblical texts or to the literary study of the text itself. Rather, they seek an interdisciplinary conversation with other academic and non-academic discourses. They encourage a critical analysis of biblical scholarship in light of contemporary concerns. And they challenge contemporary "flesh-and-blood" readers to consider the ethical consequences of their interpretations.[16]

Rape and the Case of Genesis 34

Since biblical cultural criticism regards all interpretative approaches as constructs of "real readers," the examination of these constructs identifies the views and agendas of the readers. Such an examination works particularly well in the case of Genesis 34, the story about the rape of Dinah. Containing a complex account, the chapter provokes scholars to state clearly their views on rape. Therefore, the interpretations of Genesis 34 show whether biblical scholars accept or criticize those views. They exemplify the connection between biblical scholarship and contemporary assumptions about rape.

Only a relatively limited number of interpretations exist because Genesis 34 is not a popular story among critical interpreters.[17] One reason might relate to the literary position of the chapter. Placed within the Jacob cycle (Gen 25:19–35:22), Genesis 34 is often classified as an independent later source difficult to date within Israelite history. Although the existing interpretations are often short, they contain excellent information about assumptions concerning rape in biblical scholarship.

The story in Genesis 34 is as follows: Dinah, the daughter of Leah and Jacob, is raped by Shechem, the prince of the land, when she goes to visit women in her neighborhood. Lusting after her, Shechem abducts Dinah and asks his father, Hamor, to assist him with his plan to marry her. In the meantime Dinah's father, Jacob, and her brothers hear about the rape. The brothers react strongly. When Shechem and

---

16. Pamela J. Milne, "Toward Feminist Companionship: The Future of Feminist Biblical Studies and Feminism," in *Reading the Bible: Approaches, Methods and Strategies*, ed. Athalya Brenner and Carole Fontaine (Sheffield: Sheffield Academic, 1997), 55–56.

17. Note that major feminist biblical publications do not interpret the chapter in detail, e.g., Phyllis Trible, *Texts of Terror* (Philadelphia: Fortress Press, 1984); Letty M. Russell, ed., *Feminist Interpretation of the Bible* (Philadelphia: Westminster Press, 1985); Katheryn Pfisterer Darr, *Far More Precious Than Jewels: Perspectives on Biblical Women* (Louisville: Westminster John Knox, 1991); J. Cheryl Exum, *Fragmented Women: Feminist (Sub)versions of Biblical Narratives* (Valley Forge, PA: Trinity Press International, 1993).

Hamor negotiate the marriage, the brothers request that all the Canaanite males in the town be circumcised. While the male She-chemites lie in pain after the circumcision, Dinah's brothers attack the city and kill all the males, including Shechem and Hamor; they then abduct the women and children of the city. When Jacob hears about these actions, he condemns his sons. They ask in return if their sister should be treated like a prostitute. With that question the story ends.

The summary demonstrates that this narrative includes complicating factors, such as the revenge of Dinah's brothers. The following examination does not highlight these factors, but concentrates instead on the rape. Often this focus evokes fear and fury. Rape victim-survivors and their supporters are reminded of the enormous injustice and powerlessness they have experienced. Others want to resolve the emotions by emphasizing the complications of the story. The focus on rape, however, confronts the extent of rape-supportive scholarship and culture. Such a confrontation is certainly not easy.

The present essay assumes a feminist value system "to demonstrate more transparently the importance of our [feminist biblical scholars'] contributions to the goals of the feminist movement."[18] Since the 1970s feminist scholars have researched the problem of rape.[19] They explore it from the perspective of the victim-survivor, trace the history of contemporary rape prevalence, and argue that numerous strata of society contribute to the high statistics. Grounded in feminist assumptions, this essay demonstrates that prevailing interpretations of Genesis 34 support what some feminists have called the contemporary "rape culture."[20]

Obfuscating Rape: Contemporary Interpretations of Genesis 34

Scholars employ various arguments to interpret the rape in Genesis 34. Four are particularly significant. One refers to a textual argument, another to historical considerations, the next to source-critical observations, and the last to an anthropological comparison. They are all based on standard scholarly methodologies.

18. Milne, "Feminist Companionship," 60.
19. For an analysis of the feminist work on rape, see Susanne Scholz, *Rape Plots: A Feminist Cultural Study on Genesis 34* (New York: Peter Lang, 2000), 19–44. For an abbreviated version of this analysis, see Susanne Scholz, "Through Whose Eyes? A 'Right' Reading of Genesis 34," in *Genesis*, ed. Athalya Brenner, The Feminist Companion to the Bible, Second Series 1 (Sheffield: Sheffield Academic, 1998), 150–71.
20. For an elaboration of this concept see Emilie Buchwald, Pamela R. Fletcher, and Martha Roth, eds., *Transforming a Rape Culture* (Minneapolis: Milkweed, 1993).

What Is Love? A Textual Argument

Already the beginning verses of Genesis 34 present a challenge for many readers.[21] Did Shechem fall in love with Dinah (v. 3) after he raped her (v. 2)? Was "it" not rape because he loved her? Contemporary Bible versions translate only hesitantly that Shechem raped Dinah. For example, the NRSV reads in verse 2b: "He seized her and lay with her by force." The REB presents the same verse slightly modified: "He took her, lay with her, and violated her." The new JPS *Tanakh* translation states that he "took her and lay with her by force." Showing some hesitancy in verse 2, many translations accept verse 3 as a straightforward reference to love. The NRSV states: "And his soul was drawn to Dinah, daughter of Jacob: he loved the girl, and spoke tenderly to her." The REB insists: "But Shechem was deeply attached to Jacob's daughter Dinah; he loved the girl and sought to win her affection." The new JPS *Tanakh* translation concedes: "Being strongly drawn to Dinah daughter of Jacob, and in love with the maiden, he spoke to the maiden tenderly." These translations exemplify that contemporary Bible committees emphasize the description of love in verse 3 after an initial moment of force, violence, or even rape in verse 2.

Contemporary scholars support this decision. Terence E. Fretheim reasons that "many-faceted love" overrules the rape, so that "this turn of events shifts the reader's response to Shechem in more positive directions."[22] Indeed, "Shechem proceeds to act in a way *atypical* of rapists: He clings to Dinah . . . loves her . . . and speaks to her heart. . . . The latter phrase *may* cause Dinah's positive response" [emphasis added]. Furthermore "Shechem seek(s) to make things right." He offers generously to marry Dinah, although "such generosity was certainly not necessary." The marriage proposal suggests to Fretheim that "Shechem's offer was in Dinah's best interests" within the legal tradition of ancient Israel.

While Fretheim stresses Shechem's love and generosity, he describes Dinah's brothers as suspicious characters and finally as unacceptable: "They use religion as a vehicle for their deception." A reference to Genesis 49:5–7 supports this negative view about Dinah's brothers. Fretheim claims that the "sharp and unambiguous judgment (indeed, a curse!) by Jacob on the violence of Simeon and Levi must stand as the

---

21. For a complete discussion of interpretations from 1970 to 1996, see Scholz, *Rape Plots*, 91–127.
22. This and the following quotes come from Terence E. Fretheim, *The Book of Genesis: Introduction, Commentary, and Reflections* (Nashville: Abingdon, 1994), 574–81.

primary clue about how we should interpret this chapter (Gen 49.5-7)." For this scholar the violence of the brothers and not the rape constitutes the interpretative key. He recommends following Jacob's model and rejecting the brothers because they use "their sister's predicament as an excuse to perpetrate violence." They kill the "rapist and lover of Dinah." Rejecting the brothers, Fretheim underlines Shechem's good intention, the love and generous marriage offer. Shechem turns into an "atypical rapist."

Sharon Pace Jeansonne also highlights verse 3. Interested in the "relevance of the women within the ancestral history of Israel,"[23] she asks where a reader's "sentiments" should lie when Genesis 34 ends. She finds in the narrative "unresolved ambiguities." For example, she asks whether Shechem was "sincere in his professed love" and concludes that "Shechem truly loved Dinah after the assault." For Jeansonne, love demonstrates the "many aspects of this crime and its repercussions" in a story characterized by ambiguities.

George W. Coats offers a concise interpretation that also stresses the significance of verse 3.[24] He announces that the problem arises when "Shechem rapes Dinah but also loves her" and wants "to convert the *strained* relationship into a permanent one" (emphasis added). The brothers, however, oppose Shechem's "folly." The story is, therefore, a story about the men: the brothers, "principally Simeon and Levi," and Shechem along with his father Hamor. Acting violently, the brothers plunder the city, which "leads to complications in the relationship between Israel and Shechem." And so the "simple plot [is] focused not on the rape of Dinah by Shechem, but on the rape of Shechem by the brothers of Dinah." Hence Coats titles his interpretation as "Rape of Shechem." The rapist becomes the raped one, and the rape of Dinah becomes an act of love. Coats transforms the biblical narrative substantially.

Once in Ancient Israel: Historical Considerations

Some scholars refer to the historical circumstances in ancient Israel to explain Genesis 34.[25] Danna Nolan Fewell and David Gunn claim that

23. This and the following quotes come from Sharon Pace Jeansonne, *The Women of Genesis: From Sarah to Potiphar's Wife* (Minneapolis: Fortress Press, 1990), 87–97.
24. This and the following quotes come from George W. Coats, *Genesis with an Introduction to Narrative Literature*, FOTL 1 (Grand Rapids: Eerdmans, 1983), 234.
25. The historical argument is problematic for three reasons. First, scholars have questioned the historical reliability of the Hebrew Bible as a source for reconstructing ancient Israel's history; e.g., Philip R. Davies, *In Search of "Ancient Israel"* (Sheffield: JSOT Press, 1992); and Keith Whitelam, *The*

Shechem acts appropriately within the "narrow limits of [Israelite] society."[26] He offers marriage, which would give Dinah a respected status. Therefore, "if sympathy is being accumulated, it seems to us to be sympathy for Shechem." Fewell and Gunn characterize their reading as feminist because they do not identify Dinah as "a helpless girl to be rescued" but as "a young woman who could have made her own choices—limited though they might have been—had she been asked." Although both scholars acknowledge that to advocate a woman's marrying her rapist might itself seem to be dangerous and androcentric advocacy they argue that "the story world" offers no "other liberating alternatives."[27]

Irmtraud Fischer likewise considers the marriage proposal an exonerating factor in ancient Israel. Subordinating the narrative to laws in Exodus 22:15–16 and Deuteronomy 22:23–27, she argues that Shechem tries at least to restore the legal requirements after the rape. Thus Shechem does not "brutally" use his power against the other tribe. He has intercourse with Dinah before marrying her; this is the problem of Genesis 34.

> By raping, he [Shechem] disregards law and custom and especially the personal integrity of the woman. However, the young man tries to restore them by officially negotiating a marriage and by accepting all conditions.[28]

For Fischer, the narrator does not consider rape as the problem of Genesis 34. Rather, the narrative exemplifies the fact that marriage negotiations of the family of Sarah and Abraham are often deceptive. When foreign men approach the women of this family, the foreigners and not the "patriarchs" are endangered.

Invention of Ancient Israel: The Silencing of Palestinian History (London: Routledge, 1996). Second, a detailed and extensive treatment on the issue of rape does not exist for ancient Israel, so that scholarly explanations remain selective and incomplete. Third, the date and the literary location of this narrative within the Jacob cycle (Gen 25:19–35:22) are very much disputed. Many scholars believe that Genesis 34 was added to the Jacob cycle; e.g., Eduard Nielsen, *Shechem: A Tradition-Historical Investigation* (Copenhagen: Gad, 1955); for an examination of Genesis 34 within the Jacob cycle, see Peter L. Lockwood, "Jacob's Other Twin: Reading the Rape of Dinah in Context," *Lutheran Theological Journal* 29 (1995): 98–105. See also Walter Brueggemann, *Genesis*, IBC (Atlanta: John Knox Press, 1982), 274: "Historically, we can say little about the narrative."

26. Danna Nolan Fewell and David M. Gunn, "Tipping the Balance: Sternberg's Reader and the Rape of Dinah," *JBL* 110, no. 2 (1991): 193–211.

27. For a critique of their view, see Meir Sternberg, "Biblical Poetics and Sexual Politics: From Reading to Couunterreading," *JBL* 111, no. 3 (1992): 463–88; Paul Noble, "'Balanced' Reading of the Rape of Dinah: Some Exegetical and Methodological Observations," *Biblnt* 4 (1996): 173–204.

28. Irmtraud Fischer, *Die Erzeltem Israels: Feministisch-theologische Studien zu Genesis 12–36* (Berlin: de Gruyter, 1994), 233. All translations are mine unless indicated otherwise.

Gerhard von Rad also uses a historical approach. He proposes that Genesis 34 be read as a reflection of ancient Israelite tribal history.

> The narrative seems to go back to the time when Israelite tribes were not yet settled in Palestine but on their way thither in search of new pastures. . . . By some catastrophe they were pushed out of the territory around Shechem and other tribes could settle there later. The essential intention of the narrative in its final form is to present this prehistorical conflict of Simeon and Levi. But like many sagas it has changed the political proceedings into a conflict of fewer single persons and accordingly illustrated it on the level of the personal and universally human.[29]

Reconstructing tribal history, von Rad regards the characters as personifications of the different tribes and groups in Canaan. Rape becomes an unspecified catastrophe. The particular features disappear for the sake of larger historical considerations.

Sometimes references to ancient Near Eastern texts place Genesis 34 into a historical framework. Nicholas Wyatt compares the biblical story with such texts and classifies it as a relic of an archetypal marriage rite similar to "the basic plot of premarital love present in Ugaritic and Akkadian texts."[30] To fit the comparison, Wyatt must change the vocabulary of Genesis 34:2. He proposes to switch the stem of ʿnh from the piel to the qal, so that the verb translates as "to make love." This suggestion enables Wyatt to maintain that "the essence of the affair between Shechem and Dinah turns out to be substantially that of the other ancient Near Eastern form." Changed into a premarital love story, Genesis 34 remains, however, unique in one aspect. The account includes the "untimely death of one of the partners." And so Wyatt claims that this narrative "is hardly a tale of love requited and brought to fruition: it is *au contraire* a tale that ends in tragedy." Subordinating the biblical account to ancient Near Eastern texts, Wyatt reconstructs a story about a sacred marriage ritual. Unfortunately, in this version the bridegroom dies.

An Original Love Story: Source-Critical Observations

Source criticism provides another venue to discuss the rape. Dividing Genesis 34 into two literary sources, scholars differentiate between an

---

29. Gerhard von Rad, *Genesis: A Commentary*, 3rd ed. (London: SCM, 1972), 335.
30. This and the following quotes come from Nicholas Wyatt, "The Story of Dinah and Shechem," *UF* 22 (1990): 433–58.

early love story and a later edition. The original love story does not include the rape. Ita Sheres reads Genesis 34 "in its unredacted, reconstructed state."[31] This original form of the story does not contain the rape "since structurally and linguistically it is difficult to accept his [Shechem's] 'rape' of Dinah." Sheres hypothesizes that in the original story the heroine Dinah goes out to seek a husband, finds him in Shechem, and becomes his legitimate wife. Based on the original story, the final edition contains the elements that portray Shechem sympathetically. Accordingly, Sheres claims that "Shechem is the only person in the tale sympathetic to Dinah." He is depicted as "a man in love."

> If one is to find male compassion in the story, one has to turn to Shechem, "the stranger," who after the rape falls in love with Dinah and realizes that he must "console the girl" before proceeding with official, ritualized courtship. Excluding all the other difficulties that this peculiar order of events suggests, it is fair to observe (as the text *unambiguously* does) that the only man sympathetic to Dinah is Shechem, the presumed villain of the piece. In fact, it can be easily argued that Shechem's attitude is not only the *most human* but also the *most credible*: how else could he have expected to live with Dinah, whom he had raped, as his wife?

Sheres considers Shechem as the "most human" and "most credible" character.[32] The editors, attempting to change this view of the original story, "put the final stamp on the portrait of Dinah as well as on those of all the other men and women in the text; and the specific manner in which Dinah appears in the text is due mainly to their ideological convictions." The redactors add the rape and the "bloody confrontation" between the Shechemites and the two Israelite tribes. They also place the blame on Dinah because "she undertook the forbidden [by the redactors] act of 'going out to see the women of the land.'" According to Sheres's reconstruction, rape becomes a consequence of "her [Dinah's] *unthoughtful* behavior and [is] an *instant* punishment for disobeying the rules spelled out by the men of the tribe,"[33] all later invented by biblical editors and redactors.

Erhard Blum posits two sources. The original source emphasizes the innocence of Shechem and "the unreasonableness of the revenge of

---

31. This and the following quotes come from Ita Sheres, *Dinah's Rebellion: A Biblical Parable for Our Time* (New York: Crossroad, 1990). This and the following quotes are from pages 3–18 and 105–37.
32. Judith S. Antonelli calls Sheres's characterization of Shechem "as the good guy" "a strange twist of logic"; see her book *In the Image of God: A Feminist Commentary on the Torah* (Northval, NJ: Aronson, 1995), 94.
33. Sheres, *Dinah's Rebellion*, 8 and 17 (emphasis added).

Simeon and Levi." This source promotes a "pro-Shechemite position," which a later editor changes. In the earlier version, according to Blum, "the narrator does not tire of stressing the sincerity of Shechem's courtship for Dinah: v. 3 in the account of the narrator: his love for Dinah; v. 4: his intention to pay any bride price; v. 19 an interjection: Shechem's devotion to fulfill the condition." Hence Blum insists: "It is beyond question that *after* his deed Shechem meets his duty in every respect. After all he desires to marry Dinah and he even agrees to pay an excessive bride price."[34] For Blum, the original narrator denounces unambiguously the brothers by juxtaposing Shechem's love to the fraternal vengeance. Only a later Judaic, secondary tradition softens the image of the brothers. Similar to other source critics, Blum construes an original love story that questions the proportion of the fraternal revenge to Shechem's "passion."

Seeking "to reconstruct the original source," Yair Zakovitch articulates how source criticism explains Genesis 34. He observes: "The sequence of actions at the beginning of the story is difficult: Shechem lay with the girl and ravished her (v. 2), and only afterward became infatuated with her and sought to persuade her (v. 3)."[35] The original story presented "Shechem's innocent attraction to Dinah and Jacob's sons' treacherous exploitation of the situation in order to plunder the city." It did not contain "the rape element," claims Zakovitch. Because of the anachronism in verse 7, the awkward syntax regarding the "defiling of Dinah in vv. 13 and 27, and the "real tension over which of the brothers attacked the city of Shechem" in verses 25–31, later editors added verses 2b, 5, 7ab, 13a, 13b, 17, 25a, 25b, 27, 30, and 31. Editors also assimilated the original story to two biblical texts: the story of the rape of Tamar (2 Samuel 13) and Jacob's curse of his two sons (Gen 49:5–7). The assimilation of Genesis 34 to these texts results in a contrived later story in which the rape explains the fraternal violence.

Insider versus Outsider: An Anthropological Comparison

Some scholars use an anthropological argument. They maintain that fear of the Canaanite neighbors motivates a narrative that struggles between integration and exclusion. Lyn M. Bechtel proposes such an interpretation. She suggests that Genesis 34 reflects the dispute within

---

34. This and the following quotes come from Erhard Blum, *Die Komposition der Vatergeschichte* (Neukirchen-Vluyn: Neukirchener Verlag, 1984), 210–29.
35. The quotes are from Yair Zakovitch, "Assimilation in Biblical Narratives," in *Empirical Models for Biblical Criticism*, ed. Jeffrey H. Tigay (Philadelphia: University of Pennsylvania Press, 1985), 175–93.

Israel. As a group-oriented society Israel was divided as to whether to interact with non-Israelites and to cross tribal boundaries.[36] The characters represent the different positions. Personified by Dinah and Jacob, one faction wants to interact with outsiders; personified by the brothers, "the militant folks," the other faction, vote for separation and group "purity." The writers of Genesis 34 oppose the excluding position, Bechtel believes: "The story seems to be challenging this attitude [of the brothers] by showing the potential danger in which it places the group."

Bechtel explains that in a group-oriented society like ancient Israel individuals lived and worked to serve the good of the group. In such a society the differentiation between "us" and "them" was essential. "Closely knit" boundaries had to be maintained. The activities of individuals strengthened the boundaries. Marriage was a group affair, and sexual intercourse perpetuated the values of the family and clan. Sexual intercourse became shameful when it lacked family or community bonding. Dinah and Shechem, however, are "two unhanded people" when they have "intercourse." The question is therefore not whether rape occurred but whether the "sexual intercourse" between Dinah and Shechem was shameful.

Referring to texts like Deuteronomy 22:23–29, Bechtel maintains that Shechem does not threaten the social bonding of the community. He tries to win the approval from the other group. He proposes marriage and offers many goods. This behavior indicates to Bechtel that the intercourse between Dinah and Shechem is not shameful. Bechtel claims: "The text stresses that these are honorable men [Shechem and his father Hamor]" and that "the overall action of Shechem . . . is one of honor." Thus she concludes: "Throughout the text there is no indication that Dinah is raped. The description of Shechem's behavior and attitude does not fit that of a rapist. . . . All of this diminishes the likelihood that rape was seen to have occurred."

Excusing Shechem, Bechtel considers the brothers as the villains. They are stuck in an exclusionary group-oriented behavior that threatens to destroy the whole group, and they retreat to unjustifiable vengeance. Similar to scholars who use other hermeneutical approaches, Bechtel explains: "Ironically, if there is a rape in this story, it is Simeon

36. This and the following quotes come from Lyn M. Bechtel, "What if Dinah Is Not Raped? (Genesis 34)," *JSOT* 62 (June 1994): 19–36.

and Levi who "rape" the Shechemites."[37] Again, the killing turns to rape and the rape into acceptable sexual intercourse.

Similarly, Walter Brueggemann promotes Genesis 34 as a discussion on xenophobia. For him, the theme is "Israelite accommodation to non-Israelites in the land . . . a much disputed issue in Israel."[38] In this reading, "the liaison of Dinah and Shechem" refers to the interaction between Canaanites and Israelites, which Brueggemann considers to be the result of a "seduction." Israel, however, considers "intermarriage" as "perversion." Therefore, "the report on Shechem is obviously given from a polemical Israelite perspective." Judging the brothers, Brueggemann states that "this narrative evidences the unsophisticated and irrational response of a passion unencumbered by reflection." The brothers are not interested in "accommodation, cooperation, or even ratification." Vengeance dominates them. "Fixed on the narrow sexual issue," they are "blind to the larger economic issues, blind to the dangers they have created, blind to the possibilities of cooperation, and blind even to the ways they have compromised their own religion in their thirst for vengeance and gain." Brueggemann understands that Jacob despairs over his sons. Thus he writes that the father's attempt to achieve a "more pragmatic settlement" with Shechem makes more sense than the fraternal response. Thus, in the end, Brueggemann regrets that Jacob could not prevail against the "more sectarian and destructive settlement" of his sons.

Ethical Responsibilities for the Interpretation of Genesis 34 from a Feminist Perspective

"It is . . . important to avoid complicity with the rape cultures, ancient and contemporary, that would have us deny that the crime is violent or blame the victims of sexual assault," Harold C. Washington demands.[39] The previous examination, however, demonstrates that interpretations of Genesis 34 contain numerous assumptions complicit with a contemporary belittlement of rape. Scholars suggest that the rapist "really" loved Dinah. They find rape less harmful in ancient Israel. They maintain that in ancient Israel a marriage could redeem the rape, that the story reflects a tribal conflict with Canaanite neighbors, or

---

37. For a detailed criticism of Bechtel's reading, see my book *Rape Plots*, 109–12; see also the brief critique of Harold C. Washington, "Violence and the Construction of Gender in the Hebrew Bible: A New Historicist Approach," *BibInt* 5, no. 4 (1997): 357.
38. This and the following quotes come from Brueggemann, *Genesis*, 274–80.
39. Washington, "Violence," 359.

that Genesis 34 narrates a sacred marriage ritual similar to other ancient Near Eastern texts. Further, interpreters identify an original love story and relegate the rape to a later edition. They explain the events with the dynamics of group-oriented societies in which sexual intercourse is only problematic when it threatens the community.

Yet biblical cultural critics propose that "real readers" are always located, interested, and socially and historically conditioned. As such, their interpretations reflect cultural assumptions of their time. If this suggestion is correct, interpretations of Genesis 34 mirror a culture that minimizes rape, sympathizes with rapists, and blames victim-survivors. Although feminists have worked to change these perceptions for over twenty-five years, interpretations of Genesis 34 continue to perpetrate androcentric views. Unfortunately, scholars do not investigate their assumptions critically, even when they call their readings feminist. Supporting the marriage proposal of Shechem, they do not criticize the rapist or his deed.

The interpretations and the critique of this essay reflect a division in contemporary society. A majority undervalues the injustice perpetrated by rape and considers other factors as more important. A minority, the feminist view, sides with raped victim-survivors and stresses the evil of rape. This split appears most clearly when rape occurs in complex circumstances like those in Genesis 34. In 1997, a similarly complex story occurred in Lima, Peru.[40]

> Late one night more than three months ago, a group of drunken men in their 20s raped a 17-year old girl who was on her way home from work in the crime-ridden Villa El Salvador district of Lima. After the young woman told her family about the assault, her father and brother tracked down the three rapists, who lived in their neighborhood. Her father wanted to kill them, said the young woman, who told her story on condition that she be identified only by her first name, Maria Elena. Her brother wanted to beat them. She wanted to press charges. But when one of the rapists offered to marry her, her family put pressure on her to accept, and she finally yielded after being threatened by the men who had raped her.[41]

As in Genesis 34, a young woman is raped and the rapist offers to marry her. Whereas the brothers of Dinah reject the marriage proposal, the

---

40. I chose this example because the story is similar to Genesis 34. Numerous rape stories within the United States are reported regularly. For more information, see, e.g., Bureau of Justice Statistics, "Rape and Sexual Assault," https://www.bjs.gov/index.cfm?ty=tp&tid=317&bd=-5#768#1366#1#n.
41. Calvin Sims, "Justice in Peru: Victim Gets Rapist for a Husband," *New York Times*, March 12, 1997, A1, A12.

family of Maria Elena pressures her to accept. The penal codes of Peru and fourteen other Latin American countries exonerate a rapist if he offers to marry the raped victim-survivor and she accepts. Some penal codes exonerate the rapist even if the raped victim-survivor rejects the offer. The newspaper quotes Peruvians as saying that "marriage is the right and proper thing to do after a rape" because "a raped woman is a used item. No one wants her."

Peruvian women's rights groups were outraged about the legal situation in their country. They were fighting for the removal of the law because it degraded women and was legally unsound. Beatriz Merino Lucero, the president of the congressional committee on women and a Harvard-trained lawyer, comments:

> To believe in 1997 that it is intelligent and moral for a rapist to marry his victim as a mechanism for pardon shows me that some of my colleagues in Congress don't fundamentally understand what rape is. If we know that rape is the worst act of violence against a woman, that it attacks her most intimate sense of security and places her in a situation of disadvantage, how can we assume that a woman in this state can have a life with the person who abused her?[42]

The example from Peru demonstrates the contemporary division on the issue of rape. Feminists and their organizations define rape as "the worst act of violence against a woman." Others believe that rape devalues the victim-survivor. The previous analysis demonstrates that biblical scholars have participated in this debate, siding with the non-feminist view.

Only a few exceptions exist, such as the interpretation of Alice A. Keefe. Her reading focuses on the rape in Genesis 34, considering it as "a way of speaking of its [Israel's] struggle to retain a distinctive and separate cultural identity."[43] The rape "serves as an expression of Israel's vulnerability to being dominated, taken over and absorbed by the other peoples, particularly by urban Canaanite culture." Keefe regards Dinah as a metaphoric character through whom Israel imagined itself as a violated woman. Rape was a literary element necessary for Israelite authors to imagine a future of wholeness. Although an understanding of rape as a "metaphor" for Israel's vulnerability is problematic, Keefe acknowledges the rape as the central event in

---

42. Ibid., A12.
43. This and the following quotes come from Alice A Keefe, "Rape of Women/Wars of Men," *Semeia* 61 (1993): 94.

Genesis 34. Most interpretations, however, do not. They also ignore the "flesh-and-blood" consequences of their interpretations. One scholar expresses his concern about this lack. Responding to Fewell and Gunn, who support the marriage between Dinah and Shechem, Meir Sternberg exclaims: "Tell it not to rapists, publish it not in the streets" because "some would call it [their interpretation] a license to rape."[44]

If, then, interpretations, "no matter how rational, systematic, and scientific,"[45] connect to the cultural assumptions of their day, what are the ethical responsibilities for interpreting Genesis 34? Certainly progressive Bible readers cannot afford to read this narrative while disregarding the prevalence of rape in contemporary society. If biblical cultural critics observe correctly that the Bible shapes culture and culture shapes the Bible, interpreters cannot reinterpret, minimize, or ignore the rape of Dinah anymore. They have to take the rape seriously and express their clear disapproval of the rapist. At stake are the ethics of biblical studies in a culture that has often used the Bible to support injustice and discrimination. Biblical cultural studies challenge such usage and offer opportunity to read the Bible in an ethically responsible way.

The next chapter examines an African-Mali cinematic appropriation of Genesis 34 as it emerges in the film *La Genèse*, produced and directed by Cheik Oumar Sissoko in 1999. The question is whether the film coalesces with the centuries-old convention and sidelines the rape of Dinah in order to address androcentric-postcolonial concerns in biblical-visual storytelling.

44. Sternberg, "Biblical Poetics," 476, 474.
45. Aichele and Phillips, "Introduction," 15.

11

"Belonging to All Humanity": The Dinah Story (Genesis 34) in the Film *La Genèse* (1999) by Cheick Oumar Sissoko

African movies have a difficult time finding a large audience. This is also true for *La Genèse*, produced by the Malian film director Cheick Oumar Sissoko. The movie, which covers the narratives found in Genesis 23–37, has received no reviews from biblical or religious studies scholars. The scant reviews on the film have appeared mostly in publications in the fields of communication and film studies. These evaluations emphasize that *La Genèse* is a highly unusual viewing experience for a Western audience because the movie places Africa at the center.[1] For instance, the communication professor Walter C. Metz observes that Sissoko's film presents "a uniquely African interpretation,"[2] based on a postcolonial perspective of the Genesis stories. Another reviewer, David Sterritt, makes a similar point when he states: "Combining its Old Testament story with vivid African imagery, the film may have confusing moments for moviegoers used to traditional Western treatments of this mater. For those willing to meet it on its own terms, however, it

1. Walter C. Metz, "Adapting Genesis," *Literature Film Quarterly* 35 (2007): 236.
2. Ibid., 229.

offers rich new perspectives on a timeless subject."[3] Metz even finds in *La Genèse* the translation philosophy of Walter Benjamin: "A translation touches the original lightly and only at the infinitely small point of the sense, thereupon pursuing its own course according to the laws of fidelity in the freedom of linguistic flux."[4]

It is true that Sissoko's film does not exactly follow the detailed content of Genesis 23–37.[5] This may be the characteristic African style of *La Genèse*, although some film scholars emphasize that there is no "authentic African cinema."[6] Sissoko's hermeneutical interest is not a literal rehearsal of the biblical text; rather he relates these narratives to current African society and changes the biblical text creatively for viewers to identify themselves with the story and to learn from it.[7] Thus his goal is not to produce a historical retelling of the biblical tale or to keep intact the biblical chronology. Instead, the director interprets those Genesis narratives that he finds significant for the contemporary African context in Mali. Interestingly, the film begins with Dinah's story (Genesis 34).

Sissoko's *La Genèse* changes the biblical story line dramatically as he restructures "the Bible's content as a template for understanding the lived experience of contemporary Africans."[8] For Sissoko, as well as other African film directors, "the concerns of contemporary Africa"[9] are always at the center, and the biblical tales in Genesis turn into "post-colonial allegory of fratricide in Africa."[10] The film, focusing on the topic of "brotherly betrayal,"[11] presents a "racial rehistoricization" of the biblical narratives.[12] Sterritt provides the following summary of the film:

---

3. David Sterritt, "Trio of Films Show Faith in Religious Themes," *Christian Science Monitor*, December 3, 1999, 15.

4. Walter Benjamin, "Theses on the Philosophy of History," in *Illuminations*, ed. and with an introduction by Hannah Arendt, trans. Harry Zohn (London: Fontana/Collins, 1970), 80. Metz refers to Benjamin in "Adapting Genesis," 229.

5. See also the incorrectly mentioned chapters and verses in the essay by Metz, "Adapting Genesis," 231. For instance, Esau's declaration, "Then I will kill my brother, Jacob," is not found in Genesis 41 but in Gen 27:41.

6. Lindiwe Dovey, introduction to *African Film and Literature: Adapting Violence to the Screen* (New York: Columbia University Press, 2009), 8.

7. Ibid., 9.

8. Metz, "Adapting Genesis," 231.

9. Ibid., 231. Many African movies follow this hermeneutical pattern; see, e.g., Teresa Hoefert de Truègano, "African Cinemas," *World Literature Today* (October-December 2003): 14–18, esp. 16: "Many films today explore the complexities of daily life and what modernity means for Africa."

10. Ibid., 231.

11. Metz, "Adapting Genesis," 233; also see ibid., 235: "an allegorically meaningful investigation of contemporary Africa."

12. Lindiwe Dovey, "Humanizing the Old Testament's Origins," in *African Film and Literature*, 271.

Genesis, directed by Mali filmmaker Cheick Oumar Sissoko, retells the biblical story of Jacob and Esau with an eye toward illuminating today's widespread conflicts between clans, tribes, and nations that have differing visions of what constitutes a decent and constructive way of life.[13]

The film thus focuses on the following question: Why do the various group in African fight against each other rather than collaborate? The film, of course, "is an indictment of the allegorical fratricide—brothers killing each other due to colonialism's political destabilization—that threatens to keep the African continent in the throes of the nineteenth century."[14] Sissoko describes his hermeneutical interests with the following statement:

> Fratricidal conflicts come about because of decentralization mandated by the World Bank and the IMF, which makes people struggle among each other for what little power is left. I needed a text to deal with this. . . . Around this same time a friend of mine in France showed me a script proposal dealing with Genesis chapters twenty-three through thirty-seven. I said, my God, it's what we need. . . . Genesis belongs to all humanity. . . . Today, in Mali, the primary conflict is between the Soninkè and the Fulani. This is a fratricidal conflict. I wrote the script of this film about fratricide five years ago, and it shows what is happening in my country right now, in the southwest and in the northeast. Something like one hundred and fifty people died recently in a conflict between the Soninkè and the Fulani. There are also conflicts between Arabs and Maures and in the area around Gao. All this is because of decentralization, the economic crisis, and the poor government of Mali. The World Bank and the United States say this is democracy, but that is not true. . . . What I represent is the outcome of the decentralization, the conflict. In the film, you have peasants and farmers. They live together for centuries. They know each other very well, and they share many things. But because they know each other so well, they also have many reasons to hate each other. In the film, like right now in Mali and across Africa, they are choosing to focus on these. Why? They share customs, they marry together. But because of poverty, because of money, there is all this jealousy and envy and ultimately fratricide.[15]

In other words, Sissoko presents the biblical stories included in *La Genèse* as a plea for "the reconciliation of the African brothers"[16] culminating in a "redemptive ending."[17] This reconciliation occurs at the

---

13. Sterritt, "Trio of Films," 15.
14. Metz, "Adapting Genesis," 235.
15. Ray Privett, "I Make Films about the Big Problems of Our Continent: An Interview with Cheick Oumar Sissoko," *Cineaste* 25, no. 2 (2000): 39–40.
16. Metz, "Adapting Genesis," 232.

very moment when brothers again respect their familial relationships.[18] Sissoko thus places the Genesis tales into a large allegorical framework that aims for the unification of the African continent. It considers the fraternal conflicts since the colonial era solvable and desires to see Africa as a united force in the world.[19]

Sissoko's film is significant because it does not regard the Bible as a colonial text. Instead, in Sissoko's visual reading, the Bible becomes an African tool of liberation that makes an essential contribution to social justice in the postcolonial era. In the process Sissoko's biblical interpretation takes on midrashic characteristics, which communicate this new perspective. The film is thus a good example for what newer trends in biblical scholarship describe as "social location." This approach assumes that every biblical interpretation is always grounded in a specific social context. Thus it is not the text itself nor the original historical setting behind the text that shape biblical meanings, but readers grounded in their social locations who, consciously or unconsciously, create them. By systematically applying this hermeneutical insight, Sissoko succeeds in turning the selected stories of Genesis into African tales that illuminate current violent events in the African context with selected biblical stories. This approach transforms the Bible into a source of hope toward fraternal reconciliation, even among enemy groups and after much bloodshed.[20] Despite this important issue, however, the film is permeated by an unmistakable androcentrism. The following analysis focuses on this aspect on the film.

In any reading that focuses on social location, it is vitally important to understand which narratives are included, how they are told, and likewise which tales are excluded. For instance, the proposal that Sissoko's film is permeated by an androcentric perspective helps explain why the majority of female characters in Genesis 23–37 (38) remain in the background; or why Dinah, who plays such a central role in the text, ultimately remains on the margins of *La Genèse*. Clearly, the film is mainly concerned with the fate of the brothers, their conflicts, and their reconciliation, even when a female character seemingly stands at the center of the encounter. This essay describes the content of *La*

17. Ibid., 234.
18. Ibid.
19. Ibid., 235–36.
20. Dovey, "Humanizing the Old Testament's Origins," 272–73.

Genèse, provides background information on Sissoko, the director, and critiques the androcentric features of this film.

The Content of *La Genèse* and Cheick Oumar Sissoko

The film begins with Esau, played by the internationally known Malian musician and actor, Salif Keita, and his group chasing Jacob, his brother. The film's opening sequence establishes key features of the film. The actors speak in the local dialect of Mali called Bambara. The setting dramatically showcases the countryside of Mali, particularly the renowned northeast mountain area of Hombori Tondo. Finally, in several scenes Esau's men are dressed in traditional hunter clothing.[21] Following this sequence, the movie moves to the story of Dina (Genesis 34). Here Sissoko deviates considerably from the biblical text by depicting Jacob as a father mourning for his son, Joseph (Gen 37:34). In this sequence, Jacob sits in the semi-dark of his hut while Dinah washes Joseph's shirt in the center of the courtyard of four huts. Her mother, Leah, also appears in this scene, napping with several children in the midday heat. The very slow movement of the activities and the close-ups of each character communicate how the family strains under this psychological tension. Further, Joseph's betrayal by his brothers, having implicitly occurred prior to this scene, allows the ramifications of the fraternal conflict to appear with full force.

The next scene in the film shows how Dinah, approaching Shechem in the field, tries to flirt with him. However, he becomes annoyed with her flirtatious advances, especially since a couple of boys tease him as they watch the scene. Shechem therefore runs after Dinah, catches her, and, carrying her on his shoulders, brings her to his hut. At this point, the camera stays outside the hut and focuses on the faces of the many villagers there. All of them are waiting in the shade during the midday heat. Eventually, Shechem comes through his hut's door and closes his pants in full view. Then his father, Hamor, clearly annoyed with this development, approaches his son and agrees to visit Dinah's father to propose marriage between their children. After his proposal is made, Dinah's brothers seemingly agree, demanding only that Shechem and all male inhabitants of Hamor's village are circumcised prior to the

---

21. Sissoko reconstructs all costumes and the village settings according to Mali traditions; see Olivier Barlet, "'La Genèse' by Cheikh Oumar Sissoko (Mali)," *Africultures: Les Mondes en Relation*, April 30, 1999, http://tinyurl.com/lejo5ok. See also Debra Boyd-Buggs, "Les costumes de Kandioura Coulibaly pour La Genèse," in *Cinemas africains, uns oasis dans le desert*, ed. Samuel Lelièvre (Condé-sur-Noireau, France: Corlet, 2003), 117–21.

wedding. Yet, on the third day, Jacob's sons attack the village and kill every man, boy, and male infant, all of whom are weakened due to the recent circumcision. This scene ends any further references to Genesis 34, although many of this story's characters continue to appear in the film.

When Jacob hears of the attack, he cries out in deep mourning. He then begins walking to visit Hamor who, unlike the biblical narrative, has survived the attack. Jacob takes Dinah with him, and the two fathers talk with each other in proverbial sentences. Notably, Hamor observes how the world has become as evil as prior to the deluge. Both men decide thereupon that only a meeting of the nations will be able to overcome the evil in the world. At the end of their conversation Jacob hands over Dinah to Hamor.

The following scene shows how the various African nations arrive at the meeting. This kind of meeting does not exist in the book of Genesis, but it makes it possible to weave several other narratives of Genesis 23–37 (38) into the film. During the various speeches and proverbial exchanges among the meeting's participants, Dinah appears repeatedly. She laughs hysterically, wearing a white dress and dancing in the midst of the gathered crowd, and at one point her father almost pushes her to the ground.

The depiction of these activities and speeches abruptly ends with a theater-like performance that tells the story of Judah and Tamar (Genesis 38). The performance begins with some of the gathered men mentioning the biblical characters, and then it continues with a flashback depiction of the narrative. Then the film returns to the gathering, and in another flashback Jacob tells one of his sons how his father, Isaac, searched for a bride (Genesis 24). Jacob's romanticizing commentary, "That is how we lived before the rift," is vehemently protested by Esau. Another of Jacob's sons then asks why Esau wanted to kill his brother. As a response, Jacob tells the story of the lentil soup in Genesis 25, in which Esau sells his right of primogeniture to Jacob. Since biblical chronology is not of interest to the film, Sissoko adapts the narratives into the cinematic story line to support the main point of the film: fraternal fight and fratricide are deeply rooted in the past and continuously poison the relationships of the various African nations to this day.

The climax of the film occurs in the last part of the movie. There, Jacob fights against the angel of God (Genesis 32), which is followed by the fraternal reconciliation (Gen 34:4.9.12). In the film Esau announces the new name of his brother, and he also insists that Jacob must now be addressed as "Israel" because "he was strong against God." Jacob's sons and Dinah play a central role in the grand finale. It shows the sons of Jacob walking together toward Egypt. The motionless Esau, Jacob, Hamor, and Dinah stand at a small hill watching the slow-moving group of men depart. Then, in a final and static panoramic shot, the scene disappears, leaving the audience with a truly epic feeling about the future of these people.

The movie does not include every story and detail of Genesis 23–37 (38). For instance, the tale of the pregnancy competition between Leah and Rachel, including their enslaved women, Bilhah and Zilpah, is omitted (Gen 29:31–30:24). The story of Jacob, who with the help of his mother deceives his father to receive a blessing, is also excluded (Genesis 27). The same is true of any reference to Rachel, who dies giving birth to Benjamin (Gen 35:16–21), and the single verse reporting the rape of Bilhah by Reuben (Gen 35:22). The genealogy in Genesis 36 is hinted at in several conversations among the elders during the gathering of the nations. Since Joseph disappeared already prior to the movie's beginning, Joseph's dreams are not retold in the film (Gen 37:1–11). The story of the endangered ancestress Rebekah is also absent (Gen 26:1–16). The movie only mentions those biblical narratives that advance Sissoko's hermeneutical goal, which seeks to elaborate on the origins of fratricide and the possibilities of fraternal reconciliation. Midrashic-like interpretations of the biblical texts are the result.

La Genèse is not Sissoko's first movie. The filmmaker who was born in Mali in 1945 and went to France, the former colonial power over Mali, to get an education as a filmmaker. He became internationally known with the movie *Finzan* in 1990,[22] which deals with the oppression of women in "African patriarchy."[23] The film depicts the stories of two African women. After the death of her husband one of the women is forced to marry again, and the other woman endures genital mutilation against her will. In 1995, Sissoko established himself as an internationally recognized filmmaker with another movie called *Guimba: The*

---

22. See, e.g., Laura DeLuca und Shadrack Kamenya, "Representation of Female Circumcision in Finzan, a Dance for the Heroes," *Research in African Literatures* 26, no. 3 (1995): 83–87. Already in 1986, Sissoko made the film *Nyamanton* (The garbage boys), hailed as "another landmark in the development of African cinema . . . because it links the politics of film production with the aesthetic of African cinema in new ways"; see Manthia Diawara and Elizabeth Robinson, "De Nouvelles Perspectives de la Cinematographie Africaine: Une interview de Cheick Oumar Sissoko," *Young Cinema & Theatre* 4 (1988): 3–4.
23. Metz, "Adapting Genesis," 236.

Tyrant. This film centers on a power-hungry and greedy African dictator who is eventually overthrown by the people.

Sissoko belongs to a generation of African filmmakers who intend their films to make social and political contributions to the development and advancement of their countries.[24] He thus wants his films to nurture the "emerging consciousness of our people."[25] For this reason Sissoko grounds his works in African life and culture to offer a counterbalance to globalizing and neocolonial structures, as well as to develop an "indigenous cinematic aesthetic."[26] Accordingly, Sissoko's political activism is entirely unsurprising. In 1996, together with Oumar Mariko, he founded a political party and, in 2002, he was appointed the secretary of culture in Mali. Finally, in 2007, Sissoko was nominated to be the minister of national education, but he was not appointed to this governmental position.

Dinah in Africa: Androcentrism in Fratricide and Reconciliation

In *La Genèse*, Sissoko brings attention to the problem of fratricide, suggesting the possibility for fraternal reconciliation. Brothers stand at this film's center, although the decision to begin the movie with Genesis 34 gives unexpected attention to the female character of Dinah. The film begins with her, and she remains present at its conclusion. Yet despite Dinah's impressive role, the film is not ultimately interested in her fate. The story of Dinah serves only as Sissoko's starting point to engage the topic of fratricide and fratricidal wars between Jacob's sons and the son of Hamor. Male battles are Sissoko's primary concern as he seeks to imagine an end to this violence. The prologue to the film communicates this idea. Imitating the scrolling script of the *Star Wars* saga, Sissoko describes the three male family clans as follows:

Troit cents ans après le deluge, deux clans se déchirent:

[*Three centuries after the Flood two tribes formed:*]

---

24. Teresa Hoefert de Turégano, "African Cinemas," *World Literature Today* (October-December 2003): 18. See also Smaba Gadjigo, "Africa through African Eyes," *Research in African Literatures* 23, no. 4 (1992): 97–105.
25. Privett, "I Make Films about the Big Problems of Our Continent," 38.
26. N. Frank Ukadike, "African Films: A Retrospective and a Vision for the Future," *Critical Arts: A South-North Journal of Cultural & Media Studies* 7, no. 1 (1993): 55. For a discussion on the financial challenges of translating such a vision into a movie within the postcolonial setting of West Africa, see Teresa Hoefert de Turégano, "Sub-Saharan African Cinemas: The French Connection," *Modern & Contemporary France* 13, no. 1 (2005): 71–83.

– le clan de l'éleveur Jacob et de ses fils [*the tribe of the breeder of Jacob and his sons*]

– le clan des cultivateurs sédentaires dont le chef est Hamor [*the tribe of the farmers with Hamor as the leader*]

Un troisiéme clan, le peuple des chasseurs conduit par Esaü voe uns haine mortelle á

Jacob, son frère cadet, depuis que celui-ci lui a subtilisè so Droit d'aînesse.

Reclus dans son campement, Jacob pleure son fils Joseph qu'il croit mort.

[*A third tribe consisting of hunters is led by Esau who feels lethal hatred against Jacob, his younger brother, ever since he gave up his firstborn right to him.*

Turned away from the world in his yard Jacob mourns over his son, Joseph, whom he believes to be dead.]

A tous ceuxqui, de par le monde,

Sont victimes de conflits fratricides

A tous ceux qui font la paix.

[*To all the victims of fratricide—To all who make peace*] (0:27–36)[27]

This opening refers to the three male tribal leaders in a way not found in the biblical text. In Genesis, Hamor is hardly associated with the figures of Jacob and Esau. Yet in the film all three are presented as equal patriarchs: Jacob the breeder, Hamor the farmer, and Esau the hunter. The opening also states that Jacob mourns for his son Joseph, whom he believes to be dead, as it is reported in Genesis 37:34: "Then Jacob tore his garments, and put sackcloth on his loins, and mourned for his son many days" (NRSV). Thus the end of the selected biblical texts stands at the very beginning of the film so that the following events appear in a completely different light than in the biblical chronology (0:01–2:05). In the film the Joseph story is the framework through which all of the ensuing events, including the story of Dinah, flow. Moreover, from the first minute onward violence infiltrates everything that is told in *La Genèse*. This is at least the view of film critic, Lindiwe Dovey, who classifies the implied death of Joseph as the first act of violence in the film.

---

27. The numbers throughout this essay refer to the film's minutes and seconds for easy reference.

She considers Dinah's rape as the second act of violence,[28] a surprising assessment given that the film does not contain an explicit rape scene.

The presentation of the so-called rape scene, the verbal confrontation between Dinah and Hamor, and the final scene of fraternal reconciliation demonstrate that *La Genèse* is permeated by a strong androcentric perspective. In his film, Sissoko ignores women's experiences and insists that the fraternal reconciliation alone promises African unity and independence. This exclusionary position should be questioned given that it ignores at least 50 percent of the population. It does not take full advantage of the potential of the biblical stories to envision a just and equitable future for all.

Blaming the Victim and Dinah's Flirting

As mentioned previously, the first scene in *La Genèse* does not follow the text's chronological order, beginning with Genesis 23, and instead the film starts with Genesis 34 (0:37–1:21). After a long panoramic shot with three short interruptions, in which a younger brother appears twice and Leah once, Dinah is shown in the middle of the courtyard surrounded by four huts, all belonging to Jacob, the patriarch of the family. Dinah is the first person in a close-up shot. The scene takes place outside in the heat of the afternoon. Dinah is washing a piece of clothing in a round wooden container placed on the sandy floor. It is quiet, and there is no sound except for the washing of the piece of clothing. Standing with straight legs, Dinah bows down deep into the container, and we see her long arms and then her face. She looks to the right to her younger brother who, watching his sister, sits in front of an open entrance to one of the huts. Then Dinah looks to the left, where her mother, Leah, takes a nap. Then she looks back to the piece of clothing in her hands. The next camera shot is inside Jacob's hut, where he sits and mourns. The absence of any conversation communicates the presence of profound tension. The long silence puts Dinah into the tension's center, but it is unclear what the problem is. What does Dinah have to do with Jacob's grief over Joseph?

The scene shows that Dinah is a major if not the central character for the development of the events in the story. Still, the film maintains a thoroughly androcentric perspective, as the rape scene clearly illustrates. Here, Sissoko's retelling emphasizes Dinah's flirtatious advances to Shechem. Further, the film highlights the tacit acceptance of this

---

28. Dovey, "Humanizing the Old Testament's Origins," 258.

event by the Hamorite villagers, which is only contrasted by the mild anger portrayed by Shechem's father, Hamor. Even Leah's response indicates this androcentric view when she calls Dinah a "whore." The charge of androcentrism also explains why Jacob hands his daughter over to the other tribe without any hesitation.[29] He does not give a high value to his daughter and thus finds it easy to deliver her to Hamor, whose son first had sex with her. This at least is the androcentric assessment of the situation that the film presents as a fact and does not critically interrogate.

The rape scene, which the film calls "deflowering," shows Dinah on the edge of a pasture where a herd of cows grazes (9:27–11:23). Two small boys are playing there. Dinah approaches the area, and she looks repeatedly around, looking at a male teenager who, as it turns out, is Shechem. He is working in the field when Dinah calls his name: "Shechem, Shechem!" Hearing this, the two young boys who are close by tease Shechem. Their reaction implies it is not the first time that Dinah has come looking for Shechem. She has been interested in him already for some time. Yet he is annoyed at the mockery. He chases after Dinah, catches her, and throws her over his shoulder, running away with her. In response to this development, one of the boys asks the other boy: "Has he finally done it?"

But is this a depiction of a rape scene? According to Dovey, this question can be answered in the affirmative. This is true even though the rape is not represented explicitly, given that the scene conforms with the "typical modesty of African representations of violence."[30] Yet the scene also enables another interpretation that views Dinah as the one who provokes and even desires the ensuing encounter. After all, in the film Dinah seeks Shechem's attention. She finds him and speaks to him whereas he merely responds when he feels challenged by the two boys. Only then does Shechem run after her and catch her. The story looks different in Genesis 34. There Dinah goes out "to see the daughters of the land" but is seen by Shechem who rapes her.

The film characterizes Dinah as the one who approaches Shechem and thus voluntarily gets herself "endangered," even though she also places her robe over her hair as a sign of chastity. Her curiosity, her flirtatiousness, and the ensuing provocations lead to the events

---

29. Film critics who do not know about biblical scholarship justify Shechem's deed, saying that Shechem wanted to marry Dinah and Hamor helped him to reach this goal, as "reasonable men would find a way out of this situation"; see James M. Wall, "Tribal Conflict," *Christian Century*, November 3, 1999, 1043.
30. Dovey, "Humanizing the Old Testament's Origins," 258.

according to the proverb that Hamor mentions in his speech when he tries to convince Jacob to agree to the marriage between Shechem and Dinah. Jacob asks: "Have my brothers come in peace?" And Hamor replies: "I am here on account of a woman. Can there be peace when a woman's involved?" (21:52–22:22).

This extremely misogynist proverb does not exist in Genesis 34. Is this not an African proverb that places the cause of the fraternal hatred between the tribe of Jacob and the Hamorites onto Dinah? In the film, the proverb is not further commented on by either patriarch, although the visual direction of the camera might serve as a possible critique. In the very moment in which Hamor recites the proverb the camera focuses on a woman with children. The woman sits peacefully with her children, which seems to stand in direct opposition to Hamor's speech. However, the sexist proverb maintains on the verbal level that, according to androcentric perspective, all ensuing events go back to Dinah, as she was the one who initiated contact with Shechem. This is at least one possible interpretation of this scene when one considers the significance of gender.

The next scene in the film shows the Hamorites waiting in front of the house into which Shechem and Dinah withdrew (11:24–13:47). The villagers do not speak initially, but then they run Dinah and her family down. The scene ends with a victory song of the women when a woman steps out of the house and lifts up a white sheet with a blood stain on it. According to Dovey, this is the celebration of the rape, but the scene resembles the celebration of the bride's virginity taken in the "first night," a classic patriarchal custom. Interestingly, women take center stage in this scene as if they were the ones particularly welcoming this act. Women and men tolerate Shechem's deed, and their words express suspicion toward Dinah. Nobody seems to recognize an act of violence in the event to be stopped or prevented. Although the biblical text of Genesis 34:2–3 is read out loud, including that "Shechem rapes Dinah" (16:47–17:25),[31] the mention of these verses follows the cinematic depiction and could easily be missed. After all, visual impressions are much stronger than later recited Bible verses.

31. The Bible verse is spoken in Bambara, but the English subtitles quote it like this: "Shechem, son of Hamor, Prince of the land, abducted Dinah, Jacob's daughter. He lay with her and raped her, but then he fell in love with her with all his heart and all his soul, and he consoled her." Since I do not understand Bambara, I do not know how the Bible verse is translated into Bambara.

Dinah Talks Back and a Slap in the Face

The androcentric perspective, permeating the movie, is also apparent in another scene that follows the "rape scene" (14:17–15:21). After Shechem demonstratively closes his trousers, his father comes up the steps. Hamor looks at his son for a long moment and then turns silently away from him with an angry face. Then he passes him, enters the inside of the house, and approaches Dinah, who sits on the floor opposite from the door. In the next scene Hamor accuses Dinah of having seduced Shechem. Dinah defends herself, and the dialogue taking place between both characters offers an important insight into the androcentric perspective depicted in the film. The scene is remarkable not only because Dinah speaks eloquently, but also because the film does not unambiguously side with Dinah. Both positions are introduced, but Hamor has the first and the last word. Moreover, Hamor slaps Dinah in the face and calls her naughty:

Hamor: You're Jacob's daughter Dinah. There aren't enough jackals to satisfy you bitches. You come sniffing around our houses . . . and rouse the blood of our princes?

Dinah: Princes carry gold to their in-laws. They speak softly at their weddings. But if the ass requests a wife his father-in-law covers his ears and his brothers-in-law flog him.

Hamor: Shechem, you are a prince among fools!

Dinah: When the baby ass mates with a gazelle, that doesn't cure his braying.

(He slaps her in the face.)

Hamor: How insolent!

The dialogue between Dinah and Hamor, which is a fictional creation, does not offer any solutions to this conflict. It begins with Hamor's accusation that Dinah provoked the man. Dinah defends herself with a metaphorical response that challenges Hamor's assumption of Shechem's being a prince. Dinah seems to know very well that her male relatives disapproved of Shechem's holdings. Yet her words do not show that Dinah views the act as a rape. Dinah's proverb about the baby donkey and the gazelle hints at the possibility that she regards herself of higher social standing than Shechem. Hamor slaps her in the face, and his comment about her attitude reinforces this reading. However, the exchange does not clarify what happened between Dinah and Shechem, leaving it unnamed and ambiguous. Consequently, the film shows little sympathy for Dinah, who talks back to Hamor. The film does not call out the possibility of sexual violence, and it does not condemn what happened between them. Instead, sexual violence appears in metaphorical speech only. The film, however, makes clear that Hamor goes to Jacob proposing marriage between his son and Dinah. In this way, then, vague allusions strengthen the androcentric perspective in the short scene between Hamor and Dinah, turning Dinah into an acceptable bride and future wife of Shechem.

Fraternal Reconciliation as the Foundation for African Unity

Another example from *La Genèse* fortifies the thesis that the film favors an androcentric perspective. It is the climactic ending (1:34:18–1:39:56), in which Jacob's sons run toward their father in the desert. The latter is exhausted after his struggle with God's angel, lying on the ground. Esau and Dinah are also present, and they stand like mythic figures on the side. This is the central reconciliation scene that takes place between Jacob and Esau. It represents the desired fraternal reconciliation and the end of African fighting.

Cinematically, the scene is an impressive midrash on the Jacob-Esau story that also creates several "unbiblical" constellations and connections.[32] For instance, it is an invention of the film to first show Dinah with Esau and then have her appear on the side of her father even though Jacob had previously handed her over and thus disowned her. It makes it difficult to understand Dinah's role. She gives a speech to her brothers in which she asserts her will to "love him [her "husband"] dearly," and she also tells them that Joseph will forgive them. She almost functions as a kind of angel who helps the brothers find the right direction into the future. She moves as though she has already left the mortal-human sphere and promoted only what is good. Her white clothes could be interpreted to symbolize her higher level.

In this last film scene Dinah is the only female character. Other women appear earlier in the film but only briefly and once; they are silent or speak only when a man is asking them to. For instance, Dinah's mother, Leah, appears in the film's beginning whereas Dinah is present throughout the movie, although she is often silent, speaks briefly only a few times, and laughs in a crazy way during the meeting of the nations. One of the brothers even calls her "crazy," and Dinah's

---

32. Also observed by Dovey, "Humanizing the Old Testament's Origins," 272: "The choreography of the film's final shot clearly symbolizes Sissoko's message of reconciliation and restorative justice."

responses are not always comprehensible. It is, for instance, unclear why she sits next to Esau in the last scene. It seems that this and other scenes depict the relationships in a meditative fashion. The dialogues are composed in short, poetic sentences that sound biblical but do not appear in the book of Genesis. This is also true for the final scene, which cannot be found in Genesis 23–37, and is narrated with a male voice. In *La Genèse* the prince of Egypt is Joseph. Even Jacob is called a prince in the scene that depicts the conversation between Hamor and Esau. In the final scene Hamor asks: "Who changes the name of princes on this earth?" Esau responds: "God fought with him all night and today his name is Israel, for he was strong against God." Esau answers Hamor's question only indirectly by mentioning God, indicating where the authority rests. Dinah does not play any role at all.

The movie thus culminates in the reconciliation of the primal brothers, Jacob and Esau. In the center of the events stand the brothers, as opposed to Dinah, who merely assists the brothers in finding a path toward reconciliation in the next generation. In the process the third "brother," Hamor, is taught what the relationship between the primal brothers really looks like. Esau corrects Hamor, explaining to him that Jacob should no longer be called Jacob because he is now called Israel. Jacob also advises one of his sons that Dinah is his sister, and he then explains to all of his sons that Esau is "my brother. Do as he tells you." The reconciliation scene demonstrates that reconciled brothers are not jealous of each other anymore but respect each other in order to build a future together. The same applies to the children of Jacob. The sister helps her brothers accept Joseph as their brother and trust that all will be well with them because of him. In her speech she compares Joseph to her "husband," emphasizing that she loves Shechem. Accordingly, the film depicts a path toward fraternal reconciliation that Sissoko holds up to his African "brothers" as the ideal. Only one female character participates in this process. She makes no demands about her own needs, although her situation would certainly benefit from some support and attention. Yet in the film she is the one supporting the brothers, caring about their welfare, and she wants nothing in return.

In short, Dinah does not stand in the center, but rather the primal brothers (Jacob and Esau), the sons of Jacob, and their fraternal relationship to Joseph. Thus androcentrism permeates the reconciliation scene, which is concerned solely with the reconciliation of the brothers. The sister disappears, and her own aspirations, interests, and expectations remain unaddressed. This explains why the film omits so many stories from Genesis 23–37, although it would have been easy to integrate them, as the entire film is one long midrash. It is certainly a major cinematic invention that the brothers do not go to Egypt to get food during the famine but to reconcile themselves with their brother. In this film, the brothers and their problems with each other are the central concern.

Mass Rape in African Wars and *La Genèse*

Although Sissoko's sociopolitical goal of fraternal reconciliation is certainly most welcome, the androcentric perspective of *La Genèse* appears blatantly in yet another scene. It deals with the murder of the men of the Hamorite tribe. The film stays close to the biblical text (Gen 34:25–29), depicting the gruesome killing in a five-minute-long scene (34:52–40:27). The murder of the male villagers by Jacob's sons constitutes the center of the cinematic depiction, and the murder is cinematically presented with many aesthetic means. The music dominates, and only scrapes of words and phrases can be heard. The attack by the sons, who ride toward the unarmed villagers on black horses, begins at sunrise. Just a moment earlier, the circumcised men are shown in pain, walking bent over or lying in pain on the floor. It is unquestionably clear that they are unable to defend themselves. Shechem appears in a close-up as he leaves his house, hobbling slowly and cautiously, accompanied by the concerned Dinah. Immediately thereafter, Shechem is the first man to be killed by a spear while this shout is heard: "For the dowry of Dinah, sister of Dan!" Then it is suddenly night, and fire burns down the straw roofs of the huts. We hear cries, horse whickering, and the sound of horse hoofs, and we see several running figures illuminated by the fire. It is chaotic, and swords and daggers stab their victims. We can only hear the voices of Jacob's sons, who shout to each other in short sentences:

Jacob's son: Kill all the men folk.

Jacob's son: Put an end to Hamor's lineage!

(Killing goes on.)

Jacob's son: Have you seen Hamor?

Jacob's son: Where is that son of a bitch?

Jacob's son: Nobody's seen him.

(Crying infant)

Jacob's son: What about this one?

Jacob's son: Kill *all* the men folk.

All of them.

These few sentences are part of a long scene. It is the most brutal moment of the film, in which no blood is seen at all, which is its most remarkable aspect, especially compared to murder scenes in many Western movies, such as Mel Gibson's fondness for gory staging. Some film critics, such as Dovey, emphasize this characteristic as a significant difference in Sissoko's movie. Dovey states: "What sets Sissoko's audio-visualization of violence apart from, for instance, Mel Gibson's graphic depiction of violence in *The Passion of the Christ* (2004) is that Sissoko eschews using special effects and emotionally charged extra-diegetic music as a way of evoking a facile mimetic response from the viewer in the acceptance of the filmmaker's own construction of 'victim' and 'villain.'"[33]

Yet if Sissoko's representation of African conflicts, as for instance occurring among the Mali Soninkès and Fulanis or in Congo, Sudan, or Guinea, is depicted realistically, another important characteristic is omitted. The omission pertains to the fate of African sisters whose experiences in military conflict are scarred by gang rapes and sexual violence. Why does Sissoko not include their fate in his film? Is it because in Genesis 34 only men are murdered? Sissoko's midrashic approach could have been creative here, especially since in Genesis 34:29 the brothers take the Shechemite women as captives. Yet since Sissoko's main concern has to do with fraternal murder, he does not include a scene on this verse in the film, and so he misses an opportunity to depict African women's experiences. The "sisters" do not count.

Sissoko's decision is regrettable as gang rapes are part of many contemporary conflicts in the world, including Africa. The reports of gang rapes in military conflicts in Africa and elsewhere are distressing. They are always committed by men who are soldiers and members of militia groups, even including UN troops. A Congolese doctor offers a telling report from his work at the southern Kivu province in Congo, where he treated victim-survivors of the most violent gang rapes occurring since 1994. The gynecologist comments on the gang rapes: "We don't know

---

33. Dovey, "Humanizing the Old Testament's Origins," 270.

why these rapes are happening, but one thing is clear. . . . They are done to destroy women."[34] In addition, in Guinea gruesome rape scenes occurred in a soccer stadium in which soldiers raped women randomly, killing them afterward.[35] Finally, reports from Darfur in Sudan indicate that during military actions women are raped on a huge scale as a genocidal strategy.[36]

In Africa and elsewhere women are the ones who in murderous attacks are usually also brutally violated in the form of gang rapes. So the question remains why Sissoko did not make this pertinent issue a central topic in a film that emphasizes the significance of Genesis 34. Could it be that Sissoko missed out on the "revolutionary possibilities for change in both women and men" in *La Genèse*, as observed by the film critic Salem Mekuria, referring to Sissoko's earlier film *Fizan*?[37]

The observation that an androcentric perspective permeates *La Genèse* explains why violence, killing, and massacres are depicted as exclusively male suffering, even though African conflicts regularly include mass rapes of women, often with ensuing murder. Sissoko reduces the problem of fratricide and fraternal reconciliation to men, and so the experiences of women disappear. The film is not open to feminist and gender-oriented perspectives. Sissoko's hope for fraternal reconciliation aims for postcolonial unification in Africa from which at least half of the population is excluded in his film. It is thus questionable that Sissoko's vision can be realized.

Postcolonial and Androcentric: Concluding Comments

Sissoko's film wants to participate in the West African cinematographic trend that "redefines what it is to be human."[38] This trend pursues a new vision of humanity that expands the historical view of the secularized and still Christian-dominated West to include a critique

34. Jeffrey Gettleman, "Rape Epidemics Raises Trauma of Congo War," *New York Times*, October 7, 2007, http://tinyurl.com/mtnd7kd.

35. Adam Nossiter, "In a Guinea Seized by Violence, Women Are Prey," *New York Times*, October 6, 2009, http://tinyurl.com/l4yu6v2.

36. See, e.g., http://www.amnesty.org/en/library/info/AFR54/076/2004: "This report finds that rape and other forms of sexual violence in Darfur are being used as a weapon of war in order to humiliate, punish, control, inflict fear and displace women and their communities. These rapes and other sexual violence constitute grave violations of international human rights and humanitarian law, including war crimes and crimes against humanity. The report also examines the consequences of rape which have immediate and long-term effects on women beyond the actual physical violence."

37. See Salem Mekuria, "Specificities: Other Cinema: (Post)colonial Cinema, Rituals and African Womanhood," *Social Identities* 5, no. 4 (1999): 501.

38. Dovey, "Humanizing the Old Testament's Origin," 269.

of violence and perhaps even suggests that it is bigger than this critique. Still, violence belongs to this vision about humanity, and viewers are asked to relate to the depicted violence both critically and "compassionately."[39] By placing his film into the Western Christian tradition, Sissoko claims Genesis and the Bible as a source for humanity. Although Sissoko is a Muslim, he attributes considerable significance to the Bible. In his opinion, all humans have the right to interpret the Bible regardless of their background.[40] Thus, in La Genèse Sissoko reminds us of our human commonalities when he connects the Genesis stories with the African continent.

Unfortunately, Sissoko excludes the experiences of the "other" half of humankind. In this sense, he places himself into the other long-lasting Western tradition that has ignored the experiences of women for far too long. It is regrettable that Sissoko continues this tradition and ignores the feminist-postcolonial potential of Genesis 23–37 (38) in envisioning African unity and independence. However, many Western European films are certainly not much better, even when there are exceptions to this rule, such as Anonyma: Eine Frau in Berlin (Max Färberböck, 2008). One must wonder why Sissoko integrated androcentric notions so uncritically in La Genèse. Could it be that the biblical text itself caused him to do so? Or did he assume that the Bible can only be read in an androcentric way? Unfortunately, Sissoko did not seem to be acquainted with hermeneutically innovative readings of Genesis 23–37 (38). His decision to begin the film with Dinah and to keep her present to the end is unusual. However, Dinah is a male-identified character who is unable to change her own situation and who depends on the goodwill of her father and father-in-law. She is also the only female character who has an ongoing role in the film in which men, brothers and fathers, advance the narrative of fratricide and fraternal reconciliation. Women and their experiences do not play a role in it. This is regrettable because La Genèse presents a cinematic interpretation of the Genesis stories that creatively and contextually develops the genre of Bible movies.

It also has to be emphasized that Sissoko's imaginative screen adaptation of the Genesis stories results in a very impressive Bible film. The cinematographic aesthetics create a lively and memorable viewing experience that vitalizes a rarely seen landscape and human relationships due to the film's gravity, slowness, and taciturnity. Moreover,

39. Ibid.
40. Ibid., 274.

the cinematic "otherness" of the film transports the Bible into the present era unlike many other biblical films. The music plays a significant role in this transfer because it emphasizes important moments. For instance, the music begins very quietly, increasing in volume, when Jacob recognizes his brother, Esau, for the first time: "He is my brother. Do as he tells you." The music indicates that this is the very moment of hope for Africa. Yet Sissoko's message of hope is only focused on the brothers and visually excludes half of the population. The idea that the Bible belongs to all of humanity is thus not fully realized in *La Genèse*. Still, *La Genèse* needs to be seen by many people so that Sissoko will perhaps make another film that takes advantage of the full potential of the Bible as a feminist-postcolonial source belonging to all humanity.

That this task is not easy is explored in the next chapter, which considers the (feminist) state of biblical studies in light of the US-American Title IX debates.

12

How to Read Biblical Rape Texts with Contemporary Title IX Debates in Mind

In the last five years, a considerable change has taken place in the public discourse on sexual harassment, sexual violence, and rape, especially within institutions of higher education. In April 2011, the Office for Civil Rights issued a "Dear Colleague" letter that explains to schools, colleges, and universities their obligations, under Title IX of the United States Education Amendments 1972, to eliminate sexual harassment, including sexual violence. The letter defines sexual harassment in a broad way, stating:

> Title IX of the Education Amendment of 1972 (Title IX), 20 U.S.C. §§ 1681 et seq., and its implementing regulations, 34 C.F.R. Part 106, prohibit discrimination on the basis of sex in education programs or activities operated by recipients of Federal financial assistance. Sexual harassment of students, which includes acts of sexual violence, is a form of sex discrimination prohibited by Title IX. In order to assist recipients, which include school districts, colleges, and universities (hereinafter "schools" or "recipients") in meeting these obligations, this letter explains that the requirements of Title IX pertaining to sexual harassment also cover sexual violence, and lays out the specific Title IX requirements applicable to sexual violence. Sexual violence, as that term is used in this letter, refers to

physical sexual acts perpetrated against a person's will or where a person is incapable of giving consent due to the victim's use of drugs or alcohol. An individual also may be unable to give consent due to an intellectual or other disability. A number of different acts fall into the category of sexual violence, including rape, sexual assault, sexual battery, and sexual coercion. All such acts of sexual violence are forms of sexual harassment covered under Title IX.[1]

The letter defines sexual violence as a form of sexual harassment. This view is derived from Title IX's prohibition against sexual harassment as a form of sex discrimination. The effort to combat sexual violence on college campuses on the basis of Title IX has been important, especially in light of the fact that Title IX has been on the books since 1972.

It is crucial to understand that this interpretation of Title IX, as it has been advanced by the US government and the White House under President Obama, is owed to student initiative. In February 2011, sixteen students of Yale University filed a complaint that identifies Yale University as a "sexually hostile environment which prevents women from participating in campus life as fully as men."[2] On March 31, 2011, the Office of Civil Rights announced an investigation of Yale University for possible violation of Title IX. Since then, many other Title IX complaints have been submitted. The documentary film *The Hunting Ground*,[3] produced by Amy Ziering, investigates the issue of sexual assaults on US campuses; it focuses on a team of alumnae led by Andrea Pino and Annie E. Clark, who, as students at the University of North Carolina, Chapel Hill, experienced rape and sexual assault in 2012 and 2007 respectively. In 2013, the team of five former students

---

1. Russlynn Ali, Assistant Secretary for Civil Rights, "United States Department of Education/Office for Civil Rights/The Assistant Secretary: Dear Colleagues (April 4, 2011)," in *Prevent, Handle and Investigate Complaints of Sexual Assault and Violence on College Campuses* (Mechanicsburg, PA: Pennsylvania Bar Institute, 2014), 133–34. See also online at https://www.whitehouse.gov/sites/default/files/dear_colleague_sexual_violence.pdf.

2. Claire Gordon, "Title IX Complaint against Yale Has a Case," *Huffington Post*, April 1, 2011, http://tinyurl.com/mvuyknw. See also Lisa W. Foderaro, "At Yale, Sharper Look at Treatment of Women," *New York Times*, April 7, 2011, http://tinyurl.com/ksns9jw. The report on a survey, conducted by the Association of American Universities that was released on September 21, 2015, included 150,000 students from 27 universities, including Yale University. According to the survey, 27 percent of undergraduate women said they were victims of nonconsensual sexual contract through force or in situations when they were incapacitated and unable to consent; among undergraduate men, the rate was 8 percent. Thirteen percent of undergraduate women said they suffered incidents involving nonconsensual sexual penetration or attempted penetration. Twenty-three percent of students said sexual assault is very or extremely problematic at the school. The survey response rate was 52 percent. For details on this and the other 26 universities where the survey was conducted, see Nick Anderson and Susan Svrluga, "What a Massive Sexual Assault Survey Found at 27 Top U.S. Universities," *Washington Post*, September 21, 2015, http://tinyurl.com/n928qgb.

3. For more information, see http://thehuntinggroundfilm.com/.

filed a Title IX complaint against University of North Carolina. My own university, Southern Methodist University (SMU), also had to deal with Title IX complaints. In December 2014, SMU was found in violation of the federal gender-equity law for its handling of sexual harassment and assault cases.[4] Many other US colleges and universities have been found to violate Title IX requirements, and the Office of Civil Rights (OCR) has been investigating more than one hundred schools since 2011.[5] Predictably, the agency has been thoroughly overwhelmed by an extensive backlog of Title IX investigations on cases of campus sexual assault.[6]

I have been impressed with what a federal government investigation can do to compel institutions of higher education to deal with the centuries-old problem of sexual violence. When I began researching biblical rape texts in the mid-1990s, nothing like this was happening, and during the past twenty years, I have witnessed academia's general reticence to address sexual violence. Yet I also realize that rules and regulations coming down from the federal government will not eliminate the epidemic of sexual violence on campus and in society. Rape-prone assumptions, theories, and practices are far too deeply ingrained in human history, culture, politics, economics, and religion, and I am intentionally saying "human" history, while I also recognize that we must be historically, culturally, and geopolitically specific in understanding "rape cultures" anywhere. This essay explores whether the Title IX debate on US campuses ought to shape feminist scholarship on sexual violence and rape in the academic field of biblical studies in three sections. The first section surveys feminist theories on rape since the 1970s; the second section analyzes the contributions of feminist exegesis on biblical rape texts since the 1980s; and the third section discusses two critical limitations as they exist in current feminist

---

4. Tyler Kingkade, "Southern Methodist University Violated Sexual Harassment and Assault Cases," *Huffington Post*, December 11, 2014, http://tinyurl.com/mr2puxl.
5. The Chronicle of Higher Education presents the extensive list at "Title IX: Tracking Sexual Assault Investigations," https://projects.chronicle.com/titleix/.
6. See, e.g., Tyler Kingkade, "Harvard Law Gave More Rights to Accused Students in Sexual Harassment Cases, Feds Find," *Huffington Post*, December 30, 2014, http://tinyurl.com/llgyukz; Tyler Kingkade, "Probe Finds Princeton University Violated Title IX in Its Handling Of Sexual Assault Cases," *Huffington Post*, November 5, 2014, http://tinyurl.com/mwcqcxn. For a summary review, see Tyler Kingkade, "Here's What We Learned about Sexual Assault at 27 Top Universities," *Huffington Post*, September 22, 2015, http://tinyurl.com/l7lnbby. For concerns about OCR being understaffed to handle the many Title IX complaints, see, e.g., Russell Westerholm, "Education Department Overwhelmed with Title IX Complaints, OCR Seeking Monetary Aid," *University Herald*, May 7, 2015, http://tinyurl.com/mvo84rb.

biblical exegesis on sexual violence. A conclusion encourages feminist interpreters to move beyond a "cop-out" hermeneutics.

Forty Years in the Wilderness: A Brief Survey of Feminist Theories on Rape

This, then, is the moment in which US-grassroots feminists use the Title IX legislation to end sexual violence in its various manifestations. It is a locally and temporally specific moment that has taken place in the United States since 2011. Other countries have different laws or no laws at all, and so they must find other ways of eliminating sexual violence in their societies. It needs to be emphasized that, since the 1970s, feminists from all over the world have extensively studied sexual violence and contributed to questioning long-standing assumptions and biases about it. Importantly, feminists have theorized the phenomenon of sexual violence from the perspectives of victim-survivors, tracing the origins, causes, and reasons for the contemporary prevalence of rape. They have rejected the age-old traditions of ignoring, obfuscating, and silencing victim-survivors' experiences.

The cornerstone publication that has propelled feminists to openly address the problem of sexual violence is Susan Brownmiller's 1975 book titled *Against Our Will: Women, Men, and Rape*.[7] For the first time, the hitherto silenced topic of rape is claimed as a feminist issue, bringing sexual violence to the forefront of feminist analysis around the globe. Brownmiller's volume relies on the foundational premise that biological sex differences between women and men cause rape. She asserts that "we cannot work around the fact that in terms of human anatomy the possibility of forcible intercourse incontrovertibly exists. This single factor may have been sufficient to have caused the creation of male ideology of rape."[8] Brownmiller proposes, and this explanation has raised a lot of red flags in feminist-gendered theoretical circles ever since, that in prehistoric times men discovered their genitalia as "weapons," "along with the use of fire and the first crude stone axe."[9] To Brownmiller, rape is part of the male biological predisposition. The various chapters in her book present the historical evidence for "man's structural capacity to rape and women's corresponding structural vulnerability . . . as basic to the physiology of both our sexes."[10] Moreover,

7. Susan Brownmiller, *Against Our Will: Women, Men, and Rape* (New York: Bantam, 1975).
8. Ibid., 4.
9. Ibid., 5.

"male nature" created rape to keep "all women in a state of fear" at all times.[11] In short, biology grounds Brownmiller's analysis about the origins and prevalence of rape. Her work illustrates over and over again that, due to the "accident of biology," human anatomy brought "forcible intercourse incontrovertibly" into existence.[12]

Brownmiller is the first feminist thinker to define sexual violence as a feminist issue, but other feminist thinkers quickly criticized her essentializing and naturalizing explanations. One of them is Catherine MacKinnon, who challenged this kind of "feminist naturalism." She suggests instead that rape be viewed as an expression of sexuality, "the dynamics of control by which male dominance . . . eroticizes and thus defines man and woman, gender identity and sexual pleasure."[13] More specifically, MacKinnon regards sexuality as an "experience of power in its gendered form" in which "sexuality is violent" and "violence is sexual."[14] Most importantly, MacKinnon defines rape as a societal problem, not as a "biologically inevitable" phenomenon. To her, it consists of "men's power" over women, and only when this power is dismantled will women be liberated from male oppression.[15]

Numerous other historical, cultural, and philosophical studies on rape appeared from the 1970s into the 1980s.[16] From the late 1980s to the early 1990s, feminists of color and postmodern feminist theorists rose to challenge essentialized, naturalized, and monosectional discourse about the origins and pervasiveness of rape. One of them is historian, Jacquelyn Dowd Hall. She recognizes Brownmiller's work as an "important milestone" but also criticizes her biological and thus universalizing, presumably timeless notions of rape. Like feminist thinker Bettina Aptheker and others, Hall looks for historical intersectionality to explain the collaboration of women with sources of power. For instance, she asserts that rape and lynching need to be studied together to illuminate the practice of rape in ways that biological explanations cannot. In her view, the contemporary prevalence of rape is a kneejerk response to women's increasing societal, political, and

10. Ibid., 4.
11. Ibid., 5.
12. Ibid., 4.
13. Catherine MacKinnon, *Toward a Feminist Theory of the State* (Cambridge, MA: Harvard University Press, 1989), 137.
14. Ibid., xiii, 179.
15. For a succinct and clear discussion and critique of MacKinnon's feminist position, see, e.g., Katharine T. Bartlett, "MacKinnon's Feminism: Power on Whose Terms?" *California Law Review* 75, no 4 (1987): 1559–70.
16. For a survey on feminist studies on rape, see my "Defining Rape: Feminist Scholarship on Rape since the 1970s," in *Rape Plots: A Feminist-Cultural Study of Genesis 34* (New York: Lang, 2000), 19–44.

economic rights since the 1970s, despite the fact that many women are
still economically dependent on men. Historical intersectionality supports her position, as black Americans, who gained political rights after
the Civil War (1865), lacked economic independence in the Jim Crow
era (1877–1960s) and thus suffered persecution by lynching. Hall urges
feminists to recognize the historical intersectionality of lynching and
rape, as it illustrates the sociopolitical dynamics regarding the phe-
nomena of racialized murder and gender violence. It also demonstrates
that a feminist analysis of rape "must make clear its stand against all
uses of violence for the purpose of oppression."[17] Accordingly, Hall
argues that feminist explanations based on biology are utterly insufficient and inadequate.[18]

These and many other studies ground feminist theories within ever-
expanding notions about the analytical complexities of sexual violence. They recognize sexual violence as standing within a complex
network of structures of domination such as racism, classism, or ecological violence. As feminist writer, Susan Griffin, puts it already in
1971: Rape is an expression of power structures that do not only vic-
timize women but also contribute to "raping Black people and the
very earth we live upon."[19] Another well-known feminist thinker, bell
hooks, makes a similar point over a decade later: "Feminist efforts to
end male violence against women must be expanded into a movement
to end all forms of violence."[20] When rape is understood as being part
and parcel of general patterns of violence in society, feminists escape
essentializing notions about rape. They then recognize that patriarchal oppression is not the only reason for sexual violence but intersects
with racism, classism, and imperialism. Feminists have to embrace this
broader framework to avoid promoting stereotypical ideas about rape,
women, and men.

In short, the intersectional approach to thinking about rape has
been very important to feminist analysis since the 1970s. In her essay

17. Jacquelyn Dowd Hall, "'The Mind That Burns in Each Body': Women, Rape, and Racial Violence," in *Powers of Desire: The Politics of Sexuality*, ed. Ann Snitow, Christine Stansell, and Sharon Thompson (New York: Monthly Review Press, 1983), 346.
18. Other early feminist thinkers, such as Susan Griffin and bell hooks, argue similarly. They, too, sug-gest that scholars study rape within systemic structures of oppression; see Susan Griffin, "Rape: An All-American Crime," *Ramparts* (1971): 35; bell hooks, "Feminist Movement to End Violence," in *Feminist Theory: From Margin to Center* (Boston: South End, 1984), 130; Lynn A. Curtis, "Rape, Race, and Culture: Some Speculations in Search of a Theory," in *Sexual Assault: The Victim and the Rapist*, ed. Marcia J. Walker and Stanley L. Brodsky (Toronto: Heath, 1976), 131; Angela Y. Davis, *Women, Race and Class* (New York: Random House, 1981). See also my book *Rape Plots*, 35–40.
19. Susan Griffin, "Rape," 35.
20. hooks, "Feminist Movement to End Violence," 130.

"Rape, Race, and Culture: Some Speculations in Search of a Theory," Lynn A. Curtis addresses the need to link rape and race in the United States.[21] Early radical feminist, Angela Y. Davis, also stresses that "any attempt to treat it [rape] as an isolated phenomenon is bound to flounder."[22] Instead, feminist theory must connect gender, race, and class to account for the pervasiveness of rape. Davis proposes:

> The class structure of capitalism encourages men who wield power in the economic and political realm to become routine agents of sexual exploitation. The present rape epidemic occurs at a time when the capitalist class is furiously reasserting its authority in face of global and internal challenges. Both racism and sexism, central to its domestic strategy of increased economic exploitation, are receiving unprecedented encouragement. It is not a mere coincidence that as the incidence of rape has arisen, the position of women workers has visibly worsened. So severe are women's economic losses that their wages in relationship to men are lower than they were a decade ago. The proliferation of sexual violence is the brutal face of a generalized intensification of the sexism which necessarily accompanies this economic assault.[23]

This kind of analysis, which has not lost its eerie relevance even today, insists on connecting the analysis of rape to other forms of oppression and correlating it with women's ongoing economic vulnerability and relative political powerlessness.[24]

More recent explanations advance postmodern feminist views on rape. An influential position comes from feminist thinker, Sharon Marcus, who defines rape as a "gendered grammar of violence."[25] In this grammar, men are the agents of violence and women the subjects of fear. Language constructs reality, and so rape-prone societies are "subject to change" if rape is understood as a "linguistic fact."[26] When rape is understood as a linguistic fact, one has "to ask how the violence of rape is enabled by narratives, complexes and institutions which

21. Lynn A. Curtis, "Rape, Race, and Culture: Some Speculations in Search of a Theory," in Walker and Brodsky, *Sexual Assault*, 131.
22. Davis, *Women, Race and Class*. See also my book *Rape Plots*, 35–40.
23. Davis, *Women, Race and Class*, 200.
24. For a more updated comparison of wages between women and men, see, e.g., WeNews Staff, "Part 5: Women's Median Wages Compared to Men's in the Same Jobs, 2011," *Wenews*, May 20, 2012, http://tinyurl.com/lbppfo6. See also "Women's Pay Compared to Men's from 1960 to 2013," *The Numbers* (blog), *Wall Street Journal*, September 23, 2014, http://blogs.wsj.com/numbers/womens-pay-compared-to-mens-from-1960-to-2013-1774/; Christina Huffington, "Women and Equal Pay: Wage Gap Still Intact, Study Shows," *Huffington Post*, April 9, 2013, http://tinyurl.com/k5zhuzj.
25. Sharon Marcus, "Fighting Bodies, Fighting Words: A Theory and Politics of Rape Prevention," in *Feminists Theorize the Political*, ed. Judith Butler and Joan W. Scott (New York: Routledge, 1992), 383.
26. Ibid., 388.

derive their strength not from outright, immutable, unbeatable force but rather from their power to structure our lives as imposing cultural scripts."[27] In Marcus's postmodern feminist analysis, then, the study of rape turns into an examination of the linguistic grammar of sexual violence as it appears in cultural, artistic, literary, and even religious traditions, conventions, and texts. Clearly, the postmodern feminist approach differs significantly from early feminist views, although, like them, it rejects essentializing and naturalizing notions. It stresses that "cultural scripts" construct our notions about rape and are complicit in the production of rape; rape-prone societies will change only when cultural scripts are changed. Accordingly, rape-prone societies will run out of power because people will not be convinced by them anymore; only then will rape end.[28] In short, postmodern feminist theorists argue that cultural scripts have long been complicit in the production of rape. They need to be uncovered and deconstructed from feminist perspectives.

Unfortunately, the postmodern feminist analysis never took off in full force because, in the mid- to late 1990s, feminist scholarly enthusiasm for the investigation of sexual violence declined. The danger of essentializing discourse was so deeply felt that sexual violence almost vanished from feminist scholarship during the early 2000s.[29] Although sexual violence has remained visible and pervasive, especially during the wars in Bosnia and Congo, postmodern feminist theorists were just too suspicious of essentializing, naturalizing, and ahistorical latencies in cultural-feminist approaches to pursue the investigation of cultural scripts on rape. The feminist-theoretical interest in addressing sexual violence was only rekindled in the late 2000s, when renewed publicity about rape in the US military and on US college campuses reenergized feminist grassroots movements. The current focus on rape in the United States thus remains highly practical in orientation, seeking to end sexual violence through the systematic enforcement of US law. As of January 2017, it remains to be seen whether the incoming Trump administration will support the current Title IX interpretation; it is expected that it will not.[30]

27. Ibid., 387.
28. For a powerful critique of Marcus's argumentation, see, e.g., Kelley Anne Malinen, "Thinking Woman-to-Woman Rape: A Critique of Marcus's 'Theory and Politics of Rape Prevention,'" *Sexuality & Culture* 17 (2013): 360–76.
29. When it did show up, it emphasized the dangers of essentializing and ahistorical analysis; see, e.g., Christine Helliwell, "'It's Only a Penis': Rape, Feminism, and Difference," *Signs* 25, no. 3 (2000): 789–816.

Coming Out of the Wilderness of Almost Two Millennia: Three Decades of Feminist Scholarship on Biblical Rape Texts

It took until 1984, almost ten years after the publication of *Against Our Will*, for a feminist Bible scholar to produce a scholarly-exegetical study on sexual violence in the Bible. Until then, scholarly books in the academic field of biblical studies had basically ignored, silenced, or marginalized biblical rape texts. The exegetical task fell to Phyllis Trible, who in her pioneering book, *Texts of Terror: Literary-Feminist Readings of Biblical Narratives*,[31] brings to the Bible-reading public's attention four stories that include three sexually violated women, Hagar (Genesis 16 and 21), Tamar the royal daughter (2 Samuel 13), the so-called concubine (Judges 19), and Jephthah's daughter, murdered by her father, (Judges 11). The shock value of the feminist-literary exposure cannot be underestimated because this was the first feminist-scholarly book ever published on sexual violence in the Bible. Poignantly, Trible acknowledges that she found the strength to write this book only after her previous volume, *God and the Rhetoric of Sexuality* (1978). She states: "Without the joy of the first book, I should have found unbearable the sorrow of the second. Ancient tales of terror speak all too frighteningly of the present."[32]

Other feminist biblical scholars followed Trible's lead, and in the next three decades they produced exegetical studies on sexual violence and rape in journal articles and books. In 1993, J. Cheryl Exum published a book chapter titled "Raped by the Pen."[33] Analyzing violence against women in biblical narrative, Exum acknowledges that "raped by the pen is not the same as raped by the penis."[34] She quotes feminist theorists, such as Andrea Dworkin, Susan Brownmiller, and Ellen Rooney, to maintain that "patriarchal texts can neither fully nor successfully ignore or suppress women's experience."[35] Overall, Exum's essay demonstrates what she promises from the start: it investigates how "literary rapes perpetuate ways of looking at women that encourage objectification and violence."[36] It exposes the literary mechanisms

---

30. For an early commentary on this possibility, see, e.g., Jake New, "Campus Sexual Assault in a Trump Era," *Inside Higher Ed*, November 10, 2016, http://tinyurl.com/lwkeqex.
31. Phyllis Trible, *Texts of Terror: Literary-Feminist Readings of Biblical Narratives* (Philadelphia: Fortress Press, 1984).
32. Ibid., xiii.
33. J. Cheryl Exum, *Fragmented Women: Feminist (Sub)versions of Biblical Narratives*, 2nd ed. (Bloomsbury T&T Clark, 2015; 1st ed., Sheffield: JSOT Press, 1993).
34. Ibid., 135.
35. Ibid., 161.

that silence and marginalize the female characters in Judges 19 and 2 Samuel 11. More specifically, Exum looks at Judges 19, the narrative about the gang rape of the so-called concubine, describing it as one of the "most gruesome and violent in the Bible,"[37] and juxtaposes it to the Bathsheba and David story in 2 Samuel 11. Exum's detailed comparative study culminates in a careful evaluation of the male gaze and an inquiry into the exegetical responsibility of reading biblical rape stories by taking biblical "women's word for it."[38] It is a courageous, bold, and forward-looking essay that explicitly addresses rape as a methodological and hermeneutical concern in feminist biblical exegesis.

After Trible's 1984 book, it took another eleven years before a monograph focused again on sexual violence in biblical literature. In 1995, Renita J. Weems produced a book-length investigation of sexual violence in prophetic literature titled *Battered Love: Marriage, Sex, and Violence in the Hebrew Prophets.*[39] The book presents a historical-literary analysis of the so-called marriage metaphors in biblical prophecy. Using historical and literary methods, Weems explains how biblical prophets, such as Hosea, Jeremiah, and Ezekiel, tried to convince male Israelites to compare their relationship with God to a husband who sexually threatens and violates his wife. The book argues that "the Bible's culture takes for granted women's limited roles and goes out of its way at times to reinforce the notion that women's sexuality poses a dangerous threat to the social order."[40] The study also maintains that male Israelites must have felt profoundly insulted being asked to identify with a sexually violated woman because their androcentric convictions told them, as well as generations of male interpreters, that the divine husband was justified in punishing his wife whose behavior had violated the patriarchal order. Weems is cautious about what to do about this biblical position because, in her view, the reinterpretation of "marriage as a metaphor in the Bible . . . does very little to change" the persistent efforts to "rationalize violence against women."[41]

Since 2000, the dam has been broken in biblical studies, and comprehensive and detailed investigations have consistently appeared on the topic of sexual violence and rape in biblical literature. In 2000, Gerlinde

---

36. Ibid.
37. Ibid., 136.
38. Ibid., 161.
39. Renita Weems, *Battered Love: Marriage, Sex, and Violence in the Hebrew Prophets* (Minneapolis: Fortress Press, 1995).
40. Ibid., 119.
41. Ibid.

Baumann authored a book in German that was translated three years later into English as *Love and Violence: Marriage as Metaphor for the Relationship between Yahweh and Israel in the Prophetic Books*.[42] Like Weems, Baumann offers a linguistic-historical feminist study of the so-called marriage metaphor in prophetic literature, especially Hosea, Jeremiah, Ezekiel, Lamentations, and Isaiah, with a particular focus on the relationship between God as the husband and Israel as his wife. Baumann is keenly aware of the tensions between her historical reconstructions of the biblical use of the marriage metaphor and contemporary feminist views on sexual violence. The detailed and careful linguistic and historical evaluations of vocabulary, grammatical constructs, and historical considerations make this an exegetically rich investigation.

Another volume to appear in the same year was my own monograph, *Rape Plots: A Feminist Cultural Study of Genesis 34*,[43] in which I analyze Genesis 34 as a cultural-literary artifact in past and present commentaries. The study's feminist cultural approach contextualizes nineteenth-century and contemporary biblical readings within the cultural context of concurrent literary artifacts, such as nineteenth-century forensic textbooks. The study uncovers the pervasiveness of cultural scripts favoring the rapist and obfuscating the rape. It also proposes a solution beyond rape-prone cultural scripts with a feminist reading of Genesis 34 that aligns with feminist views about rape as they have been articulated since the 1970s.

A few years later, in 2003, Cheryl A. Kirk-Duggan produced an anthology titled *Pregnant Passion: Gender, Sex, and Violence in the Bible*.[44] The volume features twelve essays that investigate both the Old Testament and the New Testament in light of gender, sexuality, and violence, although some essays focus on topics unrelated to rape. The book employs intertextual, anthropological, psychological, and gender-theoretical approaches to examine biblical texts, such as Genesis 34, the book of Esther, and the poems on "Daughter Zion" (e.g. Amos 5:2; Mic 1:13; Isa 1:8), in conjunction with extensive histories of biblical interpretation. As Kirk-Duggan explains, the book unsettles conventional interpretations and the ideologies of sexuality and gender in

---

42. Gerlinde Baumann, *Love and Violence: Marriage as Metaphor for the Relationship between Yahweh and Israel in the Prophetic Books*, trans. Linda M. Maloney (Collegeville, MN: Liturgical Press, 2003); original German title: *Liebe und Gewalt: Die Ehe als Metaphor für das Verhältnis JHWH—Israel in den Prophetenbüchern*, Stuttgarter Bibelstudien (Stuttgart: Katholisches Bibelwerk, 2000).
43. Scholz, *Rape Plots*.
44. Cheryl A. Kirk-Duggan, *Pregnant Passion: Gender, Sex, and Violence* (Atlanta: Society of Biblical Literature, 2003).

such interpretations, showing how they perpetuate violence against marginalized people, including women.

In 2004, Cheryl Anderson published her study on the construction of gender and violence in legal biblical texts. Titled *Women, Ideology, and Violence: The Construction of Gender in the Book of the Covenant and Deuteronomic Law*, the five chapters present biblical and ancient Near Eastern legislation on gendered violence in light of critical theory. Anderson maintains that there are two different categories of biblical legislation. Some laws treat both women and men in the same way, which Anderson classifies as "inclusive." Other laws treat women differently from men, which she categorizes as "exclusive." Anderson then shows that the latter body of laws constructs gender within the paradigm of "male dominance/female subordination," and, informed by critical theory, the study demonstrates that those laws do not merely describe but constitute violence against women.[45]

In 2006, Mary Anna Bader offered a multimethodological study of two biblical narratives, Genesis 34 and 2 Samuel 13. Titled *Sexual Violation in the Hebrew Bible: A Multi-methodological Study of Genesis 34 and 2 Samuel 13*, the volume argues for sexual violence as a complex methodological issue in the Hebrew Bible.[46] The work employs intertextuality and narrative criticism for investigating the two biblical stories within a web of themes and vocabulary as defined in ancient Israel and as heard by contemporary readers.

In the same year, Hilary B. Lipka delivered her study, *Sexual Transgression in the Hebrew Bible*,[47] which examines many biblical texts on sexual violence as part of what Lipka classifies as sexual transgression. A more detailed analysis of her work follows below.

In 2007, Joy A. Schroeder's work, *Dinah's Lament: The Biblical Legacy of Sexual Violence in Christian Interpretation*,[48] explored how Christian, mostly male commentators of the early church and the medieval period, interpreted the biblical rape stories of Dinah (Genesis 34), the Levite's so-called concubine (Judges 19), Tamar (2 Samuel 13), Potiphar's wife (Genesis 39), and Susannah (Daniel 13). A wealth of references to primary sources and ancient biblical commentaries enriches

---

45. Cheryl Anderson, *Women, Ideology, and Violence: The Construction of Gender in the Book of the Covenant and Deuteronomic Law* (London: T&T Clark, 2004).
46. Mary Anna Bader, *Sexual Violation in the Hebrew Bible: A Multi-methodological Study of Genesis 34 and 2 Samuel 13*, StBibLit 87 (New York: Lang 2006).
47. Hilary B. Lipka, *Sexual Transgression in the Hebrew Bible* (Sheffield: Sheffield Phoenix, 2006).
48. Joy A. Schroeder, *Dinah's Lament: The Biblical Legacy of Sexual Violence in Christian Interpretation* (Minneapolis: Fortress Press, 2007).

the portrayal of the consistent androcentric bias in the history of Christian interpretation. This bias blames women for sexual violence, reinforces the notion that women should stay at home to protect their virginity, and characterizes women as enjoying rape or as having brought upon themselves male "desire." The study demonstrates abundantly the mostly androcentric ways in which sociocultural assumptions shape the interpretation history of the biblical narrative under consideration.

Another study appeared in 2007, written by Carleen Mandolfo and titled *Daughter Zion Talks Back to the Prophets: A Dialogical Theology of the Book of Lamentations.*[49] This literary interpretation of sexual violence centers on the female voice in Lamentations 1–2 and the (male) divine voice in prophetic speech. Informed by the dialogical linguistics of Mikhail Bakhtin and Martin Buber's dialogic philosophy, the study tracks the prophetic marriage metaphor through several prophetic texts and brings them into dialogical conversation with the book of Lamentations, especially with its woman figure. By using a dialogical hermeneutic, Mandolfo addresses issues of power, subjectivity, and alterity, always mindful of the historical contexts from which the various biblical poems emerged. Her study aims "to contribute to the dethroning of biblical authority as it is now construed,"[50] and in this sense the volume is more about imperial power politics in general than about sexual violence. At the same time, Mandolfo hopes that her work will ensure an end to "monologic" justifications of divine justice.

In 2008, Frank M. Yamada examined three rape narratives (Genesis 34; Judges 19; 2 Samuel 13) with literary methods in his monograph, *Configurations of Rape in the Hebrew Bible.*[51] He suggests that each narrative belongs to a similar category of texts in which the plot describes a clear pattern of escalating violence. The increasing violence begins with the rape of a woman by one man or several men and thereafter escalates into male-on-male violence and major sociopolitical upheavals. The well-structured and reasoned argumentation presupposes a strictly formalistic understanding of literary criticism that centers on the narrator in the selected biblical rape narratives.

In 2010, Caroline Blyth published her volume, *The Narrative of Rape in Genesis 34: Interpreting Dinah's Silence,*[52] which explores similarities

49. Carleen Mandolfo, *Daughter Zion Talks Back to the Prophets: A Dialogical Theology of the Book of Lamentations* (Atlanta: Society of Biblical Literature, 2007).
50. Ibid., 5.
51. Frank M. Yamada, *Configurations of Rape in the Hebrew Bible*, StBibLit 109 (New York: Lang, 2008).

and connections between past and present notions of sexual violence as they appear in interpretations of Genesis 34. The study makes an important plea to read from the perspective of raped victim-survivors. For this purpose Blyth employs testimonies from contemporary women who experienced sexual assault, and she uses their stories to expose the variously articulated rape "myths" and prejudices about sexual violence in biblical readings.

Another book to appear in 2010 was my work entitled *Sacred Witness: Rape in the Hebrew Bible.*[53] The book posits that rape texts are common, if not ubiquitous, throughout biblical prose and poetry. Firmly placed within feminist theories on rape, the study recovers the Hebrew Bible from its current marginalization as an intellectual and cultural resource for the feminist study of rape. Honoring the perspectives of raped victim-survivors, it turns biblical literature into sacred texts about rape.

Never before in biblical research has the topic of rape featured as prominently as in this growing list of books. A considerable number of scholarly journal articles supplements the monographs.[54] However, it is also important to realize that feminist Bible scholars have turned their attention to sexual violence and rape only *after* feminist theorists have begun focusing on other issues. To be sure, biblical scholarship, including feminist biblical scholarship, is not a trendsetter but consistently in the position of catching up with sociocultural, political, and intellectual developments.

52. Caroline Blyth, *The Narrative of Rape in Genesis 34: Interpreting Dinah's Silence* (Oxford: Oxford University Press, 2010).
53. Susanne Scholz, *Sacred Witness: Rape in the Hebrew Bible* (Minneapolis: Fortress Press, 2010).
54. See, e.g., Stephanus Philippus Nolte, "A Politics of the Female Body: Reading Susanna (LXX Additions to Daniel) in a Brutalized South African Society," *Biblische Notizen* 168 (2016): 147–61; Caroline Blyth, "Lost in the 'Post': Rape Culture and Postfeminism in Admen and Eve," *The Bible & Critical Theory* 10, no. 2 (2014): 1–10; Paul A. Kruger, "Women and War Brutalities in the Minor Prophets: The Case of Rape," *Old Testament Essays* 27, no. 1 (2014): 147–76; Keree Louise Casey, "What Part of 'No' Don't You Understand? Talking the Tough Stuff of the Bible: A Creative Reading of the Rape of Tamar (2 Sam. 13:1–22)," *Feminist Theology* 18, no. 2 (2010): 160–74; Yael Shemesh, "Rape Is Rape: The Story of Dinah and Shechem (Genesis 34)," *ZAW* 119, no. 1 (2007): 2–21; Sarojini Nadar, "'Texts of Terror': The Conspiracy of Rape in the Bible, Church, and Society: The Case of Esther 2:1–18," in *African Women, Religion, and Health: Essays in Honor of Mercy Amba Ewudziwa Oduyoye*, ed. Isabel Apawo Phiri and Sarojini Nadar (Maryknoll, NY: Orbis; Pietermaritzburg: Cluster, 2006), 77–95; Gravett, Sandie, "Reading 'Rape' in the Hebrew Bible: A Consideration of Language," *JSOT* 28, no. 3 (2004): 279–99; Ellen J. van Wolde, "Does 'innâ Denote Rape? A Semantic Analysis of a Controversial Word," *VT* 52, no. 4 (2002): 528–44; Beth R. Crisp, "Reading Scripture from a Hermeneutic of Rape," *Theology & Sexuality* 7, no. 14 (2001): 23–42; F. W, Dobbs-Allsopp and Tod Linafelt, "The Rape of Zion in Thr 1,10," *ZAW* 113, no. 1 (2001): 77–81.

Two Limitations in Feminist Biblical Exegesis on Sexual Violence

In light of the growing scholarly discussion on sexual violence in biblical literature, two limitations stand out and perhaps explain the persistent hesitancy to locate biblical interpretation within feminist insights so prominently articulated in the contemporary Title IX debate. For instance, one such insight stresses that feminist analysis needs to side with the raped victim-survivor; another feminist conviction emphasizes that raped victim-survivors are not to be blamed for the sexual assault. A first limitation consists in the fact that many feminist bible scholars adhere to the principles of the scientific-empiricist epistemology. This tendency is surprising, especially since feminist exegete, Elisabeth Schüssler Fiorenza, has written so abundantly on the considerable shortcomings of this epistemological position. One quote from her many books shall suffice to illustrate her critique of the scientific-empiricist paradigm:

> Although the scientific-positivist paradigm demands objectivity, disinterestedness, and value-neutrality in order to control what constitutes the legitimate, scientifically established, true meaning of a text, it is patently *kyriocentric* and *Eurocentric*.[55]

At stake is here the exegetical relationship to the structures of power. Moreover, the adherence to positivism is a particularly *white* feminist hermeneutical preference because many minority-positioned exegetes —feminist, womanist, and otherwise—talk openly about the disciplinary pressures that ask them to avoid, downplay, or even reject socially located readings of the Bible.[56] Is the adherence of (white feminist) Bible exegetes to the empiricist-scientific epistemology related to the need to please "the fathers" and to keep tenure-track or adjunct teaching positions? Why are white feminist and nonfeminist scholars so reticent to venture into epistemologically and hermeneutically more adventurous territories when the topic is sexual violence? Please note that I am observing a tendency here, not an absolute condition.

Yet the effects of this tendency are considerable. I will mention only one example to illustrate the limitations of the scientific-empiricist

---

55. Elisabeth Schüssler Fiorenza, *Democratizing Biblical Studies: Toward an Emancipatory Educational Space* (Louisville: Westminster John Knox, 2009), 68. See also two of her other books: *Rhetoric and Ethic: The Politics of Biblical Studies* (Minneapolis: Fortress Press, 1999); *The Power of the Word: Scripture and the Rhetoric of Empire* (Minneapolis: Fortress Press, 2007).
56. See, e.g., Gay L. Byron and Vanessa Lovelace, eds., *Womanist Interpretations of the Bible: Expanding the Discourse* (Atlanta: SBL Press, 2016).

epistemology in biblical interpretation on rape. It comes from Lipka's comprehensive study, *Sexual Transgression in the Hebrew Bible*.[57] Lipka articulates the chosen hermeneutical position in the following three sentences, which make her study such a good illustration:

> I argued that we can only talk about a concept of rape in a biblical text if two elements are present. First, there must be evidence of some belief on the author's part that the sexual act is forced upon an individual against his or her will. Second, there must be evidence of a conception that this forced act violates the victim on a personal level.[58]

Lipka establishes two requirements in her hermeneutical analysis of sexual violence in biblical literature. The first requirement relates to the preference of authorial meaning. This highly modern preference assumes that it is possible, desirable, and relatively obvious to know what the original authors thought about sexual violence. The second requirement prioritizes the individualism of the victim-survivor, yet another modern assumption, as it has developed since the emergence of the Western modern worldview since the sixteenth century. It stresses the priority of the individual over the collective. Thus, perhaps unsurprisingly, Lipka treats biblical rape texts with a historical-literary approach that tries to decipher what the text meant to the Israelite writers. Importantly, however, Lipka does not explain why she makes the two requirements so central to her analysis or even how she came up with them in the first place.

Obviously, then, Lipka privileges intentional meaning to a socially located hermeneutic. But why? Confusion and silence about the rationale prevail. While Lipka acknowledges the existence of rape in biblical literature, she does not consistently use the vocabulary of rape. The inconsistency is already obvious in the choice of the book's title that classifies sexual violence as "sexual transgression."[59] Why sexual transgression and not rape? Lipka argues that her study is broader than rape, as it also includes texts about incest, adultery, and other sexual activities. But does the terminological choice of "sexual transgression" not ultimately minimize and obfuscate rape? In my view, the phrase "sexual transgression" contributes to the silencing effect we encounter even today when it comes to rape and sexual violence in the Bible and elsewhere. "Transgression" implies "wrongdoing" without clarifying

---

57. Lipka, *Sexual Transgression in the Hebrew Bible*.
58. Ibid., 220.
59. For Lipka's detailed explanation on the meaning of "sexual transgression," see ibid., 22.

who is doing the wrong and so leaves open the idea that the victim-survivor and the perpetrator are both "transgressing."

Furthermore, Lipka's claim to present the views of the original authors relies on terminology that suggests objectivity, universality, and value neutrality. She believes the phrase "sexual transgression" avoids anachronism, and she repeatedly states that she wishes to avoid "imposing our own cultural meanings upon ancient texts."[60] Yet this very empiricist-scientific goal is, of course, unattainable because an escape from particularity, locatedness, and partiality is impossible.[61] It also affirms the prevailing structures of domination because it does not side explicitly with the victim-survivor and does not question the existing power structures. Predictably, then, Lipka's study leaves unaddressed questions of power, intersectionality, and issues of social location. Certainly, her work is not unique in this regard, as this epistemological maneuver appears in many other publications.[62] The widespread reluctance of disrupting the enduring dominance of the empiricist-scientific paradigm characterizes many studies of biblical rape texts to this very day.

A second limitation stands out in feminist exegesis on sexual violence in the Bible. It pertains to the dearth of substantive feminist exegetical discourse on method and methodology. Esther Fuchs has long observed this lack in feminist biblical studies,[63] and I concur with her assessment. To date, there are no extensive discussions on method and methodology among feminist exegetes in general and among feminist exegetes reading biblical rape texts in particular. More often than not, feminist exegetes employ this or that method in service of this or that biblical rape text, but they do not explain what makes this or that reading feminist or not.[64] We are in dire need of meta-level considerations as they have taken place in other fields of feminist inquiry such as sociology, anthropology, or feminist studies in general.

60. Ibid., 247.
61. One of my favorite post-postmodern writers who elaborates on this point is Jeffrey T. Nealon, *Post-postmodernims or, The Cultural Logic of Just-in-Time Capitalism* (Stanford: Stanford University Press, 2012).
62. For other examples, see, e.g., M. I. Rey, "Reexamination of the Foreign Female Captive: Deuteronomy 21:10–14 as a Case of Genocidal Rape," *JFSR* 32, no. 1 (2016): 37–53; Alexander I. Abasili, "Was It Rape? The David and Bathsheba Pericope Re-examined," *VT* 61, no. 1 (2011): 1–15; see also n43.
63. Esther Fuchs, *Feminist Theory and the Bible: Interrogating the Sources*, Feminist Studies and Sacred Texts (Lanham, MD: Lexington, 2016).
64. See, e.g., Pamela J. Milne and Susanne Scholz, "On Methods and Methodology in Feminist Biblical Studies: A Conversation," in *Feminist Interpretation of the Hebrew Bible in Retrospect*, vol. 3, *Methods*, ed. Susanne Scholz (Sheffield: Sheffield Phoenix, 2016), 19–34.

Much more remains to be said about the absence of feminist exegetical discourse on method and methodology,[65] but I want to highlight another important point made by feminist theorists. Often they explain that feminist knowledge aims to contribute to social change and that methods and methodologies ought to be selected accordingly. Feminist practice shapes the choice of method, and the range of methods in feminist scholarship in general is astounding. Among the methods are participatory research, ethnography, discourse analysis, comparative case study, cross-culture analysis, conversation analysis, oral history, participant observation, and personal narrative. I wonder why feminist Bible exegetes have not usually followed the feminist principle that feminist practice shapes the choice of method. Instead, we have usually limited ourselves to text-based methods dominant in biblical studies. Why have we not developed participatory research methods in the feminist interpretation of the Bible? Why have we not relied on comparative case studies or cross-cultural analysis?

Asked differently, why have we adhered to the existing spectrum of methods as they are traditionally defined in the field of biblical studies and not attempted to boldly go where few Bible exegetes have gone before? In light of the current Title IX debate, it seems timely to remember anew that feminist exegesis is always implicated in "processes of politicization, diversity and continuity in political struggles over time."[66] This insight may help reduce the tendency in feminist biblical scholarship to assimilate to the status quo of the field. It might also assist feminist exegetes to contest the viability of kyriarchal ideologies in biblical interpretation, especially when they involve biblical rape texts. In short, it is high time to read biblical rape texts as sites of struggle over meaning-making, authorization, and power, to lean on Schüssler Fiorenza's feminist-exegetical framework.

Beyond a "Cop-Out" Hermeneutics: Concluding Comments

The question I address in this essay is whether the Title IX debate on US campuses ought to shape feminist scholarship on sexual violence and rape in the academic field of biblical studies. My own position is clear: I endorse an explicit connection between biblical interpretation on the one hand and feminist theories and practices on the other

---

65. For additional comments on this issue, see Susanne Scholz, "Introduction: Methods and Feminist Interpretation of the Hebrew Bible," in Scholz, *Methods*, 1–16.
66. Nancy A. Naples, "Feminist Methodology," in *The Blackwell Encyclopedia of Sociology*, ed. George Ritzer (Malden, MA: Blackwell, 2007), 4:1705.

hand. Consequently, I consider so-called historical-empiricist explanations that reject the existence of sexual violence in the ancient worlds of biblical texts as a "cop-out" hermeneutics. This cop-out hermeneutics attempts to accommodate and perhaps even to please the fathers and lords in the field and probably also in religious organizations. Could such epistemological and methodological hedging explain why feminist biblical interpretations on sexual violence are still relatively uncommon, not only in the field but also and especially beyond it? I wonder what would need to happen for alternative biblical meanings to be taken for granted as much as heteronormative, androcentric, and kyriarchal readings that are published with such abiding and abundant regularity.

In the meantime, I take my clues from the current Title IX movement. I read biblical texts from the perspectives of victim-survivors and deconstruct kyriarchal conventions, habits, and argumentation structures as they have been produced in the extensive interpretation histories of the Hebrew Bible. For the past twenty years, I have contributed to reading biblical rape texts within the context of feminist theoretical and practical concerns.[67] It has not always been easy, but what else is new? For instance, I encountered active administrative resistance from male-performing deans in two different institutions of higher education. Fortunately, I never encountered any difficulties in getting my written word out into the world, thanks to forward-looking acquisition editors. Meanwhile national and international reports on rape in the world are still pervasive. Feminist biblical scholars cannot give up; we have to continuously develop counternarratives, as exegetical resistance to the classification of biblical rape stories as tales about marriage, love, or even consensual sex is urgent. As feminist Bible scholars, we need to move beyond a cop-out hermeneutics and produce biblical readings that align with the legal efforts to take seriously the Title IX debate so that one day soon biblical rape texts will no longer be read in ways that support the silence, obfuscation, and marginalization of violence, including sexual violence, so pervasive in the world even today.

---

67. See, e.g., my *Sacred Witness* and "How to Read the Bible in the Belly of the Beast: About the Politics of Biblical Hermeneutics within the U.S.A," in *La Violencia and the People's Life: Politics, Culture, and the Interpretation of the Hebrew Bible*, ed. Susanne Scholz and Pablo Andiñach, Semeia Studies (Atlanta: SBL Press, 2016), 137–61.

The next chapter explores the considerable challenges that feminist Bible scholars encounter when they position feminist biblical exegesis as the core of biblical studies.

13

Biblical Studies Is Feminist Biblical Studies, and Vice Versa: About the Conceptualization of Feminist Biblical Studies as the Core of Biblical Studies

Biblical studies is feminist biblical studies, and vice versa. This assertion does not suggest normalizing or domesticating feminist biblical studies into the field of biblical studies. It is not a gesture of incorporation, and it does not presume the hegemonic construction of feminist biblical studies. It is also not about the rhetorical placement of feminist biblical scholarship into a position of power within kyriarchal academia. Most certainly, it does not aim to advance a neoliberal assimilatory rhetoric that produces docile bodies submitting to sociopolitical, economic, and cultural domination; it favors the erasure of boundaries and the elimination of traditional regimes of authority.[1]

Rather, the assertion that biblical studies is feminist studies, and vice versa, brings out of the closet the centrality of feminist biblical

---

1. For an analysis of this position, see the excellent discussion by Teresa J. Hornsby, "Capitalism, Masochism, and Biblical Interpretation," in *Bible Trouble: Queer Reading at the Boundaries of Biblical Scholarship*, ed. Teresa J. Hornsby and Ken Stone (Atlanta: SBL Press, 2011), 137–55.

studies in a field in which feminist scholarship is still largely absent, and if not absent, then merely tolerated as a niche research area that does not impede on the construction of normality in biblical studies. The assertion wants to trouble those normative regimes and interrogate hermeneutical and methodological claims that have contributed to exclusionary practices regarding feminist work. It also hints at an alternative to the existing epistemological hegemonies and structures of power. In short, it highlights the ongoing indecency of feminist biblical studies. Or, as Marcella Althaus-Reid would have put it, the assertion stresses the indecency of the margins becoming the knowledge center and of feminist biblical studies becoming the shifting and moving foundation for an alternative reading theory and praxis that does not collapse into the prevalent power paradigm. In this sense, then, the claim provokes a queering, not an assimilationist, vision of biblical studies.[2]

The many introductory textbooks flooding the current book market in biblical studies illustrate the gigantic obstacles that stand in the way of such a queering approach to the field. Textbook after textbook—whether it is the historical-literalist retelling by John J. Collins, Michael D. Coogan's "brief" historical-literary introduction, Christopher Stanley's "comparative approach," or Stephen L. Harris's "nonsectarian guide"—gives feminist biblical scholarship little to no visibility and recognition.[3] They ignore feminist work, theory, and accomplishment because, to them, it is profitable to marginalize feminist exegesis.[4] In fact, this factor is often the reason why even highly recognized academic publishing houses go along with the hegemonic denial of feminist biblical scholarship's impact on the field.

A case in point is a newly published textbook by Ben Witherington III, *Reading and Understanding the Bible*.[5] In September 2014, the book's publisher, Oxford University Press, advertised the volume in an email

---

2. Marcella Althaus-Reid, "From Liberation Theology to Indecent Theology: The Trouble with Normality in Theology," in *Latin American Liberation Theology: The Next Generation*, ed. Ivan Petrella (Maryknoll, NY: Orbis), 20–38, esp. 27–29.

3. John J. Collins, *Introduction to the Hebrew Bible* (Minneapolis: Fortress Press, 2004); Michael D. Coogan, *A Brief Introduction to the Old Testament: The Hebrew Bible in Its Context* (London: Oxford University Press, 2009); Christopher D. Stanley, *The Hebrew Bible: A Comparative Approach* (Minneapolis: Fortress Press, 2010); Stephen L. Harris, *Understanding the Bible*, 7th ed. (New York: McGraw Hill, 2007).

4. I know of only two exceptions: Sandra L. Gravett et al., eds., *An Introduction to the Hebrew Bible: A Thematic Approach* (Louisville: Westminster John Knox, 2008); Susanne Scholz, ed., *Biblical Studies Alternatively: An Introductory Reader* (Upper Saddle River, NJ: Prentice Hall, 2003).

5. Ben Witherington III, *Reading and Understanding the Bible* (New York: Oxford University Press, 2015).

praising the author as a "world-renowned biblical scholar" who "shows students how to read and understand the Bible in the context of the ancient world that produced it."[6] This is high acclaim for a New Testament professor who teaches at Asbury Theological Seminary, a theologically conservative school that treasures the Bible as "the only written Word of God, without error in all it affirms" and as "the only infallible rule of faith and practice."[7] Witherington is not modest either when he calls himself "one of the top evangelical scholars in the world."[8] Is this simply Oxford University Press's advertisement strategy to sell more copies of a book that covers both the Hebrew Bible and the Greek Bible? Or does the publisher seek to promote theological conservatism with a nod toward historical criticism and so to reinforce normative notions about the academic study of the Bible? What's the politics of this apparently innocuous book advertisement?

Indeed, historical assertions organize Witherington's textbook. One section is entitled "Surveying the Terrain, Studying the Map," and another chapter title, punning on the Gospel of Mark, advises: "Let the reader understand." The mention of readers affirms the familiar distinction between "the ancient text" and "the mistaken reader,"[9] turning readers into mere receivers of biblical meaning historically reconstructed. Further reinforcing the quest for historical origins while simultaneously reinforcing Christian theological conservatism, another section of the book is titled "Unearthing the Treasure." It includes retellings of various sections of the Bible, with titles such as "Historical Narratives, "The Psalms," "Isaiah," "The Prophecy and Parables of Jesus," and "Paul." His seamless literal-historical retelling of the Christian canon, which provides a characteristic pre-Holocaust Christian emphasis on the prophetic literature in the Hebrew Bible as a precursor and promise to "the prophecies and parables of Jesus" (the title of chapter 13) rehearses the classic anti-Jewish and thus supersessionist Christian approach to the Bible. Does Witherington not legitimate his conservative-theological reading by relying on historical criticism as an objective method that justifies ignoring feminist and other emerging hermeneutical approaches to the Bible?

---

6. The email was sent by Oxford University Press's highered.us@oup.com on September 25, 2014, which I received in my inbox at 9:03 a.m. See also the website blurb at http://tinyurl.com/k29tg4f: "World-renowned biblical scholar Ben Witherington III shows students how to read and understand the Bible in the context of the ancient world that produced it."
7. See Asbury Theological Seminary, "Our Statement of Faith," http://tinyurl.com/mkb3x52.
8. See the bio on the homepage of Dr. Ben Witherington III, http://www.benwitherington.com/.
9. Witherington, *Reading and Understanding the Bible*, 4.

The assertion that feminist biblical studies is biblical studies, and inversely, stands in obvious opposition to such textbooks. It claims that feminist biblical interpretation is not only a specialized area within the field of biblical studies; it is not to be excluded when we talk about the "real deal" of biblical scholarship but stands at the center of the academic study of the Bible. Esther Fuchs states it well when she writes that feminist Bible scholars have built "a genuinely autonomous field of studies" that reshapes "the future of Biblical Studies as a whole."[10] This restructuring does not aim to own the "Master's House," as Athalya Brenner feared,[11] but to foster "political engagement for epistemological transformation."[12] In short, many introductory textbooks, omitting feminist research, offer incomplete and inaccurate retellings of the field. They repress the queering moves that have taken place in biblical studies during the past forty years.

Heterarchy Instead of Patriarchy: The Historical-Conceptual Critique by Carol Meyers

Such a "queering" of biblical studies is, however, not even always endorsed by those who pioneered connections between feminism and the field of biblical studies. Carol Meyers, for instance, relegates feminist exegesis to a semi-bygone era. She considers some of its concepts as "inappropriate," "inaccurate," and even "incorrect."[13] To be sure, the critique of feminist biblical scholarship has been ongoing, as it should be in the spirit of productive and collegial debates. Thus Meyers is not the only feminist scholar criticizing feminist biblical scholarship. Genderqueer feminist Bible critics, too, bemoan co-optative and assimilatory tendencies in feminist exegetical work.[14] Yet these kinds of challenges rarely make it into the conversation of the whole field. Meyers's critique of feminist biblical scholarship is a significant exception as it appeared in the form of a presidential address at the annual meeting of the Society of Biblical Studies in 2013. Her critique reached a broad readership in the field and perhaps even beyond. It challenges

---

10. Esther Fuchs, "Biblical Feminisms: Knowledge, Theory and Politics in the Study of Women in the Hebrew Bible," *BibInt* 16, no. 3 (2008): 224.
11. Athalya Brenner, "Epilogue: Babies and Bathwater on the Road," in *Her Master's Tools? Feminist and Postcolonial Engagements of Historical-Critical Discourse*, ed. Caroline Vander Stichele and Todd G. Penner (Atlanta: Society of Biblical Literature, 2005), 333–38, esp. 338.
12. Fuchs, "Biblical Feminisms," 225.
13. Carol Meyers, "Was Ancient Israel a Patriarchal Society?," 133, no. 1 *JBL* (2014): 22–23.
14. See, e.g., Deryn Guest, *Beyond Feminist Biblical Studies* (Sheffield: Sheffield Phoenix, 2012); Esther Fuchs, *Feminist Theory and the Bible: Interrogating the Sources* (Lanham, MD: Lexington, 2016).

the concept of patriarchy in feminist reconstructions of ancient Israel as a gendered society. Meyers observes that feminist historians assume far too quickly that ancient Israelite society was "patriarchal." They present Israelite women as a homogeneous group that lacked any sociopolitical rights and responsibilities, and they depict Israelite women as the property of Israelite men, as utter victims of male domination. Rejecting such gross historical generalization, Meyers challenges feminist historians to develop a nuanced reconstruction of Israelite women's lives.

More specifically, Meyers argues that since nineteenth-century intellectual discourse invented the notion of patriarchy, its use should be discontinued in historical reconstructions of ancient Israel. Meyers grounds her argumentation in recent research in classical studies and "third-wave feminist" archaeological studies to show that the concept of "patriarchy" is "not flexible enough to accommodate the reality of daily household activities and interactions."[15] According to Meyers, it "interferes with attempts to understand the complex gendered patterns of life in ancient Israel," and assumes incorrectly "an unduly negative view of women's lives in the biblical past."[16] Yet Meyers also clarifies that her position does not presume the existence of gender equality in ancient Israel. On the contrary, Meyers acknowledges that considerable gender inequities characterized Israelite social life, and many biblical references to patrilineality and male control of female sexuality illustrate this fact. What is needed, according to Meyers, is a differentiated view in which Israelite men's dominance is recognized as "fragmentary, not hegemonic."[17] Male supremacy in ancient Israel must be described as socially complex in ways that the nineteenth-century notion of patriarchy does not allow. In fact, patriarchy should be replaced with the term *heterarchy*. This term, originating from the social sciences, allows historians to describe more adequately the existence of simultaneous and multilayered power structures of gender.

Meyers's proposal, on the surface at least, seems reasonable. It is highly probable that women's agency in the ancient Israelite context was varied and complex. The trouble is that Meyers's argumentation is not grounded in feminist hermeneutical considerations. In fact, her proposal undermines feminist biblical scholarship in four ways. First, Meyers rejects feminist biblical scholarship as outdated. In her view,

---

15. Meyers, "Was Ancient Israel," 26.
16. Ibid.
17. Ibid., 27.

it is stuck in nineteenth-century intellectual discourse on the concept of patriarchy, and is unaware of more recent social-scientific developments that make this term obsolete. Second, Meyers neither engages nor values feminist contributions to biblical historiography. When she observes that "the all-inclusive concept of male dominance and concomitant female victimhood, as articulated by second-wave theorists," still appears "in the publications of many feminist biblical scholars,"[18] she rightly challenges feminist exegetes for making generalizing historical claims about ancient Israelite gender performances. Yet she distances herself from these studies by rejecting rather than debating them in any detail. Feminist biblical publications appear in only 10 out of 109 footnotes. Even those feminist historical works that Meyers acknowledges as providing "examples of women exercising power and authority in households and in larger society"[19] do not play a central role in her analysis. She dismisses them as deficient and ultimately as insignificant. Third, Meyers puts earlier feminist biblical research into competition with what she classifies "third-wave" feminist archaeological work. She places earlier feminist scholarship against later feminist work without acknowledging that the current feminist generation stands on the shoulders of the former. This kind of rhetorical move plays into the hands of those for whom feminist scholarship as a whole is irrelevant. One could thus argue that Meyers's approach is almost as detrimental as the neglect of feminist research in malestream Bible textbooks. Neither one of them advances a feminist conceptualization of biblical historiography; rather, both rely on a clichéd and abbreviated descriptions in which feminist scholarship loses. In other words, Meyers not only disregards earlier feminist biblical scholarship but also creates a competitive analysis in which younger faceless feminist historians supersede the previous generation of feminist scholars.[20]

Fourth and finally, a significant epistemological insight of the last twenty years remains invisible in Meyers's approach. It is the intellectual-cultural move from the scientific-empiricist to the postmodern epistemology in (biblical) hermeneutical work.[21] After all, even secular historians argue convincingly that gender notions as we assume them

---

18. Ibid., 16.
19. Ibid., 16n50: "To be sure, other feminist biblical scholars provide examples of women exercising power and authority in households and in the larger society; however, they do not explicitly critique the patriarchal model."
20. The names of the so-called third-wave scholars appear only in the footnotes; see ibid., 24–25.
21. For one of the earliest introductions to postmodernism in biblical studies, see, e.g., A. K. M. Adam, *What Is Postmodern Biblical Criticism?* (Minneapolis: Fortress Press, 1995).

today were defined in the nineteenth century.[22] In other words, there simply is no way of reconstructing gendered Israelite historiography independently from contemporary assumptions about gender.[23] This epistemological insight implies that Meyers's reconstruction of Israelite women's lives presupposes *contemporary* notions of gender, whether or not they are grounded in a differentiated view of patriarchy. In this sense, then, any historiography about ancient Israel is already "anachronistic," as we are always "stuck" in contemporary concepts, assumptions, and vocabulary. We are unable to describe Israelite gender dynamics as they were practiced once upon a time because historical reconstructions are always located in a historian's context. Said differently, historical reconstructions are always hermeneutically biased, not objective, and never value neutral. Consequently, the historical goal of reconstructing an "accurate" and "correct" history of women's lives in ancient Israel is an epistemological fantasy of the nineteenth century. It also assumes a view of gender that is stuck in the heteronormative gender paradigm criticized by queer theorists since the 1990s.[24] Another biblical feminist scholar, Esther Fuchs, thus observes unambiguously: "Missing in feminist historical criticism of the Hebrew Bible is an awareness of the methodological and theoretical questioning of fundamental premises, concepts, and inquiries in the study of history as such."[25]

In short, Meyers's desire to get rid of the modern concept of patriarchy in contemporary feminist and nonfeminist biblical historiography does not locate itself in constructive conversation with feminist theories and feminist biblical scholarship. Rather, it legitimizes its position with references to the social sciences (anthropology) and classical studies. This is fine in itself, but it is not a feminist scholarly move. It also does not explain why contemporary white, black, or brown, Christian, Jewish, or secular, Eastern, Western, queer, trans, bi, intersex, able-bodied or dis-abled, poor, middle-class, employed or living on dividends, female or male or inbetween or beyond people should care about Meyers's efforts to develop a gendered historiography of ancient Israel. As Mukti Barton observes, white Europeans and North

---

22. See, e.g., Hayden White, *Metahistory: The Historical Imagination in Nineteenth-Century Europe* (Baltimore: Johns Hopkins University Press, 1973).

23. See, e.g., Keith Whitelam, *The Invention of Ancient Israel: The Silencing of Palestinian History* (New York: Routledge, 1996).

24. See, e.g., Judith Butler, *Gender Trouble: Feminism and the Subversion of Identity* (New York: Routledge, 1990).

25. Esther Fuchs, "The History of Women in Ancient Israel: Theory, Method, and the Book of Ruth," in Vander Stichele and Penner, *Her Master's Tools*, 211.

Americans stand in a long tradition of decontextualizing, depoliticizing, and individualizing Bible interpretations that adhere to "the myth of pure objectivity" and value neutrality while they avoid "the stark reality" of injustice, racism, sexism, and oppression.[26] It seems that Meyers's address does not escape this controversial hermeneutical tradition. Yet this predicament is certainly not unique to her work alone but shared by much scholarship in biblical studies.[27]

Toward "Emancipatory Radical Democratic Biblical Knowledges": The Proposal of Elisabeth Schüssler Fiorenza

So how then should we conceptualize biblical studies as feminist biblical studies, and vice versa? Elisabeth Schüssler Fiorenza offers some interesting suggestions when she talks about the rhetoric of empire.[28] She observes that mainstream biblical scholars, focusing on historical criticism, read "biblical texts as documents of the past."[29] When they make contemporary connections, they stress the "spiritual, purely religious, individualistic appropriation" of those texts.[30] In contrast, those on the margins of biblical studies examine "the interpersonal interactions between readers and text as well as the significance of social-religious location for biblical readings for today."[31] This differently directed approach requires that biblical interpretation be understood as a sociopolitical and cultural-political practice. It takes seriously its public responsibility "because the Bible has shaped and still shapes not only the church [as well as the synagogue, one might add] but also the cultural-political self-understanding of the American imagination."[32] Biblical interpretation, according to Schüssler Fiorenza, should thus be conceptualized "as an integral part of emancipatory struggles for survival, justice, and well-being," and ought to be grounded in the needs and wants of "wo/men struggling for survival and change."[33] When Bible scholars follow this advice, they abandon the antiquarian project and "translate wo/men's quest for self-esteem and justice into the

---

26. Mukti Barton, "The Bible in Black Theology," *Black Theology* 9, no. 1 (2011): 57–76, esp. 74, 62.
27. See, e.g., Richard D. Nelson, *Historical Roots of the Old Testament (1200–63 BCE)* (Atlanta: SBL Press, 2014).
28. Elisabeth Schüssler Fiorenza, *The Power of the Word: Scripture and the Rhetoric of Empire* (Minneapolis: Fortress Press, 2007).
29. Ibid., 53.
30. Ibid.
31. Ibid.
32. Ibid., 56.
33. Elisabeth Schüssler Fiorenza, *Democratizing Biblical Studies* (Louisville: Westminster John Knox, 2008), 13.

language and research goals of the academy."[34] People's issues, their problems, and their needs become central so that the academic study of the Bible will then produce "emancipatory knowledge and liberating insights" for them.[35]

This kind of scholarship includes both deconstructive and constructive modes of analysis, as it "understands the Bible and its own work of interpretation and education as a site of struggle over meaning-making, authorization, and symbolic power."[36] Schüssler Fiorenza's proposal implies that questions of "the power of scripture and its authority" have to be addressed.[37] She structures the concept of power in two ways. On the one hand, power appears as "structural-pyramidal power" that expresses itself vertically in "kyriarchal relations of domination."[38] On the other hand, it combines with power "operating horizontally as an ideological network of relations of domination,"[39] intersecting with gender, race, sexuality, class, empire, age, and religion. Each of these reinforces the others, and together they effect "dehumanizing exploitation and othering subordination."[40] The understanding of this twofold power structure in the world, as well as the fostering of "critical and constructive exchanges and learning,"[41] shape the task of biblical studies. Its goal is to produce "emancipatory radical democratic biblical knowledges" in which feminist knowledge is an integral and central part.[42]

In this sense, Schüssler Fiorenza defines biblical studies as feminist biblical studies, and vice versa. Her book, *Changing Horizons: Explorations in Feminist Interpretations*,[43] makes this point in a discussion about the purpose of feminist analysis in biblical studies. Schüssler Fiorenza explains: "Biblical research and scholarship must be done in the interest of *all* wo/men and engender a radical democratic societal, cultural, religious, and personal transformation."[44] It requires "a reconceptualization of biblical studies in critical feminist terms"[45] so that biblical

---

34. Ibid.
35. Ibid.
36. Ibid., 15.
37. Schüssler Fiorenza, *Power of the Word*, 56.
38. Ibid., 57.
39. Ibid.
40. Ibid.
41. Elisabeth Schüssler Fiorenza, "Toward a Feminist Future of the Biblical Past," in *Empowering Memory and Movement: Thinking and Working across Borders* (Minneapolis: Fortress Press, 2014), 535.
42. Ibid.
43. Elisabeth Schüssler Fiorenza, *Changing Horizons: Explorations in Feminist Interpretations* (Minneapolis: Fortress Press, 2013).
44. Ibid., 296.
45. Ibid., 297.

studies becomes "a rhetorics and ethics of inquiry and transformation."[46] It resists the neoliberal, corporate-driven, and technocratic belief in objectivist and disinterested research, and it turns biblical studies into "a critical rhetoric of inquiry that treats biblical texts and scholarly interpretations as arguments rather than as descriptive statements or the*logical doctrines."[47]

Interestingly, genderqueer scholar Deryn Guest indirectly endorses Schüssler Fiorenza's reconceptualization of biblical studies when Guest defines the exegetical project as an interrogation of "dominant voices on religion, gender and sexuality" from the position and politics of minoritized people, such as LGBTQI people. In fact, Guest reminds biblical scholars that "in biblical studies we are in the enviable position of being the experts on the very texts currently used to both uphold and challenge current religious/state policies on adoption, marriage, civil partnerships, who can serve as ministers, and so forth."[48] In other words, to Guest, biblical interpretation is not an antiquarian task but stands in direct conversation with contemporary society. Guest suggests that biblical studies "provide ammunition for policy-making in both church/synagogue and state" and "affect the actual lives of LGBTI citizens, often profoundly."[49] Reconceptualized in this way, the field of biblical studies is central to contemporary cultural-religious conversations over sociopolitical practices.

Are We There Yet? Feminist Biblical Studies as an International, Interreligious, Interracial, and Intercultural Field of Study

The idea of making marginalized people's voices and experiences the center of biblical studies is neither new nor limited to feminist hermeneutical discussions. For instance, Vincent L. Wimbush reasons that "making African American experience the starting point for the academic study of the Bible is likely to have an effect upon all aspects of the field—the definition and orientation, structure of curricula, programs, and research projects, relationships with other disciplines, fields, and programs, recruitment of students and faculty."[50] He notes

---

46. Ibid., 300.
47. Ibid., 292.
48. Guest, *Beyond Feminist Biblical Studies*, 163.
49. Ibid.
50. Vincent L. Wimbush, "Interrupting the Spin: What Might Happen if African Americans Were to Become the Starting Point for the Academic Study of the Bible," *Union Seminary Quarterly Review* 52, no. 1–2 (1998): 75. He asks succinctly on p. 64: "What might happen if African American experience were the starting focal point, the foreground, for the academic study of the Bible?"

that an African American biblical hermeneutics centrally placed within the field would make it impossible for exegetes to limit their task to narrowly defined textual work, what he characterizes as "the fetishization of a certain class-specific cultural textual-interpretive practice."[51] Instead, it would open up the field to the "complexity of social dynamics as social textu(r)alization."[52] The field would then focus on the complex interactions of society, culture, and sacred texts, including the Bible; it would position scholars to investigate society and culture as inspired by the Bible, and vice versa. This hermeneutical refocusing act would ensure that the field of biblical studies, a remnant of a "rather narrow slice of the culture" from which it emerged, namely, "North Atlantic European-American high Protestantism and Catholicism," would move out of its self-imposed academic-intellectual isolation.[53] What is true for the conceptualization of biblical studies as African American biblical studies is also true for feminist biblical studies. By making feminist biblical studies central to biblical studies, everything changes in biblical studies.

So why is it so difficult to make feminist biblical studies the focal point of biblical studies? Put another way, why has the field of biblical studies not become feminist biblical studies? There are, of course, many reasons, but Schüssler Fiorenza mentions four important ones in *Changing Horizons*.[54] One reason relates to the problem of feminist co-optation into the hegemonic academic expectations of the field. Feminist scholars want to get and to hold on to their academic positions. It requires that they conform to the professional standards of academia and the field. They have to publish, receive grants, and become recognized as members of the guild. The temptation of dutiful daughterhood is manifold and, of course, includes ignoring feminist lineage, names, and topics in research and teaching. Another reason relates to the lack of institutionalizing feminist scholarship in universities and colleges, as well as isolating feminist academic work from feminist commitment and activism. Yet without grounding feminist research within movements for progressive change, feminist biblical scholars are endangered to be "trivialized, silenced, and forgotten" not only in the academy but also in feminist discourse in the world. It is thus crucial to create institutional infrastructures. Yet another reason

---

51. Ibid., 65.
52. Ibid., 75.
53. Ibid., 76.
54. Schüssler Fiorenza, *Changing Horizons*, 301–4.

pertains to the ongoing dominance of the positivist-scientific paradigm that often limits feminist exegesis to "women in the Bible." This paradigm ensures that nonfeminist interpreters dismiss feminist interests and goals as biased and thus unscholarly. It classifies as unscientific any consideration of the sociopolitical, economic, and cultural-religious struggles of real people. A fourth and final reason relates to the ongoing feminist reticence to develop solidarity and alliances across all kinds of marginalized discourses in biblical studies. This, in turn, belies the necessity of developing countervisions and dissident strategies in feminist exegetical scholarship. Such reluctance disconnects feminist exegesis from intersectional and socially located analysis.

All of these reasons explain why it is so difficult for feminist biblical studies to gain traction in the field. Yet there is another key reason that explains why feminist biblical studies are marginalized in biblical studies. It has to do with the profound political-economic changes currently taking place in institutions of higher education in North America and elsewhere. The increasingly corporate, neoliberal, and technocratic forces mold, move, and define what is supported, valued, and taught in contemporary colleges, universities, and schools of theology. Henry A. Giroux describes succinctly the effects of these forces when he states:

> Four decades of neoliberal policies have resulted in an economic Darwinism that promotes privatization, commodification, free trade, and deregulation. It privileges personal responsibility over larger social forces, reinforces the gap between the rich and poor by redistributing wealth to the most powerful and wealthy individuals and groups, and it fosters a mode of public pedagogy that privileges the entrepreneurial subject while encouraging a value system that promotes self-interest, if not an unchecked selfishness. Since the 1970s, neoliberalism or free-market fundamentalism has become not only a much-vaunted ideology that now shapes all aspects of life in the United States but also a predatory global phenomenon.[55]

The neoliberal policies of privatization, commodification, deregulation, and "financialization"[56] have had a profound impact on higher education today. They decrease democratic education and reduce the value of critical thinking, as Giroux observes:

---

55. Henry A. Giroux, *Neoliberalism's War on Higher Education* (Chicago: Haymarket, 2014), 1.
56. For the latter dynamic, see the important analysis by Costas Lapavitsas, *Profiting without Producing: How Finance Exploits Us All* (London: Verso, 2013).

> The neoliberal paradigm . . . abhors democracy and views public and higher education as a toxic civic sphere that poses a threat to corporate values, power, and ideology. . . . Similarly, critical thought, knowledge, dialogue, and dissent are increasingly perceived with suspicion by the new corporate university that now defines faculty as entrepreneurs, students as customers, and education as a mode of training.[57]

In short, the market-driven corporate dynamics of higher education instrumentalize academic work for commercial purposes and financial gains. Institutions of higher education sell themselves as workplace-training facilities, disregarding their tradition and competency of fostering the liberal arts unencumbered by immediate financial gains. Although it would be worth pondering to what extent institutions of higher education supported such goals in the past.[58] It is clear that neoliberalism diminishes the status of the liberal arts, including biblical studies, as they do not accommodate the profit-driven, technocratic, and corporate educational agenda. The liberal arts do not deliver measureable products, to be calculated on spreadsheets and listed with quantifiable outcomes. Learning, teaching, and research in the liberal arts consist of cumbersome and long-winding processes without immediate, linear, and measurable outcomes. Yet the neoliberal environment of higher education does not have patience for such work, and so it sidelines and divests from it. At some schools, entire departments have closed or have been greatly reduced, including departments of physics, philosophy, anthropology, or modern languages.[59] Because neoliberal interests endorse business, engineering, and technology departments, the advancement of the so-called STEM fields is in full force. There, the educational payoff is quantifiable and leads to lucrative postcollege employment. Consequently, the neoliberal rationale exerts considerable pressure on departments of religious and theological studies, as well as on schools of theology, where Bible courses are often limited to basic courses preserving the theological status quo. Since such an environment does not encourage creativity and innovation, the position of the nineteenth-century curriculum continues to prevail.

It is thus unsurprising that, defined by "hierarchical domination, bureaucratic control, hostility to radical research and teaching, and

---

57. Ibid., 30.
58. Stephen D. Moore and Yvonne Sherwood, *The Invention of the Biblical Scholar* (Minneapolis: Fortress Press, 2011).
59. See my discussion in chap. 2 of this book.

anathema to free thinking,"[60] this neoliberal climate does not foster innovation in the teaching and research agendas of religious and theological studies. There is little incentive to expand teaching and research into innovative and creative directions. Fear about diminishing tenure-track or tenured positions is always a factor, if euphemistically called "contingent" faculty do not already fill most teaching slots because, as Hector Avalos states it so bluntly, it is very likely that there is "no job for you."[61] It is probably not accidental that this situation occurs at the very moment when the field has begun hiring people excluded for centuries. Marc Bousquet, author of *How the University Works: Higher Education and the Low-Wage Nation*,[62] makes this very point when he observes:

> Generally speaking, if the field pays someone with a doctorate less than a bartender, there's going to be a bunch of women in that discipline. If the field pays per-course wages of $2,000 to adjunct labor, you're a lot more likely to find women than in fields where per-course wages are $20,000. . . . In general, the more a discipline has been permatemped since the 1980s, the more women it has hired.[63]

This is depressing stuff.

Nevertheless, those of us working in feminist biblical studies *must* continue developing biblical studies as an international, interreligious, interracial, and intercultural intellectual field of research. We need to provide critical insight into the structures of domination as they pertain to biblical interpretation. We have to make our work acceptable to the intersections of gender, race, class, physical abilities, nationalism, colonialism, or heteronormativity, and we should provide intellectual rationale and analysis to global struggles for justice. We also need to insist on developing biblical studies as an academic location that critically investigates the manifold sociopolitical, economic, cultural, and religious conditions that require change. We have to articulate sociopolitical, economic, cultural, and religious alternatives, and recognize existing divisions, including those based on gender, as asymmetric power relations that have profoundly defined, limited, and

60. Anthony J. Nocella II, Steven Best, and Peter McLaren, eds., *Academic Repression: Reflections from the Academic-Industrial Complex* (Baltimore: AK Press, 2010), 13.
61. Hector Avalos, *The End of Biblical Studies* (Amherst, NY: Prometheus), 316.
62. Marc Bousquet, *How the University Works: Higher Education and the Low-Wage Nation* (New York: New York University Press, 2008).
63. Marc Bousquet, "Lady Academe and Labor-Market Segmentation: The Narrative of Women's Success via Higher Education Rests on a House of Cards," *Chronicle of Higher Education*, October 29, 2012, http://tinyurl.com/keoklsx.

distorted the interpretative work in biblical studies. We need to collaborate with each other, and we need to do whatever we can to build institutions and research agendas that open up spaces for the next generation of feminist Bible scholars, teachers, and readers. Tat-siong Benny Liew calls for "intercommunal conversations across minority groups,"[64] and womanist exegetes, Gay L. Byron and Vanessa Lovelace, affirm "that interpreting sacred texts cannot be done independent of the communities with whom we read and to whom we are accountable."[65] In my view, feminist exegetes need to be part of these conversations and also be connected to their communities of accountability. In fact, many feminist and genderqueer Bible scholars have already reached out and engaged in this kind of "multipolar or multicentric" discourse, despite the difficulties of establishing it within our own institutional locations. In sum, those of us creating "alternatives" to the status quo in biblical studies need to insist that biblical studies is feminist biblical studies, and vice versa, even when some universities, colleagues, and publishers ignore, sideline, or marginalize feminist biblical studies even today.

The next chapter offers additional insights into the power dynamics involved as feminist exegetes translated the Bible into inclusive German. It will become clear why secular and religious critics reacted so harshly to the feminist translation effort, especially when the responses are examined in light of translation theories and theories on barbarism. The sociopolitical, cultural, and exegetical challenges to feminist biblical scholarship illuminate lingering and reasserting colonizing attitudes and empire hierarchies not only in ecclesial but also in secularized German settings during the last couple of decades.

---

64. Tat-siong Benny Liew, "What Has Been Done? What Can We Learn? Racial/Ethnic Minority Readings of the Bible in the United States," in *The Future of the Biblical Past: Envisioning Biblical Studies in a Global Key*, ed. Roland Boer and Fernando F. Segovia (Atlanta: SBL Press, 2012), 282–83.
65. Gay L. Byron and Vanessa Lovelace, "Introduction: Methods and the Making of Womanist Biblical Hermeneutics," in *Womanist Interpretations of the Bible: Expanding the Discourse*, ed. Gay L. Byron and Vanessa Lovelace (Atlanta: SBL Press, 2016), 15.

14

Barbaric Bibles: The Scandal of Inclusive Translations

In 1940, Walter Benjamin declared that "there is no document of civilization which is not at the same time a document of barbarism."[1] This is certainly the case for the various Bible translations that have been used by self-declared civilizers who brought them to those whom they classified as "barbarians," who, in turn, often read them in civilizing ways while the civilizers treated them barbarically. What is civilizing to some is barbaric to others, although it is not as interchangeable as it seems. Historic power structures, epistemological claims to authority, and hegemonic structures of sociopolitical control and domination are always already present, ready to advance such practices. The intense and often rather harsh debate on the first inclusive German Bible translation is not an exception to these dynamics. This essay elucidates some of them as they have become apparent with the German publication of the *Bibel in gerechter Sprache* (*BigS*; Bible in just language).[2]

---

1. Walter Benjamin, "Theses on the Philosophy of History," in *Illuminations*, ed. and with an introduction by Hannah Arendt, trans. Harry Zohn (London: Fontana/Collins, 1970), 258.
2. Ulrike Bail et al., *Bibel in gerechter Sprache* (Gütersloh: Gütersloher Verlagshaus, 2006). The book publication is in its fourth edition. The Bible has a website: https://www.bibel-in-gerechter-

Why the Viciousness? About Secular and Religious Responses to the First Inclusive German Bible Translation

The translation of the Bible into inclusive German—sensitive not only to gender but also to racial-ethnic issues, such as anti-Judaism in Christian biblical hermeneutics, and social-class dynamics—has brought enormous and long-overdue publicity to progressive German theological scholarship, as it has been developed during the past forty years. It has also proved to be an extremely controversial Bible translation. Even prior to the publication date in October 2006, a firestorm of vicious, hateful, and brutally negative criticism appeared in major German-language news outlets, reaching a general public far beyond the theological and ecclesial press. The forcefulness of the negative assessment of the *BigS* has been stunning, especially since it occurred in a thoroughly secularized society. Initially, the secular press commented on the translation with tongue-in-cheek titles. For instance, the weekly magazine *Der Spiegel*, comparable in status to *Time* magazine, introduced readers to the *BigS* with headlines such as "Umstrittene Übersetzung: Die Schlange hatte mehr drauf" (controversial translation: the serpent was smarter)[3] and "Wortsalat im Garten Eden" (gobbledygook in the garden of Eden).[4] The daily and nationally distributed newspaper *Frankfurter Allgemeine Zeitung* declared that the new translation was "Nicht zum Gebrauch im Gottesdienst geeignet" (Not suitable for use in worship settings),[5] and the local daily newspaper, *Kölner Stadt-Anzeiger*, believed the *BigS* was "Die Bibel aus dem Gleichstellungsbüro" (The Bible of the equal opportunity office).[6]

The actual discussion in the secular press was seriously negative. For instance, Robert Leicht, a journalist of the weekly *Die Zeit*, questioned the legitimacy of the project already in April 2006. He alleged that the inclusive translation confuses the distinction between translation and interpretation, thereby misrepresenting the *Urtext* (source

---

sprache.de/. All translations from the original German into English are mine, unless indicated otherwise.

3. "Umstrittene Übersetzung: Die Schlange hatte mehr drauf," *Der Spiegel*, October 25, 2006, http://tinyurl.com/kkxp5g9.

4. Matthias Schulz, "Wortsalat im Garten Eden," *Der Spiegel*, October 30, 2006, 190, http://tinyurl.com/le5z9ws.

5. "Nicht zum Gebrauch im Gottesdienst geeignet," *Frankfurter Allgemeine Zeitung*, June 5, 2007, http://www.faz.net/aktuell/politik/bibel-in-gerechter-sprache-nicht-zum-gebrauch-im-gottes-dienst-geeignet-1433739.html.

6. Katharina Eckstein, "Die Bibel aus dem Gleichstellungsbüro," *Kölner Stadt-Anzeiger*, June 6, 2007, http://tinyurl.com/mp86dky.

text).[7] Other secular journalists charged that the translation overturns Luther's principle, according to which the words of the translation should follow the literal meaning of the source text. They complained that the new translation "does not allow the text to speak for itself" and "reverses the principle into its absurd opposite."[8]

Full-blown attacks, however, came from Christian theologians and ecclesial bodies. For instance, Ulrich Wilckens, a retired bishop and translator of a well-known New Testament German translation, accused the *BigS* editors and translators of "heresy" and a "simply wrong translation."[9] Other German theology professors complained that this Bible translation "goes behind the ideas of the Protestant Reformers . . . [by] serving theological and political interests"[10] of the translators only. Still others judged that the *BigS* "hits rock bottom in the modern history of Bible interpretation."[11] And systematic theologian Ingolf U. Dalferth declared the inclusive translation to be "theologically bankrupt" and "philologically, historically, and theologically useless."[12]

Various church bodies also submitted unsympathetic assessments soon after the translation was published. In March 2007, the highest committee of the Evangelische Kirche Deutschland (EKD), the umbrella organization of the Protestant regional churches in Germany, explained that the new translation would not be authorized for worship use and not replace the 1984 Luther translation.[13] The EKD committee (*Rat der EKD*), criticizing the translation for its lack of *Worttreue* (lit.: "fidelity to the word"), mandated that the *BigS* serve only as a

7. Robert Leicht, "Kein Wort sie wollen lassen stahn," *Die Zeit*, April 6, 2006, http://tinyurl.com/ktvvr7e. See also the discussion by academic theologians such as Ingo U. Dalferth, "Der Ewige und die Ewige: Die 'Bibel in gerechter Sprache'—weder richtig noch gerecht, sondern konfus," *Neue Zürcher Zeitung*, http://tinyurl.com/l27eedo. And even some feminist theologians of the first generation opposed the translation; see, e.g., Elisabeth Gössmann, "Anfang der Weisheit: Die weibliche Tradition der Bibelauslegung und die 'Bibel in gerechter Sprache,'" *Neue Zürcher Zeitung*, December 14, 2006, https://www.nzz.ch/articleEPVQL-1.83077.
8. Heike Schmoll, "Befreit zur religiösen Mündigkeit," *Frankfurter Allgemeine*, October 30, 2006, 1.
9. Ulrich Wilckens, "Theologisches Gutachten zur 'Bibel in gerechter Sprache'," *epd-Dokumentation*, April 24, 2007, 30. For a detailed analysis of Wilckens's "Gutachten" that counters his position, see Luise Schottroff, "Stellungnahme zum theologischen Gutachten von Ulrich Wilckens zur Bibel in gerechter Sprache," *epd-Dokumentation*, July 24, 2007, 34–37.
10. Jens Schröter, "Kritische Anmerkungen zur 'Bibel in gerechter Sprache,'" *epd-Dokumentation*, April 24, 2007, 19. See also his "Übersetzung und Interpretation: Bemerkungen zur 'Bibel in gerechter Sprache,'" *epd-Dokumentation*, July 24, 2007, 21–27. See also Jens Schröter and Ingolf U. Dalferth, eds., *Bibel in gerechter Sprache? Kritik eines misslungenen Versuchs* (Tübingen: Mohr Siebeck, 2007).
11. Ulrich H. J. Körtner, "Bibel oder nicht Bibel: Das ist hier die Frage! Zur Kritik der 'Bibel in gerechter Sprache,'" *epd-Dokumentation*, April 24, 2007, 23.
12. Dalferth, "Der Ewige und die Ewige."
13. "Die Qualität einer Bibelübersetzung hängt an der Treue zum Text: Stellungnahme des Rates der EKD zur 'Bibel in gerechter Sprache,'" *epd-Dokumentation*, April 24, 2007, 14–15.

"supplementary edition of the Bible" (*eine ergänzende Bibelausgabe*). It claimed that the *BigS* collapses translation and interpretation, as its emphasis on inclusivity distorts the biblical text. The EKD committee also came close to rejecting the translation's goals of gender justice, its elimination of anti-Judaism, and its promotion of social justice when it criticized the *BigS*'s notion of "just language" in the following statement:

> The notion of "just language" or "just language use" is unclear. It is also unclear why the three chosen criteria of "gender justice," "justice regarding the Christian-Jewish dialogue," and "social justice" should succeed in "addressing the biblical foundational topic in a special way." Used as translation principles, these criteria turn into preconceived ideas with which the text is read. This approach does not serve the understanding of the biblical text at all.[14]

Other ecclesial bodies also disapproved of the inclusive translation. The Protestant Lutheran Churches of Germany (VELKD) published a statement on March 6, 2007, in which it declared:

> The "Bibel in gerechter Sprache" is not authorized from any ecclesial committee.... [It] is *ungeeignet* [lit.: "unsuitable"] to be used as an exclusive Bible translation.... [The translators] project modern assumptions into it which contradict the Reformation that impressed deepest respect upon the Holy Scripture.[15]

Similarly, Catholic leaders distanced themselves from the first inclusive German Bible. Elmar Fischer, bishop of Feldkirch in southern Germany, cautioned that the translation is not authorized for worship use.[16] The Austrian bishops advised that Bible translations be kept apart from "restrictive ideologies" (*einengenden Ideologien*). In their view, the new translation "is only sometimes useful and even then only when read together with other *authentic* Bible translations."[17]

The outrage, coming down from both secular and ecclesial venues, is unusual, although the *BigS* has also received positive endorsement, including financial support, from many theological and ecclesial

---

14. Ibid., 14.
15. "Beschluss zu neueren deutschen Bibelübersetzungen: Bischofskonferenz der Vereinigten Evangelisch-Lutherischen Kirche Deutschlands," *epd-Dokumentation*, May 29, 2007, 36.
16. "'Bibel in gerechter Sprache' nicht für die Liturgie zugelassen," *Katholischer Nachrichtendienst*, March 7, 2007, http://tinyurl.com/mr966k5.
17. "'Bibel in gerechter Sprache' ungeeignet für Liturgie und Schule," *Katholischer Nachrichtendienst*, March 16, 2007, http://tinyurl.com/k3qt98w (emphasis added).

groups and laypeople.[18] Yet this essay explores why the appraisals of the *BigS* were so sweepingly and relentlessly negative. It proposes that the negative evaluations reflect strongly held and defended notions about intellectual, cultural, and theological superiority, hegemony, and power, usually tucked away behind post-Holocaust and postunification rhetoric of liberalism and human rights. In other words, the massive and quick rejection by secular and religious institutions and individuals of public authority—the press, various church bodies, and individual scholars—reveals for a short but fully visible moment the colossal forces present in German-speaking culture endorsing empire hierarchies, gender inequalities, and "otherness" as politically, socially, and religiously acceptable structures in social life.

This, then, is the scandal of the first inclusive German Bible translation. It exposes a reactionary worldview in which democratic sensibilities remain elusive when secular and religious institutions of authority are confronted with progressive theological propositions in the German-language context. Said differently, the publication of the *BigS* offers a unique opportunity to understand the current state of the collective German psyche when its symbolic heritage is challenged. As it emerges from the sociopolitical, religious, and geopolitical borderlands of intellectual-academic German institutions, the *BigS* encourages the decolonization of scholarly, social, and religious habits, conventions, and spaces within the German-language context. Yet it is exactly for this reason that the vicious responses to the first inclusive German Bible translation represent a unique window into the intellectual

---

18. See, e.g., the Protestant regional church, the Evangelische Kirche in Hessen Nassau (EKHN). This regional church has a long tradition of endorsing feminist and liberation theologians—such as Luise Schottroff, who is one of the *BigS*'s editors—and of promoting progressive theological movements and teachings. The EKHN supported the work of this Bible translation financially and with personnel. In March 2007, the highest officer of the EKHN ("Kirchenpräsident"), Peter Steinacker, published a letter in which he encouraged the congregations of the EKHN and related institutions to study the translation and to develop their own positions; see Peter Steinacker, "An die Kirchengemeinden und Einrichtungen in der EKHN: Brief des Leitenden Geistlichen Amtes der Evangelischen Kirche in Hessen und Nassau (EKHN) zur 'Bibel in gerechter Sprache,'" *epd-Dokumentation*, May 29, 2007, 36–37. Also the *Nordelbische Evangelisch-Lutherische Kirche* endorsed the study and use of the *BigS*, not following the recommendations of the Lutheran Church organization in Germany (VELKD) and the EKD; see "Erklärung zur Bibel in gerechter Sprache: Kirchenleitung der Nordelbischen Kirche," *epd-Dokumentation*, July 24, 2007, 28–34: "Nach Ansicht des Theologischen Beirats machen die theologischen Erwägungen es nicht erforderlich, dass die Kirchenleitung sich den Beschluss der Bischofskonferenz der VELKD vom 06.03.2007 und die Stellungnahme des Rates der EKD vom 31.03.2007 zu eigen macht. . . . Unter Abwägung aller dieser Aspekte ist schließlich im Einzelfall eine verantwortliche Entscheidung für oder gegen die Verwendung der 'Bibel in gerechter Sprache' zu treffen. Ein besonders geeigneter Ort im Gottesdienst kann die Verwendung als Lesung des Predigttextes sein" (33). The *Evangelische Kirche im Rheinland* also endorsed the study and use of the *BigS*.

empire forces in the German-language setting that are usually kept undercover, tucked away, and not spoken about in public.

Two intellectual-academic discourses help illuminate why critics of the *BigS* felt so comfortable in rejecting the historic accomplishment of translating the Bible into inclusive German. The discourses come from translation studies and theories of barbarism. Both of them shed light on the significance of the geo-intellectual dynamics at work in the vehement and harsh rejection of the new translation. The following analysis explains the theoretical developments in the field of translation studies, demonstrating that critics of the *BigS* rely on scholarly outdated views about the nature, purpose, and function of translated texts. The analysis also brings scholarship on barbarism into the conversation to expose critics of the *BigS* as upholders of empire forces. A conclusion encourages Bible readers to welcome the first inclusive German Bible translation as a cultural-theological opportunity to strengthen and foster democratic sensibilities in the German-language context and beyond.

From Textual Fidelity to Products of Geopolitics: The Contribution of the Field of Translation Studies

When we look at the field of translation theories as it has emerged in modern Western thought, the impetus to translate the Bible into vernacular European languages, such as German, in the sixteenth century CE is a good starting point. After all, with the emergence of the empiricist-scientific epistemology, Western Bible readers came to reject hermeneutical models advanced by earlier Jewish and Christian interpreters.[19] The Protestant Reformation, aligning with the newly developing empiricist-scientific epistemology, insisted on *sola Scriptura* (only Scripture) as the basis for biblical translation. Interpreters claimed this principle to create independence from doctrinal and ecclesial hermeneutical conventions and restrictions. By reading the Bible directly and without interference from church authorities, Reformers and their descendants limited hermeneutical procedures to the *sensus litteralis*, which ignored traditional structures of authority for the establishment of biblical meaning. To be sure, the history of the Bible

19. For a historical survey, see, e.g., Eugene A. Nida, "Bible Translation," in *Routledge Encyclopedia of Translation Studies*, ed. Mona Baker (London: Routledge, 1998), 22–28; John Sandys-Wunsch, *What Have They Done to the Bible? A History of Modern Biblical Interpretation* (Collegeville, MN: Liturgical Press, 2005).

and its translations into Greek, Latin, and other vernacular languages is complex and complicated.[20] Yet the Protestant Reformation insisted on the idea that Bible translations are literalist-linguistic achievements transforming the original Hebrew, Aramaic, or Greek texts into *formal* equivalents in manifold target languages.

This notion of translation was modified in the 1960s when Eugene A. Nida proposed a "new concept of translation."[21] He called it "dynamic" or "functional equivalence." Central to Nida's translation theory was the idea of finding the *dynamic* or *functional* equivalent in the target language. The replication of stylistic characteristics such as rhymes, chiasms, or parallelisms was secondary because the translation had to be in tune with the sensibilities of readers, their word choices, and their contexts. According to Nida, a translation is only "legitimate" when readers understand it, and so it does not matter anymore if a translation "correctly" represents a source text's formal expressions.[22]

In the 1980s, the field of translation studies moved beyond Nida's theory when Hans J. Vermeer developed the *skopos* theory, which emphasizes that the purpose of a translation determines which translation strategy to employ. Accordingly, translations only succeed if they reach their functional goals in the target language.[23] Gone are the days of translating source texts as "literally" as possible because proponents of the *skopos* theory insisted that translations ought to communicate the purpose of a text in the target language. Other developments, too, moved translation theorists from a reliance on the literalist-formal or functional-equivalence models to approaches in which translations are recognized as participants within systemic processes taking place in the target-language context. For instance, Itamar Even-Zohar explained: "Translation is no longer a phenomenon whose nature and borders are given once and for all, but an activity dependent on the relations within a certain cultural system."[24] Similarly, in

---

20. For a description, see, e.g., Philip A. Noss, ed., *A History of Bible Translation* (Rome: Edizioni de storia e letteratura, 2007).

21. Eugene A. Nida and Charles R. Taber, *The Theory and Practice of Translation* (Leiden: Brill, 1982), 1. He articulated his views for the first time in Eugene A. Nida, *Toward a Science of Translating* (Leiden: Brill, 1964). For a discussion on Nida's work in the context of recent biblical translation studies, see, e.g., Stephen Pattemore, "Framing Nida: The Relevance of Translation Theory in the United Bible Societies," in *A History of Bible Translation*, ed. Philip A. Noss (Rome: Edizioni de storia e letteratura, 2007), 217–63.

22. Nida and Taber, *Theory and Practice*, 2.

23. Jeremy Munday, *Introducing Translation Studies: Theories and Applications*, 2nd ed. (London: Routledge, 2008), 87. See also Christina Schäffner, "Skopos Theory," in Baker, *Routledge Encyclopedia of Translation Studies*, 235–38.

24. Itamar Even-Zohar, "The Position of Translated Literature within the Literary Polysystem," in *The Translation Studies Reader*, ed. Lawrence Venuti (London: Routledge, 2004), 204.

1990, Susan Bassnett and André Lefevre maintained that translators need to take into account the interactions between translation and culture. They argued that translations stand in "cultures" shaped by context, history, and conventions.[25] In other words, translations engage the sociopolitical, cultural, and social dynamics of the target-language setting.

In the 1990s, the prominent translation theorist Lawrence Venuti went even further. He focused on the centrality of translators, articulating his ideas in the influential book, *The Translator's Invisibility*. It begins with the following sentences:

> "Invisibility" is the term I will use to describe the translator's situation and activity in contemporary Anglo-American culture. . . . What is remarkable here is that this illusory effect conceals the numerous conditions under which the translation is made, starting with the translator's crucial intervention in the foreign text.[26]

According to Venuti, translators are undervalued as the producers of translations, although they are the ones negotiating the countless cultural differences between source text and target language. Translators perform the difficult task of "double writing" and "double reading," and so they intervene into "a present situation" from "a foreign past."[27] In other words, Venuti highlighted the fact that translators shape the reception of translated texts and they do so by employing two main methods. Either translators stabilize the status quo or they resist homogeneous adaptations by foreignizing the text.[28] In either case, translators stand at the crucial nexus of translating the source text into the target language. They have the linguistic power to prevent "an appropriation of foreign cultures for domestic agendas, cultural, economic, and political." Venuti thus explained that "the most urgent question facing the translator . . . [is], What to do? Why and how do I translate?"[29] Said differently, Venuti placed translators at the center of the translation process, as there is no translation without them. Determining the nature, purpose, and function of

---

25. Susan Bassnett and André Lefevre, *Translation, History and Culture* (London: Pinter, 1990). The development of feminist translation studies stands in this tradition; see, e.g., Sherry Simon, *Gender in Translation: Cultural Identity and the Politics of Transmission* (London: Routledge, 1996).
26. Lawrence Venuti, *The Translator's Invisibility: A History of Translation* (London: Routledge, 1995), 1–2.
27. Ibid., 312.
28. Lawrence Venuti, *The Scandals of Translation: Towards an Ethics of Difference* (London: Routledge, 1998), 5.
29. Ibid., 19.

the translation, translators decide whether their translations will comply with the status quo or challenge hegemonic expectations of the target language's cultures.

Venuti also observed that translators have endured their invisible status for far too long. In his view, the reasons for their invisibility relate to the hierarchical and authoritarian structures put in place by the publishing industry. Since publishers must sell, they look for translations that affirm the status quo in the target-language culture. Domesticated translations provide the cohesive and smooth reading experience in the target language that readers prefer. Yet domesticated translations also keep translators invisible as the crucial intermediaries between source text and target language.[30] In contrast, foreignized translations represent "a disruption of target-language cultural codes,"[31] as foreignization makes readers "recognize the linguistic and cultural difference of foreign texts."[32] Publishers fear that readers will not like translated books that seem strange, are difficult to read, and perhaps even criticize the target-language context. Other theorists also highlighted the central function of translations in the translation process. For instance, Michael Cronin observed that translators "are constantly moving backwards and forwards between languages. They are sensitive to the liminal, in-between zones that increasingly characterize contemporary consciousness and global cultural evolution."[33] Foreignized translations ensure that translators are visible in the business of translating text from the source text to the target-language context.

In short, contemporary translation theorists recognize that translations participate in geopolitical, economic, and cultural power dynamics, and translators are central to the task of translation. As they evaluate how to engage those forces, they decide whether a translation submits to or resists the target-language culture. Consequently, theorists advise that translators think critically about the translation process as not to reinforce asymmetric exchanges between the source text and the target-language culture.[34] Translation theorists, abandoning the literalist-formal model, have replaced it with the cultural-studies

30. See also Peter Fawcett, "Ideology and Translation," in Baker, *Routledge Encyclopedia of Translation Studies*, 106–11.
31. Ibid., 42.
32. Venuti, *Scandals of Translation*, 41.
33. Michael Cronin, "Deschooling Translation: Beginning of Century Reflections on Teaching Translation and Interpreting," in *Training for the New Millennium: Pedagogies for Translation and Interpreting*, ed. Martha Tennent (Philadelphia: John Benjamins Publishing, 2005), 262.
34. See Venuti, *Scandals of Translation*, esp. 158–89.

paradigm. They recognize translations as products of geopolitical, social, cultural, and economic dynamics that shape translations. Since the act of translation does not take place in neutral space, it is up to the translators to decide how to align their translations within the historically grown networks of power.[35]

The conceptualization of the translation process as a multifaceted web of power relations has serious consequences for thinking about the *BigS*. Obviously, the argument that the *BigS* violates literalist-formal translation principles is too narrow and old-fashioned to make sense in light of contemporary translation theories. The *BigS*'s critics favor domesticating translations whereas the *BigS* offers a foreignizing translation that challenges the sociopolitical and cultural status quo. Yet the viciousness of the *BigS*'s critics goes beyond outdated views about the nature, purpose, and function of translations. As the *BigS*'s critics reject the idea that translations are "necessarily embedded within social contexts,"[36] another explanation model is necessary to grasp the magnitude of the critics' stance. After all, some of the critics are thoroughly secular and do not usually comment on Bible translations. The question thus is why so many secular and religious critics felt so compelled to assess the first inclusive German Bible translation in such negative ways. Clearly, they responded from a deeply emotional place, indicating that significant power dynamics were at stake for them. To understand these dynamics, contemporary theorists on barbarism help explain why critics rejected the first inclusive German Bible translation so vehemently, persistently, and viciously.

Beyond Civilizing Translations: The Contributions of Theories on Barbarism

As we have seen, translation theorists maintain that translations are geopolitical products that engage webs of power relations within a target language's culture. Consequently, translations are not merely literal-formal or equivalent renderings of the source text, but translations always engage the target language's context. Theorists on barbarism allow us to take this notion even further. They suggest that, like any other written text, translations either reinforce or challenge

---

35. See, e.g., Mona Baker, "Translation Studies," in Baker, *Routledge Encyclopedia of Translation Studies*, 277–80.
36. Michaela Wolf, "Introduction: The Emergence of a Sociology of Translation," in *Constructing a Sociology of Translation*, ed. Michaela Wolf and Alexandra Fukari (Philadelphia: John Benjamins, 2007), 1.

assumed power relations about intellectual and cultural hegemony and superiority. Thus translations turn into either civilizing tools of empire or inferior products of "the barbarians." If the latter, they are viewed as "other," lacking power in the empire. Said differently, translations invite rigorous debates about status and power on a highly abstract-symbolic level. In the case of the *BigS*, the translation compels even secular critics to comment on a religious topic that is normally only negotiated on the margins of secularized German society.

More specifically, theorists on barbarism investigate the dynamics of colonizing beliefs, habits, and practices, including within the intra-colonial experiences of British and French societies. Theorists tend to ignore the German context because Germany did do not have an extensive colonial past due to curtailed imperial ambitions after the so-called World War I (1914–1918) and the Nazi era (1933–1945). Yet the limited colonial experience has not prevented German culture from adhering to notions of national-cultural superiority and intellectual hegemony. Without a doubt, the Nazi era is the most extreme expression of this problem, but it has presented itself also in many other time periods in Germany, though luckily with far less violent consequences. Thus, for instance, the characterization of postwar West German culture as being populated by "frustrated colonialists"[37] strikes a chord, including the effort here to comprehend the harsh assessment of the *BigS*.

A look at the theological discourse in Germany illustrates the widespread acceptance of hegemonic assumptions about civilization and barbarism during the last couple of centuries. After all, German scholarship dominated the academic field of Protestant theology from the late eighteenth century CE until the late 1960s, perhaps even into the early 1970s. For instance and significantly, it was customary for Christian theology students from almost anywhere, including the United States, to earn graduate credentials at German theology departments and then return home to high renown and status. This one-way path of learning was not limited to theological studies but also existed in many other academic fields.[38] In Germany, the intellectual,

37. Martin Braach-Maksvytis, "Germany, Palestine, Israel, and the (Post)colonial Imagination," in *German Colonialism: Race, the Holocaust, and Postwar Germany*, ed. Volker Langbehn and Mohammad Salama (New York: Columbia University Press, 2011), 295.

38. For general studies on the relationship of German colonialism and culture, see, e.g., Sebastian Conrad, *German Colonialism: A Short History* (Cambridge: Cambridge University Press, 2012); Michael Perraudin and Juergen Zimmerer, eds., *German Colonialism and National Identity* (New York: Routledge, 2011); Britta Schilling, *Postcolonial Germany: Memories of Empire in a Decolonized Nation*, Oxford Historical Monographs (Oxford: Oxford University Press, 2014). For a detailed study on German

scientific-scholarly, and theological colonial impetus is still taken for granted, as the negative responses to the *BigS* indicate. Due to a general lack of postcolonial analysis in German Bible scholarship, critics of the *BigS* articulate their negative assessment in light of colonizing assumptions about the "other." The general unawareness of colonizing ideas and assumptions made it easy for critics to dismiss the expertise of the fully credentialed group of *BigS* translators. It did not matter to the critics that many of the translators are internationally recognized scholars who enjoy productive teaching and research careers even abroad. Instead, critics of the *BigS*, utterly unaware of their colonizing stance, took for granted their national-cultural superiority and intellectual hegemony. Their negative reviews thus resemble the imperial attitude of a colonizer who classifies the other as inferior, as standing in opposition to the dominant and "civilized" position which is culturally approved, socially respected, and epistemologically dominant. Accordingly, critics felt at ease to reject the *BigS* as a useless, bankrupt, and even heretical translation. In short, they regarded it as barbaric.

As theories of barbarism have articulated the meaning of barbarism and civilization, three theorists helpfully discuss the distinction between civilization and barbarism. First, Tzevetan Todorov, a Franco-Bulgarian philosopher, proposes two ways of thinking about barbarism. One way has emerged since the so-called Enlightenment. A relative definition, it regards barbarity as an "optical illusion" because it fails to understand others. It assumes that the move from a barbaric state of thinking and treating others to a civilized state of thinking requires empathy with the other. Empathy turns the stranger, the other, the barbarian into an acquaintance, somebody who is known, and who does not need to be condemned or feared. The other way relies on the term *barbarian* in an absolute sense in which the barbaric is seen as something that "exists in itself."[39] Here barbarism becomes something that "is within us, as well as being in others; no people, no individual, is immune to the possibility of carrying out barbaric acts."[40] In other words, barbarism is identified as a deeply held quality, and the challenge is to define the distinction between the barbaric and

---

Protestant churches in German colonies, see, e.g., Hanns Lessing et al., eds., *The German Protestant Church in Colonial Southern Africa: The Impact of Overseas Work from the Beginnings until the 1920s* (Wiesbaden: Harrassowitz, 2012); Susannah Heschel, "Theology as a Vision for Colonialism: From Supersessionism to Dejudaization in German Protestantism," in *Germany's Colonial Pasts*, ed. Eric Ames et al. (Lincoln: University of Nebraska Press, 2005), 148–64.

39. Tzevetan Todorov, *The Fear of Barbarians: Beyond the Clash of Civilizations*, trans. Andrew Brown (Chicago: University of Chicago Press, 2010), 20.

40. Ibid., 21.

the civilized. The various definitions have in common an essentialized view of barbarity. Todorov puts it this way: "No culture is barbarian in itself, no people is definitively civilized; all can become either barbarian or civilized. This is what defines the human race."[41]

The trouble is that Todorov does not reflect critically on how the standards about civilization and barbarism are set. He affirms that "we" can try to reach the standards of civilization, but he does not explain who "we" are and why the standards he selects are superior to others. Still, his discussion raises the issue of the binary relationship between barbarism and civilization, and so it helpfully suggests that the relationship between barbarism and civilization is bundled together. Neither one can or ought to be rejected or exclusively affirmed because all of them depend on each other.

When one applies the essentialized view on barbarism to Bible translations, it becomes clear that translators have to continuously negotiate what the standards are for whom, where, and why. After all, according to Todorov, all translations have the potential to be used in barbaric ways. Accordingly, the *BigS* is as good or as bad as any other authoritative translation, and critics of the *BigS* ought to take this idea seriously. Since they did not, one could argue—tongue in cheek—that their harsh rejection is quite barbaric and in need of more civilizing deliberation.

Second, another important theory about barbarism comes from the literary critic, Maria Boletsi. She employs the concept of barbarism "as a theoretical concept in cultural critique" that describes "some of the epistemological and comparative operations it [barbarism] can trigger from within or from the margins of dominant discourses and modes of representation."[42] To Boletsi, therefore, the term *barbarism* is not an essentializing concept about otherness but a "critical intervention" with which to examine "the contact zones between heterogeneous discourses, narratives, or knowledge regimes." The goal is to identify "transformative potential."[43] In other words, to Boletsi, the notion of barbarism does not describe a lack, an absence, or a negative state that opposes the positive state of civilization.[44] Rather, barbarism

---

41. Ibid., 51.
42. Maria Boletsi, *Barbarism and Its Discontents* (Stanford: Stanford University Press, 2013), 2.
43. Ibid., 3.
44. See, e.g., *Shorter Oxford English Dictionary on Historical Principles*, 2002: "uncivilized nature or condition; uncultured ignorance; absence of culture; barbaric style [in art etc.], unrestrainedness"; *Oxford American Dictionary and Thesaurus*, 2003: "the absence of culture and civilized standards"; *Webster's New International Dictionary*, 1913: "ignorance of arts, learning, and literature; barbarousness."

offers unexpected, innovative, and nontraditional ways of knowing and understanding. It fosters the exploration of margins and contact zones between barbarism and civilization, and so it interrupts conventional workings of language, thinking, and ways of life. She states:

> Barbarism, then, oscillates between two main functions: it reinforces the discourse of civilization that needs it as its antipode but it also nurtures a disruptive potential, through which it can interrupt the workings of the very same discourse that constructs the category of the barbarian for the sake of civilization's self-definition.[45]

What Boletsi's discussion of barbarism explains is the fact that any discourse of civilization needs its opposition—barbarism—to justify its civilizing qualities and practices. By needing the other, it acknowledges that there are other ways of thinking, doing, and living. Boletsi explains that the goal is to imagine ways of constructing "the other" and the "barbaric" not as threatening, inferior, or illegitimate but to take it as an alternative, a different option that is otherwise just like you and me. The other wants to be recognized, seen, and understood, even though it does things differently from how we do things. In this sense, then, otherness is not a zero-sum game but a matter of difference in degree. The other is not "totally" other, but it resembles "us" in more ways than we customarily acknowledge when we try to win the rhetorical battle. Applied to the *BigS*, Boletsi's understanding of barbarism suggests that, indeed, the *BigS* is a translation like any other Bible translations. All of them are interpretations because every translation is always an interpretation. There are different translations, to be sure, and we disagree on the merits of each, but our disagreements do not mean that only the *BigS* is wrong, even heretical, and other translations are not. Undeniably, the inclusive German Bible translation disrupts the assumed center, as it challenges dominant ways of translating the Bible into German. It teaches that there are many ways of translating this culturally and religiously influential book into contemporary German.

Third, yet another theory about barbarism has been proposed, and it too helps understand why the secular and religious critique of the *BigS* was so vicious. This theory comes from religious studies scholar, Santiago Slabodsky, who characterizes theories of barbarism "as one of the most provocative rhetorical resources of imperial projects."[46] He

---

45. Boletsi, *Barbarism and Its Discontents*, 6.

observes that all enemies of all kinds of empires are always branded with the term *barbarism*. Trying to find a way out of this branding system, Slabodsky proposed that those who have been classified as "barbarians" need to reappropriate this term and mobilize it "for self-consciousness . . . in their counter-narratives."[47] In his own effort of decolonizing "modern Jewish experiences through the optic of the Manichean civilization/barbarism dualism,"[48] Slabodsky explores how European depictions of Jews as non-Westerners, as barbarians, shifted to an acceptance of Jews as integral members of Western civilization in the post-Holocaust era. Tracing Jewish barbarism in several Jewish political projects that "reformulated the Manichean dualism during the last articulation of the normative passage from barbarism to civilization,"[49] Slabodsky wants to contribute to the disruption of intellectual hegemonies, especially in the North. He shows that some thinkers have successfully reappropriated the concept of barbarism so that the West turns out to be barbaric. Others give barbarism a positive value that turns the binary of civilization and barbarism on its head. In his own project of decolonizing contemporary Judaism from its civilizational position, Slabodsky is hesitant to propose an easy way out of this binary. In his view, neither a reappropriation nor a positive counternarrative of barbarism is a solution for "future Jewish engagements with global politics."[50]

If Slabodsky's idea about barbarism is applied to the debate on the *BigS*, inclusive translations remind us of the fact that every inclusive translation is a way of subverting, foreignizing, and "barbarizing" that which is classified an "authorized" translation. In this sense, then, the *BigS* encourages conversation about the perceived "civilized" status of the various Bible translations, whether it is Luther's Bible translation of 1545 or the *BigS* of 2006. Yet critics of the *BigS* were far removed from such explorations, as they were busy defending their positions of intellectual status, authority, and hegemony. They denied that their harsh rejection of the *BigS* executes a colonizing position over the "other." The question is if Slabodsky sides with the inclusive Bible translators, as it seems unlikely that he will find the counternarrative of the *BigS*

46. Santiago H. Slabodsky, "Emmanuel Lévinas's Barbarisms: Adventures of *Eastern* Talmudic Counter-Narratives Heterodoxly Encountering the South" (PhD diss., University of Toronto, 2009), 16.
47. Ibid., 20.
48. Santiago Slabodsky, *Decolonial Judaism: Triumphal Failures of Barbaric Thinking* (New York: Palgrave Macmillan 2014), 4.
49. Ibid., 7.
50. Ibid., 201.

in itself transformative. It seems more likely that he would encourage Bible scholars to investigate the "failed history"[51] of the barbarian tradition in biblical exegesis as the starting point for a future of decolonial Bible interpretation. To be sure, the *BigS* plays a significant role in this failed history, but it would also require more information on the historical contexts, functions, and roles of Bible translations to further contextualize the viciousness of the *BigS*'s critics.

In other words, the three theories on barbarism suggest that the secular and religious assessments of the *BigS* are so harsh because the first inclusive German Bible translation exposes the intellectual colonialism in German-speaking culture. As the colonizing process took place in Germany mainly on the level of academic discourse and scientific research rather than on the level of geopolitical expansion and colonial occupation, Bible translations have usually served as theoretical, "civilizing" tools of empire.[52] The *BigS* represents a serious challenge to this tradition, and for this reason the first inclusive German Bible translation received responses far more vicious than any other German Bible translation in recent memory. Yet when one regards the *BigS* as barbaric and as a subversive tool that fosters resistance and alternative views about the world, the question is whether it offers a convincing counternarrative to the intracolonial status quo. After all, for the first time in the history of the German language more than fifty mostly female Bible scholars produced an inclusive Bible translation that attends to issues of gender, anti-Judaism, and class. Does it successfully circumvent hegemonic forces, embedded within the German-speaking theological heritage, and so is the *BigS* indeed a "barbaric" alternative to other German Bible translations?

This is a complicated question. According to Slabodsky, barbarians of the world need to unite and "develop a conceptual community." In his case the community of barbarian Jews needs to unite with the barbarians from the global South,[53] as he states provocatively: "The disruptive project should not be done in dialogue with Rome."[54] The vicious critique of the *BigS* indicates that neither Rome nor Berlin wishes for any dialogue. It is thus high time that German inclusive Bible translators

---

51. Ibid.
52. A new German-language Luther translation approved by the entire ecclesial Protestant hierarchy was published in 2017 in honor of the five-hundredth anniversary of the Protestant Reformation. It is praised as "scientifically precise and at the same time linguistically on point" (*wissenschaftlich präzise und zugleich sprachlich treffend*). For more information, see "Die Lutherbibel 2017: Was ist neu?," Deutsche Bibel Gesellschaft, http://tinyurl.com/mv7ohqw.
53. Slabodsky, *Decolonial Judaism*, 327.
54. Ibid., 328.

look South and connect with those who are in the process of decolonizing translations in Africa, Asia, South America, and anywhere else.[55] The trouble is that global-South barbarians do not always recognize German barbarians as barbarians. The legacy of European colonialism and its geopolitical reaches of political, economic, and intellectual-religious supremacy are so well-known that resistance within the colonizer's countries is often unrecognizable to global-South barbarians. It is such a complicated dynamic that sometimes the barbarians themselves, living inside the colonizer's lands, do not even recognize it. They, too, get confused about their allegiances because the colonizer's land is their home and they are their sisters and brothers, their children, and their children's children.

About Welcoming Barbarian Translations in the West: Concluding Comments

I want to be clear at this point: I do not think that deeply held and defended hierarchies and notions of otherness are limited to German-language Bible translations and their critics. On the contrary. But I do think that perhaps—and the issue will require further investigation—certain characteristics are typical of the German-language setting because of local histories and traditions. This essay highlights that the viciousness and forcefulness of the secular and religious critique of the *BigS* are a unique and collective expression of empire attitudes in German-language culture. After all, inclusive English translations have not received such widespread and extensive responses that would be comparable to the first and only inclusive German Bible translation.[56] In fact, the English-speaking public, as well as religious organizations, largely ignore inclusive English Bible translations, and so lay audiences

---

55. See, e.g., Gosnell L. Yorke and P. Renju, eds., *Bible Translations and African Languages* (Nairobi, Kenya: Acton, 2004); Johnson Kiriaku Kinyua, "A Postcolonial Analysis of Bible Translation and Its Effectiveness in Shaping and Enhancing the Discourse of Colonialism and the Discourse of Resistance," *Black Theology: An International Journal* 11, no. 1 (2013): 58–95; Gosnell L. Yorke, "Bible Translation in Africa: An Afrocentric Perspective," *The Bible Translator* 50, no. 1 (2000): 114–23.

56. In English, see, e.g., *The Inclusive Bible: The First Egalitarian Translation* (Lanham, MD: Rowman & Littlefield, 2007); *The Contemporary Torah: A Gender-Sensitive Adaptation of the JPS Translation* (Philadelphia: Jewish Publication Society, 2006); *New International Version Popular Edition, Inclusive Language* (London: Hodder & Stoughton, 1997); Victor Roland Gold et al., eds., *The New Testament and Psalms: An Inclusive Version* (New York: Oxford University Press, 1995).

rarely know about them.[57] This is a remarkable difference to the German-language context.[58]

In sum, secular and religious critics defend positions of empire, as contemporary translation theories and theories about barbarism indicate. The critics focus on gender, but when one looks carefully, they uphold colonizing attitudes that favor empire hierarchies about "otherness" structuring the political, social, and religious life in German-speaking society even today. This, then, is the scandal of the *Bibel in gerechter Sprache*: it illustrates that deeply rooted democratic sensibilities remain elusive when secular and religious people and institutions encounter the first ever inclusive German Bible translation. Surprisingly, the power struggle is still openly fought over a Bible translation despite the secular nature of the early twenty-first-century German-language context. It demonstrates that German-language culture still cares deeply about the Bible. Yet it also still defends the Bible within a framework of empire religiosity. In addition, this religiosity is largely unconsciously articulated, and so it is difficult for critics to recognize their colonizing assumptions. In this sense, then, the *BigS* and its translators have made a crucial cultural, political, and religious contribution to the exposure of empire attitudes in contemporary German culture. The *BigS* defies such attitudes about the other, the "barbarian," by offering an alternative to empire religion. It posits that it is no longer necessary to be civilized into Martin Luther's colonizing Bible translation.

Most importantly, then, the first inclusive German Bible translation

---

57. An exception comes from several publications from the Christian Right focused on "gender-neutral" Bible translation; see, e.g., Vern S. Poythress and Wayne A. Grudem, *The Gender-Neutral Bible Controversy: Muting the Masculinity of God's Words* (Nashville: Broadman & Holman, 2000); D. A. Carson, *The Inclusive Language Debate: A Plea for Realism* (Grand Rapids: Baker, 1998). For an analysis of this and related publications, see Karen Strand Winslow, "Recovering Redemption for Women: Feminist Exegesis in North American Evangelicalism," in *Feminist Interpretation of the Hebrew Bible in Retrospect*, vol. 2, *Social Locations*, ed. Susanne Scholz (Sheffield: Sheffield Phoenix, 2014), 269–89.

58. See also Susanne Scholz, "The Bible as 'Men's' Word? Feminism and the Translation of the Old Testament/Hebrew Bible," *Lectio difficilior: European Feminist Journal for Feminist Exegesis* (October 2010): http://tinyurl.com/n25rcga; Susanne Scholz, "The *Bibel in gerechter Sprache (BigS)*: The Secular Press, *Kirchenherren*, and Theology Professors React to a New German Inclusive Bible Translation," *SBL Forum* (April 2008): http://tinyurl.com/myemrds. See also the related articles published in the same venue: Irmtraud Fischer, "Why the Agitation? The Status of the *Bibel in gerechter Sprache* in Academia and the Churches," trans. and ed. Susanne Scholz, *SBL Forum* (April 2008): http://tinyurl.com/lw6hgt6; Wolfgang Stegemann, "Translation or Interpretation: Intense Controversy about the New German Translation of the Bible," trans. and ed. Susanne Scholz, *SBL Forum* (April 2008): http://tinyurl.com/nxgrqnc; Luzia Sutter Rehmann, "What Is the *Bibel in gerechter Sprache*? Assumptions, Process, and Goals of a New German Bible Translation," trans. and ed. Susanne Scholz, *SBL Forum* (April 2008): http://tinyurl.com/kgw3eph; Marie-Theres Wacker, "The New Inclusive Bible Translation in the Context of (Post)modern Germany," trans. and ed. Susanne Scholz, *SBL Forum* (April 2008): http://tinyurl.com/kphg7fr.

is a uniquely constructive contribution in support of a democratically organized society. We should not be surprised that, instead of celebrating this accomplishment, the German Protestant church has already superseded the *BigS* with an officially authorized new translation. Predictably, inclusive language is not part of that translation. In light of this situation, perhaps the scandal about the first inclusive German Bible translation is that its critics dug in their heels. It resulted in the production of yet another empire-friendly translation, published in celebration of the five-hundredth anniversary of the Protestant Reformation in Germany.[59] Barbarian (feminist) Bible translators and exegetes unite!

---

59. Martin Luther, *Die Bibel nach Martin Luthers Übersetzung—Lutherbibel revidiert 2017: Jubiläumsausgabe 500 Jahre Reformation* (Stuttgart: Deutsche Bibelgesellschaft, 2016). For more information, see "Lutherbibel 2017," Deutsche Bibel Gesellschaft, http://tinyurl.com/latvpcv.

Index of Authors

Dobbs-Allsopp, F. W., 272
Douglas, Kelly Brown, 205
Dovey, Lindiwe, 240, 242, 247–50, 252, 255–57
Dozeman, Thomas B., 140
Drell, Lauren, 45
Driver, G. R., 101, 114
Dube, Musa W., 75–76, 220
Dunn, James D. G., 53
Dussel, Enrique, 69

Ebeling, Erich, 108
Eckstein, Katharina, 296
Eligon, John, 176
Elmore, John M., 38
Engelmann, Angelika, 101, 103
Eshelman, Raoul, 162
Eshkenazi, Tamara Cohn, 207
Eugene, Toinette, 199
Evans, Craig A., 16
Even-Zohar, Itamar, 301
Exum, J. Cheryl, 208, 220, 223–26, 267–68
Eyre, C. J., 111

Fahey, Johannah, 40
Fahim, Kareem, 175
Faiola, Anthony, 35
Fander, Monika, 71
Farley, Edward, 8
Felder, Cain, 54–55
Ferguson, James, 37
Ferris, Robert W., 6–7
Fewell, Danna Nolan, 80–81, 206, 229–30, 238
Finkelstein, Jacob J., 106, 110
Fischer, Elmar, 298
Fischer, Irmtraud, 139, 154, 230, 312
Fish, Stanley, 41
Fitzpatrick, Elyse, 153

Flanders, Henry Jackson, 19
Fletcher, Pamela R., 95, 227
Foderaro, Lisa W., 41, 260
Fogel, Reuben Seth, 145
Fontaine, Carole, 207
Forkas, Effie, 145–46
Foskett, Mary F., 141, 219
Fowler, Robert M., 58
Frenz, Albrecht, 89
Fretheim, Terence E., 228–29
Freyne, Seán, 223
Frick, Frank S., 19
Frymer-Kensky, Tikva, 101, 104–5, 206–7, 209
Fuchs, Esther, 84, 202, 209–10, 215, 220–21, 275, 282, 285
Fukuyama, Francis, 35
Fulbrook, Mary, 70
Fulton, Lauren, 144

Gafney, Wilda C. M., 204
Gaventa, Beverly Roberts, 197
Gerstenberger, Erhard, 36, 79, 135
Gettleman, Jeffrey, 50, 176, 256
Gifford, Carolyn De Swarte, 193
Giroux, Henry A., 33, 169, 290
Gold, Victor Roland, 311
Goldstein, Elyse, 83–84
Gordon, Claire, 260
Goss, Robert E., 4, 155, 218
Gössman, Elisabeth, 155, 297
Graham, Susan Lochrie, 207
Grant, Jacquelyn, 205
Gravett, Sandie, 104, 272, 280
Gray, Patrick, 197
Greenberg, Moshe, 103
Greenstein, Edward L., 225
Gregg, Paul, 23
Griffin, Susan, 264
Groothuis, Rebecca Merrill, 149

Index of Ancient Sources